The MAILBOX®

The Idea Magazine For Teachers™

INTERMEDIATE

1995–1996
YEARBOOK

Becky S. Andrews, Editor

The Education Center, Inc.
Greensboro, North Carolina

The Mailbox® 1995–1996 Intermediate Yearbook

Editor In Chief: Margaret Michel
Intermediate Grades Editorial Director and Senior Editor: Becky S. Andrews
Editorial Manager: Julie Peck
Associate Editors: Irving P. Crump, Christine A. Thuman
Contributing Editor: Peggy W. Hambright
Copy Editors: Lynn Bemer Coble, Jennifer Rudisill, Gina Sutphin
Staff Artists: Jennifer T. Bennett, Cathy Spangler Bruce, Pam Crane, Teresa Davidson, Susan Hodnett, Sheila Krill, Rebecca Saunders, Barry Slate, Donna Teal
Editorial Assistants: Elizabeth A. Findley, Wendy Svartz

ISBN 1-56234-138-3
ISSN 1088-5552

Printed in the United States of America.

The Education Center, Inc.
P.O. Box 9753
Greensboro, NC 27429-0753

Contents

Teacher Resource Ideas

Step Right Up To A New Year!

Back-To-School Ideas From Our Subscribers

It's already August (wasn't it only yesterday that you finished final report cards?), and you're just a step away from the start of another year. Help your students begin the year on the right foot by including the following creative subscribers' ideas into your back-to-school plans.

Wish You Could Have Been There!

Let your students create their own back-to-school bulletin board in a snap! Duplicate a class supply of the postcard pattern on page 10 on white or light-colored construction paper. On his postcard, have each student write a message to a friend (or you) describing how he spent his summer vacation—being sure to mention any places he visited. Instruct the student to address his postcard and draw a fun stamp. Mount the finished postcards in the middle of a bulletin board entitled "Wish You Could Have Been There!" Along the border of the display, mount a variety of postcards collected from places you've visited. Since some of your students may not have had opportunities to travel farther than their hometown, be sure to include postcards of your area as well. After the class leaves for the day, take time to study the postcards and assess your new students' writing abilities. *Laura Gill-Williams—Grs. 4/5, Hawthorne Elementary, Tulsa, OK*

Dear Eddie,
What a great summer I had! My family took several neat trips. We went to Branson, Missouri. While we were there we went to a lot of musical shows. Then we visited St. Louis. Have you ever seen the Gateway Arch? It's huge!
Your friend,
Pablo

Eddie Richards
1500 Lafayette Court
Williamston, OK 70892

Goldfish Grab

There's nothing fishy about this first-day icebreaker! Fill a large bowl with a variety of goldfish-shaped crackers. Have each student grab a handful. For each fish a student holds, have her share something about herself with the rest of the class. At the end of the icebreaker, move into a math lesson during which students use the crackers as counters for word problems or as manipulatives for making patterns. Of course, eating the tasty treats at the end of the lesson is the best part of all! *Susan M. Reed—Gr. 4, Ebenezer Elementary, Lebanon, PA*

Step Right Up To A New Grade!

Here's an activity that answers the question, "What can my kids do on the first day while I'm greeting students?" In preparation, duplicate two copies of the sneaker pattern on page 10 for each student. Cut out the sneakers; then, for each student, glue two sneakers onto a large sheet of white construction paper as shown. Before students enter your room, place a paper and a glue stick on each desk. Provide a variety of lettering stencils and markers or crayons on a centrally located table. Write the following instructions on the board:

1. Use the stencils on the table to trace your first name on your paper. Return the stencils when you are finished.
2. Decorate your name and shoes with your favorite colors. If you don't have your own markers or crayons, use the ones on the table.
3. Decorate the rest of your paper to reflect your hobbies or favorite activities.

Later in the day, have each student introduce himself to the class by sharing and explaining his poster. Display the posters on a wall with the title "Step Right Up To _____ Grade!" *Lynn Marie Gilbertson—Gr. 4, James Sales Elementary, Tacoma, WA*

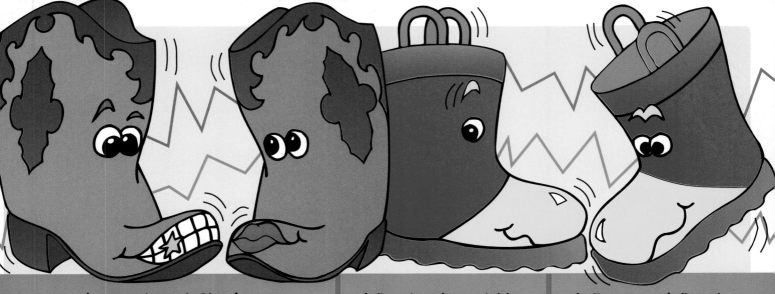

Appointment Clocks

Here's a unique way to help students get to know each other better. Give each student a copy of the "My Appointment Clock" pattern on page 11. Explain that each child will have three minutes to get the blanks on her clock filled in with the names of six classmates. Each time a student signs a classmate's clock, that classmate must write her name in the same blank on the other child's clock. For example, if Sue signs the six o'clock blank on Alice's clock, Alice must sign the six o'clock blank on Sue's clock. Sue and Alice then have made a six o'clock appointment. Set a timer for three minutes; then have students walk around the room to get their clocks filled in.

After the session, announce that it's time for two o'clock appointments. Have each student meet with the partner listed on his two o'clock space. During a two-minute period, have these partners interview each other about special interests, hobbies, families, etc. At the end of the period, announce that it's time for four o'clock appointments; then have students switch partners according to their clocks. Use the clocks anytime you'd like pairs of students to review for a test, discuss a literature selection, or complete an assignment. *Beth Gress, Mt. Gilead, OH*

Name **Min**

My Appointment Clock

A Poster About Me

Looking for an independent project for students to complete on the first day? Duplicate the reproducible activity on page 12 for each child. Place several inkpads (to complete the fingerprint space on the poster) at a table, along with a supply of markers and crayons. Have each child complete and color his poster. Let students mount their finished posters on construction paper after sharing them with the class. Display the posters on a back-to-school bulletin board. *Beth Gress*

Self-Esteem Builder

Take steps early in the year to bolster your students' self-esteem. For homework during the first week, I ask each child to bring in an object that illustrates one way that she is unique and special. My students have brought in items such as sports trophies, favorite drawings, photographs, and original stories. This simple activity sets the stage for a year of building self-esteem and appreciating our differences. *Sherri Kaiser—Gr. 4, Walnut Grove Elementary, Suwanee, GA*

A Teamwork Puzzle

As a reading specialist, I worked with a teacher whose back-to-school theme was "Teamwork." To further develop the theme, I photographed the entire class; then I took the developed photo to a drugstore where I had it made into an 11" x 14" jigsaw puzzle. I removed 31 pieces at random from the puzzle and put them into a paper bag. The assembled puzzle—missing the 31 pieces—was left on a classroom table.

At school the next day, I led the class in a discussion of teamwork—emphasizing the importance of the individual to the entire group. Then I had each of the 29 students and the classroom teacher take a puzzle piece from the bag. I took the last piece. One by one we fitted our pieces into the puzzle until the whole picture (or "team") was complete. The puzzle remained on the table for the rest of the year and became a favorite free-time activity. *Patricia Cassel— Reading Specialist, Maywood Hills Elementary, Bothell, WA*

Brown-Bag It!

A terrific getting-to-know-you activity is in the bag with this fun-filled idea! Give each student a copy of the "Brown-Bag It!" reproducible on page11 and a small brown lunch bag. Read through the instructions with the class, discussing the types of items students might bring for each category. Encourage students to use a photograph for no more than one category. Have each student collect her items at home and bring them to school in the lunch bag the next day. (To prevent students from bringing very large items, inform them that they are not to switch the lunch bag for a brown grocery bag.) The next day, let each child share the contents of her bag. To check on listening skills, call out an item that was shown and see if students can identify its owner and why it was shared. *Beth Gress, Mt. Gilead, OH*

Fifteen Questions

Combine a fun icebreaker with a review of famous people. Label construction-paper strips (one per student) with the names of well-known people from the past or the present, and/or famous fictional characters. Tape a strip on the back of each student; then instruct him to walk around the room and ask 15 classmates yes/no questions (one question per classmate) about the person written on his strip. Besides being introduced to new classmates, students will receive practice in some valuable skills such as questioning techniques, memory, and attention to detail. When each student has asked 15 questions (or earlier—if someone makes a correct guess within 15 questions), let each student remove his strip to reveal his mystery identity. *Judith Brinckerhoff—Gr. 6, Hanaford School, East Greenwich, RI*

Extracurricular Encouragement

To inform my students of the extracurricular clubs and activities offered at our school, I decorate a bulletin board with a giant hand and the title "Drake Deals A Great Hand!" In the hand, I place several giant playing cards: each decorated with a picture to illustrate a particular club or activity. For example, one card is decorated with a mask to symbolize our school's Drama Club. Another card is labeled with musical notes to represent the school's chorus. To add a fun finishing touch, I staple pieces of confetti and streamers made from curling ribbon to the display. *Dot Weld— Grs. 5 & 6, Drake Middle School, Auburn, AL*

Welcome-Back Coupons

Welcome your new class in style with this fun activity. For each student, duplicate a page of back-to-school coupons such as those shown below. Cut out each page of coupons; then cut the coupons in half and put the pieces in a Ziploc® bag along with a low-fat cookie, a stick of sugarless gum, or another treat. Place one of these bags on each child's desk on the first day of school. As students enter the room, instruct them to tape the matching pieces together to reveal their surprise treats. *Brenda H. McGee—Gr. 4, Meadows Elementary, Plano, TX*

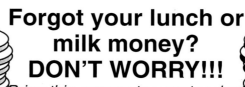

Free Snack During Break Time
Good for today or any day!

Forgot your lunch or milk money? DON'T WORRY!!!
Bring this coupon to your teacher.

Lost Your Pencil? NO PROBLEM!
Trade in this coupon for a brand-new one.

Need an encouraging word?
Show this coupon to your teacher and get ready to be encouraged!

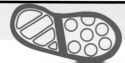

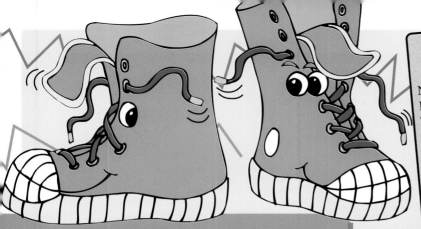

Back-To-School Miniforms

Use the handy miniforms on page 14 to save time and make classroom management a breeze.

- **Be A Television Terminator!:** Place a stack of these coupons in a basket on your desk. Encourage students to take a coupon home, complete it, and have a parent sign it to verify that his child didn't watch any television that night. (You may want to exempt news shows or educational programs.) The following day, have students place their signed coupons in a second basket. Periodically draw a few names from this basket and award "Television Terminator" prizes such as pencils, stickers, or notepads to the winners. Discard the remaining signed coupons and begin the challenge again.
- **Artwork Label:** Duplicate a supply of these labels to attach to your students' art projects.
- **Please Remember…:** Staple this reminder onto papers that need to be returned, notes that need to be signed, incomplete homework assignments that must be finished, or requests to parents for supplementary materials. Duplicate the form on brightly colored paper so that it's sure to grab the proper person's attention.
- **Student Information Card:** Have students or parents complete copies of this form at the beginning of the year. Keep the stack handy in your desk to use as a quick reference.

Beth Gress, Mt. Gilead, OH

The Big D Is Coming

Last year our students weren't the only ones to enjoy a few back-to-school surprises. Several weeks after school started, signs reading "The Big D Is Coming!" began to appear in the teachers' lounge and workrooms. Curiosity mounted as later signs read "Come To The Big D On Friday Afternoon!" The Big D turned out to be a "D-essert" party for the staff—complete with ice cream and a wide array of toppings. This delicious treat was a super way for all of us to celebrate a successful start to a new year. *Jennifer Overend—Gr. 6, Aprende Middle School, Chandler, AZ*

"Graph-tastic" Facts

Get acquainted with your new class, and introduce a super math lesson at the same time with this graphing activity. Have each student or pair of students select a topic on which to interview classmates. Students might ask about such subjects as birthday months, hair or eye colors, types of pets, numbers of family members, favorite ice-cream flavors, or numbers of books read over the summer. Provide time for students to interview classmates and compile their data. Give each child a copy of a class roster to insure that all information is complete.

After students have compiled their data, give each child a copy of the open graph on page 13. Walk students through the process of titling their graphs and filling in the categories along the bottom. Provide colorful markers with which students can complete their bar graphs. Display the graphs on a bulletin board entitled "The Greatest Class Ever—Bar None!"
Beth Gress

No Horsing Around

Discussing classroom rules is an important first-week task that doesn't have to be boring for your students. After discussing our class rules, I post the "Schoolhouse/horse Rules" poster shown above. My students get a real chuckle out of the puns and figurative language used in the rules. For an extended activity, I have each cooperative group choose an animal and write a list of school rules based on it. Groups begin by brainstorming words associated with their animals; then they skim encyclopedia articles for more words to add to their lists. Finally they use their word lists to create posters similar to my example. *Annette Manley, Ft. Caroline Elementary, Jacksonville, FL*

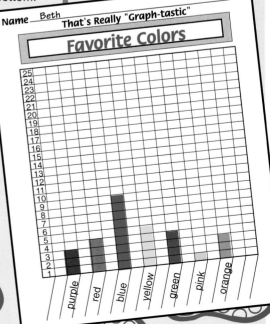

Name _Beth_   That's Really "Graph-tastic"
Favorite Colors

purple red blue yellow green pink orange

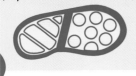

Patterns

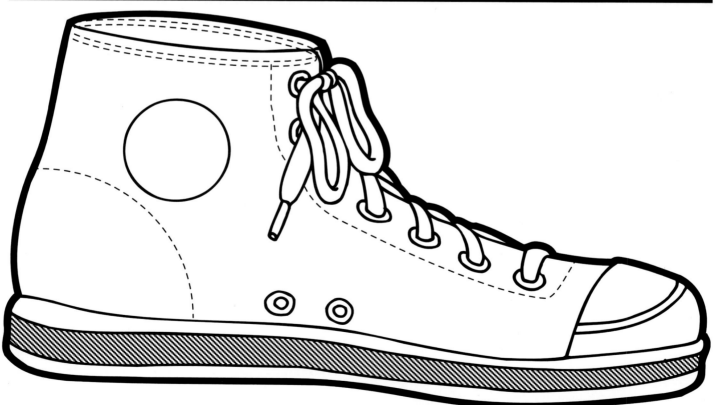

Note To Teacher: Use the postcard pattern with "Wish You Could Have Been There!" on page 6. Use the sneaker pattern with "Step Right Up To A New Grade!" on page 6.

Name _____

My
Appointment Clock

©The Education Center, Inc. • *THE MAILBOX®* • *Intermediate* • Aug/Sept 1995

Note To Teacher: Use with "Appointment Clocks" on page 7.

Name _____   Back to school

Brown-Bag It!

Read the following list of categories. After you get home today, find one item to represent each category. (The item must be small enough to fit into the lunch bag that your teacher will give you.) Try to find items that are 3-D and unique. Bring your bag to school tomorrow. Be prepared to share the contents of your bag with your classmates.

CATEGORIES

- a hobby or free-time activity that you enjoy
- one of your favorites (food, color, music, book, etc.)
- future plans or goals
- something you'd like to do better
- a place you'd like to visit
- something special about your family
- the best part of summer vacation
- something that reminds you of a memorable event or time in your life
- something that you really dislike
- a talent or special ability that you have

©The Education Center, Inc. • *THE MAILBOX®* • *Intermediate* • Aug/Sept 1995

Note To Teacher: Use with "Brown-Bag It!" on page 8. Provide each student with a copy of this reproducible and a small paper lunch bag.

11

A Poster All About...

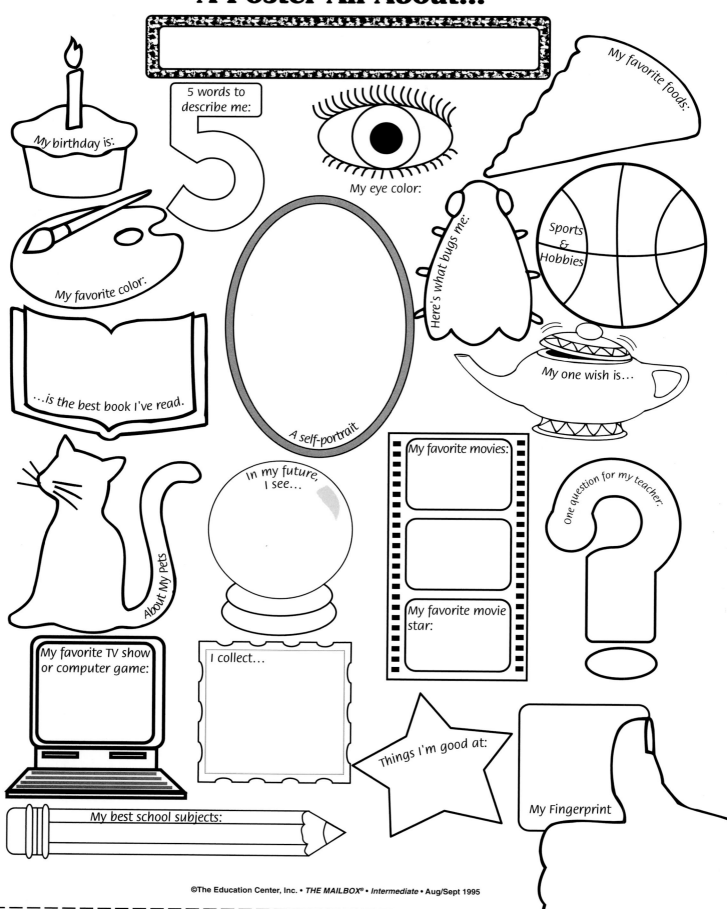

My birthday is:

5 words to describe me:

My eye color:

My favorite foods:

My favorite color:

Sports & Hobbies

...is the best book I've read.

Here's what bugs me:

My one wish is...

A self-portrait

About My Pets

In my future, I see...

My favorite movies:

My favorite movie star:

One question for my teacher:

My favorite TV show or computer game:

I collect...

Things I'm good at:

My Fingerprint

My best school subjects:

Note To Teacher: Use with "A Poster About Me" on page 7.

Name(s) ____________________ Making a bar graph

That's Really "Graph-tastic"!

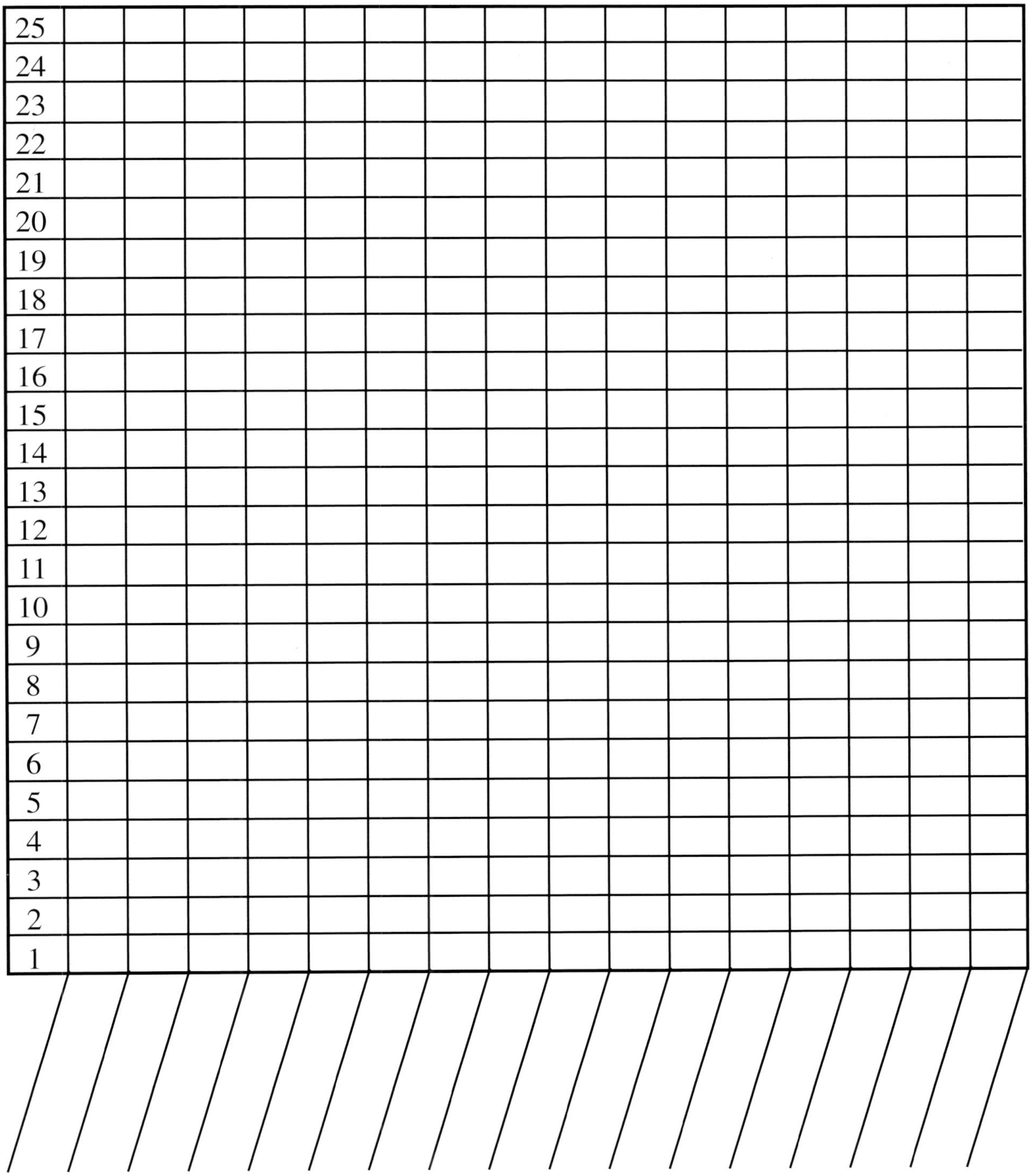

25
24
23
22
21
20
19
18
17
16
15
14
13
12
11
10
9
8
7
6
5
4
3
2
1

Note To Teacher: Use with " 'Graph-tastic' Facts" on page 9. Have each student write the title of his graph in the box at the top; then have him write the categories in the spaces along the bottom. (Depending on their data, you may wish to advise students to skip spaces between the categories in order to spread out the bars.) Finally have the student illustrate his data by drawing and coloring bars on his graph.

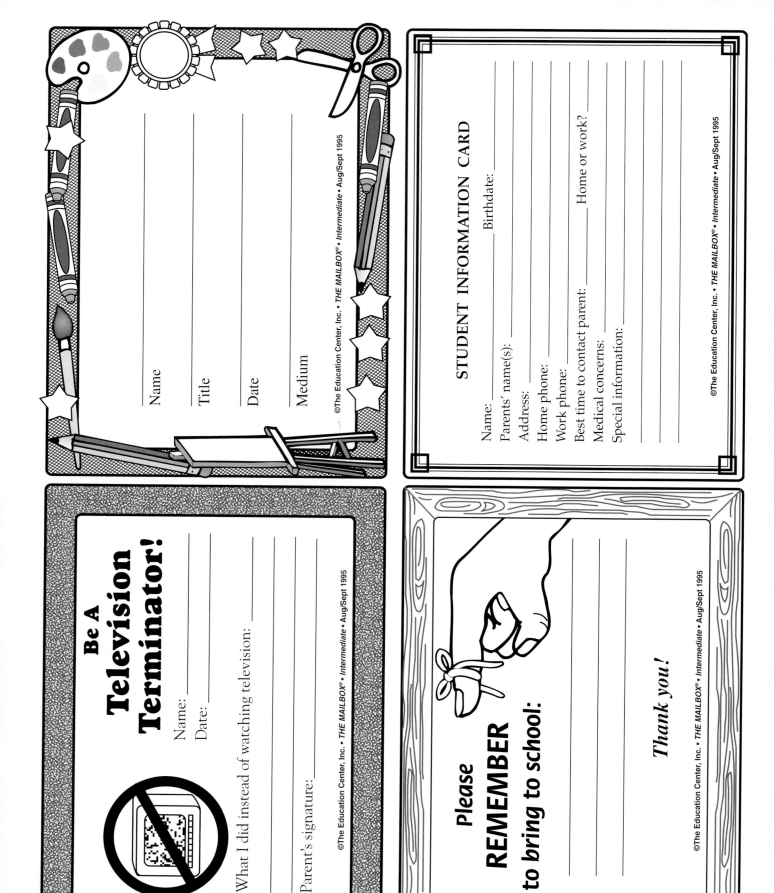

Name

Title

Date

Medium

STUDENT INFORMATION CARD

Birthdate: _____

Name: _____

Parents' name(s): _____

Address: _____

Home phone: _____

Work phone: _____

Best time to contact parent: _____ Home or work? _____

Medical concerns: _____

Special information: _____

Be A Television Terminator!

Name: _____

Date: _____

What I did instead of watching television: _____

Parent's signature: _____

Please REMEMBER to bring to school:

_____

Thank you!

Note To Teacher: Use with "Back-To-School Miniforms" on page 9.

Spur Them On!

Teacher-Tested Ideas For Motivating Students

Motivating students—it seems to get tougher every year. But never fear! Our subscribers are ready to share their most successful motivational strategies. So saddle up to the following classroom-proven ideas and get ready to spur your students on to a great year!

The ABCs Of Student Motivation

For a handy reminder about how to motivate your students, take a look at the colorful poster on page 20. Filled with quick tips on motivating and encouraging students, these words of wisdom will vitalize your teaching and refocus your energies in a snap. Mount the poster on a wall near your desk or inside the door of your teacher's closet—wherever it can be reached when you need help motivating a student. *Poster written by Barb Witteman, Miami University, Oxford, OH*

Student-Of-The-Day Bookmarks

Encourage attendance with the help of a Student-Of-The-Day calendar. Duplicate a supply of the award bookmarks found on page 22. Cut out the bookmarks and store them in a basket. At the start of each month, write a student's name and an interesting historical fact or famous person's birthday in each school day on a large calendar. Explain to the class that the child whose name is listed in a particular space will be that day's honored student.

Each morning have the student of the day read his fact to the class. During the day, allow the honored child to run errands and perform special tasks for you. As a thank-you gift, let him pick a bookmark from the basket. Not only does the student earn extra strokes for being helpful, but he also has a special class privilege to look forward to. *Therese Durhman—Gr. 5, Mountain View School, Hickory, NC*

First And In Front
Step up to the front of the class and be the line leader on this day:

Hang Ten!
Enjoy ten minutes of FREE time at the computer or the center of your choice.

Munch With Me!
For being such a great helper, enjoy a special lunch with the teacher on this day:

Class Test Average

In my class, tests aren't a dreaded evil, but a fun class challenge! Each time my students take a test, they try to work together to beat our previous class test average. This challenge encourages my students to work harder on their individual scores in order to bring up the class average. When we beat our average, everyone has a reason to celebrate! *Roseann Graf—Gr. 6, Oak Ridge Elementary, Chino Hills, CA*

"Berry" Good Spellers

Motivate your students to prepare for spelling tests with a "berry" easy idea! Duplicate a class supply of the berry pattern on page 22. Have students color and cut out their berries; then have them store the cutouts in personal work folders. When a child scores 100 percent on a spelling test, use a hole puncher to punch out one of the numbers on her berry. After all ten numbers have been punched, reward the student with a No Homework Pass (see the pattern also on page 22); then give her another pattern so that she can continue this "berry" motivating project. *Betty Wastlick—Gr. 4, St. Mary's School, Richland Center, WI*

I'm A "BERRY" Good Speller!

Homework Motivator

To encourage students to complete their homework, fill a small trunk with inexpensive treats; then close and padlock the trunk. Place the padlock's key on a ring with two similar keys. Duplicate the homework incentive chart on page 21 for each student. Also duplicate a supply of the key pattern.

After checking homework, stamp one space on the chart of each student who completed his assignment. When the last box on a row is stamped, give the child a No Homework Pass (see the pattern on page 22) and a paper key. On Friday, let each student who earned a paper key choose one key from the ring and try to open the padlock. If he picks the right key, allow the lucky student to select a treat from inside the trunk. *Linda Eller—Gr. 6, Idlewild Elementary, Memphis, TN*

You're "Topps®" With Me!

Whenever a student in my class is the only child to make 100 percent on an assignment or test, I reward her with an unusual—and highly popular—award. First I give the hardworking student a certificate labeled "Super Student Topps® Award"; then I give her a package of Topps® sports cards. Depending on the season, I give my students basketball, baseball, football, or hockey cards manufactured by the Topps® company. My students enjoy this incentive and love being among my "Topps®" students. *Pamela J. Spring—Gr. 4, Anna Jarvis Elementary, Grafton, WV*

Name ____

Social Studies Quiz
The Civil War

1. Choose one of these famous people and explain what role he/she played in the Civil War:

_____ _____ _____

_____
_____
_____

2. Explain the difference between an abolitionist and a secessionist:_____
_____
_____

3. On the back of this page, make a chart that compares and contrasts the North and the South.

Name ____

Division Test

1. 32$\overline{)576}$ 2. 23$\overline{)345}$ 3. 43$\overline{)685}$

4. 19$\overline{)710}$ 5. 92$\overline{)987}$ 6. 72$\overline{)989}$

7. Explain what mistakes were made in solving these problems. Write your explanations on the back of this test.

a. $\begin{array}{r}38r29\\42\overline{)1515}\\-125\\\hline365\\-336\\\hline29\end{array}$ b. $\begin{array}{r}45r41\\51\overline{)2346}\\-204\\\hline306\\-255\\\hline41\end{array}$

Colorful Tests

When duplicating tests, I run off two or three copies on colorful paper. On test day, I randomly distribute the tests; then I challenge students who get the colorful copies to make an A. I reward students who meet that challenge with a No Homework Pass. (See the pattern on page 22.) My students try harder to prepare for tests since they never know when they might receive a "colorful" copy. *Brenda N. Dalton—Gr. 6, Cradock Middle School, Portsmouth, VA*

The Great Behavior Raffle

To motivate good behavior and homework completion, I started the Great Behavior Raffle. On Friday each student who completed all work and exhibited responsible behavior gets to place his name in my raffle box. Once a month I pull a name out of the box and reward the lucky student with an inexpensive gift. I also photograph the child holding his prize; then I mount the photo on a piece of poster board that is displayed in my classroom year-round. This display is a great visual reminder of how doing the right thing pays off! *Christel S. Pedota—Gr. 5, St. Agnes Of Bohemia School, Chicago, IL*

Friday Challenge

Keep your students on task all week long by instituting a Friday Challenge. Pair up with another teacher in your grade level. On Monday announce to students that your partner's class has challenged yours to an activity on Friday (a kickball game, a geography bee, etc.). Only students who stay on task throughout the week will be included in the challenge. You'll be amazed at the quality of work your students will produce with this easy incentive. *Eileen J. Harford—Grs. 5 & 6, Orchard Middle School, Solon, OH*

Meal Tickets

To inspire my students to excel, I designate certain lessons as "meal ticket" activities. After the lesson is taught, I write clear expectations for my students' work on the board. As the children work through the lesson, I move about the room making comments and offering feedback. I also distribute small pieces of paper labeled "Meal Ticket" to students who are working on task. At the end of the lesson, those students write their names on the tickets and drop them into a bucket. Once a month I draw two tickets. Each winner and a friend come to my house for dinner and dessert. It's amazing what kids will do for a little spaghetti and ice cream at the teacher's house! *M. J. Goewey—Gr. 5, River Road Elementary, Eugene, OR*

Catch 'Em Doing Good!

At the beginning of the school year, I give each of my students an incentive chart with 20 spaces. Each time a student exhibits responsible behavior, I stamp one or two spaces on his chart. When the student has earned 20 stamps, he can cash in his chart for a special privilege, such as an extra half hour of computer time. Or he can choose to fill another sheet and cash in all 40 spaces for a reward of even greater value, such as a night of no homework, a chance to serve as another teacher's helper, or joining another class for recess. Focusing on positive behaviors—now *that's* motivating! *Mary Pio—Gr. 4, Madie Ives Elementary, Miami, FL*

Name_____

You're GRRR-eat!

Marvelous Monday

Starting off the week on a positive note is a great motivator. On Monday have each student draw the name of a classmate from a basket. Have the student write a positive note about his classmate and then deliver it. After reading the note, have the classmate store it in his special "Marvelous Monday" folder. Encourage students to pull out their folders anytime they're discouraged or need a lift. When you see a folder out on a child's desk and it's not Marvelous Monday, you'll know that somebody needs a little extra encouragement. *Dawn Helton—Gr. 4, Read-Turrentine Elementary, Silsbee, TX*

A Gripping Motivator

When I notice a student staring into space during writing workshop, I know that writer's block must be the culprit. To motivate that child to move past the block, I quietly go to her desk and put a brand-new pencil gripper on her pencil. While it may not write words on the paper, the gripper lets the student know that I understand her struggle. Sometimes that little gesture is enough to motivate a student to start writing. *Maxine Pincott—Gr. 4, Oliver Ellsworth School, Windsor, CT*

The Breakfast Club

Want to create a hunger for doing their best in your students? At the end of each month, reward students who have turned in all assignments and maintained responsible behavior by making them members of the Breakfast Club. One morning during the next month, invite this group of industrious students to join you 20 minutes before school for a delicious breakfast of doughnuts and juice. *Roseann Graf—Gr. 6, Oak Ridge Elementary, Chino Hills, CA*

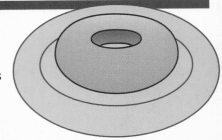

Motivational Moolah

Here's an idea that is especially effective during the last quarter of the school year when motivation is likely to hit an all-time low. Duplicate a supply of "motivational moolah" bills (or use play money). Announce to students that they will be able to earn the money for such behaviors as turning in assignments on time, keeping desks tidy, following class rules, and completing extra-credit work. Conversely, they will be fined for breaking class rules, not turning in work, and exhibiting irresponsible behavior. Mount a poster listing ways to earn money and fines (see the example). Have each student make a simple ledger in which to record his earnings and fines. Allow students to use their money to buy class privileges such as extra computer or recess time. Or encourage them to save their bucks to spend at an end-of-the-year "white elephant" auction, stocked with items donated by students and their families. *Eileen J. Harford—Grs. 5 & 6, Orchard Middle School, Solon, OH*

Ways To Earn $

• Turn in completed, well-done assignment	$5.00
• Extra-credit book report	$5.00
• Clean tote tray and table	$10.00/week
• Test Scores	
(a) 90%–100%	$10.00
(b) Improvement of one letter grade	$5.00
• Working on a bulletin board	$5.00–$20.00
• Working in the library or office	$5.00–$20.00

Fines

• Messy desk	$10.00
• Disruptive behavior during a lesson or work period	$10.00
• Not turning in an assignment on time	$10.00
• Breaking a school rule	$10.00
• Showing disrespect to another student or an adult	$20.00

Gold Pencil Award

When one of our students has turned in all assignments and maintained responsible behavior during the month, we reward her with a special certificate and a metallic gold pencil. Our students are proud of these unique pencils, representative of their outstanding accomplishments. *Roseann Graf and Sue Winans—Gr. 6, Oak Ridge Elementary, Chino Hills, CA*

Help From Local Businesses

For unique awards, I browse through local phone books and newspaper ads looking for businesses that have the same names as my students. I contact each of these businesses and ask if it can donate items labeled with the company's logo; then I use these articles as rewards. My students have received hats, key chains, mugs, and many more fun items—all emblazoned with their names! We've found car dealerships, retail stores, pharmacies, and grocery stores that are more than willing to help youngsters achieve through these free rewards. *Uber Adams—Gr. 5, Jefferson Elementary, Butler, PA*

Goodie Grab Bags

Three's the magic number when it comes to motivating my students! I fill three separate bags with a different array of treats. In one bag, I place a variety of candy. I fill another bag with inexpensive items such as pencils, erasers, and notepads. The last bag is filled with homework passes and other special coupons. (See those featured on page 22.) When I want to recognize a student for exceptional effort, I let her "grab" a reward from the bag of her choice. *Theresa O'Connell—Gr. 5, Our Lady Of Grace School, Greensboro, NC*

Auction Coupons

What intermediate kid wasn't born to shop? With that fact in mind, I motivate my students by holding an auction every other month. I begin by duplicating and cutting out a supply of small coupons. On Friday, I give a coupon to each student who has exhibited good effort and behavior during the week. Students store their coupons in envelopes. About four or five times a year, I hold an auction during which students can spend their coupons on baked goods (donated by parents) and other inexpensive items. *Nancy Murphy—Gr. 5, Converse School, Beloit, WI*

Monthly Raffle

Here's another super idea for using the incentive chart on page 21. Give each student a copy of the chart. Stamp spaces for positive behavior, improvement, and quality work. When all of the spaces on a student's chart have been stamped, give him the option of using it to purchase a No Homework Pass (on page 22) or saving it to use at an end-of-the-month raffle. Collect a variety of items from yard sales, discount stores, free gifts in the mail, etc. On the last Friday of the month, hold a raffle during which students can exchange their charts for the items. *Debbie Patrick—Gr. 5, Park Forest Elementary, State College, PA*

Class Puzzle

In addition to rewarding individual efforts, I like to honor my students as a class for responsible behavior. I begin by having students choose a celebration they would like to work towards, such as a pizza party. I then draw and laminate a picture that represents the party, such as a pizza. I cut the picture into 10 to 12 pieces, which I store with a roll of tape in a Ziploc® bag. Whenever I catch the class as a whole on task or cooperating, I choose someone to select a piece and add it to the puzzle. The day after the puzzle has been completed, we choose a new theme and celebrate! *Eileen J. Harford—Grs. 5 & 6, Orchard Middle School, Solon, OH*

We All Scream For Ice Cream!

Divide the class into teams of five to six students each. On a bulletin board, post a large ice-cream cone for each team. Award points to teams each time a member exhibits responsible behavior, completes an assignment, shows kindness to a classmate, etc. At the end of the day, reward the team that has accumulated the most points with a paper scoop to place on its cone. When a team earns six scoops, reward it with an ice-cream treat. *Beverly Langland—Gr. 5, Trinity Christian Academy, Jacksonville, FL*

What if I get ZONKED?

BAG #1

BAG #2

BAG #3

Pam Crane

Who's The "Hottest" Class?

There are certain times—right before a holiday, at the beginning of spring, during the last month of school—when getting students to act responsibly becomes extra challenging. Solve that problem with a little friendly competition. Challenge another class to a contest based on whole-class behavior. Ask the teachers of special classes such as music, art, and P. E. to award points to a class that exhibits responsible behavior. Record the points for each class on a large paper thermometer posted outside the classroom door. At the end of the contest, reward the winning class with a video party. *Beverly Langland—Gr. 5*

Let's Make A Deal!

For a fun motivational activity, play a game of "Let's Make A Deal!" Set a goal for students such as reading 120 minutes a week. On Friday have each child who met the goal write his name on a slip of paper and drop it into a basket. Draw three names. Give each winner a small reward, such as a piece of candy; then give him a chance to trade his treat for what's in Bag #1, Bag #2, or Bag #3. After the three winners have made their choices, reveal the contents of each bag. Two of the bags should contain items such as pencils, bookmarks, stickers, or notepads. But one bag should contain a "zonk" prize such as your autograph or a paper clip. Students will love the excitement and pure fun of this motivator! *Jim Eaton—Gr. 6, Parkside Elementary, Normal, IL*

The ABCs Of Motivating Students

Accept each student for who he or she is.

Be positive in everything you do, and model this attitude for your class.

Communicate with all parents on a regular basis. Send "good news" notes home to celebrate students' achievements.

Develop a consistent plan for discipline. Treat everyone equally.

Eye contact is important. Arrange your classroom so that you can see every child.

Form teaching strategies that allow every student to become actively involved in the learning process.

Give yourself a pat on the back regularly—you can't motivate others if you're not motivated too.

Have students critique your lessons so that you can improve your techniques.

Introduce lessons in an exciting manner.

Join students in cooperative groups. Student interaction is a positive learning experience.

Keep students on task by walking around the room and conferring with them regularly.

Learn each child's name as soon as possible, and use it often.

Make each child feel special with a smile or an encouraging word.

Never let other students put down another child's answer, even if it is not correct.

Objectives provide structure and lesson continuity.

Provide feedback on all student work, including tests, as soon as possible.

Quietly listen if a student needs to talk to you.

Remember that relevant activities encourage student participation. Let students help plan your lessons.

Smile! Smile! Smile!

Take time to reflect on your lessons and how you motivated your students.

Use tasteful humor, and don't be afraid to laugh.

Vary the way you teach; provide a variety of activities.

Wait and give students a chance to respond.

X-cellent work and effort deserves to be recognized. Give at least one "good news" note to a child each day.

You can have students design and put up bulletin boards, giving them ownership of their classroom.

Zero in on the strengths of each child.

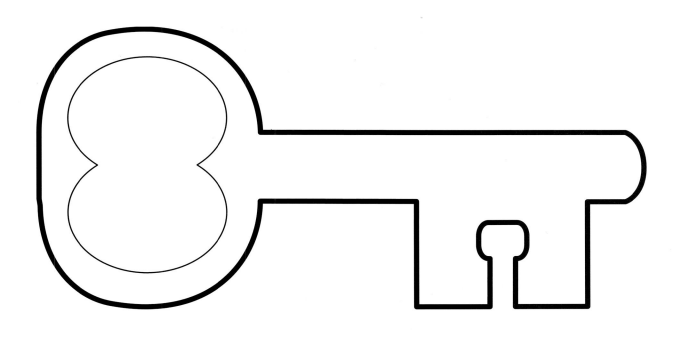

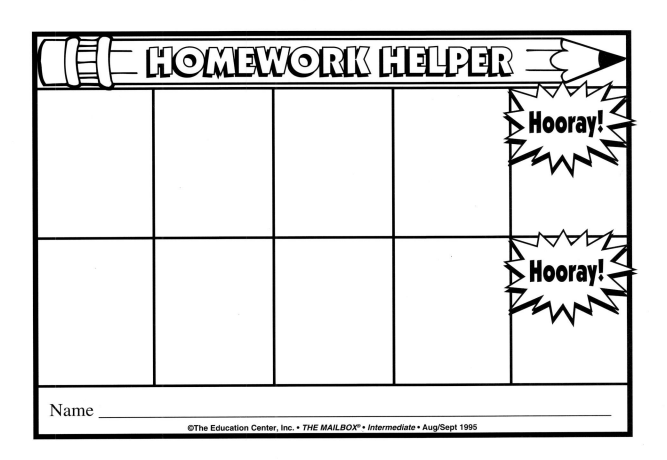

HOMEWORK HELPER

Hooray!

Hooray!

Name _____

Pattern

Use with " 'Berry' Good Spellers" on page 15.

1   10

I'm A **"BERRY"** Good Speller!

2   9

3   8

4   7

5   6

Patterns

Use with "Student-Of-The-Day Bookmarks" on page 15. Also use the No Homework Pass with " 'Berry' Good Spellers" on page 15, "Homework Motivator" and "Colorful Tests" on page 16, "Goodie Grab Bags" on page 18, and "Monthly Raffle" on page 19.

NO HOMEWORK PASS

Assignment:

_____

Name:

_____

Hang Ten!

Enjoy ten minutes of FREE time at the computer or the center of your choice.

Munch With Me!

For being such a great helper, enjoy a special lunch with the teacher on this day:

_____ .

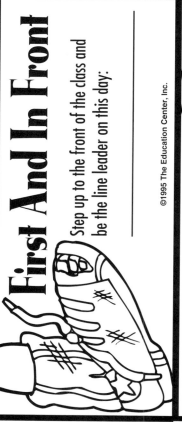

First And In Front

Step up to the front of the class and be the line leader on this day:

_____

How SWEET It Is!

Because your help was so sweet,

See your teacher for a special treat!

EXTRA! EXTRA!

For your extraspecial help, enjoy 15 minutes of free reading time!

Pulling Together

Our Subscribers' Tips For Effective Parent-Teacher Conferences

Even the most veteran teacher may get a little nervous when the time for parent-teacher conferences rolls around. But according to our subscribers, a conference is a time for open communication and positive plans for the future. Use the following suggestions from teachers like you to ensure productive and meaningful parent-teacher conferences.

Conference Highlights For Parents

During a parent-teacher conference, so much is discussed that it's often difficult for a parent to remember everything once he leaves. During each of my conferences, I take lots of notes on bright notepaper. I include several positive comments about the student, suggestions for how the parent can help at home, and news about upcoming projects and due dates. The parent is able to talk freely, while I converse and take notes at the same time. At the end of the conference, I give my notes to the parent to keep as a home reference.

Karen L. Stephani—Grs. 5–6
Roosevelt School
Plover, WI

Students' Self-Evaluations

Try this icebreaker to get end-of-term conferences started on the right note. Each child in my class writes a self-evaluation of her accomplishments during the term, then lists behavior and academic goals for the upcoming term. She reads this composition to her parent at the beginning of the conference. This gives the child a chance to communicate with both her parent and me, plus proudly share her accomplishments. Students' self-evaluations are always right on target!

Nancy Murphy—Gr. 5
Converse School
Beloit, WI

Evening Meeting With Parents

At the beginning of the year before Open House, I meet with all parents in the evening so that those who work outside the home are able to attend. I discuss my expectations for the upcoming year and ask parents to share what expectations they have. I also provide an overview of the year. This meeting opens the lines of communication and helps parents feel more at ease when it's time for individual conferences.

Dawn Helton—Gr. 4
Read-Turrentine Elementary
Silsbee, TX

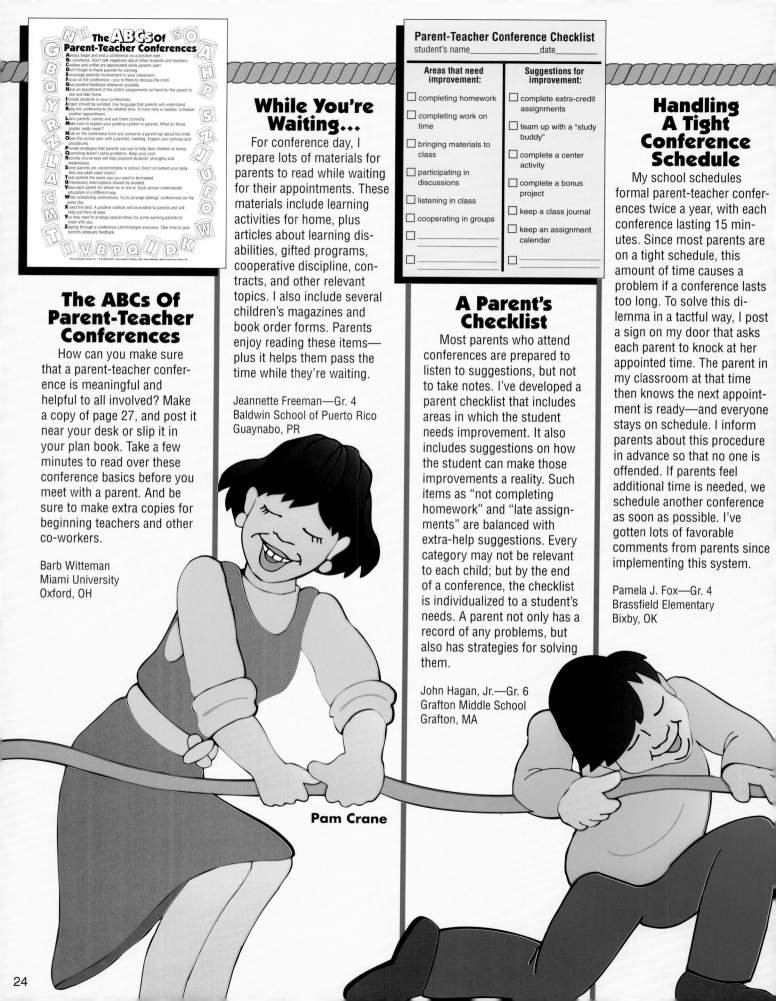
The ABCs Of Parent-Teacher Conferences

How can you make sure that a parent-teacher conference is meaningful and helpful to all involved? Make a copy of page 27, and post it near your desk or slip it in your plan book. Take a few minutes to read over these conference basics before you meet with a parent. And be sure to make extra copies for beginning teachers and other co-workers.

Barb Witteman
Miami University
Oxford, OH

While You're Waiting...

For conference day, I prepare lots of materials for parents to read while waiting for their appointments. These materials include learning activities for home, plus articles about learning disabilities, gifted programs, cooperative discipline, contracts, and other relevant topics. I also include several children's magazines and book order forms. Parents enjoy reading these items— plus it helps them pass the time while they're waiting.

Jeannette Freeman—Gr. 4
Baldwin School of Puerto Rico
Guaynabo, PR

Parent-Teacher Conference Checklist

student's name_____ date_____

Areas that need improvement:	Suggestions for improvement:
☐ completing homework	☐ complete extra-credit assignments
☐ completing work on time	☐ team up with a "study buddy"
☐ bringing materials to class	☐ complete a center activity
☐ participating in discussions	☐ complete a bonus project
☐ listening in class	☐ keep a class journal
☐ cooperating in groups	☐ keep an assignment calendar
☐ _____	☐ _____
☐ _____	☐ _____

A Parent's Checklist

Most parents who attend conferences are prepared to listen to suggestions, but not to take notes. I've developed a parent checklist that includes areas in which the student needs improvement. It also includes suggestions on how the student can make those improvements a reality. Such items as "not completing homework" and "late assignments" are balanced with extra-help suggestions. Every category may not be relevant to each child; but by the end of a conference, the checklist is individualized to a student's needs. A parent not only has a record of any problems, but also has strategies for solving them.

John Hagan, Jr.—Gr. 6
Grafton Middle School
Grafton, MA

Handling A Tight Conference Schedule

My school schedules formal parent-teacher conferences twice a year, with each conference lasting 15 minutes. Since most parents are on a tight schedule, this amount of time causes a problem if a conference lasts too long. To solve this dilemma in a tactful way, I post a sign on my door that asks each parent to knock at her appointed time. The parent in my classroom at that time then knows the next appointment is ready—and everyone stays on schedule. I inform parents about this procedure in advance so that no one is offended. If parents feel additional time is needed, we schedule another conference as soon as possible. I've gotten lots of favorable comments from parents since implementing this system.

Pamela J. Fox—Gr. 4
Brassfield Elementary
Bixby, OK

Pam Crane

The Week In Review

This organizational plan helps me prepare for conferences. Each week I store my students' checked papers in a large basket; then I distribute them on Friday afternoon. Students look over their papers, read my comments, and note their grades. Each child also receives his portfolio folder and a sheet entitled "My Week In Review" (see the example). Each student chooses two papers that he wants to place in his portfolio and completes his week-in-review sheet; then he staples these three items together. I set guidelines for the types of papers (e.g., two from each subject) that I want students to choose. At conference time, I share the child's week-in-review sheets and accompanying assignments with the parent. If the student attends the conference, I invite him to share his papers with his parent.

Joan Fate—Gr. 4
Whittier Elementary
Clinton, IA

Family-Teacher Conferences

About two weeks before conference day, each of my students takes home a notice that lists available time slots for appointments. When all of the notices have been returned, I send a confirmation letter to each parent. This letter includes the designated conference time, plus several encouraging comments about the child's progress. I ask the parent to respond by writing some positive statements about his child and his child's work. The student is also encouraged to add comments about his successes in school. In addition to these three items, I also ask that the parent and child cooperatively list any questions or concerns that they may have. When it's conference time, I encourage both the parent and child to attend—and to bring the letter. During the conference, we review the student's progress, discuss any questions and concerns, and write a brief plan of action for continued success. I later send a follow-up postcard thanking the parent for taking part in the conference.

Phil Forsythe
Northeastern Elementary
Bellefontaine, OH

Business Card Swap

I designed a personal business card, then photocopied it onto pink and blue tagboard. During Open House and conferences, I distribute these laminated cards to parents. I also ask parents for their business cards, which I keep in a file box. If it's more convenient for a parent, I'm able to contact him or her during the workday. Parents also have my number in case they need to reach me.

Maxine Pincott—Gr. 4
Oliver Ellsworth School
Windsor, CT

Parent's Guide

Conference minutes can pass by so quickly—and there's so much information to cover! To take better advantage of this precious time, I provide each parent with a copy of my "Parent's Guide To Mrs. Graf's Sixth Grade." This one-page outline explains my classroom policies and procedures. Parents really appreciate this guide and refer to it all year long.

Roseann Graf—Gr. 6
Oak Ridge Elementary
Chino Hills, CA

Parent Questionnaire

For a truly successful conference, plan for it! I always send home a parent questionnaire about two weeks before scheduled conferences. (See the reproducible on page 28.) I ask parents to respond to the questions so that I can better help them—and myself— prepare for our meeting. With this completed questionnaire as a guide, I can lead a much more organized conference!

Ann Nicklawske McGee—Gr. 4
Oakdale Elementary
Oakdale, MN

My Must List

For an effective conference, I always review my "must list":

1. Begin by saying something positive about the child.
2. Include the child in all or at least part of the conference. Ask for the child's suggestions.
3. Ask the parent what results he wants to see.
4. List actions that will be taken as a result of the conference.
5. Make a copy of the list for my files. Then give the list to the parent and child.
6. Suggest a follow-up call in two to four weeks to check progress.

Jane H. Reiser—Gr. 6
Jones Lane Elementary
Darnestown, MD

Plan Ahead!

I've found that planning for a conference is vital. Before a conference, I list three positive things about the student; jot down two subjects in which the student is doing well, plus his strengths in those areas; list questions I want to discuss with the parent; and note any plan that I can share with the parent to help with a particular problem area.

During the conference, I share these notes with the parent. I ask if she has any questions and if she would like her child to join us. If so, I invite the student's questions and comments. To conclude the conference, the parent, student, and I devise a plan for improvement. We also set a date to check on the progress of the plan.

Jean A. MacCoy—Gr. 5
St. Barnabas School
DeLand, FL

The ABCs of Parent-Teacher Conferences

Always begin and end a conference on a positive note.

Be courteous. Don't talk negatively about other students and teachers.

Cookies and coffee are appreciated while parents wait!

Don't forget to thank parents for coming.

Encourage parental involvement in your classroom.

Focus on the conference—you're there to discuss the child.

Give positive feedback whenever possible.

Have an assortment of the child's assignments on hand for the parent to see and take home.

Include students in your conferences.

Jargon should be avoided. Use language that parents will understand.

Keep the conference to the allotted time. If more time is needed, schedule another appointment.

Learn parents' names and use them correctly.

Make sure to explain your grading system to parents. What do those grades really mean?

Note on the conference form any concerns a parent has about his child.

Open the school year with a parents' meeting. Explain your policies and procedures.

Provide strategies that parents can use to help their children at home.

Quarreling doesn't solve problems. Keep your cool.

Records you've kept will help pinpoint students' strengths and weaknesses.

Some parents are uncomfortable in school. Don't sit behind your desk. And use adult-sized chairs!

Treat parents the same way you want to be treated.

Unnecessary interruptions should be avoided.

Value each parent for whom he or she is. Each person understands education in a different way.

When scheduling conferences, try to arrange siblings' conferences on the same day.

X-pect the best. A positive outlook will be evident to parents and will help put them at ease.

You may need to arrange special times for some working parents to meet with you.

Zipping through a conference shortchanges everyone. Take time to give parents adequate feedback.

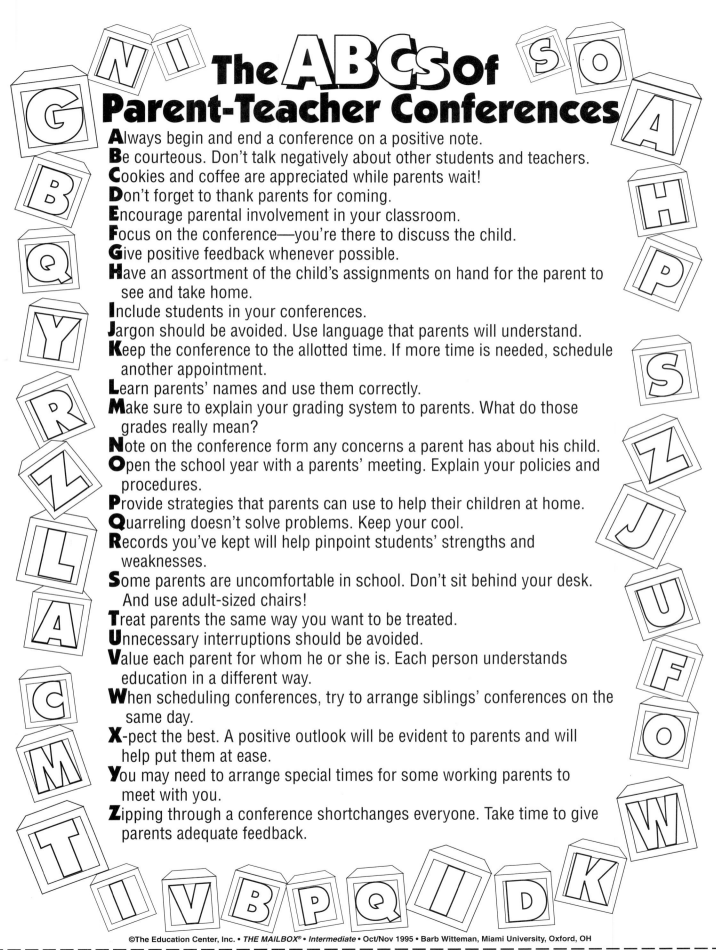

©The Education Center, Inc. • THE MAILBOX® • Intermediate • Oct/Nov 1995 • Barb Witteman, Miami University, Oxford, OH

Note To The Teacher: Use with "The ABCs Of Parent-Teacher Conferences" on page 24.

Let's Pull Together!

_____
date

Dear _____,

    Would you please take a few minutes to answer the questions below? Your responses will help us prepare for our upcoming conference. I look forward to meeting with you on _____

_____.

    Please return this questionnaire before our scheduled conference day.

               Thank you,

- What subject(s) does your child enjoy most?_____
  Why?_____
  _____
  _____

- What subject(s) seems difficult for your child?_____
  Why?_____
  _____
  _____

- About how much time does your child spend each night with homework and reading?
  _____

- Does your child participate in any after-school activities?_____
  If so, list them: _____
  _____

- Please list any concerns that you think we should address during our conference:
  _____
  _____
  _____
  _____
  _____

©The Education Center, Inc. • *THE MAILBOX*® • *Intermediate* • Oct/Nov 1995 • Idea by Ann Nicklawske McGee—Gr. 4, Oakdale Elementary, Oakdale, MN

Note To Teacher: Use with "Parent Questionnaire" on page 26.

IT COMPUTES!

How do teachers like you make the most of their classroom computers? Find out from our "techno-wise" subscribers.

Computer Station Organizer

Want to eliminate the question, "Whose turn is it?" Organize your computer station with a three-ring binder filled with laminated construction paper cut to fit (one sheet per student). Open the binder so that it stands freely (similar to a chart stand). Use a wipe-off marker to write a student's name on each page. When a student is finished with the assigned computer task, he flips the page over to show the next person in turn. When all of the sheets have been used, simply flip the entire set back to the first sheet and repeat the process. Using wipe-off markers will enable you to reuse the notebook again and again.

Patti Derr—Gr. 5
Northwest Area Elementary
Reading, PA

Computer Keyboard Covers

Looking for an inexpensive way to help your students practice memorizing the computer keyboard? Obtain the lid from a box of duplicating paper and cut away a flap from one of the long sides. Place the lid over the keyboard with the open side facing the student. Direct the student to place his hands inside the opening, under the box lid, and onto the keyboard. This allows the student to type without looking directly at the keyboard. Decorate the lid with Con-Tact® paper for a more attractive cover.

Kelly Howell—Gr. 6, Macedonia Elementary, Canton, GA

Font IDs

Help students easily identify your computer's fonts with this tip. Make a list of all the fonts on your computer by typing the name of each font in its own style. Print a copy of the font list and attach it to the wall near your computer. Students can quickly scan the list to decide which fonts they want to use.

Jennifer Overend—Gr. 6, Aprende Middle School, Chandler, AZ

Computer Bulletin Board

Here's a fresh idea for a bulletin board featuring computer terms. Use different fonts on the computer to type the terms and phrases you wish to highlight. After printing, cut out the terms and arrange them on a bulletin board around the title, "Computer Kids Are Cool, Calm, and Connected!"

Sue Reed—Gr. 4
Ebenezer Elementary
Lebanon, PA

Welcome To Our Pad!
Open House Ideas From Our Subscribers

Looking for some fresh ideas to make Open House a hoppin' event? Take a look at this collection of creative suggestions from the experts—our subscribers!

Glad You Could Visit!

On a table near the classroom door, I place a sign-in sheet for parents who attend our Open House. After they leave, I write a brief thank-you postcard to each parent who visited; then I drop the postcards in the nearest mailbox on the way home. The parents are always very appreciative of this extra effort I take just to say, "thanks." What a simple way to strengthen the all-important parent/teacher relationship! *Deena Block—Gr. 4, G. B. Fine Elementary, Pennsauken, NJ*

May We Quote You?

Involve the whole family in this writing project—and create a bulletin board that's perfect for Open House! About a week or two before your scheduled Open House, send home a reproducible asking parents and other family members to complete the sentence, "I've learned that…." Include a sample or two, such as "I've learned that most of the things I worry about never happen." Ask each family to send as many quotes as it would like. Post all responses on a "May We Quote You?" bulletin board for visitors to enjoy during Open House. *Brenda H. McGee—Gr. 4, Meadows Elementary, Plano, TX*

Snappy Silhouettes

To create an eye-catching Open House display, I use an overhead projector to make a silhouette of each student in my class. With a white pencil, I outline each child's profile on black paper; then I cut out the silhouette, mount it onto white paper, and frame it with red paper strips. These silhouettes are attached to my students' chairs and "greet" parents at our Open House. *Nancy Barra—Gr. 5, McCormick Elementary, Chicago, IL*

Fred

Looks just like me!

I've learned that as you go through life, always stop and eat the houseflies.

Treasure Hunt

Early in the year, reserve a bulletin-board space for each student. As the year progresses, have students select assignments and artwork to display in their spaces. Then, about a week before Open House, have each student complete the following activities:

1. Decorate a large, unsigned manila envelope.
2. Write an unsigned letter welcoming his parents to Open House.
3. Draw a self-portrait (also unsigned).

For Open House, place each student's collection of work from the bulletin board in his envelope. Put the envelope and the student's letter on his desk. Display students' self-portraits in the empty spaces on the bulletin board. When parents arrive for Open House, invite them on a treasure hunt to find their children's desks and portraits. *Jan C. Fox, Mariemont Elementary, Sacramento, CA*

Graffiti Charts

For Open House, hang several pieces of colorful bulletin-board paper outside your classroom. On each one write a sentence starter such as, "We love to…," "The funniest thing that ever happened was…," and "I really like it when my parent/child…." Place a bucket of colorful markers nearby; then invite parents and their children to fill the charts with their responses. *Debbie Schneck—Gr. 4, Fogelsville Elementary, Schnecksville, PA*

Welcome, Mom And Dad!

A few days before Open House, my students write letters to their parents. I place a copy of each student's letter in his portfolio. Then, on Open House night, each child's original letter is placed on his desk. Parents love these letters, which they take home as keepsakes of their child's year in the fourth grade. At the end of the year, each student writes another letter—this time to a student in the third grade. We compare this letter to the one written earlier for Open House. Students are surprised and delighted to see how their writing has improved over the year. *Maxine Pincott—Gr. 4, Oliver Ellsworth School, Windsor, CT*

A Student-Run Open House

Let your class take care of your Open House, from creating the invitations to baking healthy snacks! Have students greet parents, describe important aspects of the classroom, and answer any questions as best as they can. You can sit in the background with parents and help when the need arises. Students love having this responsibility, and your load is lightened a little! *Jodi Augustine—Grs. 4/5, The Montessori School, P.S. 27, Yonkers, NY*

Barry Slate

The winner of this delicious, chewy, and oh-so-slimy garden slug is...

DOOR PRIZES

And The Winner Is...

Motivate an interest in Open House by awarding some simple door prizes. Decorate your classroom with inexpensive houseplants or flower arrangements. At the close of Open House, have each guest drop his nametag in a box. Then draw names and award the plants to the winning parents. Reward the child of each lucky parent with a book, homemade gift, or other small item. *Patricia Dancho—Gr. 6 Language Arts, Apollo-Ridge Middle School, Spring Church, PA, and Debbie Schneck—Gr. 4, Fogelsville Elementary, Schnecksville, PA*

Time Travelers

Everyone in our school gets into the act when planning for Open House! Each year we teach an all-school unit prior to Open House. This past year our theme was history. Each teacher prepared a lesson based on a period in history (for example: the Victorian era). Then students "traveled through time" by rotating through the classrooms and creating projects related to the various time periods. On Open House night, parents and guests became time travelers too as they visited each classroom and observed the students' projects. *The Ames School Staff, Riverside, IL*

Frogs At Valley Forge

The Contribution Of Frogs To The Revolutionary War... The Untold Story.

Fourth-Grade Stars

Prior to Open House, I videotape each of my students answering the question, "What do you like best about fourth grade?" On Open House night, I play the tape for parents and guests. Both students and parents love to watch our class stars! *Debbie Schneck—Gr. 4*

Open House Self-Portraits

During the first week of school, have students draw and cut out large, simple paper-doll patterns. On the body of the cutout, have each student write three paragraphs: a description of himself that includes hobbies, interests, and special talents; a paragraph describing what he hopes to accomplish during the school year; and a paragraph explaining how he views the world. Instruct each student to personalize and decorate his pattern so that it resembles himself. On the night of Open House, display these paper-doll people in the classroom; then challenge parents to identify their children. Give the projects to parents to take home as keepsakes of their children's school year. *Theresa Hickey—Gr. 4, St. Ignatius School, Mobile, AL*

"Guess Who?" Wall

A real eye-catcher for the students, parents, and staff of my school is my "Guess Who?" wall. I ask each student to bring to class a baby picture and a recent photo of herself. I attach each student's baby photo to the outside of a folded sheet of pink or blue construction paper. The recent photo is attached to the inside. Students add their signatures and colorful decorations around their recent photos. I display these folded sheets on the wall outside our classroom. Everyone who visits at Open House loves to guess who's who! *Susan Giesie— Gr. 4, Ben Franklin School, Menomonee Falls, WI*

"Spring With The Arts" Open House

Last spring, the second- through fifth-grade classes in my building held a "Spring With The Arts" Open House. This event highlighted all the special teachers and activities in our school, including art, music, physical education, and the media center. Parents and guests were invited to visit all areas of our building. The library and parent-teacher organization hosted a book fair, the fifth-grade choir presented a concert, physical education students showed off their tumbling skills, and artwork was displayed in the hallways. Also, popcorn and drinks were offered at a minimal cost. The response to our spring Open House was marvelous! *Sandalynn K. Henry— Librarian, West Elementary, Newcomerstown, OH*

Scavenger Hunt

A scavenger hunt is the perfect way to show off your classroom during Open House without being pulled in a hundred different directions. Make a list of children's work that is displayed in your room. During Open House, have students accompany their parents around the classroom, checking off each item on the list that they find. Or challenge students to make up scavenger hunts for their parents. Have each student create a map with directions guiding his parents to find at least three projects, pictures, papers, progress charts, or other attractions around the classroom. Not only will parents be excited to see their children's work, but students will practice two important skills: writing directions and drawing maps. *Deena Block—Gr. 4, G. B. Fine Elementary, Pennsauken, NJ,* and *Debbie Schneck—Gr. 4, Fogelsville Elementary, Schnecksville, PA*

Guest Book

As parents arrive for Open House, I ask them to write their names and addresses in our classroom guest book. I also take lots of pictures throughout the evening. When I have the film developed, I request double prints. One set of prints is added to our guest book, while others are sent home in thank-you cards written by the students. With this idea, everyone has a memento of our Open House! *Linda Stroik—Gr. 4, Jackson Elementary, Stevens Point, WI*

Communication's The Key!

Open communication between parents and teacher is the key to getting the school year off to a successful start. As parents leave Open House, give each one a stamped postcard that you have preaddressed to yourself. Encourage parents to drop you a note about any concerns as their children adjust to the new grade level. This gesture assures parents that you are eager to stay in touch! *Penny Parchem, Dallas, TX*

Parent Packets

Each parent attending my Open House receives a colorful folder entitled "Parent Packet—For The Parents Of [student's name]." Inside each packet are copies of newspaper and magazine articles relevant to education and parenting skills. I also include classroom rules, our homework policy, suggestions for encouraging reading at home, tips for assisting with schoolwork, and directions for sending work in case of absences. I also include brochures from our local park system and our community college in which I've highlighted events of interest to parents and their children. My students' parents love getting these informative packets! *Patricia Novak—Gr. 4, Meadowbrook School, Eatontown, NJ*

Classroom Tour Book

For Open House, I number bulletin boards and other places in my classroom that I want to share with parents. Then I create a corresponding tour book that includes an explanation of each numbered item. For example, #1—"This is our 'We're Letter Perfect' bulletin board where we display 100 percent spelling papers." With tour book in hand, each student takes his parents on a guided classroom tour. *Ruth Hesketh—Grs. 4/5, Spencer Williams School, Downey, CA*

Keeping Open House "Open"

Everyone can have a wonderful time at an Open House that is casual and involves parents, students, and staff. Consider the following tips:

- If your chorus gives a presentation, include some sing-along numbers so everyone can join in.
- If you have a school band or orchestra, invite parents and teachers to bring their instruments and join in a concert.
- Have a dance for students, teachers, and parents.
- Set up carnival booths for older children to demonstrate math and science "magic."
- Invite everyone to activities in common areas such as the gym, cafeteria, or hallways.
- Try not to turn Open House into a mini-conference time.
- Serve refreshments and make sure that Open House is a real social event!

Julia Alarie—Gr. 6, Essex Middle School, Essex, VT

CENTER SOLUTIONS

Organizing And Managing Your Learning Centers

Learning center is a term that means different things to different teachers. But whether it's a set of flash cards, a file-folder activity, or a tape recorder, a learning center is a great way to provide students with important skills practice and reinforcement. Use these tips from our subscribers to make the organization and management of your learning centers as easy as pulling a rabbit out of a hat!

Shoebox Centers

To solve the problem of "But I don't have any space for centers!", I use "Shoebox Centers" in my classroom. Inside each individually labeled shoebox, I place directions for the activity, all the needed materials, and an answer key. A student can take a box back to her desk to complete or work in a quiet spot on the floor. When she has completed the center, the student writes her name on an index card and leaves the card sticking out of the box. This alerts me to check her work before I leave for the day. I write my comments and a grade (if desired) on her card; then I place the card on her desk for the student to read the next morning.

Wendy Shands
Grs. 6–8 Resource
Lake City Middle School
Lake City, TN

Clever Clothespin Tip

To squeeze a little extra space for centers out of my classroom, I use an adhesive such as Qwik-Tac™ to attach pinch clothespins below or around my bulletin boards. I then clip file-folder games and other center activities to the clothespins. This simple trick makes my centers easily accessible—plus the colorful activities brighten up my classroom walls!

Jodie Sell
Wasola, MO

Centers On A Table

If you've got a chart stand and a table in your classroom, then you've got a double-duty learning center! Place the chart stand in the middle of the table. On each side of the chart stand, hang a poster labeled with directions. Students can sit on either side of the chart stand and complete a center activity. Changing the centers is as simple as changing the posters!

Sharon Caskey—Gr. 4
Lincoln Elementary
Marshfield, WI

WORK A LITTLE MATH MAGIC
Write two original word problems that include fractions. Give them to a friend to solve.

Pocket Chart Centers

A pocket chart is just the tool to manage your classroom centers program. To begin, laminate a supply of red, yellow, and green paper strips. Each week program the strips with center activities as follows:

- Red strips: activities students must complete before the end of the day
- Yellow strips: extra-credit activities students can work on after they've completed the red strip activities
- Green strips: fun activities that don't earn extra credit but still keep the brain in gear!

Place each strip in your pocket chart. Changing the strips is easy; just wipe the strips clean and reprogram them with new tasks.

Shannon Berry—Gr. 4
Heritage Christian School
Brookfield, WI

A Two-Group System

Within our fourth-grade pod, we have a combined total of 17 computers. Each day students in my class spend 30 minutes working on these computers and 30 minutes in centers. To manage this hour, I divide my class into two groups: Group 1 and Group 2. Each of these groups is subdivided into four subgroups: 1A, 1B, 1C, 1D, and 2A, 2B, 2C, 2D. While Group 1 is working on the computers, Group 2 works on centers. I assign centers using a management chart (see the illustration). For example, if Suzy is in group 2B, she will work on center #2 on Monday, center #1 on Tuesday, center #4 on Wednesday, and center #3 on Thursday. Once a student knows what her subgroup number/letter is, all she has to do is look at the chart to find her center assignment for the day. After 30 minutes are up, the groups switch.

Stephanie Speicher—Gr. 4
Elm Road School
Mishawaka, IN

	1	2	3	4
Monday	A	B	C	D
Tuesday	B	C	D	A
Wednesday	C	D	A	B
Thursday	D	A	B	C

The First 20 Minutes

My learning centers program is just the way to start the day! I divide my class into four groups. During the first 20 minutes of each morning, each student goes directly to one of four learning centers. Also during this 20-minute session, I meet with a remediation group of three or four students who work with me on any needed skills. Morning is a great time for centers, because it helps students focus on the school day ahead.

Charlotte Hinson
Bellaire Elementary
Bossier, LA

Read Chap. 6 in our novel.

Respond to Chap. 6 in your journal.

Check math homework with a partner.

Complete a crossword puzzle.

Make a word search puzzle with spelling words.

Design a book-report project.

Try to memorize the names of 10 cities in our state.

Design a bumper [...] National Pet Lovers Week.

Magic Wheel

Making sure that every student visits each of your learning centers doesn't have to be a management miracle! For a simple center-assignment tool, cut two circles—one large, one small—from poster board; then laminate the circles. Fasten the circles together with a brad as shown; then divide them into sections according to the number of student groups. Use a wipe-off marker to label the outer sections with the names of your learning centers. Label the inner wheel's sections with your student groups. Post the wheel where it can easily be seen. When you're ready for groups to move to a different center, simply rotate the inner wheel in a clockwise direction. Continue rotating the wheel until it has returned to its original position. When you want to change centers or groups, just wipe the wheel clean and reprogram it.

Merle Goess—Special Education Grs. 4–6
Albany Avenue Elementary
North Massapequa, NY

Learning Center System

Wondering how to flow 30 students through your learning centers without complete chaos? First align five extra student desks along a wall. Label each desk with a different-colored index card: Team #1, Team #2, Team #3, Team #4, and Team #5. Place a center activity on each desk. Divide your class into five numbered teams; then write each student's name on a small index card that matches the color of his team's desk label. Stack each team's name cards (name side up) on a corner of its desk.

To move students through the centers, have each child whose card is on the top of his team's stack visit his team's center. When the student is done, have him put his name card at the bottom of the stack; then have him quietly inform the student whose card is now at the top of the deck to take his turn. At the end of the day, simply rotate the activities to different desks. By the end of the week, each team will have had a chance to complete each center.

Beverly Langland—Gr. 5
Trinity Christian Academy
Jacksonville, FL

Magnetic Centers

For fun centers your students will really stick with, look no farther than your metal file cabinet. Place a strip of magnetic tape on the back of a learning center; then stick the center on the side of your file cabinet. Or use appealing refrigerator magnets to adhere your center to the cabinet.

Jeri-Lyn Flowers
Cartersville Elementary
Cartersville, GA

Simple Storage

Trying to find space for learning centers in an already-crowded classroom can be a real challenge. Make room for your learning centers with these space-saving ideas:

- Store learning centers in plastic milk crates placed on the floor along a wall.
- Purchase an inexpensive, three-tiered rolling cart. Use it to hold file-folder activities and other learning-center materials.
- Collect four same-sized cardboard boxes. Use clear packing tape or glue to attach the boxes together as shown. Place the cross-shaped storage box on a desk; then fill each section with a learning center. By positioning a chair in front of each box, you've got four instant learning stations.

Deena Block—Gr. 4
George B. Fine Elementary
Pennsauken, NJ

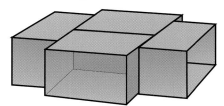

Center Choices

Intermediate kids love making choices, so I let my students choose the centers they want to work on. I label a magazine file for each subject. In each file, I place learning centers on that subject. These are centers that easily fit inside a large manila envelope or file folder. I place centers that are too large for the magazine files on shelves that are also labeled according to subject. When a student finishes his classwork, he is allowed to pick a center and take it back to his desk to complete.

Kate Luchtel—Grs. K–8 Tutor
Gardena, CA

Learning Center Tickets

Build accountability into your learning center program with this practical idea. Give each student a Learning Center Ticket, as shown, labeled with a number for each of your learning centers. Divide your class into groups—one per center. Rotate the groups through the centers at a pace that works best with your schedule (one center per day, all centers by the end of the week, etc.). When a student finishes his first center, he writes the center's name beside number 1 on his ticket; then he clips his work to the back of the ticket. As he progresses through the centers, he fills out his ticket and attaches his work. At the end of the day or week, collect work from one or two centers; then orally go over the remaining centers. Learning center tickets will increase student accountability and prevent casual attitudes about centers.

Clorinda Roache—Gr. 6
Sherwood Park Elementary
Fayetteville, NC

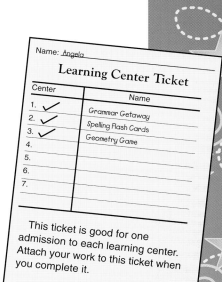

Name: Angela

Learning Center Ticket

Center	Name
1. ✓	Grammar Getaway
2. ✓	Spelling Flash Cards
3. ✓	Geometry Game
4.	
5.	
6.	
7.	

This ticket is good for one admission to each learning center. Attach your work to this ticket when you complete it.

Welcoming Your Non-English-Speaking Student

If you've just found out that you're getting a non-English-speaking pupil in your classroom, don't panic! Here are plenty of activities to help your new student feel at home with the language and the classroom—even before the language specialist arrives!

by Carolyn Dobervich and Karen Thacker

Pointing To Our Roots

Prepare your class to welcome the new student by pointing out that America is a nation of varied cultures. Emphasize this point by having each student stick a pin in a world map to point out the country(ies) from which her ancestors originally emigrated. Instruct each student to use pictures, songs, or artifacts to share something about her heritage.

The Newcomer's Bag

Non-English-speaking students thrive when treated as members of the class. However, they also benefit by working alone or with a partner. Store the following no-stress, success-based activities—along with directions—in a Newcomer's Bag. Then allow time for the non-English-speaking student to work on these activities alone or with a buddy.

- **Simple games such as Candyland®, Old Maid, Lotto, or Concentration®:** Games teach directions, vocabulary, and social skills.
- **A picture dictionary.**
- **A photo album that shows typical class activities, and labels objects and areas of the room:** Help the student become familiar with the daily routine by illustrating a clock showing the time of day by each photo.
- **A simple craft:** When the student needs a break from English, let him experiment with clay, tracing or coloring activities, or maze books. Provide materials for making bag puppets or paper dolls.
- **Magazines and catalogs to cut and paste:** Have the student cut out, categorize, and label pictures of clothing, body parts, familiar objects, and people. Challenge the student to find illustrations for action verbs such as *running*, *eating*, *standing*, and *playing*.
- **Stamps and coins:** Instruct a partner to help the student make a poster labeling American bills, coins, and stamps. Provide small change and play money so the student can practice making equivalent sets (e.g., five pennies equals a nickel), selecting the correct money to pay for items, and making change.
- **Puzzles, especially United States and world map puzzles.**
- **Books on tape:** Look for simple, popular stories such as fairy tales that the child might already know.

Campus Tour Book

Send the student and a buddy on a tour of the campus with an instant camera. Instruct the buddy to take a picture of the new student at each location. Have the two place the developed photos into a book and label each location. Then have the pair find the locations again, using the book and spoken directions such as "Go to the office" and "Let's visit the library."

The Library

Build An Alphabet Book

Give the non-English-speaking student a blank book with one page for each letter of the alphabet. As the student learns new words, instruct him to add them to the book on the appropriate pages. Also encourage the student to illustrate items on each page. As the book grows, so will the student's confidence!

Make A Calendar

Encourage the non-English-speaking student to share his culture with the class by creating a cultural calendar. On an inexpensive calendar, have him mark important holidays or remembrance days from his country. Next instruct the student to paste his own illustrations over the printed ones. Finally have him write native-language words for numbers, days of the week, and months next to the English versions on the calendar.

June: tháng sáu

Sunday chủ nhật	Monday thú hai	Tuesday thú ba	Wedr thú
2	3	4	
9	10	11	12
16	17	18	19

How To Speak English To Someone Who Doesn't

- **Speak naturally, but clearly, with pauses.** Pausing gives the student time to translate.

- **Point, pantomime, and label.** Hold or point to the objects you are talking about. Place bilingual labels on objects around the room.

- **Let the child be silent.** A long period of silence is normal in second-language learners. Students who are allowed weeks or months to listen without speaking actually learn faster.

- **Model rather than correct.** Don't be concerned with pronunciation or grammar. Instead, check your understanding by repeating correctly what you think the student tried to say.

- **Let the child rest.** It is exhausting to work in a foreign language. The non-English speaker needs opportunities to stop listening.

- **Keep checking for understanding.** In some cultures, children are taught not to answer a question with a direct "no." Give the child a hand signal or a card to place on the desk when he needs help.

- **Don't confuse conversational with academic English.** Conversation is easiest and comes first. Most children need five to seven years of language support before they are academically independent.

- **Encourage and appreciate bilingual students.** Children who are discouraged from using their native language can develop other problems and sometimes never become proficient in either language. Use a translator, a bilingual dictionary, or any other help you can get to communicate while the student's English is emerging.

13   14   15

20   21   22

Wrapping Up Another Year

Motivational Activities For End-Of-The-Year Fun & Learning

How do you keep students motivated and tuned in till the final good-byes are said? This collection of our subscribers' favorite ideas offers plenty of practical suggestions—just in time to ensure a happy ending!

It's In The Bag!

This project is a great way to review the year just completed, plus distribute photos you've taken throughout the year. Provide each student with a brown paper bag and a photo in which he's featured. Have the student paste the photo to the front of his bag. Then have the student list favorite activities and memories of the year on colorful strips of paper. Attach the completed bags—filled with the strips—to a bulletin board titled "[Your Grade] Grade: It's In The Bag!" Then send the bags home with students on the last day of school to share with their families. *Sharon Zacharda—Gr. 4, West View Elementary, Pittsburgh, PA*

Upcoming Attractions

Welcome *next* year's new students with posters created by *this* year's students! At the end of the year, provide each student with a 12" x 18" sheet of construction paper, plus a copy of the reproducible on page 45. Have each student follow the directions on the sheet to make a poster about the past year. Collect all of the completed projects and save them for next year. Then, on the first day of school, give each new student a poster so everyone will see what they have to look forward to. This project is always a hit with my students— those moving on to the next grade as well as incoming students who receive the posters. *Rita Geller—Gr. 4, Ramblewood Elementary, Coral Springs, FL*

See Ya' Later, Alligator!

Say, "See ya' later, alligator!" to each student in your class with a one-of-a-kind keepsake. Have each student cover a L'eggs® pantyhose box with green construction paper. Instruct the student to cut rows of teeth from white construction paper and paste them onto the top and bottom flaps. Provide wiggle eyes and black markers for students to complete the details of their projects. For a related writing project, have students describe favorite experiences of the past year in paragraphs titled "Now And Later." Then fill the students' alligators with Now And Later® candy. *Colleen Dabney—Gr. 6, Williamsburg Christian Academy, Williamsburg, VA*

KATIE
Student Of The Week

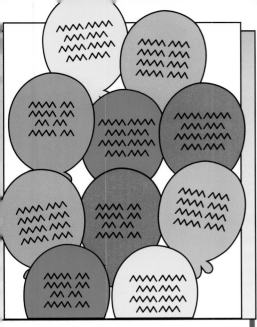

Up, Up, And Away!

Near the end of the year, I like to have my students acknowledge one another's talents, accomplishments, and admirable personality traits. I provide each student with a copy of our class roster, which also includes my name. Each student is instructed to write a positive comment beside each person's name on the roster (excluding himself). Next I give each student five or six pages of colorful balloon patterns. On each balloon, the student writes a classmate's name, his comment about that classmate, plus his signature. After cutting out their balloons, students distribute them by placing the cutouts upside down on their classmates' desks. Each student puts all of his balloons in an envelope; then I collect the envelopes. To complete the project, I attach each student's balloons to a long strip of computer paper and laminate the strip. The banners are displayed in class during the last weeks of school; then students take them home. I encourage students to hang their banners in their bedrooms and read them periodically as reminders of how wonderful they are!
Kathleen Walsh—Gr. 5, Chelsea Heights School, St. Paul, MN

The Most Important Thing

At the end of the year—as a way of "living, learning, and passing it on"—each of our fifth-grade grads completes the following statement: "The most important thing I've learned this year is...." Several statements are shared each day over our school's public-address system. They're also included in a fifth-grade graduation book. These insightful comments prove that students really do learn from one another! They're also more apt to heed tips from their classmates than from a teacher.
Kathy Williams—Grs. K–5 Counselor, Pleasant Grove Elementary, Pensacola, FL

Wrapping Up!

Take a tip from your Christmas bulletin boards and end the school year with an easy, eye-catching display. Cover your door or a bulletin board with cheerful, springtime wrapping paper or brightly colored butcher paper. Add a large bow and streamers in contrasting colors. Title the board "We're Wrapping Up A Great Year!" and you've got an attractive display that's as easy to put up as it is to take down. *Gaylin Black—Gr. 4, Angleton, TX*

We're Wrapping Up A Great Year!

We're Movin' Up To The Sixth Grade!

Name That Word

This activity is a great end-of-the-year review in any subject area. First I prepare paper strips, each labeled with an alphabet letter. (Omit *J, K, Q, X, Y,* and *Z.*) Each student draws a letter strip, then looks in his text for vocabulary words that begin with that letter. The student selects ten words and writes a definition for each one, without including the word. The next day I collect the definition sheets and redistribute them to students, making sure each child has a list other than his own. Each student reads the list of definitions he now has and supplies the words that have been defined. What an easy, fun way to review! *Paula Rush—Gr. 6, East Marshall Middle School, Gilman, IA*

Movin' On Up

Step right up to this easy, student-made hallway banner. Have each student trace an outline of her shoe on a long strip of yellow butcher paper. The shoe prints should all face the same direction when the paper is displayed horizontally. Within her shoe outline, have each student write one or two sentences about what she learned and enjoyed during the year. Or, as a variation, have students write what they are looking forward to in the upcoming year. Add the title "We're Movin' Up To The [Next Grade] Grade!" along the top edge of the paper. Display the banner in a hallway near your classroom. *Pamela Doerr—Substitute Teacher, Lancaster County Schools, Mount Joy, PA*

Class Prophecy Book

For a year-end writing project, have students create a class prophecy book. Assign each student a classmate to interview. After each student learns more about his assigned classmate's interests and hobbies, instruct him to write a paragraph predicting what that person will be doing 20 years from now. Bind the completed pages into a book to share at a year-end party. *Patricia Clancy— Gr. 5, Peter Noyes School, Sudbury, MA*

fault

ferns

forecast

friction

front

floodplain

force

fracture

fronds

fish

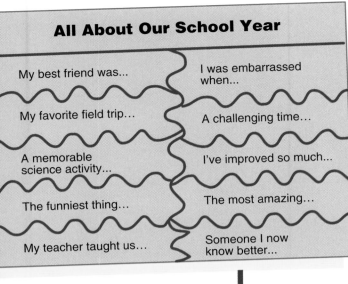

All About Our School Year

My best friend was...

I was embarrassed when...

My favorite field trip...

A challenging time...

A memorable science activity...

I've improved so much...

The funniest thing...

The most amazing...

My teacher taught us...

Someone I now know better...

All About Our School Year

For a fun art project to end the year, my students make "All About Our School Year" posters. I provide each student with an 8 1/2" x 14" sheet of art paper. The student draws wavy lines on the paper to divide it into eight to ten sections; then she labels the top of each section with a sentence starter from the list above. After completing her sentence starters, the student illustrates each one. Save these posters until next year—they'll make an appealing display to greet your new crop of students. *Denise Edwards, Mercer County Elementary, Harrodsburg, KY*

Anonymous Letters

This letter-writing activity gives students a chance to show off their writing skills and reminisce about the year. Have each student write an anonymous letter to a classmate. The letter should relate good experiences during the year and include plenty of positive comments about the letter's recipient *without* naming him or her. Collect all of the letters when they are completed. During the last few weeks of school, read a letter at the close of each day; then invite the student who wrote the letter to stand and identify the person to whom it was written. *Jeannette Freeman—Gr. 4, Baldwin School, Guaynabo, Puerto Rico*

End-Of-The-Year Alphabet Books

For our end-of-the-year open house, my fifth graders made alphabet books reflecting what they had learned during the year. After dividing into small groups, each group came up with ideas for each letter of the alphabet. Students used their notebooks, portfolios, and journals to form preliminary lists. Then each group had to choose one idea for each letter—which turned out to be quite a challenge! Next came the illustrations. Clip art, magazine pictures, and original drawings were all included in the books. Each group also decided on the materials to use to publish its book. This project was definitely fun, but it also served as a basic-skills review. Important group skills—including problem solving, cooperation, and friendship—were also evident. The students were especially proud to exhibit these books at open house. *Stephanie E. Patterson—Gr. 5, Curtis Intermediate, Weatherford, TX*

Postcards From The Heart

Every year in June, my students and I struggle with the fact that we won't see each other the following school year because they'll move on to middle school. To keep in touch, I give each student a prepaid postcard with my address printed on it. My students decorate the front of their cards and then take them home to send to me later in the summer. *Christine Smyth—Gr. 5, Hanson Elementary, Buxton, ME*

Sweet Notes, Sweet Good-byes

Saying good-byes at the end of the year is often difficult. As an alternative to exchanging address lists, I use this creative project. First I provide each student with a supply of colorful, construction-paper circles—one per classmate. Everyone is instructed to write a "short and sweet" message on each circle, as well as his name, address, and phone number. Students distribute the completed circles to their classmates. Each student then glues his circles together to resemble scoops of ice cream piled on top of each other. A brown paper cone is added at the bottom of the circles. Everyone now has a huge ice-cream cone full of sweet notes to take home on the last day of school—plus an instant student directory. Provide large envelopes so students can fold their cones and take them home intact. *Elise Nash—Gr. 5, Delaware Academy, Delhi, NY*

Class Yearbook

For a final send-off for my students, I present them with copies of my special Fifth-Grade Class Yearbook. Throughout the year, I take pictures of students involved in various activities. I also take pictures of our administrators, the office staff, and the teachers who will likely have my students next year. I lay out pages just like a yearbook, complete with captions and names. At the back of the book, I include several blank autograph pages. When I've finished my yearbook, I duplicate it on the school copier. My students are always surprised when they receive their yearbooks—special keepsakes of their year in fifth grade. *Janet Zeek—Gr. 5, Tolleson Elementary, Chandler, AZ*

The Year In Pictures

It's a challenge to keep students focused on academics during the last week of school. What better way to review the school year than by making illustrated keepsakes? Provide each student with a booklet of 12 blank pages, plus a copy of the reproducible on page 46. Before copying the reproducible, program it with special events and activities that you want students to include in their booklets. Instruct students to follow the directions on the page carefully to ensure a successful final project. Then presto! Each student has his very own illustrated story of the school year. *Rita Geller—Gr. 4, Ramblewood Elementary, Coral Springs, FL*

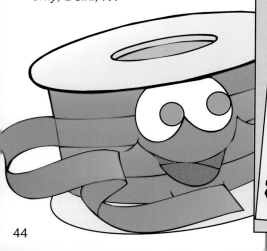

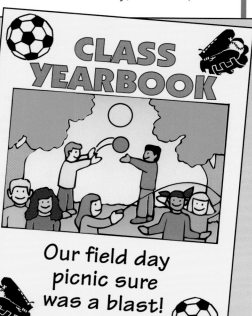

Name_____ Year-end project

Upcoming Attractions

Do you remember how you felt on the first day of school last fall? A little nervous maybe? Downright scared? Well here's your chance to help next year's students see what's in store for them. Just follow the directions below to complete a poster about this year. Next year's students will surely thank you!

Materials: One 12" x 18" sheet of white construction paper; colored markers, crayons, or colored pencils; a good memory

Directions:

A. Fold the sheet of construction paper into six equal sections; then unfold it. Illustrate the following on the front of your sheet, one item per section:

1. Write "Welcome Back To School" in big, fancy letters.
2. Draw a picture of your favorite school lunch.
3. Illustrate a scene from your favorite library book. Include the title and author of the book.
4. Draw a picture of your teacher.
5. Illustrate your favorite "special subject": art, music, P.E., etc.
6. Draw all of the school supplies that a student in your class needs.

B. Now turn over your sheet of paper. Illustrate the following on the back of your paper, one item per section:

1. Write one important class rule. Draw a neat border—flowers, stars, squiggly lines, etc.— around the rule.
2. Write the word RESPONSIBILITY in fancy letters. Write a short poem about responsibility.
3. Write the word RESPECT in fancy letters, each letter a different color. Around this box, make a border of words and phrases that describe what respect means to you.
4. Draw a picture of friends working together. Describe a time this past year when friends working together had wonderful results.

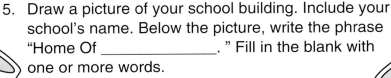

5. Draw a picture of your school building. Include your school's name. Below the picture, write the phrase "Home Of _____. " Fill in the blank with one or more words.
6. Write the name of your favorite holiday. Draw a picture of one way we observed this holiday in class.

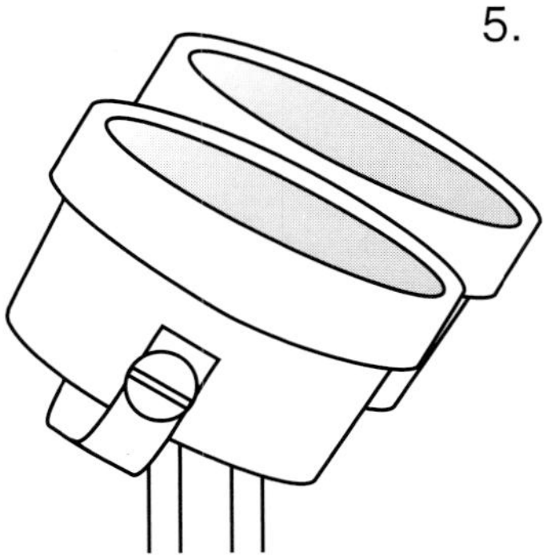

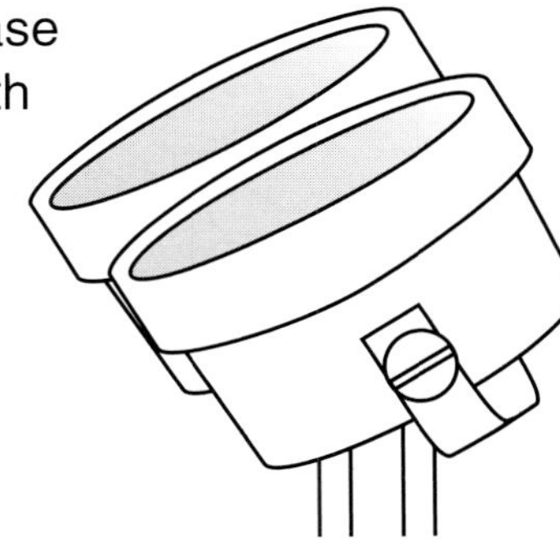

©The Education Center, Inc. • THE MAILBOX® • Intermediate • June/July 1996 • Idea by Rita Geller—Gr. 4, Ramblewood Elementary, Coral Springs, FL

Note To The Teacher: Use this reproducible with "Upcoming Attractions" on page 40.

The Year In Pictures

A *keepsake* is anything special that you save to remind you of a special time or person. Follow the directions below to make a keepsake booklet about the past year.

Materials: a blank, 12-page booklet; colored markers or crayons; glue; scissors

Directions:

1. Design a cover on the first booklet page. Include the year, your name and grade, and your school name. Add a drawing of your school.
2. Color each month's label on this page. Cut out each label and glue it to a page. Be sure to put the labels in the correct order.
3. Illustrate each page. See the ideas below for events to illustrate. Write a caption for each illustration.
4. Use the last page as an autographs page for your classmates to sign.
5. Most of all, have fun!

Ideas to illustrate:

- September: _____
  _____
- October: _____
  _____
- November: _____
  _____
- December: _____
  _____
- January: _____
  _____
- February: _____
  _____
- March: _____
  _____
- April: _____
  _____
- May: _____
  _____
- June: _____
  _____

©The Education Center, Inc. • *THE MAILBOX* • *Intermediate* • June/July 1996 • Idea by Rita Geller—Gr. 4, Ramblewood Elementary, Coral Springs, FL

Note To The Teacher: Use this reproducible with "The Year In Pictures" on page 44. Make one copy of this page and program it with special events of the past year that you want your students to illustrate. Then duplicate copies for your class.

BULLETIN BOARDS

Bulletin Boards

This bulletin board is the centerpiece of my back-to-school classroom decor based on a theater theme. I also display book posters around the classroom instead of movie posters. When students arrive on the first day, I greet them at the door and give each one a ticket. These tickets are redeemed later in the day for popcorn. What a fun way to give students a sneak preview of the great year ahead!

Susan Barnett—Gr. 6, Northwest Elementary, Fort Wayne, IN

Welcome parents to Open House with this interactive, back-to-school display. Duplicate a class supply of the fish pattern (page 60) on colorful construction paper. Have each student write his name on a fish and attach it to the board. Extend pieces of white yarn from the fishes to the top of the board. Add a small paper hook to the end of each line. During Open House, invite parents to write messages to their children on the background paper. *(For more great Open House ideas from our subscribers, see pages 30-33.)*

Sharon Zacharda—Gr. 4, West View Elementary, Pittsburgh, PA

This welcome-back bulletin board is one of my favorites! Photograph each student holding a book while sitting in a chair. Make sure that each photo shows a side view of the student and that she faces the camera. Trim each photo, leaving only the student's image. Next duplicate the desk pattern (page 60) on brown construction paper. Mount the patterns on black construction-paper squares bordered with yellow to resemble chalkboards. To complete the display, add a student photo cutout to each desk.

Susan Patee—Gr. 5, Hillside Elementary, Farmington Hills, MI

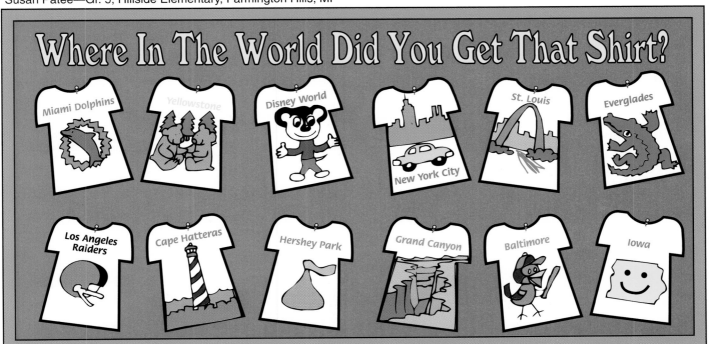

Many students return to school wearing T-shirts that feature places they've visited or their favorite sports teams. Turn these shirts into a valuable learning experience and easy-to-make display. Instruct each student to write the details about his T-shirt's origin on the pattern. Then have him turn over the pattern and decorate it to resemble his real shirt. Attach the completed shirts to the board with pushpins so they can easily be taken down and read by others.

Mary Chmelar—Gr. 4, Keota Community Schools, Keota, IA

Bulletin Boards

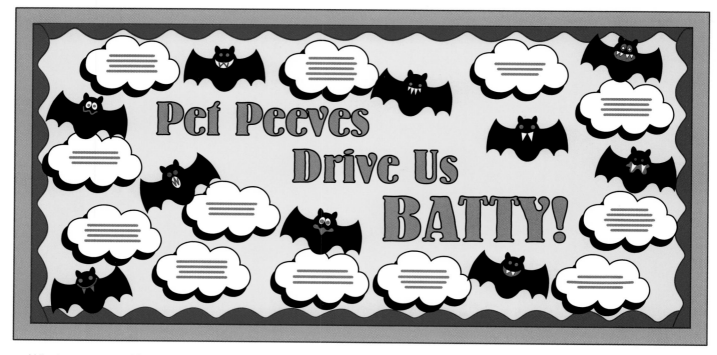

What pet peeve drives you batty? Have students interview family members and friends to find out their pet peeves. Give each student a bat pattern (see page 61) to trace on black paper. Then have him cut out the bat and embellish it with paper eyes and fangs. Instruct the student to cut out one white and one black cloud from paper; then have him describe a pet peeve on the white cloud. Arrange the bat and cloud shapes on a board as shown.

Julia Alarie—Gr. 6, Essex Middle School, Essex, VT

In October, my students complete a lesson on feelings—what causes them and how they are expressed on our faces. Each student draws a caricature of a feeling we discussed (see the list below) on a pumpkin pattern. We then feature our patch of portraits on a colorful fall bulletin board.

Lynn Marie Gilbertson—Gr. 4
James Sales Elementary
Tacoma, WA

exhausted	enraged
confused	ashamed
ecstatic	cautious
guilty	smug
suspicious	depressed
angry	overwhelmed
hysterical	hopeful
frustrated	lonely
sad	lovestruck
confident	jealous
embarrassed	bored
happy	surprised
mischievous	anxious
disgusted	shocked
frightened	shy

Sharpen skills with a November display that doubles as a learning center. Place seasonal skill sheets—such as the one found on page 296—in large pockets stapled to the board. Enlarge the body of the turkey found on page 296; then color it, cut it out, and staple it to the board. Write each child's name on a cut-out feather and add it to the display. Each time a student completes an activity, let him place a sticker on his feather.

Christine Juozitis—Gr. 4, Thomas Jefferson School, Binghamton, NY

What would your students want if they could wish for one thing—that is, one thing that would not directly benefit them? Have each student write her wish on a paper wishbone (see the pattern on page 61). Then display the wishbones with a colorful Pilgrim cutout. If desired, send additional wishbones home for parents to complete; then add these cutouts to the display.

Suzanne Hammer—Gr. 5, Louisa-Muscatine Elementary, Letts, IA

Bulletin Boards

Good work—how sweet it is! To display student papers during December, mount two candy canes on a board as shown. Duplicate the gingerbread boy on page 62 onto light brown paper. Have students cut out and color the patterns; then staple the patterns to the board along with paper candy cutouts. Duplicate the candy paper topper on page 62 on white construction paper. Give a topper to each student to cut out, color, and slip onto a favorite paper.

Michelle Fancher—Gr. 7, Immaculate Conception School, Indian Orchard, MA

To make this cheery holiday display, duplicate a tree-light pattern (page 63) on several different colors of construction paper. Have each student cut out a pattern and glue a photo of himself onto it. Mount the lights on a garland that has been attached to a board as shown.

A few days before students head home for the holidays, give each child his light and another light pattern that has been cut from tagboard. Have the student glue the colored light onto the tagboard pattern and write a message to his parents on the back. Laminate the lights; then punch a hole in the top of each one and insert an inexpensive key ring. How's that for turning a bulletin board into wonderful holiday gifts?

Jan Drehmel—Gr. 4
Korger Chestnut School
Chippewa Falls, WI

The weather outside may be frightful, but the reading incentive of this display is delightful! Duplicate copies of the snowflake book-report form on page 63. Have students cut out, color, and complete these forms when they want to recommend cool books they've read. Add a large snowman and small student-made snowflakes to the display for a wintry touch.

Gloria Twohig—Librarian, St. Matthew's School, Campbellsport, WI

For the right combination of fun and practice, cover a board with light blue paper. Use a black marker or tape to divide the paper into eight lockers. Duplicate the lock pattern on page 62. Label each lock with a math problem. Write each answer on a paper strip. Staple the strips to the lockers as shown; then challenge students to pin each lock to the correct locker. Provide an answer key. Change the locks and numbers frequently.

Colleen Dabney, Williamsburg Christian Academy, Williamsburg, VA

Bulletin Boards

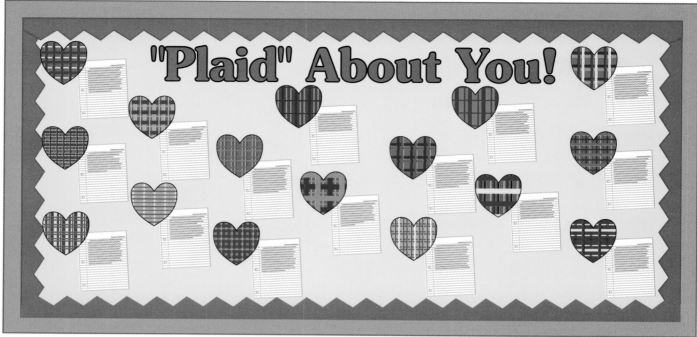

For a bright Valentine's Day display, have each student create her own heart-shaped tartan. Explain to students that a *tartan* is a plaid pattern consisting of stripes of various widths and colors. The stripes cross at right angles against a solid background. Have each student fill a sheet of white construction paper with her tartan, using colored pencils, crayons, or markers; then have her cut a heart shape from the paper. Ask each student to write a paragraph about someone she is mad about. Post the paragraphs among the hearts.

Lisa Borgo—Gr. 4, East Hanover, NJ

Post a strip of white paper decorated to resemble a piano keyboard on a board as shown. Duplicate the note pattern on page 64 on colorful paper. Each morning introduce a new vocabulary word by giving students the first few letters of the word and letting them try to guess its identity. After the word has been guessed or revealed, discuss its meaning for students to copy in their vocabulary notebooks. Label a note cutout with the word, its part of speech, and the name of the student who correctly guessed the word. When the board is completely filled with notes, let student groups create quizzes to test classmates on the words.

Chava Shapiro, Monsey, NY

The best part of this good-work display is preparing the background paper! Cover a bulletin board with white (or any light-colored) paper. Pour several colors of fluorescent paints in pie pans. Have each student gently place his hand, palm down, in a pan of paint, then make a handprint on the bulletin-board paper. When the paint has dried, use the board for highlighting students' outstanding work.

Shannon Berry—Gr. 4, Heritage Christian School, Brookfield, WI

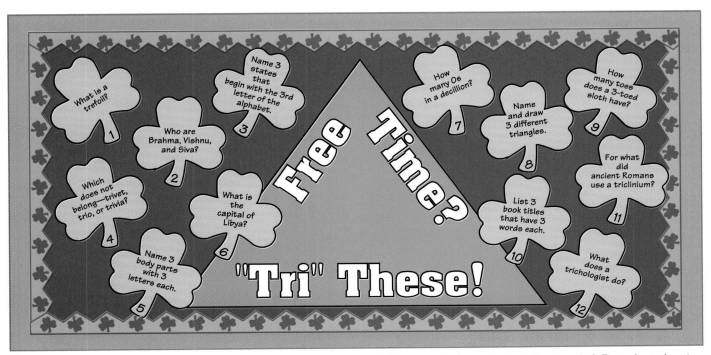

Everyone knows that Ireland's national symbol, the shamrock, is a small, three-leafed plant, right? But what about other mysteries related to the number 3? Program shamrock patterns with the research activities as shown. Have students work in groups of three and write their responses on large index cards. (See the answer key on page 308.) May the luck of the Irish be with them!

Bulletin Boards

Cultivate a love of poetry with this easy-to-make display. Have each student cut out a large flower from a discontinued wallpaper book. Post each child's flower with a sample of her original poetry. Mount additional flowers around the title to complete your garden of glorious verses!

Colleen Dabney—Gr. 6, Williamsburg Christian Academy, Williamsburg, VA

For an "udderly" awesome self-esteem activity, enlarge the cow pattern on page 65 and post it on a small bulletin board. Have each student use a black marker to decorate a white paper bag with cow spots and his name. Add a label to an empty milk bottle (or a milk carton with the top cut off) that reads "Crème De La Crème." As you observe a student exhibiting exemplary behavior or study skills, have that child label a slip of paper with his name and drop it in the bottle. At the end of the day, draw one slip from the bottle. Post that student's bag on the board; then have classmates fill the bag with written "cow-pliments" about the honored child.

Linda Archibeque Trimberger—Gr. 4
Jackson Elementary
Greeley, CO

You can bank on improving vocabularies with this interactive display! Label 24 green index cards with alphabet letters as shown. Punch a hole in the upper right corner of each card; then place the card on a metal ring. Mount the 24 rings on the board with pushpins. Punch holes in more blank cards. Store the cards in a basket labeled "Deposit Slips." When a student finds a new word in his reading, he writes it on a blank card; then he writes the definition and his name on the back of the card. The student adds, or deposits, the card into the word bank by placing it on the correct ring (behind the letter card). When you have a few extra minutes, take a ring from the board and review the words with students.

Marilyn Crenshaw—Gr. 4
David Elementary
The Woodlands, TX

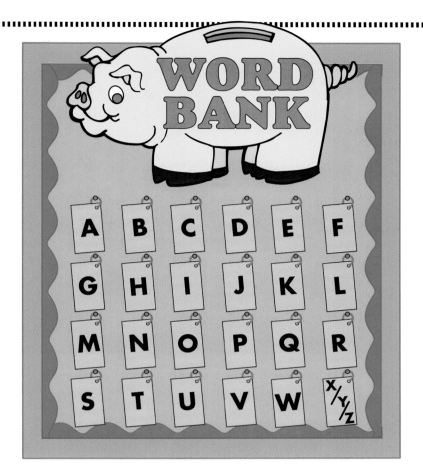

It's no puzzle to see how this eye-catching—and simple—display reinforces the concept of symmetry. Have each student cut out a large puzzle piece from colorful paper. Then have him search through magazines to find an example of symmetry. After cutting out the example, the student glues it to his puzzle piece. Use this display idea to review other important skills such as numeration or parts of speech.

Colleen Dabney—Gr. 6, Williamsburg Christian Academy, Williamsburg, VA

Bulletin Boards......................................

Send the message that actions speak louder than words. Have each student draw a large flower outline on colorful paper. On an index card, have the student write a description of a good intention she has had and how she acted on it. Post the cards and flowers on the board with a copy of the parrot pattern on page 66. Add the title and large leaf cutouts as shown.

Mrs. Bednar, Mrs. Branagan, Miss Emery, and Mrs. Pace—Gr. 6, Sayreville Middle School, Sayreville, NJ

Motivate your students to read with this sweet incentive! Challenge each child to read seven books of at least 100 pages each. Have the student's parents sign a slip verifying that the child has read each book. Each time a student brings in a book slip give him a miniature candy bar. After the student eats the candy, post the wrapper above his name on the board. Reward each student who reads all seven books with a giant candy bar and a certificate.

Philip Lang—Gr. 5
Christ Lutheran School
Rancho Palos Verde, CA

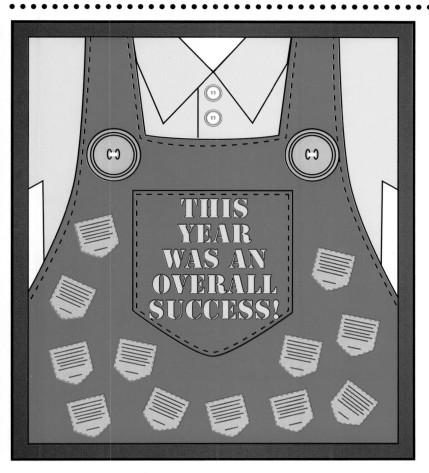

Celebrate the successful moments of your school year with this "jean-uinely" fun display! Use white, yellow, and blue paper to construct the simple shirt and overalls design on a bulletin board as shown. Use a marker to draw in the stitching and large pocket, and use paper cutouts for the buttons. Have each student cut a pocket from blue paper and draw stitching around the edges (see the example). Instruct each student to answer the following question on his pocket: "What was the most successful thing that you accomplished this year?" Post the pockets as shown.

Adapted from an idea by Colleen Dabney—Gr. 6
Williamsburg Christian Academy
Williamsburg, VA

Invite ants to your classroom for a best behavior picnic! Cover a bulletin board with a paper picnic tablecloth. Attach paper plates, food cutouts, plasticware, napkins, and recycled juice boxes to the board as shown. For each day that the students exhibit good behavior, add one copy of the ant pattern on page 66 to the board. Once 20 ants have taken over the picnic, it's time to go out to lunch! Order pizza for the class or make other special lunch arrangements.

Colleen Dabney—Gr. 6

Patterns

Use with the bulletin board on page 48.

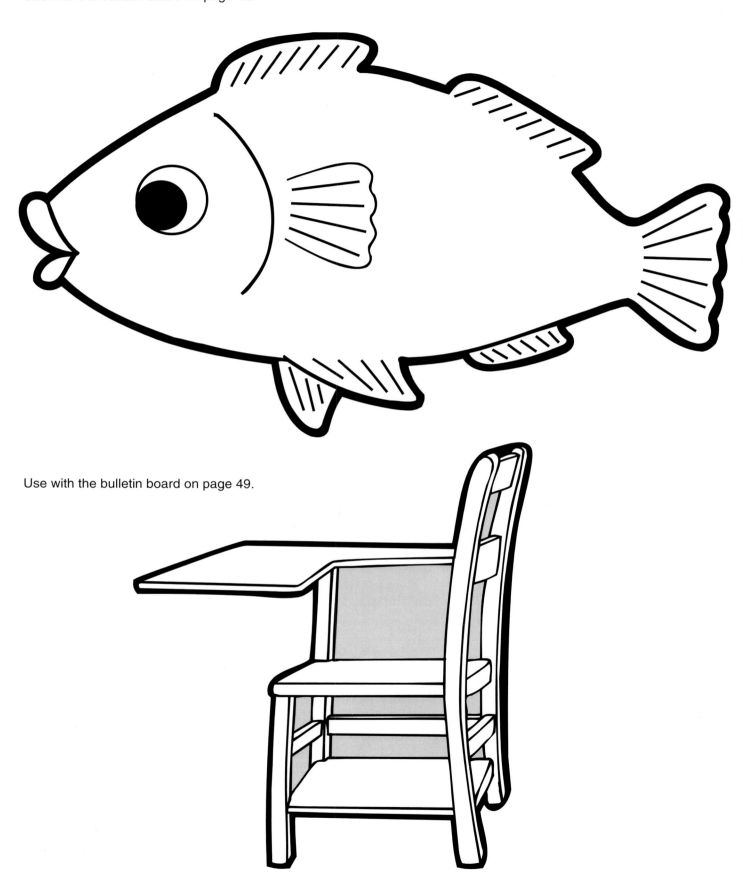

Use with the bulletin board on page 49.

Patterns

Use with "Pet Peeves Drive Us Batty!" on page 50.

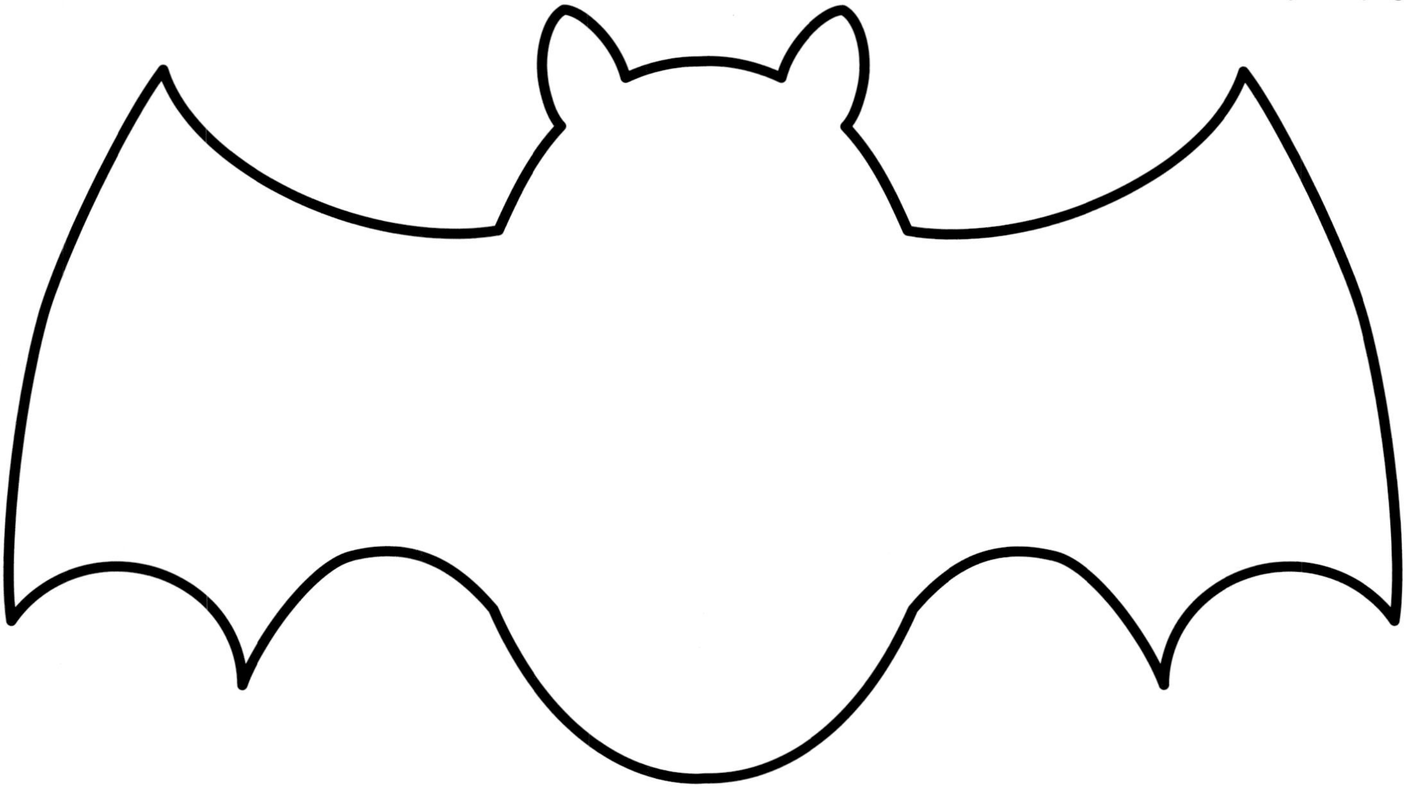

Use with "Make A Wish!" on page 51.

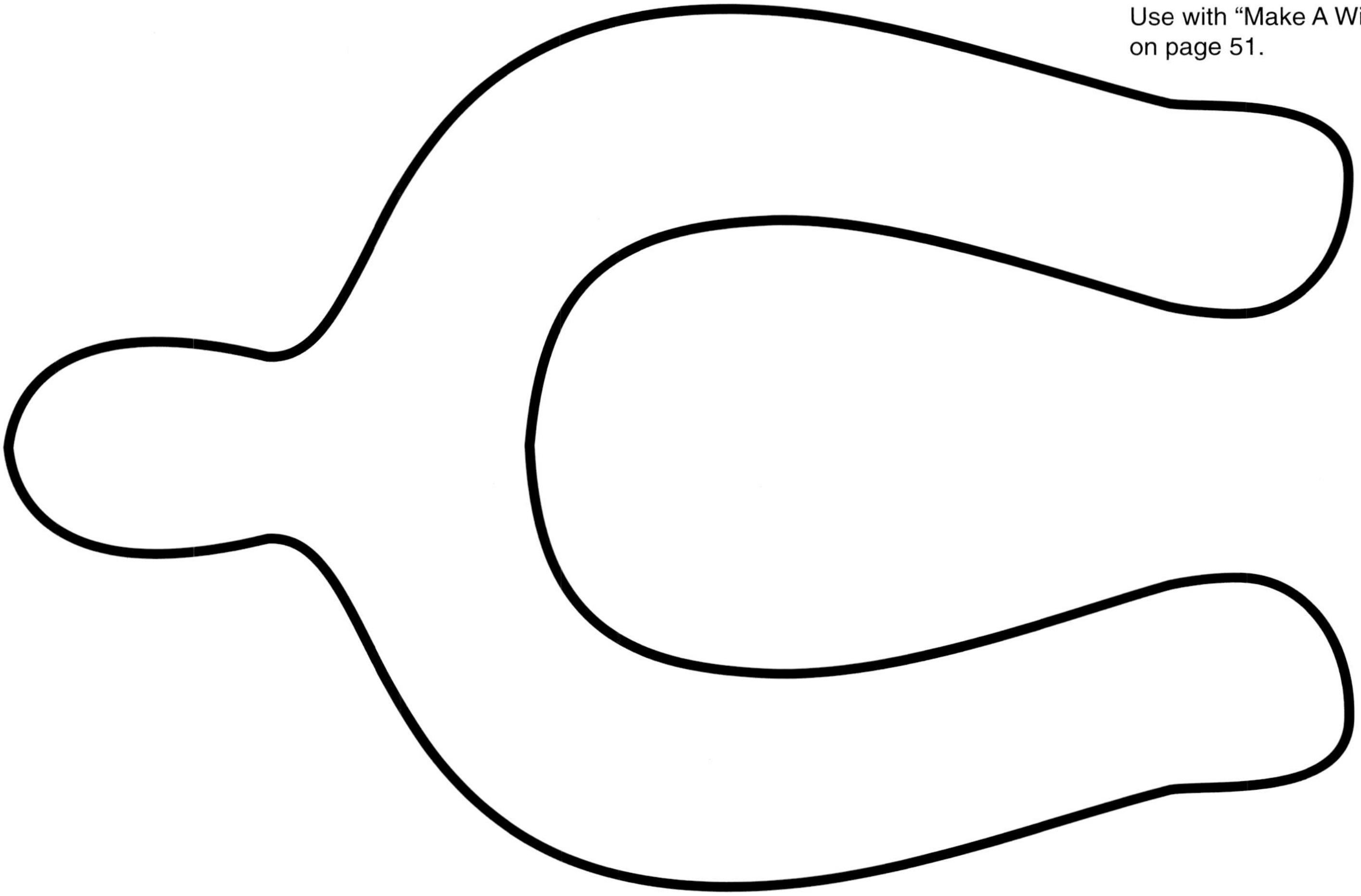

Paper Topper

Sweet!

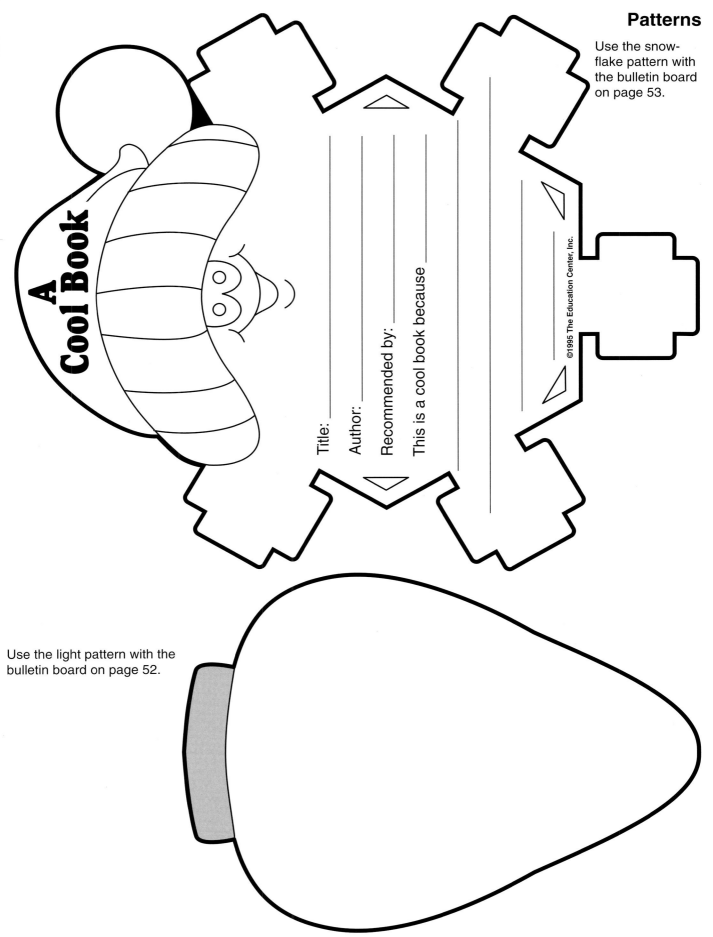

Use the snow-flake pattern with the bulletin board on page 53.

A Cool Book

Title:

Author:

Recommended by:

This is a cool book because

©1995 The Education Center, Inc.

Use the light pattern with the bulletin board on page 52.

Pattern

Use with "Take Note Of Our Key Words!" on page 54.

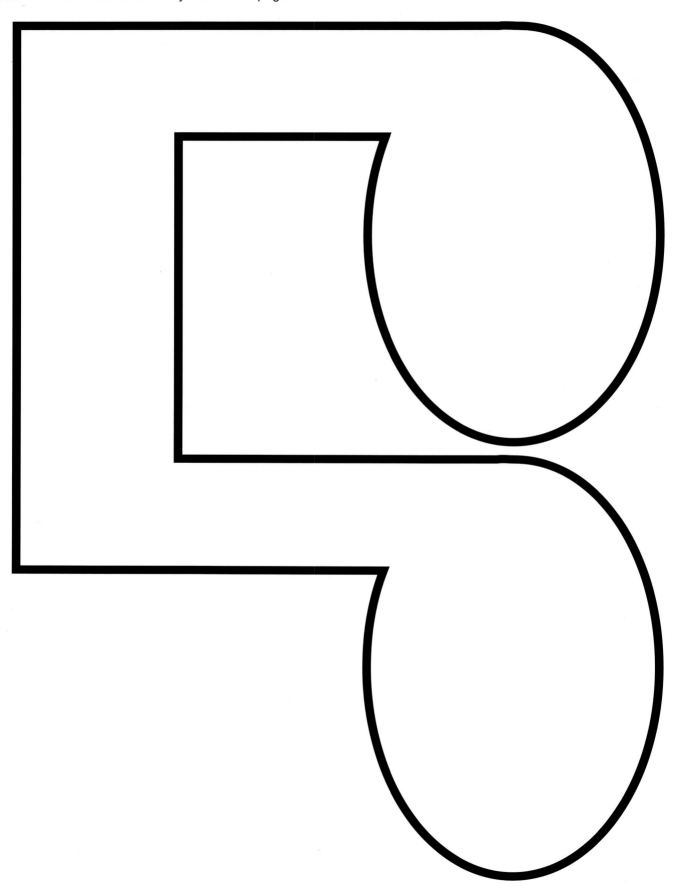

Patterns

Use with "Don't Parrot Platitudes—Act!" on page 58.

Use with "Out To Lunch!"
on page 59.

ARTS & CRAFTS

Arts & Crafts

Paper-Plate Designs

Since the days of the ancient Indian civilizations, the arts have been an important part of Mexican life. Share with your class pictures of Mexico's beautiful architecture, famous murals, and paintings. Then celebrate Mexico's Independence Day (September 16) with these colorful paper-plate designs.

Materials:
  9-inch paper plates
  pencils
  markers, crayons, and paints
  paintbrushes

Directions:
  1. Have each student lightly trace his design on a paper plate. Encourage students to include symbols that relate to Mexico's history and culture.
  2. After completing their designs, have students fill in all of the spaces on their plates with bright colors.
  3. To display the finished designs, hang them from your ceiling or use them as a border for a bulletin board.

Coletta Preacely Ellis—Grs. 5/6, Wilson Elementary, Lynwood, CA

Stained-Glass Names

Decorate your windows for Open House or for any occasion with this eye-catching, stained-glass project.

Materials for one project:
  clear plastic wrap
  piece of tagboard or other stiff paper (about 10" x 10")
  paper clips
  permanent markers—assorted bright colors and black

Directions:
  1. Provide each student with a piece of plastic wrap large enough to extend over the piece of tagboard. Have students secure the plastic wrap to the tagboard with paper clips.
  2. Have each student use permanent markers to write his name (in fat, bubbly letters) on the plastic, using a different color for each letter.
  3. Have the student outline his name with a black permanent marker.
  4. To complete the project, instruct each student to carefully cut around the black outline, then remove the paper clips and lift his name from the tagboard.
  5. Adhere these stained-glass names to your classroom windows. You may need to add a few drops of water to make the plastic wrap adhere to the glass.

Elizabeth Bourassa—Gr. 6
Olson School
Minneapolis, MN

Welcome parents and other visitors to Open House with these bright, colorful projects.

Materials:

9" x 12" white construction paper	pencils
markers and crayons	scissors
glue	black fine-tipped marker
assorted decorations such as glitter, sequins, and yarn	

Directions:

1. Have each student sketch the first letter of her first name on a 9" x 12" sheet of white construction paper. Instruct students to make big block letters that fill their sheets.
2. Instruct each student to write the remainder of her name somewhere on the letter, making sure that it is readable; then have the student outline her letter with a black fine-tipped marker.
3. Have the student cut out her letter.
4. Instruct the student to personalize her letter with symbols that represent her hobbies and interests. In addition, suggest that she use glitter, markers, crayons, sequins, yarn, and other available items for decoration.
5. Display all of the completed letters on a bulletin board or your classroom door.

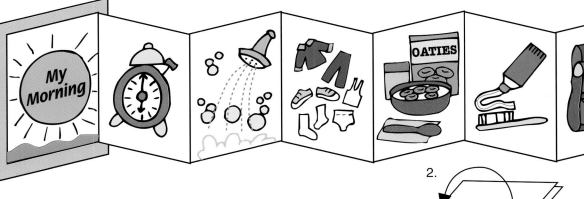

Illustrating Sequences

A stained-glass window, a comic strip, and a motion picture: they each tell a story in a series of pictures. Have students think about the many consecutive movements that they make during a day. Then have each student choose an event or time period during an average day to illustrate on the panels of an accordion book. Instruct students to use simple shapes and a minimum of detail in their illustrations.

Materials for each student:

one 9" x 12" sheet of white construction paper	scissors
two 4" x 6" pieces of tagboard	transparent tape
two 16-inch pieces of ribbon	rubber cement
crayons, colored pencils, and markers	

Steps:

1. Fold the 9" x 12" sheet of construction paper in half lengthwise. Open the sheet and cut it in half on the crease.
2. To make an "M" fold with each resulting piece of paper, fold each piece in half; then fold each end back to the folded edge as shown.
3. Tape these two pieces together, resulting in an accordion-folded 4 1/2" x 24" piece of paper.
4. Attach the pieces of ribbon to one of the tagboard pieces with rubber cement; then let it dry completely.
5. Rubber-cement a tagboard piece to each end of the paper.
6. Choose an event in your daily life to illustrate on the panels of your book. Use the first page as a title page.

Terrifying Towers

Here's a frighteningly good way to bring out your students' creativity during the Halloween season! Gather a supply of different-sized boxes (one per student). Provide students with colorful paper, markers, paints, and other craft supplies. Distribute one box to each child. After the student has covered the box with paper, instruct him to decorate the front and two sides to create a terrifying creature. Next have the student write a description of the origin, dangers, and habits of his creature; then have him attach this description to the back of his box. When all of the boxes are done, stack groups of four or five of them as shown to build several terrifying towers. Display the towers in the school lobby so that others can read and enjoy your students' monstrous creations.

Thanksgiving Wreath

When it comes to thanks, this holiday wreath says it all! Provide each student with a wire coat hanger, construction paper in a variety of autumn colors, scissors, markers, a length of ribbon, glue, a length of yarn, and other craft materials. Hang each wreath from the ceiling for everyone to read and enjoy.

Directions:

1. Pull and shape the coat hanger to create a circle.
2. Trace your hand 12 times on different-colored sheets of paper. Cut out each tracing.
3. On one side of each hand cutout, write a word or phrase that expresses something for which you are grateful.
4. Glue the hands around both sides of the wire, making sure that the writing on each hand shows. Also make sure to position the hand cutouts so that the hanger will be completely covered.
5. Complete the wreath by adding a ribbon bow, glitter, streamers, or other decorative items.
6. Tie a length of yarn from the top of your hanger for hanging.

Me And My Shadow

Spruce up your school landscape this fall with colorful side-walk art. On a sunny day, pair up students and provide them with colored sidewalk chalk. Have each pair of students find a space on the blacktop or sidewalk. Instruct one student in each pair to pose, casting a shadow on the sidewalk. (Encourage students to be creative in their poses, showing movement and personality.) As the student holds the pose, have his partner trace the outline of his shadow. Then have them switch roles to create another shadow outline. Using additional colored chalk or large paint-brushes and tempera paint, have each student add details to his shadow drawing. Let students transform their shadow drawings into famous people being studied, favorite book characters, important people populating recent current events, or life-sized portraits of themselves. Once the paint dries, invite other classes to venture outside and take a look at these shady characters.

Folksy Weather Vanes

Fall is the perfect time for a little folk art! These country weather vanes will liven up your classroom and make great holiday gifts.

Materials for the teacher:
plaster of paris
water
a bowl and spoon for mixing

Materials per student:
one empty, clean, half-pint milk carton with its top cut off
one 12-inch wooden dowel
scissors
a black, felt-tipped pen
an art knife
cardboard

acrylic paints or colored markers
glue
masking tape
a paper grocery bag that has been cut into 1/2-inch strips
newspaper

Directions for the teacher:
1. Mix the plaster of paris with water according to the directions on the box.
2. As students work on their designs (step 1 below), fill each milk-carton container with 1 1/2 inches of plaster.
3. Instruct each student to hold his dowel upright in the center of his carton until the plaster hardens enough to support the dowel. Let the plaster harden overnight.

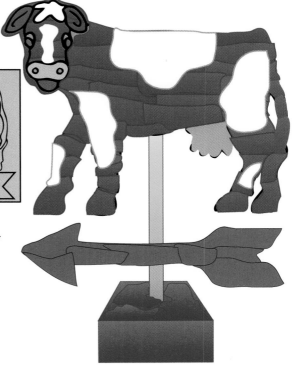

Directions for the student:
1. Draw a design for your weather vane on scrap paper.
2. Copy your design onto the cardboard using a black, felt-tipped pen. Draw an arrow on the cardboard as well (see the illustration).
3. With an adult's help, carefully cut out your design and the arrow using the art knife.
4. After the plaster has hardened overnight, peel away the milk carton. Tape the back of the weather-vane character to the top of the dowel as shown. Tape the arrow to the dowel between the character and the base as shown.
5. Lay the weather vane on its side on newspaper. Completely cover both sides of your weather-vane design and arrow with paper-bag strips that have been smeared with glue. Smooth down the strips; then let them dry and harden overnight.
6. The next day, use the black, felt-tipped marker to redraw your weather vane's details according to your rough sketch. Paint or color both sides of the weather vane and the arrow. Also paint the dowel and the plaster of paris base. Dry the display overnight.

Make the holidays bright and cheery with these easy-to-make ornaments.

Bread Dough Ornaments

Materials: white liquid glue, poured in several small containers; liquid tempera paint; two-day-old, white bread slices with the crusts removed (two or three slices per ornament); seasonal cookie cutters; glitter; rubber cement; plastic spoons and small bowls for mixing; toothpicks and tongue depressors (for decorating the ornaments); string

How To Make:

Add assorted colors of liquid tempera paint to containers of white liquid glue and mix. Tear up the bread and place the pieces in a small bowl; then add the glue mixture to cover. Knead to mix and form a dough. Flatten the dough using the palm of your hand. After placing the dough on a piece of waxed paper, cut seasonal shapes in it with cookie cutters. Use a toothpick and/or tongue depressor to decorate the ornaments with contrasting colors of glue or glitter. Let the ornaments dry for several days. Attach a loop of string to each ornament with rubber cement.

Paula Holdren
Chalfont, PA

Stained-Glass Ornaments

Materials: a 9" x 5" rectangle of clear Con-Tact® paper for each student, torn pieces of tissue paper in assorted colors, holiday patterns or cookie cutters, pencil, hole puncher, ribbon, scissors

How To Make:

Remove the back of the Con-Tact® paper. Cover the right half of the sticky side with the tissue-paper pieces (one thickness only). Fold the left side of the Con-Tact® paper over the right side, trapping the tissue-paper pieces inside. Press firmly to seal. Place a pattern on top of the Con-Tact® paper; then trace the pattern and cut out the tracing. Punch a hole in the top of the ornament and add a ribbon hanger.

Paula Holdren

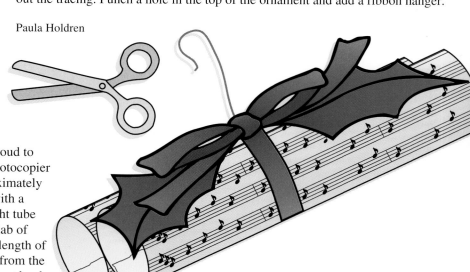

Noteworthy Ornaments

Here's a festive project that students will be proud to give as holiday gifts. For each ornament, use a photocopier to reduce two pages of Christmas music to approximately 5" x 7" each. To "age" the carols, blot each one with a damp tea bag. When dry, roll each carol into a tight tube (music side out) and fasten its loose edge with a dab of glue. Glue the scrolls together side by side. Tie a length of red ribbon around the scrolls; then fashion a bow from the ribbon ends. Attach a sprig of holly and an ornament hook to complete the project.

Here's a reason to celebrate—creative, inexpensive gifts that students can make for Christmas, Hanukkah, or Kwanzaa!

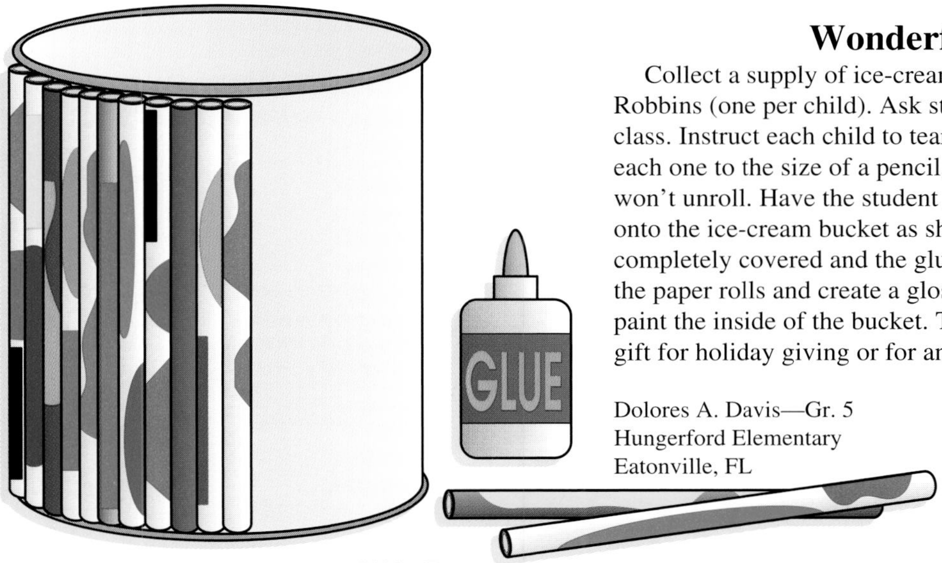

Wonderful Wastebaskets

Collect a supply of ice-cream buckets from places such as Baskin-Robbins (one per child). Ask students to bring colorful magazines to class. Instruct each child to tear colored pages from the magazines, roll up each one to the size of a pencil, then glue the edge of each page so that it won't unroll. Have the student glue these rolled-up pages closely together onto the ice-cream bucket as shown. After the outside of the bucket is completely covered and the glue has dried, spray shellac on it to reinforce the paper rolls and create a glossy finish. To complete the project, spray paint the inside of the bucket. The finished product makes a wonderful gift for holiday giving or for any special occasion.

Dolores A. Davis—Gr. 5
Hungerford Elementary
Eatonville, FL

Holiday Gift Bags

These oh-so-festive holiday gift bags can be used for years to come. Plus they offer a great way to recycle used cards and gift wrap!

Materials:

brown paper lunch bag
small piece of sponge
scissors
glitter, sequins, and other small decorations
old holiday cards
24" length of ribbon or yarn
glue

tissue paper
white paint
wrapping-paper scraps
hole puncher
newspaper
water

To Make:

1. Dampen the small piece of sponge. Open the lunch bag and place it on a newspaper-covered surface. Dip the sponge in white paint and lightly blot the entire paper bag to create a snowy effect. Let dry.
2. Fold down the top edge of the bag three-quarters of an inch to the inside, all the way around. Cut a strip of wrapping paper one inch wide and 18 inches long. Glue the wrapping-paper strip over the turned-down edge. Let dry.
3. Cut simple shapes from old holiday cards or wrapping-paper scraps. Decorate the shapes with sequins, glitter, or other items. Glue the cutouts to the bag and allow to dry.
4. Fold the bag flat. Punch holes through all thicknesses in the upper left and right corners of the bag. Each hole should be 1/2 inch from the top and side of the folded bag.
5. Thread ribbon or yarn through the holes; then tie the ends on the inside of the bag. Place a piece of tissue paper in the bag to hide that special gift.

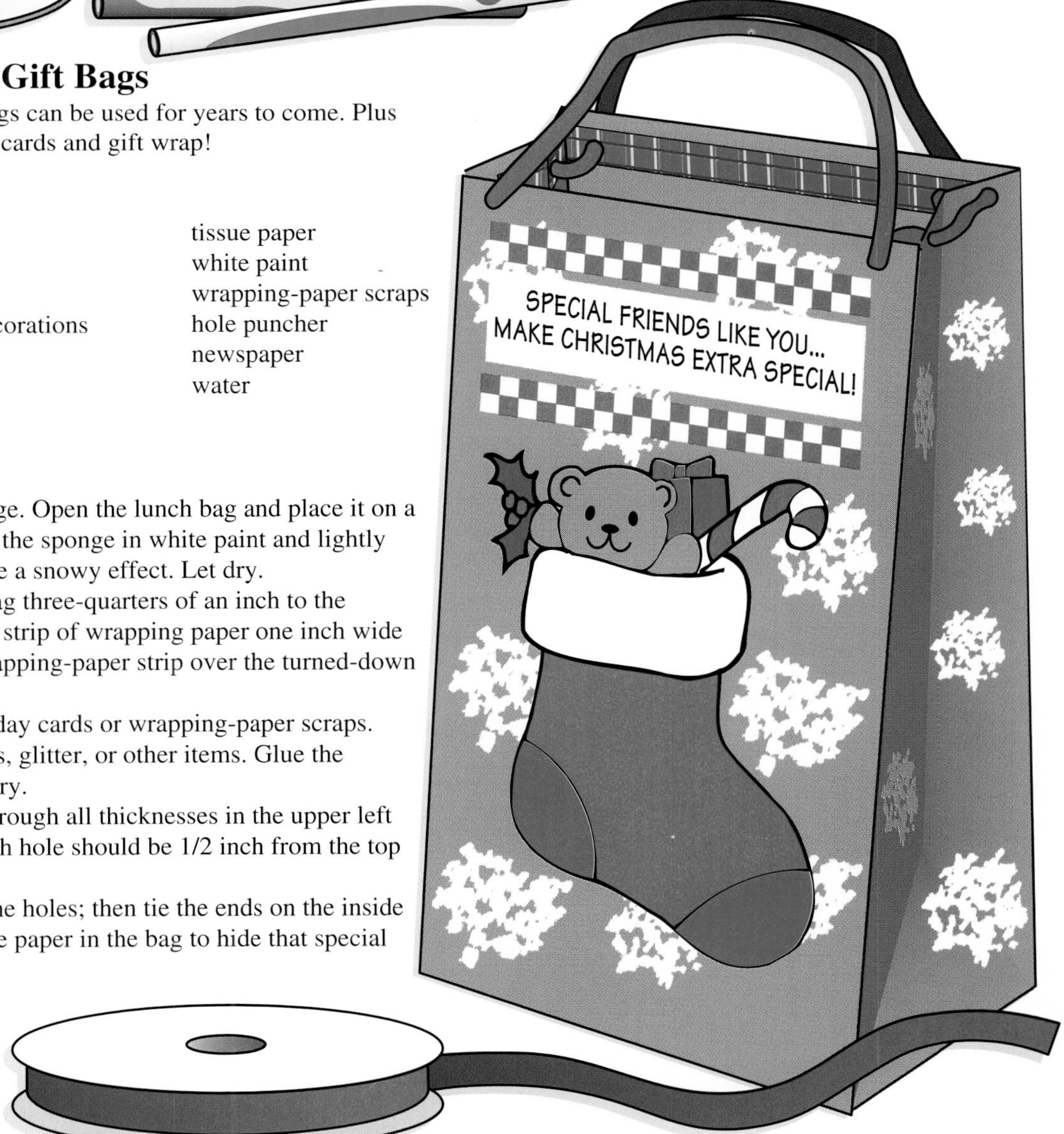

Barbara Beideman—Gr. 4
Eden Christian Academy
Pittsburgh, PA

Arts & Crafts

Spread a little holiday spirit in your classroom with these fun art projects.

Extended Art

Combine writing and art—while you recycle holiday cards—with this fun activity. Each student needs the front panel of a used holiday card, white construction paper, scissors, glue, and drawing materials. Have each student select a card, cut out a scene or picture from it, and then glue the cutout to the white construction paper. Next direct the student to extend the picture as shown. After the student has completed his art project, challenge him to write a story about the picture illustrated on it. Mount the published writing on colored construction paper and tape it to the bottom of the extended art project.

Virginia Weber—Gr. 5
Clearview Elementary
Brogue, PA

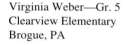 **Patterns**

petal

leaf

Poinsettia Wreath

Creating this poinsettia wreath is the perfect project for an independent art center. Make several photocopies of the patterns on tagboard for students to use as tracers. Place the patterns, needed materials, and directions for making individual poinsettias at a center. If desired, challenge each cooperative group to make enough poinsettias to create its own holiday wreath.

To make each individual poinsettia:
1. Trace six petals onto red paper and cut them out. Fold each petal in half, but crease the fold only slightly.
2. Glue the ends of the petals together to make a poinsettia. Let dry.
3. Punch three holes from a scrap of yellow paper. Glue the holes (flowers) in the center of the poinsettia.
4. Trace three leaves onto green paper and cut them out. Fold each leaf in half, but crease the fold only slightly. Glue the leaves on the back of the poinsettia.

To make a wreath:
Staple ten or more of the poinsettias in a wreath shape on a bulletin board. Or glue the poinsettias onto a classroom door or wall space that has been covered with paper. Add a bright red bow.

Dawn Helton—Gr. 4
Read-Turrentine School
Silsbee, TX

74

Stars Of Ecuador

Vividly colored Ecuadorian stars spring from a South American folk tradition. These cheerful and easy-to-make ornaments can be hung on windows, door frames, or Christmas trees. For a February display that combines multicultural studies with Valentine's Day, have students use red, pink, purple, white, and lavender yarns to make their stars. Display the star-studded projects on a large tree branch that has been spray-painted white and stuck in a deep bucket of sand.

Materials for each student:
two 3" squares of cardboard
two 5" squares of aluminum foil
   (or any colored foil or wrapping paper)
glue stick
transparent tape
about 10 yards of colored yarn or crochet thread
   (or shorter lengths of various colors of yarn or thread)

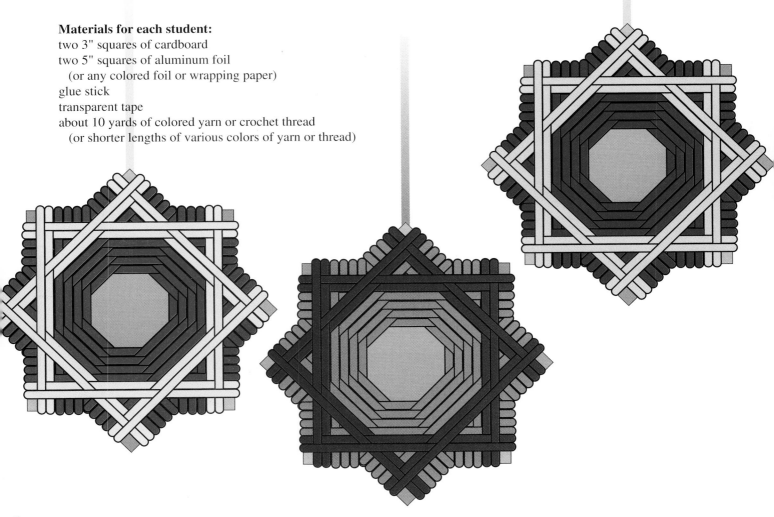

Steps:

1. Center each cardboard square in a square of foil. Fold the edges of the foil around the cardboard; then glue down the edges. (Don't worry if some cardboard shows in the middle of one side of each square.)
2. Glue the two foil-covered squares together so that the covered sides are on the outside and the squares are offset to make an eight-pointed star (see the diagram).
3. Tape one end of the yarn below a valley on one side of the star.
4. To begin, wind the yarn clockwise behind two points to a valley; then wind counterclockwise in front of three points to a valley (see the diagram). Continue winding in this pattern so that the pattern progresses around the star one point each time. As you continue adding rows, try to place the yarn rows neatly side by side, rather than stacking them on top of one another. If desired, change the color after a few rows by cutting the yarn, tying on another color, and continuing to wind.
5. After the desired number of rows have been wrapped, tie the end of the yarn to a previous row, using a double knot. Trim any yarn that is left hanging.
6. Tie a loop of yarn to a row in the ornament to make a hanger.

Beth Gress, Mt. Gilead, OH

75

Recyclable, Romantic Robots

Say good-bye to humdrum valentine holders and hello to the most unique valentine mail carriers ever! Divide your class into several cooperative groups. Give groups a couple of weeks to collect boxes, cardboard tubes, and other recyclable items. While groups are collecting their items, gather a supply of art materials such as paint, aluminum foil, and scrap construction paper.

About two weeks before Valentine's Day, challenge each group to use its recyclables to create a romantic robot that will serve as a valentine holder for the group's members. Give each group scissors, glue, rubber cement, and a roll of masking tape. Explain that the first step will be to make the robot's body, making sure it is designed with some type of receptacle for holding group members' valentines. Use a box cutter as needed to assist students with cutting that can't be done with regular scissors. After all of the robots have been assembled, let students decorate them with paint, aluminum foil, or other items. Have each group present its completed robot to the class and demonstrate where to put group members' valentines. During the week of Valentine's Day, have students write stories about their robots, explaining their origins, special abilities, and personalities. Post the robots and stories outside your classroom for a Valentine's display that isn't likely to be forgotten!

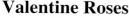

Valentine Roses

Here's a simple and sweet idea for Valentine's Day, Mother's Day, or any time you want to surprise a special someone with a one-of-a-kind gift.

Materials for one rose:
one Hershey's Kiss®
5" x 5" square of red cellophane
one 10" floral stem (from a floral shop)
two green silk leaves (each with a wire stem)
one 12" length of stretchy green floral tape

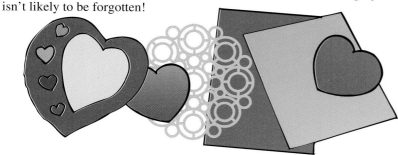

Steps:
1. Place the cellophane on the top point of the candy kiss; then gently gather the cellophane under the bottom of the kiss.
2. Bend the top two inches of the floral stem and wrap it snugly around the gathered cellophane, making a rosebud shape.
3. Beginning at the top of the stem, stretch and wrap the green floral tape snugly around the stem (covering the excess cellophane gathered under the rosebud). Add a leaf about two inches below the bud and continue to wrap for another inch. Then add the second leaf and continue wrapping.
4. Deliver the rose to your special valentine!

Valerie Hornbaker—Gr. 6
Elreka Grade School
Hutchinson, KS

An Irish Quilt

Add a touch o' art to your curriculum this March! Divide students into four cooperative groups. Have each group research a particular aspect of Ireland: its people, geography, industries, history, government, arts, recreation, etc. After the research has been completed, give each group four 7" squares of white art paper. Have the group decorate its squares with drawings and captions that illustrate its topic. Glue the completed squares in rows to resemble a quilt on a large sheet of green butcher paper (or a green paper tablecloth). Add stitches with a black marker as shown. Hang your paper quilt in a hallway so that others can learn about the Emerald Isle. For a whimsical touch, have each group create the head of a slumbering leprechaun to peek out from the top of the quilt.

Paper Pysanky

Don't wait until Easter to introduce students to the rich tradition found in Ukrainian Easter eggs, called *pysanky*. Admired all over the world for their unique beauty, these eggs are usually based on a geometrical design that contains symbols and colors of meaning to the artist. Pysanky are given to family and friends to convey one's love and best wishes during the Easter season. Though the process of making pysanky is based on the batik method of applying wax in several stages and dipping the eggs in dye, your students will love making paper versions of this lovely art form. *(Use this activity with the thematic unit on the former Soviet Union found on pages 155–162.)*

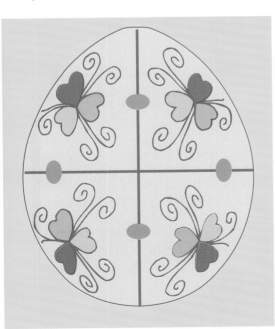

Materials:

student copies of page 82
rulers and pencils
scissors and glue

white art paper
markers or crayons
construction paper

egg-shaped templates for tracing
fine-tipped markers

Steps:

1. Use a template to trace a large egg shape in the middle of a sheet of white art paper.
2. Use a pencil and ruler to divide the egg into geometric parts (see the examples on the reproducible).
3. In real pysanky, symbols that mean something to the artist and to the person for whom the egg is being made are drawn in each section of the egg. Symbols are often repeated in a section to create a design. Think about who you would like to receive your *pysanka* (the name for a single egg); then look at the reproducible for symbols you can use (or create your own). Use a pencil to draw symbols inside the different egg sections.
4. Colors are an important part of your egg's message. Use the chart on the reproducible to help you decide how to color your pysanka so that it's suited for the person who will receive it.
5. Use fine-tipped markers to add details to your symbols.
6. Cut out your pysanka and glue it to a contrasting sheet of construction paper. Then give it to your special friend.

Simone Lepine—Gr. 5
Syracuse, NY

Enjoy the beauty and fragrances of springtime with these fun-to-make gift ideas.

Milk Jug Easter Baskets

Materials: gallon-sized plastic milk jugs; polyester fiberfill; fabric scraps; lace; scissors; pinch clothespins; ribbon; shredded newspapers or tissue paper; choice of stapler, fabric glue, or hot-glue gun; fruit, soft candy, and/or trial-size cosmetics

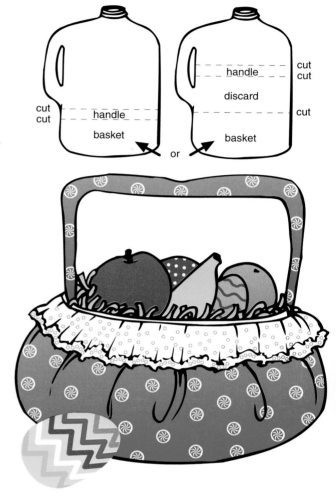

How To Make:

1. Cut off the top of a milk jug approximately two inches below the handle; save it for later use.
2. Cut a piece of fabric to fit around the bottom portion of the jug; allow for extra fabric so that it will overlap the jug's top edge.
3. Spread the cut fabric wrong side up on a flat surface; then center the bottom of the jug on the fabric.
4. To make the basket's sides soft and padded, insert fiberfill as you pull the fabric up to the jug's top edge.
5. Overlap and staple the fabric to the top edge of the jug. (You may wish to use fabric glue or a hot-glue gun instead.)
6. Cut a piece of fabric to fit the inside of the basket. Fold under the fabric's raw edge; then staple it to the edge of the basket.
7. Make a handle from the saved portion of the jug by cutting a two-inch-wide section to the length desired; then cut a piece of fabric large enough to completely cover the handle. Staple the fabric to the handle; then staple the handle to the basket's sides.
8. Glue lace around the top edge of the basket to hide the stapled area; use pinch clothespins to hold the lace in place until the glue dries.
9. Fill the inside of the basket with shredded newspaper or tissue paper; then place fruit, soft candy, trial-size cosmetics, or other such items on top.
10. Present the completed baskets to residents of a local nursing home as an Easter surprise.

Deborah Mayo—Gr. 5, Nebo Elementary, Jena, LA

Mother's Day Bath Salts

Materials: baby-food jar with lid, liquid starch, paintbrush, colored tissue paper (cut into small pieces), acrylic sealant, ribbon, cloth fabric or wallpaper, scissors, mixing bowl, Epsom salts, glycerin, perfume, food coloring, measuring spoons, measuring cup, glue

How To Make:

Paint a small area on the outside of a baby-food jar with liquid starch. Place a piece of tissue paper on the wet area and paint over it with more liquid starch. Cover the entire outer surface of the baby-food jar in this way. When the jar is dry, spray it with a coat of acrylic sealant. Allow the sealant to dry. From fabric or wallpaper, cut a circle that has a diameter of four inches. Glue it to the lid's top. Then tie and glue a bow around the lid as shown.

To make the bath salts: mix together 1/2 tablespoon glycerin and a drop of food coloring in a bowl. Add a few drops of perfume. Stir in 1 1/2 cups Epsom salts and mix well. Fill the jar, and the result is a beautiful gift of luxurious bath salts for Mom.

Paula Kear—Gr. 4, St. Mary's Elementary, Ellis, KS

Wallpaper Fan

Enlist the help of a few parent volunteers for this project. The lovely results are well worth the effort!

Materials: wallpaper samples, 1/4-inch-wide ribbon, hot-glue gun, scissors, 1/2-inch-wide rosebuds or other small craft flowers, Popsicle® sticks (1 1/2 per fan)

How To Make:

1. Cut an 18" x 5" rectangle from wallpaper (or tape two 9" x 5" rectangles end to end).
2. Fold the rectangle fan-style; then open it onto a table, making sure that each short, outer edge is folded toward the back.
3. Pick up each short side of the rectangle in a separate hand; then bring your two hands together, turning them so that your wrists are slightly touching.
4. Gently twist the rectangle so that the bottom edges of the two short ends meet.
5. Have an adult help you center a Popsicle® stick behind the fold line where the two ends meet. Hold the fan while the adult hot-glues the stick in place to make a base for the fan.
6. Next have the adult glue half of a Popsicle® stick in the center of the base so that it is at a right angle to the other stick, helping the fan to stand.
7. Carefully refold the fan at the bottom to form a semi-circle. Have the adult hot-glue the folds together on the back just above the Popsicle®-stick base.
8. Stand the fan upright. Have the adult place a dot of hot glue on the front center; then place a ribbon bow on the glue. Have the adult add another dot of glue to the center of the bow. Place a rosebud or other small flower on this dot of glue.

Mae Purrenhage—Grs. 3–5
Jackson Elementary
Fort Campbell, KY

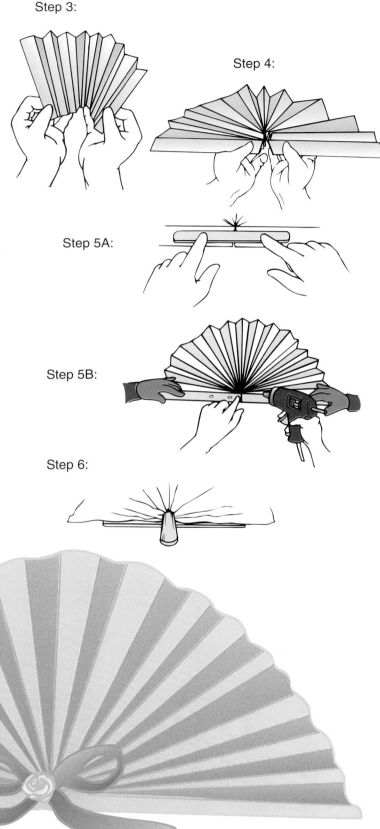

Step 3:

Step 4:

Step 5A:

Step 5B:

Step 6:

For Mom

Fun Flowers For Favorite Folks

Let your students say "thanks for a great year" to the school secretary, cafeteria workers, guidance counselor, and other staff members with this easy gift idea. Purchase a supply of small, inexpensive potted plants (one for each person you want to thank). Then have each student or pair of students complete the following steps:

1. Cut two 5-inch circles, two 4 1/2-inch circles, and two 3-inch circles from colored newspaper ads. Group the cutouts into two sets of concentric circles.
2. Make rounded cuts along the outer edge of each circle to create flower petals.
3. Roll each petal around a toothpick to create edges that are slightly curled.
4. Stack each set of three flowers in order according to size, with the largest circle on the bottom; then glue the set of three flowers together.
5. Position a straw between the two sets of flowers to serve as a stem; then glue the flowers to the straw back-to-back.
6. Cut two small circles from a laminated paper scrap. Glue one circle to the front center and one to the back center of the flower.
7. Insert the completed flower in the soil of a potted plant.

Gerrie Gutowski—Gr. 4
Sombra Del Monte School
Albuquerque, NM

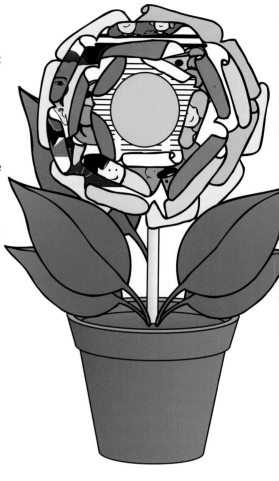

Time In A Bottle

"If I could save this year in a bottle…." What *would* be in that bottle if you could fill it with memories of the school year that's about to come to an end? Pose that question to your students; then set them loose to create these memory-filled projects.

Steps for each student:

1. Cut out a bottle shape from a large piece of white construction paper. Include a lid.
2. Write your name on your bottle's lid.
3. Use a black marker or crayon to divide the bottle into four sections.
4. Decorate the sections so that they illustrate the following topics:
   - The funniest thing that happened this year
   - Five words that describe this year
   - The most important thing I learned this year
   - An area in which I improved this year
5. Optional: Trace your bottle on a clear acetate sheet. Cut out the tracing; then tape or staple it on top of your bottle.

Post the bottles on a bulletin board titled "If We Could Save Time In A Bottle…."

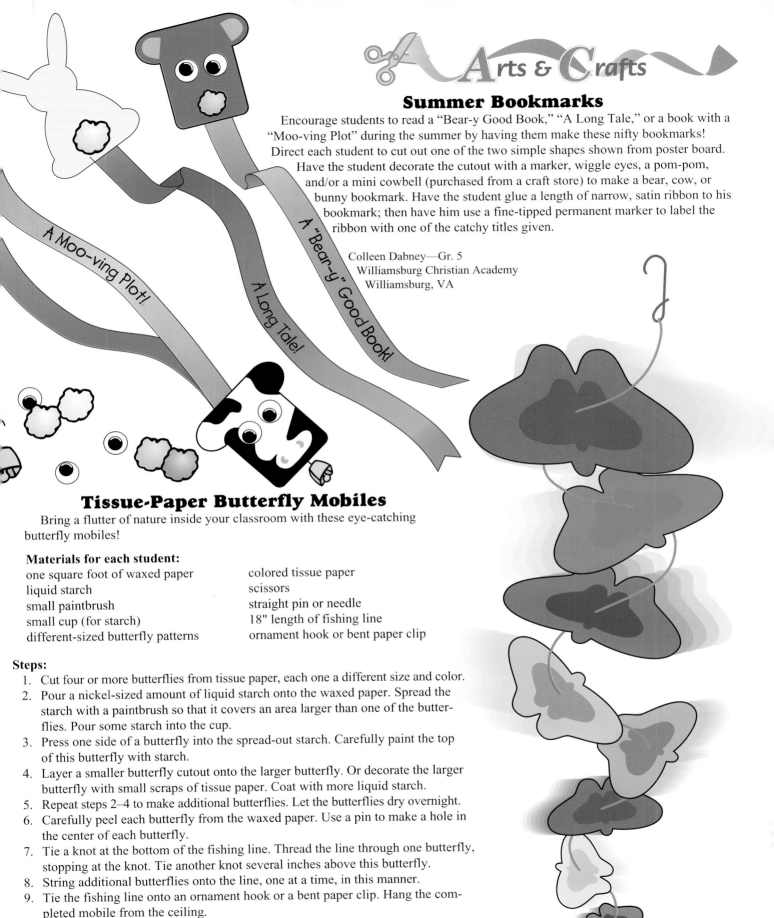

Summer Bookmarks

Encourage students to read a "Bear-y Good Book," "A Long Tale," or a book with a "Moo-ving Plot" during the summer by having them make these nifty bookmarks! Direct each student to cut out one of the two simple shapes shown from poster board. Have the student decorate the cutout with a marker, wiggle eyes, a pom-pom, and/or a mini cowbell (purchased from a craft store) to make a bear, cow, or bunny bookmark. Have the student glue a length of narrow, satin ribbon to his bookmark; then have him use a fine-tipped permanent marker to label the ribbon with one of the catchy titles given.

Colleen Dabney—Gr. 5
Williamsburg Christian Academy
Williamsburg, VA

A Moo-ving Plot!

A Long Tale!

A "Bear-y" Good Book!

Tissue-Paper Butterfly Mobiles

Bring a flutter of nature inside your classroom with these eye-catching butterfly mobiles!

Materials for each student:

one square foot of waxed paper
liquid starch
small paintbrush
small cup (for starch)
different-sized butterfly patterns
colored tissue paper
scissors
straight pin or needle
18" length of fishing line
ornament hook or bent paper clip

Steps:

1. Cut four or more butterflies from tissue paper, each one a different size and color.
2. Pour a nickel-sized amount of liquid starch onto the waxed paper. Spread the starch with a paintbrush so that it covers an area larger than one of the butterflies. Pour some starch into the cup.
3. Press one side of a butterfly into the spread-out starch. Carefully paint the top of this butterfly with starch.
4. Layer a smaller butterfly cutout onto the larger butterfly. Or decorate the larger butterfly with small scraps of tissue paper. Coat with more liquid starch.
5. Repeat steps 2–4 to make additional butterflies. Let the butterflies dry overnight.
6. Carefully peel each butterfly from the waxed paper. Use a pin to make a hole in the center of each butterfly.
7. Tie a knot at the bottom of the fishing line. Thread the line through one butterfly, stopping at the knot. Tie another knot several inches above this butterfly.
8. String additional butterflies onto the line, one at a time, in this manner.
9. Tie the fishing line onto an ornament hook or a bent paper clip. Hang the completed mobile from the ceiling.

Gail Teune—Gr. 4
Central School
Riverside, IL

Pysanky Project

Have you ever dyed Easter eggs? In one special area of our globe, called the Ukraine, people have been dyeing eggs for hundreds of years. These special eggs are called *pysanky.* They are decorated with very fancy, intricate designs. In fact, no two pysanky are alike! Pysanky contain symbols and colors that have special meanings. Each is designed to communicate special wishes for the person who will receive the egg. Pysanky are given to family and friends as gifts.

Dividing The Egg: One of the first steps in making a pysanka is to divide the egg into geometric parts. Here are examples of some traditional patterns:

Drawing The Symbols: Once the egg is divided into geometric parts, the next step is to draw pictures and symbols inside each section. In traditional pysanky, symbols are repeated in each section to create a design. Also, nature is used to represent different messages. Use some of these traditional symbols, or create some of your own.

Flowers: beauty, children, wisdom, love, charity, goodwill

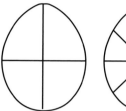

Fruits: knowledge, health, a good life, wisdom

Trees: long life, good health, strength, youthfulness

 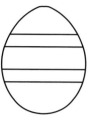   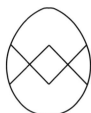

Animals: prosperity, wealth

ram's horns

Birds: fulfillment of wishes, spring, good harvest, protection

Other:

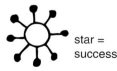 star = success

 sun = growth, good fortune

 spider = good fortune

 water = wealth

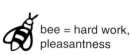 bee = hard work, pleasantness

Coloring The Egg: Colors are a very important part of the message of the pysanka. Each color has a special meaning:

white = purity
green = hope, wealth, happiness
orange = power, endurance
brown = prosperity

yellow = success, wisdom
blue = sky, air, good health
red = happiness, hope, life
purple = faith, trust

Note To The Teacher: Use this reproducible with "Paper Pysanky" on page 77.

LANGUAGE ARTS UNITS

Vocabulary Builders
Favorite Vocabulary Activities From Our Subscribers

Searching for a better blueprint for building your students' word power? If you're ready to renovate your vocabulary lesson plans, pack these creative ideas from our subscribers into your teaching toolbox!

Words From The Past

For a unique homework assignment, challenge each student to interview an older relative or friend to find examples of words that are no longer in use. Some examples might include *phonograph, icebox, buttonhook,* or *running board.* The next day, compile the students' words into a class list; then ask students to speculate why each word is no longer used. Follow up this assignment by having students suggest current words that may be lost in the future. *Isobel Livingstone, Rahway, NJ*

Puzzle Charades

There's nothing like an action-filled game to perk up flagging learning spirits! For each cooperative group, laminate a holiday decoration or poster; then cut it into eight puzzle pieces. Label a set of flash cards with vocabulary words for students to review. To play, divide your class into teams of five or six students each. Give an unassembled puzzle to each group. In turn, have a member of a team draw a vocabulary card and silently act it out, as in the game of charades. Allow the actor's team three chances to guess the word. If a team correctly guesses the word, the actor selects one puzzle piece and adds it to his team's puzzle; then that team chooses a different actor and takes another turn. If a team does not correctly guess the word, play rotates to the next team. The team that completes its puzzle first wins. *Eileen J. Harford—Grs. 5–6, Orchard Middle School, Solon, OH*

Let Your Fingers Do The Typing!

Provide practice with keyboarding skills while students review the spellings of new vocabulary words. At a center, store a supply of laminated computer keyboards made from tagboard. During free time, let a student take a keyboard to his desk and practice "typing" his vocabulary words. Use these handy tools to practice spelling words too! *Dawn Helton—Gr. 4, Read-Turrentine Elementary, Silsbee, TX*

R.I.P.
Awesome
Born: ?
Died: Sept. 14, 1995

stunning
magnificent
amazing
breathtaking

Death Of An Overused Word

When I find my sixth graders overusing a word in written or oral language (everything is "awesome" to them), we bury the word in our Tired Word Graveyard. I label a cut-out tombstone with the worn-out word; then I hang the tombstone on a classroom wall. My students help out by decorating the gravesite with paper flowers labeled with more exciting synonyms for the weary word. This eye-catching display is a motivating way to encourage my students to use a thesaurus, build their vocabularies, and breathe new life into their writing! *Maura Palmer—Gr. 6, Hampstead Middle School, Hampstead, NH*

Keep Looking!

Familiarize your students with the dictionary and new vocabulary words with this simple activity:
1. Write three numbers on a slip of paper. No number should be larger than the number of students in your class. Don't reveal the numbers to your students.
2. Write a word on the board. Instruct students to begin searching for the word in their dictionaries.
3. As students raise their hands to signify that they've found the word, assign a number to each child in numerical order.
4. When all students have found the word, ask one child to read the definition aloud as you write it on the board. Have each student copy the word and its definition in his vocabulary notebook.
5. Reveal the three numbers and ask the numbered students to raise their hands. Reward each of those students who copied the word and its definition correctly with a piece of sugarless candy or another small treat.

Remind the class that even the last person to find the word in the dictionary may get a chance to win a treat. *Redena Barton—Gr. 5, L. F. Addington Middle School, Wise, VA*

The Reinstein kids were often mischievous.

An Occasional Cow

Sometimes Imogene made sarcastic remarks.

Novel Vocabulary Bags

Each time my class starts a new novel, I post a vocabulary list for each chapter. To review these words, I give each child a paper lunch bag to decorate with her name and a scene from the book. I also give her a supply of small index cards (one per vocabulary word). On each card, the student writes a sentence that correctly or incorrectly uses one of the words. On the back of the card, the student writes *correct* or *incorrect*. After each student has completed her set of cards and placed them in her bag, pair her with a partner. Have partners take turns reading each other's cards and guessing whether the sentences are correct or incorrect. *Benita Kaplan—Gr. 4, Glyndon Elementary, Reisterstown, MD*

Quick Draw Review

When you want the entire class to review for a vocabulary test, try this fun-filled activity. Call a volunteer to the chalkboard or overhead projector. Whisper a word to the student; then have her draw pictures to illustrate the word's meaning. If a classmate correctly guesses the word, have him also explain the relationship between the pictures and the word's meaning. If correct, let him be the next artist. *Elsie B. McGill—Grs. 6–8, College Park Middle School, Hickory, NC*

The Vocabulary Express

At the beginning of the year, I post a large paper locomotive on my classroom wall (see the pattern on page 89). I also duplicate a supply of train cars (pattern on page 89). Each time my students learn a new vocabulary word, I write it on a car cutout and add it to the train. In no time, our Vocabulary Express is winding its way around the classroom, out the door, and down the hallway. At the end of each week, we review the words from the beginning of the train to its end. My kids love watching their train grow from week to week! *Bari S. Garfield—L. D., Fuchs Bet Sefer Mizrachi, Cleveland Heights, OH*

Vocabulary Express   detour   luminous

Weighty Words

I haven't found a better tool for building vocabulary than an innovative alphabet book called *The Weighty Word Book* by Paul M. Levitt (published by Manuscripts, Ltd.). For each letter of the alphabet, the author gives a short story that explains the meaning of a vocabulary word beginning with that letter. For example, the story for the letter *e* is about an ant that used to be quick and speedy when searching for food. Then one day he discovered a picnic area that provided an endless supply of tasty tidbits. Since he found a better way to solve his problem and no longer had to be quick to find food, he became the "ex-speedy ant" *(expedient)*. I read one of these stories to my class each day. My students love them and review the new words almost daily. *Therese Durhman—Gr. 5, Mountain View School, Hickory, NC*

Checkered Vocabulary

Place this review game at a learning center to provide plenty of vocabulary practice. Purchase an inexpensive game of checkers. Write each vocabulary word you want to review on a small slip of paper; then tape the slip to the bottom of a checker. Two students play the game using the rules of checkers with one exception: when Player A is ready to jump one of Player B's checkers, he must define the word attached to the bottom of the checker. If correct, Player A may jump and take the checker. If incorrect, Player B gets to take Player A's checker. Provide a dictionary at the center so players can check their definitions. *Pamela Doerr—Substitute Teacher, Elizabethtown School District, Elizabethtown, PA*

A New And Improved Word Wall

Create a visual dictionary that reminds students of vocabulary words from various units of study. Label a set of large index cards with the letters of the alphabet (one letter per card). Mount the cards alphabetically in a horizontal path along your classroom walls, placing each card at the very top of the wall. As students work on a particular unit, write each new vocabulary word on a construction-paper cutout related to the topic. For instance, label cut-out leaves with words from your plants unit or cut-out stars with vocabulary from *Number The Stars*. Post each word under its correct letter. By writing the words on topical cutouts, you'll help students locate words about a specific topic more quickly. To further assist students, post a key as shown. *Karen Andreozzi, Hugh Cole Elementary, Warren, RI*

L

latitude

longitude

labor

landscape

locate

Word Wall Key

Spelling Words

Recycling Unit

Fossils Unit

Map Skills

Recipe Unit

Current Events

ABC Vocabulary

The next time your students are lined up to go to lunch, play this quick-on-your-feet vocabulary game. Call out a topic such as proper nouns, capital cities, rivers, or book characters. At a signal, have the first student in line name a word belonging in that category that begins with *A*. The second student names a word beginning with *B*, and so on through the alphabet. It's a great way to review vocabulary in a snap! *Jim Eaton—Gr. 6, Parkside Elementary, Normal, IL*

Guess And Check

One way I help students learn new vocabulary is by teaching them different strategies for determining the definitions of unknown words. Some of these strategies include using context clues, examining the sentence that comes before or after the word, and looking at any affixes in the word. After teaching these skills, I give each child a copy of the reproducible shown and a list of new words from a literature selection. Using the different strategies, my students try to guess each word's meaning. Then they use any available source (dictionary, thesaurus, encyclopedia, textbook, etc.) to check their guesses. After my students have mastered the Guess And Check strategy with the words I provide, I ask them to look for other unfamiliar words in the selection and add them to their charts.
Laura Vazquez—Gr. 5, Charles R. Hadley Elementary, Miami Springs, FL

Guess And Check

+/-	Unknown word	Clues to its meaning	Guess the meaning.	Check the meaning using dictionary or other source.
+	coaxing- pg. 11	placed	to convince	to persuade or trying to persuade
+	gait- pg. 118	clumsy	the way they walk	particular manner of moving on foot

Super-Duper Sentences

Who doesn't like to impress friends by using a weighty word now and then? For example:
- "Have you the audacity to doubt my veracity and insinuate that I prevaricate?" *(Are you calling me a liar?)*
- "My gastronomic satiety admonishes me that I have arrived at a state of deglutition inconsistent with dietetic integrity." *(I have indigestion.)*
- "There's the anatomical juxtaposition of two orbicular muscles in the state of contraction!" *(That person is kissing someone!)*

I challenge my students to memorize these weighty sentences after we've reviewed the meanings of the new words in them. Then I have students use the words in sentences of their own. My students love to plug these words into writing workshop pieces and conversations. Parents have even added their own "super-duper sentences" to our collection. *Barbara Caplan—Gr. 5, Franklin Elementary, Reisterstown, MD*

Boob-Tube Vocabulary

On Friday my students have a homework assignment that includes the modern wonder we all love to hate—television. Over the weekend, each student is to write down five new vocabulary words that he has heard on television and wants to learn. On Monday students turn in their words; then the class reviews the compilation and chooses 15 to 20 words to learn that week. (Because I have a bilingual class, words can be in Spanish or English, which helps everyone pick up some new vocabulary in a different language.) After the words have been chosen, students define the words and explain how they could be used on a television program. *Coletta Preacely Ellis—Grs. 5/6, Wilson Elementary, Lynwood, CA*

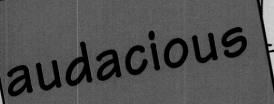

Word Of The Day

After all students have arrived in the morning, I display a large flash card labeled with the vocabulary word of the day. I ask if anyone knows the pronunciation and/or meaning of the word; then I write three sentences using it on the board. Each student copies the day's date, the new word, its meaning, and the three sample sentences in his vocabulary notebook. The flash card is added to a vocabulary wall display that grows as the year progresses. The next morning each student must use the word correctly in a sentence before entering the classroom. My students love using these new words at home. They even insist that I not allow parents to enter our classroom during Open House until the parents use a new word in a sentence too! *Jane H. Reiser—Gr. 6, Jones Lane Elementary, Darnestown, MD*

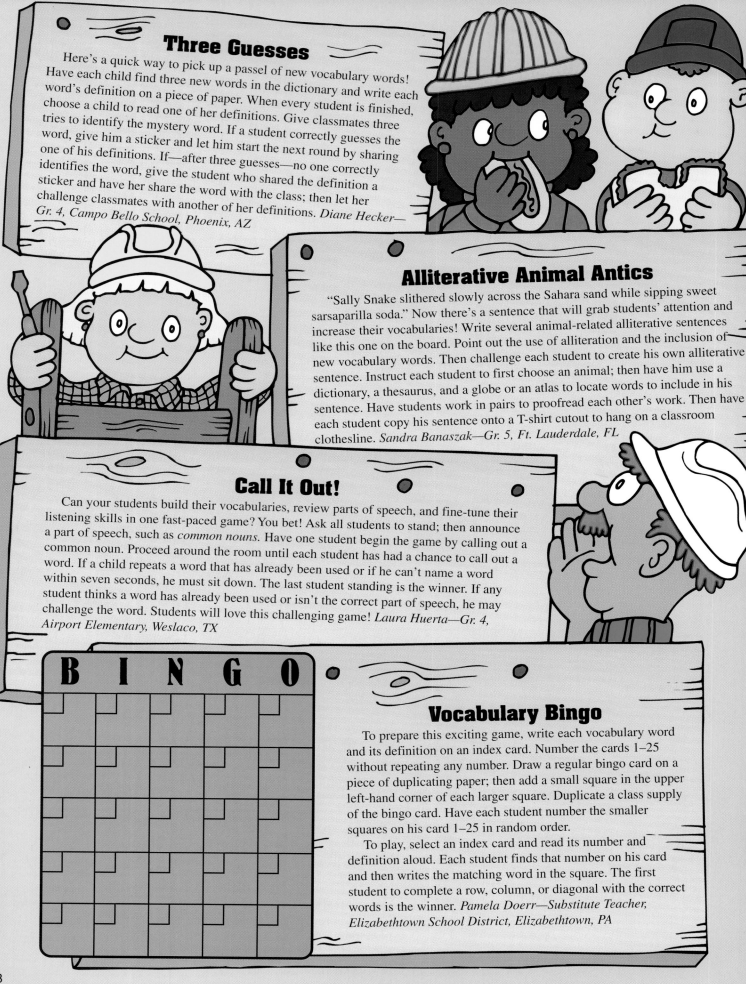

Three Guesses

Here's a quick way to pick up a passel of new vocabulary words! Have each child find three new words in the dictionary and write each word's definition on a piece of paper. When every student is finished, choose a child to read one of her definitions. Give classmates three tries to identify the mystery word. If a student correctly guesses the word, give him a sticker and let him start the next round by sharing one of his definitions. If—after three guesses—no one correctly identifies the word, give the student who shared the definition a sticker and have her share the word with the class; then let her challenge classmates with another of her definitions. *Diane Hecker— Gr. 4, Campo Bello School, Phoenix, AZ*

Alliterative Animal Antics

"Sally Snake slithered slowly across the Sahara sand while sipping sweet sarsaparilla soda." Now there's a sentence that will grab students' attention and increase their vocabularies! Write several animal-related alliterative sentences like this one on the board. Point out the use of alliteration and the inclusion of new vocabulary words. Then challenge each student to create his own alliterative sentence. Instruct each student to first choose an animal; then have him use a dictionary, a thesaurus, and a globe or an atlas to locate words to include in his sentence. Have students work in pairs to proofread each other's work. Then have each student copy his sentence onto a T-shirt cutout to hang on a classroom clothesline. *Sandra Banaszak—Gr. 5, Ft. Lauderdale, FL*

Call It Out!

Can your students build their vocabularies, review parts of speech, and fine-tune their listening skills in one fast-paced game? You bet! Ask all students to stand; then announce a part of speech, such as *common nouns.* Have one student begin the game by calling out a common noun. Proceed around the room until each student has had a chance to call out a word. If a child repeats a word that has already been used or if he can't name a word within seven seconds, he must sit down. The last student standing is the winner. If any student thinks a word has already been used or isn't the correct part of speech, he may challenge the word. Students will love this challenging game! *Laura Huerta—Gr. 4, Airport Elementary, Weslaco, TX*

B I N G O

Vocabulary Bingo

To prepare this exciting game, write each vocabulary word and its definition on an index card. Number the cards 1–25 without repeating any number. Draw a regular bingo card on a piece of duplicating paper; then add a small square in the upper left-hand corner of each larger square. Duplicate a class supply of the bingo card. Have each student number the smaller squares on his card 1–25 in random order.

To play, select an index card and read its number and definition aloud. Each student finds that number on his card and then writes the matching word in the square. The first student to complete a row, column, or diagonal with the correct words is the winner. *Pamela Doerr—Substitute Teacher, Elizabethtown School District, Elizabethtown, PA*

Use with "The Vocabulary Express" on page 85. Duplicate one copy of the engine and multiple copies of the train car on white paper; then mount each pattern onto colorful construction paper and cut out to leave a border of colored paper (see the illustration on page 85).

Forward, Then Backward

Use letters in each word below to build some four-letter words. You may skip over letters, but you may not change the order of the letters. Begin by spelling three words going forward in the word; then spell three words moving backward. (Try to avoid using obvious words such as *hand* in number 2.) Use a dictionary to check your words. The number of possible solutions may surprise you!

Example: PERSONALITY   salt, pray, slit
                              ←   tine, tarp, lose

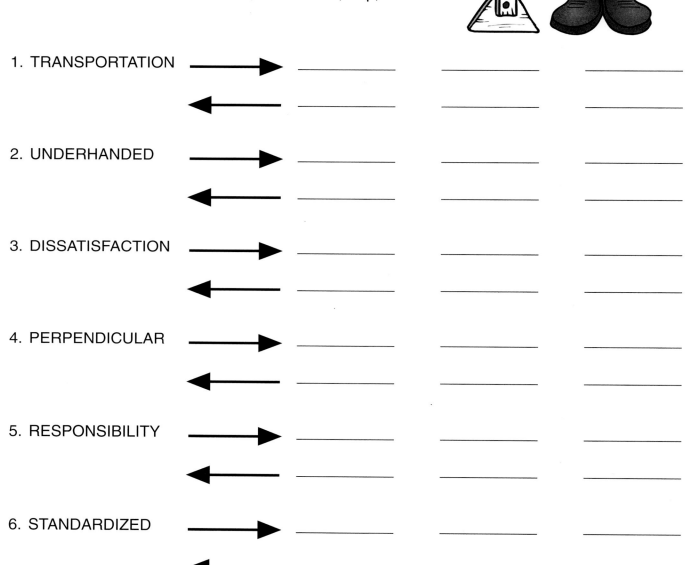

1. TRANSPORTATION ————▶ _____ _____ _____

                   ◀———— _____ _____ _____

2. UNDERHANDED ————▶ _____ _____ _____

                ◀———— _____ _____ _____

3. DISSATISFACTION ————▶ _____ _____ _____

                    ◀———— _____ _____ _____

4. PERPENDICULAR ————▶ _____ _____ _____

                  ◀———— _____ _____ _____

5. RESPONSIBILITY ————▶ _____ _____ _____

                   ◀———— _____ _____ _____

6. STANDARDIZED ————▶ _____ _____ _____

                 ◀———— _____ _____ _____

Bonus Box: Try to find at least one five- or six-letter word going forward or backward in each word above.

A Musical Journey

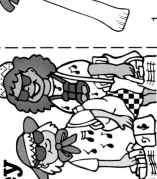

Melody Major and Dee Minor are touring the United States. In each town below, they are studying a different musical instrument. The instrument can be spelled using some of the letters in the name of the town. For example, in <u>Chillicothe</u>, Illinois, Melody and Dee learned about the *cello*. Write the name of each instrument in the blank. Use a dictionary to help you.

1. Powatan Point, OH   _____

2. Baudette, MN   _____

3. Dunsmuir, CA   _____

4. Jeffersonville, GA   _____

5. Brookside, AL   _____

6. Grand Canyon, AZ   _____

7. Reydell, AR   _____

8. Fullerton, KY   _____

9. Vermilion, OH   _____

10. El Centro, CA   _____

11. Georgetown, KY   _____

12. Jacksonburg, WV   _____

Bonus Box: Could Melody and Dee study an instrument in your town or a town nearby? Write the name of the town and the instrument on the back of this paper.

©The Education Center, Inc. • THE MAILBOX® • Intermediate • Aug/Sept 1995 • Key p. 308

Build-A-Word

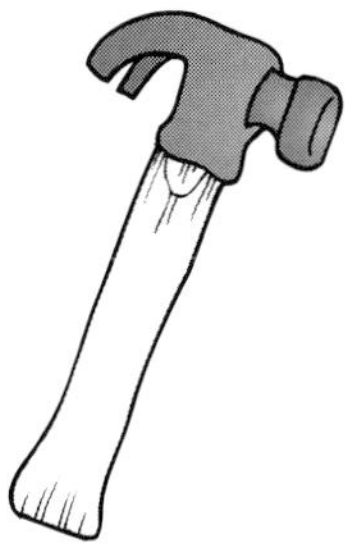

Add the letter indicated to each word below. Then rearrange the letters to spell a new word. Check your work with a dictionary if necessary.

Example: a + lock = cloak

1. a + threw = _____
2. b + dare = _____
3. c + peas = _____
4. d + pedal = _____
5. e + thaw = _____
6. f + yeast = _____
7. g + hour = _____
8. h + laws = _____
9. i + drab = _____
10. j + yell = _____
11. k + bear = _____
12. l + clear = _____
13. m + lone = _____
14. n + drag = _____
15. o + star = _____
16. p + cream = _____
17. a + tarp = _____
18. r + kind = _____
19. s + half = _____
20. t + bale = _____
21. u + gel = _____
22. v + sea = _____
23. w + ten = _____
24. x + real = _____
25. y + trap = _____
26. z + ripe = _____

Bonus Box: What two words can be spelled with these letters: **d r e n a e**? Write them on the back of this page.

©The Education Center, Inc. • THE MAILBOX® • Intermediate • Aug/Sept 1995 • Key p. 308

Zounds!

MUCH ADO ABOUT ADJECTIVES AND ADVERBS

From Shakespeare to Sandburg to Dr. Seuss, all great writers know the value of a well-placed adjective or adverb. Use the following fun activities and reproducibles to give your students plenty of practice with these descriptive parts of speech.

SWEET SIXTEEN

For this wonderfully wordy activity, all you need is 16 small index cards and a twist tie (the kind packaged with small or medium-sized plastic garbage bags) for each student. Punch a hole in the top left corner of each card. Distribute 16 cards and a twist tie to each child. Review with students that an adjective is a word that describes a person, place, thing, or thought (or idea/emotion, such as *happiness* or *anger)*. Instruct students to label four cards in their sets with a person; four cards with a place; four cards with a thing; and four cards with a thought. Direct each child to stack his cards in any order, insert the twist tie through the holes, and then twist the tie so that the cards are held securely together.

Next have students swap their card sets. Challenge each child to write an adjective describing the noun on each card in the set. Allow students to use dictionaries or thesauruses to help them. After students have finished, direct them to swap the card sets again with a different classmate. Tell students that they must write an adjective that is different from the one already written on a card. Once cards have been swapped three or four times, have students return the sets to their original owners. Hold a sharing session during which you list the students' adjectives on chart paper. Display the list in the classroom for students to refer to during writing workshop.

ME BOOKS

"I gotta be me" is the theme for this adjective-building exercise. Collect a wide variety of magazines. Have each child cut out ten pictures that he thinks illustrate his personality; then direct him to glue each picture to a separate piece of paper. Provide students with file folders in which to store their pictures. To give periodic practice with adjectives, challenge each student to pull out his Me Folder, select one picture from it, and write a paragraph explaining why that picture reflects his personality. Stipulate that the student must include at least five adjectives in the paragraph. After peer editing, have students use highlighter pens to mark the adjectives in their paragraphs. Let students share their paragraphs; then instruct them to store their written work in their folders. After students have had a chance to write paragraphs for all ten pictures, let them decorate the fronts of their folders, then staple their pictures and paragraphs inside. Send the resulting Me Books home or place them in your students' writing portfolios to save for your next parent conference.

Forsooth! Thy adjectives doth add much vigor to thy writing!

graceful
dainty
ballerina
twirling leaping

ADVERB ANTICS

Here's a quick game that puts adverbs on center stage. Choose one student to be It and to leave the room. While he's out in the hall, have the rest of the class choose an adverb, such as *rapidly.* When It returns, have him ask one member of the class to do something in the manner of the adverb that was selected. For example, It may ask a fellow student to "put on your coat in the manner of the adverb." The student who is It continues to ask for demonstrations such as this until he correctly guesses the adverb. Once the adverb is guessed, It selects a replacement and the game continues. As students play this game more frequently, they'll be on the lookout for new adverbs to use.

SAY IT WITH A CARD

I'm so glad that you are mine,
That's why I celebrate you
on this day of swine...

Students will greet this fun activity with a cheer! Ask students, parents, and co-workers to help you collect a wide variety of used greeting cards. Distribute several cards and a highlighter pen to each pair of students. First have the students identify the adjectives and adverbs in each card's text by highlighting them with the marker. After checking their work, direct the students to use a thesaurus or dictionary to find substitute words for the highlighted ones. Have the pair write the new version of each card's text on the inside front cover or back of the card. Let students share their old and new versions with the class.

As a creative follow-up, challenge each student pair to use art materials to design a new greeting card for one of the lesser-known holidays listed below. Require students to include a certain number of adjectives and adverbs in their cards. When the cards are finished, number each and post it on a bulletin board. During free time, let students number their papers and list the adjectives and adverbs they find on each card. Provide an answer key so students can check their work.

January: National Hugging Day™
February: Read To Your Child Day
March: National Pig Day
April: Thank You School Librarian Day
May: National Teacher Day
June: National Yo-Yo Day

July: Video Games Day
August: Family Day
September: World Gratitude Day
October: National Dessert Day
November: National Clean Out Your Refrigerator Day
December: Eat What You Want Day

SPECIAL ASSIGNMENT

Make practicing adjectives and adverbs a part of your daily routine with this easy-to-implement idea. Write "SPECIAL ASSIGNMENT: SEARCH FOR..." at the top of a piece of poster board; then laminate the poster and mount it on a classroom wall or chalkboard. Each morning use a wipe-off marker to write a special adverb or adjective assignment on the chart (see the example and the list shown). Have students complete the assignment in their writing journals. Sometime during the day, invite students to share their answers. Award bonus points or inexpensive treats to students who list the most words.

Search For...
- adjectives that describe your best friend.
- adjectives that describe the desert.
- adjectives that describe our classroom.
- adjectives that describe your favorite vacation spot.
- adverbs that describe how a gorilla dances.
- adverbs that describe how you eat a food you hate.
- adverbs that describe how you read your report card.
- adverbs that describe how your favorite television star might clean his/her room.

SPECIAL ASSIGNMENT:
Search For...
adverbs that describe how a gorilla dances.

Barry
Slate

THE LITERATURE LINK

Have you considered looking between the pages of a high-quality children's book for the perfect parts-of-speech activity? The following books are wonderful tools for teaching or reviewing adjectives and adverbs. After sharing a book with your class, have small groups of students create their own books on adjectives or adverbs, act out the book as a drama or puppet play, or write another chapter for the book.

Up, Up And Away: A Book About Adverbs by Ruth Heller
Many Luscious Lollipops: A Book About Adjectives by
 Ruth Heller
A Is For Angry: An Animal And Adjective Alphabet by
 Sandra Boynton

TICKET TRIOS

A trio of nouns is listed on each ticket below. In the blank of each ticket, write an adjective that could be used to describe each of the three items.

NOW PLAYING
"Much Ado About Adjectives"
Words can't describe it!

Example: _____ skin, pillow, music
Answer: *soft* (Other words may work, too.)

VOTED BEST PLAY OF 1590
ON SALE NOW!

1. _____
library
mouse
whisper

2. _____
race
ball
horse

3. _____
suit
paint
floor

4. _____
noun
fraction
English

5. _____
cactus
rosebush
porcupine

6. _____
base
degree
cousin

7. _____
gravy
pillow
mattress

8. _____
wheel
league
heart

9. _____
file
person
serving

10. _____
golf
marshmallow
poodle

11. _____
bone
money
joke

12. _____
tape
pepper
maple

13. _____
table
leg
nickel

14. _____
whistle
music
siren

15. _____
watch
coin
earrings

16. _____
bread
engine
potato

Bonus Box: Number the back of this page 3–10. Beside each number, write an adjective with that number of letters. For example, for number 3 you could write *old*.

©The Education Center, Inc. • THE MAILBOX® • Intermediate • April/May 1996 • written by Ann Fisher • Key p. 308

To Be Or Not To Be An Adverb—That Is The Question!

Each word below is really a hidden adverb. To discover each adverb, first replace the underlined letter with a different letter. Then rearrange all the letters to spell a word that is often or always used as an adverb. Write the adverb on the blank; then write a short sentence using the adverb on the rest of the blank.

Example: <u>c</u>ot   **Answer:** too

1. sla<u>w</u>   = _____

2. <u>o</u>ver   = _____

3. <u> </u>pearly   = _____

4. lemon<u>s</u> = _____

5. <u>p</u>ostal   = _____

6. <u>g</u>reen   = _____

7. <u>t</u>ended   = _____

8. woo<u>l</u>ly   = _____

9. f<u>e</u>ather = _____

10. <u>b</u>lew   = _____

11. toad<u>s</u>   = _____

12. tear<u>y</u>   = _____

Bonus Box: Use a dictionary to find the meanings of these adverbs: bombastically, concordantly, loquaciously, arduously. For each word, write a sentence using it correctly on the back of this page.

©The Education Center, Inc. • *THE MAILBOX*® *Intermediate* • April/May 1996 • written by Ann Fisher • Key p. 308

WELCOME TO WRITER'S WORKSHOP!

TIPS AND TECHNIQUES FOR TEACHING PROCESS WRITING

When we want to present the very best teaching ideas around, we go to the experts—our readers! Recently we asked you to send us your favorite process-writing tips and ideas, and the mail poured in! On the following pages, you'll find a colossal collection of classroom-proven ways to help your students become more effective writers.

JOIN IN THE FUN!

My class always settles down quickly and begins to write after a brainstorming session. Why? Because I complete the writing assignment too! When the children see me at my desk thinking and writing, it encourages them to do the same. Students write while ideas are fresh on their minds; then they revise, edit, and rewrite. They're also anxious for me to share my writing. I use my piece on the overhead as an example when teaching revising and editing techniques, especially when I don't have a student volunteer his paper for that purpose.

Denise Edwards, Mercer County Elementary, Harrodsburg, KY

ROUND-ROBIN REVISING

Try this editing technique that allows several students to check a rough draft in a short period of time. After completing a piece of writing, have each student pass his paper to the classmate who sits directly behind him (or to his right if students sit in groups). Using a timer, have each student read his classmate's paper and make editing and/or story improvement suggestions. Instruct students to use proofreading symbols within the text and make extended comments in the margins. When the timer sounds, instruct each student to pass his paper again. Repeat this process until three or four people have read a student's paper. By the time a paper reaches the last editor, it will be a real challenge to find any more errors.

*Faye K. Wells, Marion County Elementary
Buena Vista, GA*

EDITING WITH EASE

My students follow the writing-process steps throughout the year. When I noticed that many students had difficulty with the editing and revising stages, I developed a checklist (see page 101) to help both writers and editors. A writer attaches a checklist to a paper of his that needs editing. Three peers then read the piece and complete the attached checklist by recording a yes or no response to each question. The writing, along with the accompanying checklist, is turned in to me. By looking at the checklist, I'm able to quickly spot areas which the writer needs to revise. These checklists provide direct and constructive feedback to peer editors, writers, and especially me.

Maureen Roman—Gr. 6, Northwestern Lehigh Middle School, New Tripoli, PA

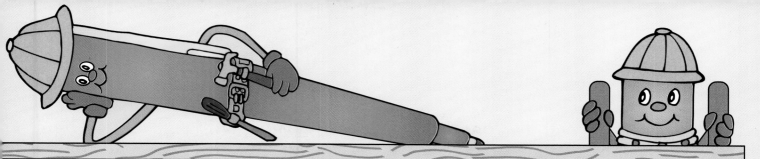

EDITING RAFFLES

In my writer's workshop, students revise each other's writings by filling out a "PQP"—which stands for "Praise, Question, Polish" (see the example). After the PQPs are completed, each student then peer edits with two other classmates. Each peer editor completes a pink editing slip (see the example), which is given to the writer. After a student has obtained a PQP and two pink editing slips, she brings them and her rough draft to me for a teacher conference. I check the forms for thoroughness and usefulness; then I place forms that are complete and truly helpful into a raffle container. Every two weeks I pull out one or more forms and reward the winning students with small prizes. Students are eager to help with revising and editing so that they have more chances in the raffle.

Julie VandeBerg—Gr. 4, Rosendale Elementary
Rosendale, WI

☆☆☆☆☆ PQP ☆☆☆☆☆
Revised by: _____
Praise: _____
Question: _____
Polish: _____

Editing Slip
Writer:
Peer Editor:
Capitalization:
Punctuation:
Spelling:
Legibility:

MAGIC REVISION MARKERS

Students often have a natural inclination to believe their written work is perfect "as is," and thus resist making efforts to revise it. To help solve this problem, I very dramatically inform my class that I had a special visit from the "revision fairy" (the tooth fairy's cousin!), who left a set of "magic" markers for my class. These magical writing utensils, which are just thin-line markers, are stored in a special container and may only be used when students revise their papers. Though my students think it's silly, the magic works! After the markers are introduced, rough drafts are always filled with colorful revision and editing marks.

Jessica G. Nardi—Gr. 6, Hillsborough Middle School
Livingston, NJ

INTRODUCING: OUR FEATURED WRITER

A student's writing needs to be recognized and shared with others besides the teacher. To accomplish this, I've created a "Featured Writer" program. Each week I publicly display one student's written work along with a photo of him. I also interview the student, asking him how he got the idea for his writing, what type of process he went through, and what his interests and hobbies are. Then I announce to the class the name of the featured writer and give a short summary about his writing. To further recognize the featured writer, I send home an award to which I've attached an incentive like a homework pass or pizza coupon. What a great way to say, "Writing is important—and so are you!"

Anne Boots, Seymour Middle School, Seymour, WI

USING POSTER ADVERTISEMENTS AS TOPICS

To make a great writing center (and do a bit of recycling in the process), I cut out lots of advertising pictures from educational poster catalogs. I store the pictures in a box located on my writing table. Each student selects a picture and completes one of the following writing activities about it:

- Write about a personal experience that the poster reminds you of.
- Use the slogan on the poster as a title and write a story about it.
- Change the poster in some way; then write about the new topic.
- Create and then describe another illustration to go with the slogan.
- Work with a partner to create and describe a way to prove that the slogan on the poster is true.

These colorful, entertaining poster illustrations make for a popular writing activity that's a snap to make!

Cindy Goodman—Gr. 4, Menlo Park Elementary, Edison, NJ

Some of my best friends are books.

Of all the things you wear, your expression is the most important.

C-U-P-S CODE

When evaluating a student's writing assignment, I use the following code: C (capitalization), U (usage), P (punctuation), and S (spelling). When a student sees one or more of these letters in the margin of his paper, he's alerted that that particular line of writing contains one or more errors. The student then revises his paper by using a dictionary, rereading his paper, or asking a peer for assistance.

Charlotte Hinson, Bellaire Elementary, Bossier, LA

Example:
We traveled in
u are spaceship to
s anuther planet.
c it was an exciting
   adventure.

TIMING CONFERENCES

When holding individual writing conferences, I use this tip to make sure everyone gets an equal turn. I begin the process by sitting between two students. The first student and I discuss his writing project, while the other child holds a stopwatch and times us. At the end of five minutes, the timer switches to the conference chair position, and a third child then keeps time. This easy and effective method ensures that no student misses his turn.

Patricia E. Dancho—Gr. 6, Apollo-Ridge Middle School, Spring Church, PA

NO SENTENCES ALLOWED!

For even your strongest writers, it can seem a bit scary to have to come up with a page or more of paragraphs related to a new writing topic. To ease those prewriting jitters, try this trick. Set a timer for five minutes; then have students list words and phrases related to the topic—no sentences allowed! When time is up, ask volunteers to each share an item or two from their lists.

Faye K. Wells
Marion County Elementary
Buena Vista, GA

FEELING THE STORY

Reach out and touch a story before writing it? That's exactly what my students do with this fun prewriting activity. First each student fills a shallow box with sand. Then he brings objects from home—such as toy soldiers, horses, dolls, trees, and cars—to create a scene in the box. I also keep a collection of small toys to use, which has grown over the years with students' donations. If a student can see a "real" scene and manipulate its elements, it can cause that creative spark to glow and grow into a terrific original story.

Janet Riddle—Gr. 4, Park Glen Elementary, Fort Worth, TX

LOOKING FOR A TOPIC?

This idea will lead to some interesting story lines! Have each child list the people, places, and activities he enjoys, making sure to include at least five items in each list. When a student is at a loss for a writing topic, he chooses one item from each list and creates a story that incorporates all three. Have students keep their lists in their writing folders and add or refer to them whenever they wish.

Pamela Doerr—Grs. K–6 Substitute Teacher
Lancaster County Schools, Mount Joy, PA

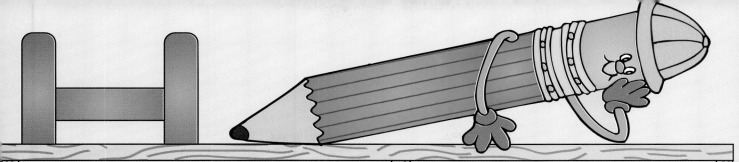

TAPING EVALUATIONS

At the beginning of the year, I ask each student to bring a blank audiocassette tape to class as part of his back-to-school supplies. Instead of only writing comments on students' papers, I can really personalize evaluations by tape-recording them. I also ask each student to tape-record his own evaluation after mine. For those students who don't have tape recorders at home, both the school librarian and I provide them for student use.

Patricia E. Dancho—Gr. 6, Apollo-Ridge Middle School, Spring Church, PA

KEEPING TRACK OF WRITING SKILLS

I love individual conferences with students during writer's workshop, but find myself bogged down trying to keep track of the skills each student needs to work on. To solve this problem, I developed a spreadsheet that helps me organize skills for each student. In the first column, I write the student's name. In the second and third columns, I ask the student to set two goals for herself, such as "remember periods" or "begin a new paragraph with each new speaker." In the fourth column, I set a writing goal for the student. In the fifth column, I record the date goals are set, while the sixth column records the date goals are achieved. Once goals have been met, students move on to new ones. My students like to know the exact areas in which they should improve, and this spreadsheet helps me to be more organized.

Carrie Hursh—Gr. 6, Whitewater Valley Elementary, Harrison, OH

student's name	student goal 1	student goal 2	Mrs. Hursh's writing goal	date goals set	date goals met
Mary O'Keeffe	Remember periods.	Begin a new paragraph with each new speaker.	Stick with your theme throughout.	3/6/96	3/20/96
David Hodnett	Think about commas.	Watch spelling.	Try more creative topics.	3/6/96	3/22/96

SPELLING ADVICE

To encourage students to revise their spelling during writer's workshop, allow them to go to the classroom computer for spelling advice. Have the computer opened to a new document on any word-processing program with a spell-check function. Students can then check the spellings of unfamiliar words. Your computer-crazy kids will love this idea, which is perfect for the one-computer classroom.

Amy Eisenberg—Gr. 6, Sudbrook Magnet Middle School Baltimore, MD

HOT TOPICS

Prepare a topics file for those students who sometimes get stuck for an idea during writer's workshop. Simply write "Hot Topics" on the cover of a red notebook. Inside, draw a line down the center of each page and label the resulting columns "Topic" and "Author." At any time, a student may list a topic that she has written about, plus her name, in the notebook. Students may also look in the notebook when they need a story idea or just a little inspiration. If someone has a question about a listed topic, she may ask the student who listed it.

Pamela Doerr—Grs. K–6 Substitute Teacher Lancaster County Schools, Mount Joy, PA

"I DON'T KNOW WHAT TO WRITE ABOUT..."

To get students excited about a writing assignment and to prevent the "I don't know what to write about" blues, I simply introduce the assignment and discuss lots of examples and ideas. After my song-and-dance is over, I give students that night to think of ideas and toss around topics. On the following day, I usually find that prewriting is a breeze and most students are anxious to get going on their rough drafts.

Amy Murray, Waterford, MI

ROUND-TABLE PEER EDITING

When teaching my class how to write an organized essay, I introduce the terms *introductory paragraph*, *thesis statement*, *supporting details*, *body paragraphs*, and *closing paragraph*. Students are then given a prompt to write about, or they create their own topics. Once rough drafts are complete, groups of four students each peer edit in a round-table session (each student reads another group member's essay, passes it to his left, reads another essay, passes it, etc.). When evaluating a classmate's essay, a student completes a reproducible checklist (see page 102). After the session is over, each student's essay is returned to him, along with the three peer-editing checklists. Students use these checklists to help them rewrite their rough drafts. If students learn to look for the basic elements in one another's work, they're more likely to include them in their own writing pieces!

Carrie Hursh—Gr. 6, Whitewater Valley Elementary, Harrison, OH

STARS AND WISHES

I model peer conferences many times before students begin on their own. To do this, I make overhead transparencies of several writings which may include published works from children's magazines, former students' papers, or writing pieces from some of my current students. After reading a piece two times, students decide on things they like about it, which we call "stars." Then we brainstorm suggestions to make the work better, called "wishes." Finally, to practice the skill of making revisions, we ask questions (each beginning "I wonder...") about other things we'd like to know about the topic.

Denise Amos—Gr. 4
Crestwood Elementary
Crestwood, KY

TITLES THAT REALLY GRAB YOU!

Here's an activity that will result in a treasure trove of attention-grabbing titles for written work. As a class, list titles from various books, movies, and television shows on the chalkboard; then discuss which of the titles are most interesting. Next have the class list title characteristics that grab the reader's attention, including interesting adjectives, adverbs, and use of detail. For example, discuss why the title *Unusual Weather* is not nearly as interesting as *Cloudy With A Chance Of Meatballs*. Work with students to improve the titles on their initial lists that need improvement.

For the next phase of this activity, have each student list possible writing topics; then have him work with a classmate to create interesting titles to go with his topics and those of his partner. Have each pair join another pair to share their titles. Finally have everyone share his attention-grabbing titles with the class.

Pamela Doerr, Grs. K–6 Substitute Teacher
Lancaster County Schools, Mount Joy, PA

LAMINATED WRITING CHECKLISTS

Do you teach writing skills to more than one class of students? If you do, laminate a class set of writing checklist forms (see pages 101 and 102 for examples). Then provide each pair of peer partners with a wipe-off pen to use when completing the checklists. At the end of the peer conferences, have students clean the checklists with a damp sponge so they're ready to use with the next class.

Patricia E. Dancho—Gr. 6, Apollo-Ridge Middle School, Spring Church, PA

DESCRIPTIVE WRITING CHECKLIST

Writer's name _____ Date _____

Directions for each peer editor:

a. Write your name in one of the three editors' boxes in the chart.

b. Answer the eight questions by writing Yes or No in each box in your column.

c. When finished, give this checklist and the attached writing piece to another editor.

d. If you are Editor #3, give the completed checklist and attached writing piece to the teacher when you have finished answering the questions.

	Editor #1	Editor #2	Editor #3

Content:

✓ Did the writer tell about a specific person, place, or thing? ....

✓ Did the writer include details that appeal to at least two of the five senses? ....

✓ Did the writer use interesting words rather than ones that are more commonly used? (For example: *trotted* or *sprinted* instead of *ran*) ....

Form:

✓ Does the first word in each sentence begin with a capital letter? ....

✓ Does each sentence end with a punctuation mark that is used correctly? ....

✓ Are commas, semicolons, apostrophes, and/or colons used correctly? ....

✓ Is the writer's handwriting legible? ....

✓ Are there any misspelled words? ....

If so, list them in the box:

©The Education Center, Inc. • *THE MAILBOX®* • *Intermediate* • Feb/Mar 1996 • written by Maureen Roman—Gr. 6, Northwestern Lehigh Middle School, New Tripoli, PA

Note To The Teacher: Use with "Editing With Ease" on page 96. If desired, use this format to develop checklists for other types of writing such as business letters, research papers, persuasive pieces, or creative stories.

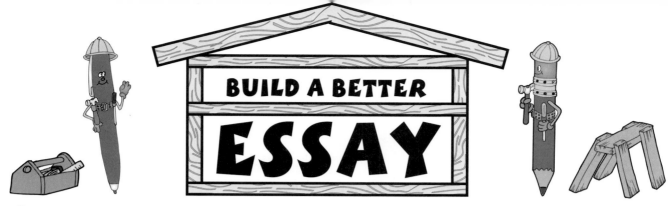

BUILD A BETTER ESSAY

Title of essay: _____

Written by: _____   Date: _____

Edited by: _____

Evaluate your classmate's essay by answering the following questions. Write your initials in either the *yes* or *no* box.

INTRODUCTORY PARAGRAPH:

1. Does the introductory paragraph have a **thesis statement** that restates the question or states the topic?   [yes] [no]

   What is the thesis statement sentence? _____
   _____

2. Does the remaining part of the introductory paragraph include **supporting details** or ideas about the thesis statement or topic?   [yes] [no]

3. How would you improve the introductory paragraph? _____
   _____

BODY PARAGRAPHS:

1. Does the first body paragraph begin with a topic sentence about the first detail in the introductory paragraph?   [yes] [no]

2. Do the remaining sentences in the first body paragraph support the topic?   [yes] [no]

3. Do each of the remaining body paragraphs begin with a topic sentence and have supporting details?   [yes] [no]

4. How would you improve the body paragraphs? _____
   _____

CLOSING PARAGRAPH:

1. In the closing paragraph, does the writer summarize his or her feelings or the facts stated in the introductory paragraph?   [yes] [no]

2. Does the writer leave the reader with a message or moral?   [yes] [no]

3. How would you improve the closing paragraph? _____
   _____

©The Education Center, Inc. • *THE MAILBOX*® • *Intermediate* • Feb/Mar 1996 • written by Carrie Hursh—Gr. 6, Whitewater Valley Elementary, Harrison, OH

Note To The Teacher: Use with "Round-Table Peer Editing" on page 100.

MATH UNITS

A Decimal Marks The Spot!

A Treasure Chest Of Activities For Reinforcing Decimal Concepts

Looking for fun, creative games and activities to help you teach decimal skills? Just dig into this treasure chest of learning experiences, all designed to help students master decimals.

by Irving P. Crump

Let's Go On A Treasure Hunt!

Help students build decimal number sense with a fun treasure hunt. To prepare for the hunt, write a decimal number on each of 16 index cards. Relate each decimal to something in the classroom, such as your height, the price of a piece of classroom equipment, the temperature, the width of a chalkboard, or the capacity of a terrarium. On four of the cards, make sure that the decimal numbers do not make sense. (For example: write 12.5 meters as the height of a bulletin board.) Before students arrive for the day, attach each card to the object that it relates to. Then have students search the classroom for the 16 cards. Challenge them to determine which cards do not make sense. Instruct students to list those four numbers on paper, then change them to numbers that do make sense.

How Many Places?

Review with students one way a decimal is often read: by saying *point* for the decimal point. When the decimal is read as *point,* each individual digit to the right of the decimal is stated. For example: 100.087 is read, "One hundred *point* zero, eight, seven." If the decimal is read as *and,* the last digit to the right of the decimal indicates the place-value family. Since the value of the 7 in 100.087 is *7 thousandths,* the number is read, "One hundred and eighty-seven *thousandths.*"

To provide additional practice with this concept, tell students that you are thinking of a number. Say, "The first digit of my number is in the hundreds place and the last digit is in the hundredths place. How many digits does my number have?" *(5)* Continue this line of questioning with other examples like those below. Ask a volunteer to write an example of each number on the chalkboard.

The first digit is in this place:	The last digit is in this place:	How many digits in this number?
ones	hundredths	3
tens	thousandths	5
hundred thousands	hundredths	8
one millions	hundredths	9
hundred millions	thousandths	12
ten thousands	tenths	6
ten millions	hundredths	10

Place-Value Punchout

Extend students' understanding of decimal place value with a simple calculator exercise. Write a decimal number, such as 689.21, on a chalkboard or transparency, and instruct each student to enter it in his calculator. Have partners double-check each other to make sure the number is entered correctly. Next give students a set of operations—one at a time—to perform on the number. For example: "Subtract eighty; subtract four; subtract two tenths; add thirty. What number now shows in your display?" *(635.01)* After several days of practice, try the next activity.

Down To Nothing

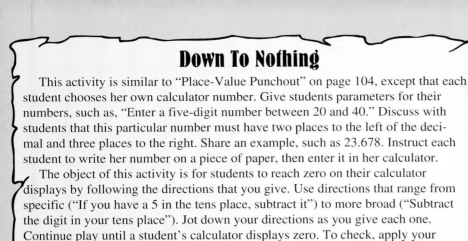

This activity is similar to "Place-Value Punchout" on page 104, except that each student chooses her own calculator number. Give students parameters for their numbers, such as, "Enter a five-digit number between 20 and 40." Discuss with students that this particular number must have two places to the left of the decimal and three places to the right. Share an example, such as 23.678. Instruct each student to write her number on a piece of paper, then enter it in her calculator.

The object of this activity is for students to reach zero on their calculator displays by following the directions that you give. Use directions that range from specific ("If you have a 5 in the tens place, subtract it") to more broad ("Subtract the digit in your tens place"). Jot down your directions as you give each one. Continue play until a student's calculator displays zero. To check, apply your directions to the winning student's original number.

Decimal Dash

Divide students into teams of five players each and provide each team with ten large index cards. Instruct each team to number its cards 1–9, and label one with a large decimal point. Advise each team to draw a line under its 6 and 9 to distinguish them from each other. Instruct each captain to collect his team's cards, shuffle them, and then deal two facedown to each team member.

To play Decimal Dash, announce to the class a decimal number that has no repeating digits, such as 136.75. At a signal, have each team turn over its cards, work together to form the decimal, and then rush to the front of the class with the correct cards to show that decimal. (Since 136.75 requires six cards, one player must hold two cards. The team members should decide who will hold two cards before leaving their places.) Award five points to each team that forms the correct number; award ten points to the fastest team.

Jackpot!

Adding, estimating, and comparing decimals—reinforce a bounty of skills with Jackpot! Provide each student with a copy of the game cards on page 106. On a chalkboard, draw the place-value wheel shown. Tell students that the object of round one is to see who can reach a total that is closest to 1 (the number on the treasure chest). To play, follow these steps:

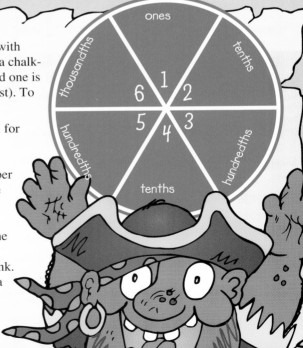

1. Roll a die and announce the number. Players check the place-value wheel for the matching place value. For example, a roll of 2 is tenths.
2. Each student chooses a digit from those listed along the card's edges. He then matches that digit with the place value and writes the resulting number in the first blank. For example: if 2 is rolled and the student chooses 8, he writes 0.8 in the blank.
3. When a digit is chosen, the player marks through it. That digit can not be used again. (Remind students that the two zeros are treated the same as the other digits.)
4. Repeat steps 1–3, with each student writing his number in the second blank.
5. Each player then adds the numbers in the first and second blanks to find a total. The total is written in the unnumbered blank.
6. Repeat steps 1–3 eight more times, adding each time until students reach their final sums.

Does any student have exactly 1.0? If not, write students' totals on the chalkboard. Compare them to see who has the total closest to 1.0. Continue play with the other rounds as students try to reach goals of 5, 10, and 20.

Jackpot! Game Cards

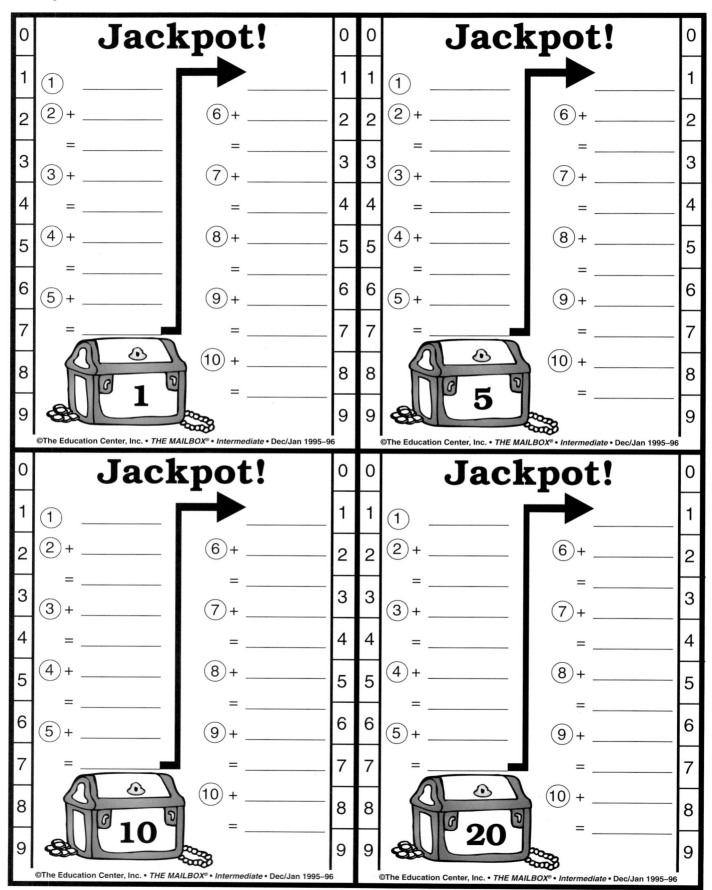

©The Education Center, Inc. • *THE MAILBOX®* • *Intermediate* • Dec/Jan 1995–96

©The Education Center, Inc. • *THE MAILBOX®* • *Intermediate* • Dec/Jan 1995–96

©The Education Center, Inc. • *THE MAILBOX®* • *Intermediate* • Dec/Jan 1995–96

©The Education Center, Inc. • *THE MAILBOX®* • *Intermediate* • Dec/Jan 1995–96

Note To The Teacher: See "Jackpot!" on page 105 for information on how to use these game cards.

Three's A Crowd!

Three numbers in each group below have something in common. Circle the letter of the number that does not belong with the other three. Write a sentence or phrase telling why you chose that number. There may be more than one right answer.

(1.) a. 17.6   b. 12.8   c. 6.4   d. 15.7
_____

(2.) a. 298.05   b. 78.92   c. 355.61   d. 156.7
_____

(3.) a. 12.34   b. 56.789   c. 456.78   d. 76.543
_____

(4.) a. 7.05   b. 7.50   c. 7.5   d. 7.500
_____

(5.) a. 68.02   b. 7.034   c. 26.01   d. 37.95
_____

(6.) a. five and five hundredths   b. five point five   c. 3.79   d. four point ninety
_____

(7.) a. six point zero eight   b. six and eight tenths   c. six point eight   d. 6.80
_____

(8.) a. eighty-one thousandths   b. 0.017   c. seven hundred fifty-six thousandths   d. 1,800
_____

Pirate Patterns

Write the next two numbers that continue each pattern. Pay special attention to the decimals in each pattern.

(1.) 6.5,   6.6,   6.7,   6.8,   _____, _____

(2.) 0.96, 0.97, 0.98, 0.99, _____, _____

(3.) 0.2,   0.4,   0.6,   0.8,   _____, _____

(4.) 0.5,   1.0,   1.5,   2.0,   _____, _____

(5.) 6.3,   6.6,   6.9,   7.2,   _____, _____

(6.) 2.4,   4.8,   9.6,   19.2, _____, _____

(7.) 4.5,   6.0,   7.5,   9.0,   _____, _____

(8.) 17,   18.5, 20.5, 22,   _____, _____

(9.) 20.0, 25.5, 31.0, 36.5, _____, _____

(10.) 0.0,   0.5,   1.5,   3.0,   5.0,   7.5,   _____, _____

It's A Living!

Have you ever heard of Anne Bonny? What about Mary Read? Do you know why these two women are famous? To find out, complete each decimal activity below. Then shade in the sections of the puzzle that have matching answers. Use a colored pencil.

1. Write the standard form of:
   a. six and eight tenths _____
   b. sixty and eight hundredths _____
   c. sixteen and eight thousandths _____
   d. sixty and eight tenths _____
   e. eight thousandths _____
   f. eight hundredths _____

2. Order the following from 1 (greatest) to 4 (least):

   _____ 16.207 _____ 6.9 _____ 16.19 _____ 16.26

   Color the decimals that match #2 and #3.

3. Find and color four decimals in the puzzle that are between 10.5 and 11.5.

   _____ _____ _____ _____

4. Find and color three decimals that have a 5 in the hundredths place.

   _____ _____ _____

5. _____, rounded to the nearest whole, equals 10.0.

6. _____, rounded to the nearest tenth, equals 17.8.

7. _____, rounded to the nearest hundredth, equals 6.08.

8. What decimal number in the puzzle is equivalent to 1/2? _____

9. What is the greatest decimal number in the puzzle? _____

10. What is the least decimal number in the puzzle? _____

Study the puzzle to help you complete the following:
In the early 1700s, Anne Bonny and Mary Read were _____s.

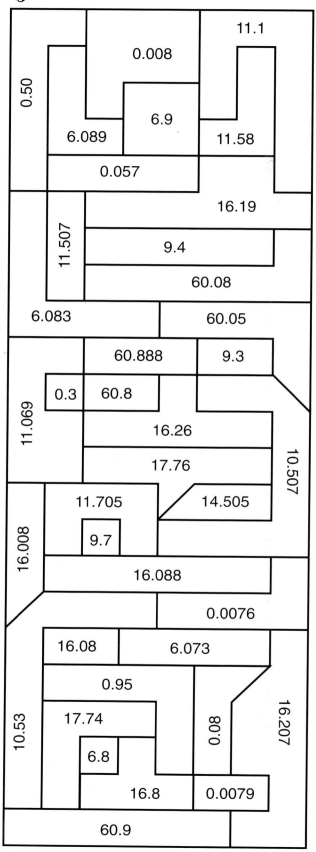

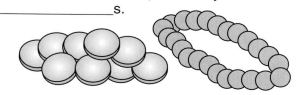

©The Education Center, Inc. • THE MAILBOX® • Intermediate • Dec/Jan 1995–96 • Key p. 309

Boasting Buccaneers

Who has the biggest pirate ship? The
fastest? The strongest crew? The cutest?
(The *cutest?*) Help these boastful bucca-
neers settle the score once and for all!

	45.87 m
	45.3 m
	42.9 m
	41.35 m

1. Which pirate ship is the longest? Fill in the chart with the ships'
names. Use these clues to help you: The *Caribbean Cruiser* is
longer than the *Yo Ho Ho* but shorter than the *Black Moon.* The
Eagle Talon is not the longest, but it's longer than the *Yo Ho Ho*
and the *Caribbean Cruiser.*

2. In a 100-meter race, the *Yo Ho Ho* had the best time. The *Eagle
Talon* beat out the *Caribbean Cruiser* by only 0.2 of a second. In
which place did the *Black Moon* finish? Complete the chart with
the ships' names.

	18.7 sec.
	18.13 sec.
	18.27 sec.
	18.5 sec.

3.
	9.62
	9.8
	9.49
	9.73

The ships' captains competed in the gangplank dive. The *Caribbean Cruiser*'s captain was beaten by the *Black Moon*'s captain by
only 0.07 of a point! The captain of the *Yo Ho Ho* whined that his
peg leg slipped on the gangplank, causing his score to be the
lowest. Complete the chart to show how the captains placed.

4.
Yo Ho Ho	5.43
Caribbean Cruiser	
Total	20.325

Which ship holds the most treasure? The *Yo Ho Ho* has 0.09 of a
ton more treasure than the *Black Moon.* The *Eagle Talon* has 4.9
tons of treasure. Complete the chart to show the amount of treasure on each ship.

5. The four ships' captains are named
Kidd, Drake, Kirk, and Morgan. These
captains have sailed the following
numbers of miles:
    5,892.5
    6,123.9
    6,875.0
    7,056.8
Read the following clues to help you
match each captain with his ship and
the number of miles he has sailed. Use
the chart to help you. Mark X for a
choice that you can eliminate. Mark ✓
for a choice that you are sure of.

	Yo Ho Ho	Caribbean Cruiser	Eagle Talon	Black Moon	5,892.5 mi.	6,123.9 mi.	6,875.0 mi.	7,056.8 mi.
Kidd								
Drake								
Kirk								
Morgan								
5,892.5 mi.								
6,123.9 mi.								
6,875.0 mi.								
7,056.8 mi.								

Bonus Box: Three
of the pirate cap-
tains were real.
Which one is
fictional? Research
to find out.

a. Either Captain Kirk or Captain Kidd has sailed the most miles.
b. Either Captain Drake or Captain Morgan is at the helm of the *Caribbean Cruiser.*
c. Captain Kirk is the captain of the *Eagle Talon,* which has sailed more miles than Captain Drake's
   ship, but fewer than Captain Morgan's.
d. The *Black Moon* has sailed 6,875.0 miles.

TAKE A CHANCE!

Exploring The Concepts Of Probability

What are your chances of winning the lottery? Why does the "house" almost always win in a casino? And more importantly, why can't you ever find a pair of black socks in a drawer filled with dark-colored ones? The odds are simply against you! Help clear up some of the mystery that surrounds probability with the following creative teaching ideas and reproducibles.

by Dr. Beth Lazerick

Brown-Bag Mysteries

Introduce the concept of probability by providing each small group of students with a brown-paper mystery bag. In each bag, include 20 (10 red, 6 blue, and 4 yellow) like items, such as cubes, links, or chips. Instruct one student in each group to select an item from its bag, without peeking, and record its color with a tally mark. That student then returns the item to the bag. Instruct students in each group to takes turns repeating these steps 19 more times for a total of 20 times. When each group has completed its tally, ask students to guess how many items of each color they think are in the bag. Have groups repeat the entire experiment to see if their guesses are logical. Record and discuss class results; then have each group examine the contents of its bag.

Even though each bag contains 10 red, 6 blue, and 4 yellow items, students may have predicted 11 red, 6 blue, and 3 yellow, or a similar combination. This prediction is based on *experimental* results. *Theoretical probability* would predict 50% red, 30% blue, and 20% yellow—no matter how many times a selection was made from the bag—because each bag contains items that are 50% red, 30% blue, and 20% yellow. Repeat the activity with bags containing other combinations of colors. Have groups of students exchange bags with each other to see if their results are similar.

Knock Out Nine!

Have each student list the digits 1–9 horizontally on a sheet of paper. Next roll two dice and name the sum. Instruct students to cross out any numbers whose addends or sum is the same as the one rolled. For example, if you roll 2 and 4 (6), students may cross out the 6 or a pair of addends that equal six: 1 + 5 or 2 + 4. Continue with rolls of the dice and have students cross out numbers until they are no longer able to do so. Anyone who cannot cross out a digit "freezes" and lays down his pencil. Continue to roll the dice until every student freezes. A student's score is the sum of his remaining digits, and the lowest score wins that round.

A single game might look like this:

Roll 6 and 1	Cross out 3 and 4	1 2 3̸ 4̸ 5 6 7 8 9
Roll 5 and 6	Cross out 9 and 2	1 2̸ 3̸ 4̸ 5 6 7 8 9̸
Roll 4 and 4	Cross out 8	1 2̸ 3̸ 4̸ 5 6 7 8̸ 9̸
Roll 5 and 2	Cross out 7	1 2̸ 3̸ 4̸ 5 6 7̸ 8̸ 9̸
Roll 6 and 4	Freeze! Score 1 + 5 + 6 = 12	1 2̸ 3̸ 4̸ 5 6 7̸ 8̸ 9̸

Follow up the game by having students work in pairs to complete the activities on page 111. When everyone is finished, ask a volunteer to list all of the possible outcomes when rolling two dice (2–12). Share with students that this set of numbers is called the *sample space*. Next list on the board all the possible ways to roll each of the sums 2–12. Ask students which outcome(s) is most likely. (7) Continue with a discussion of which would be the best moves to make for each roll when playing "Knock Out Nine!" Then play the game several more times. See if students' strategies change and scores become lower because of better planning!

It's A Sure Thing!

When you roll a *single die*, which number do you think will turn up most often? Suppose you rolled a die 30 times. How many times do you think 1 will show? ____ 2? ____ 3? ____ 4? ____ 5? ____ 6? ____ Try the following activity with a friend:

1. Take turns rolling a die 30 times. Make a tally mark (|) in the chart beside the outcome you roll each time. When your tally reaches five, make a diagonal tally mark: ⧻

outcome	number of times rolled	total
1		
2		
3		
4		
5		
6		
	total	30

2. How close were your predictions? _____

3. Why didn't you get exactly what you thought you would? _____

4. If the world were perfect, what would you expect from your 30 rolls? _____

Double Your Fun

What do you think will be the "most popular" outcome when you roll *two dice?* ____ In the chart below, list all the possible outcomes when rolling two dice.

outcome	number of times rolled	total
2		
	total	36

1. Take turns rolling two dice 36 times. Make a tally mark (|) beside the outcome you roll each time. When you reach five, make a diagonal tally mark: ⧻

2. What do you observe? _____

3. Are your results the same as the results of other pairs of classmates? _____

4. Suppose all the pairs of students in your class combined their results in a huge graph. What do you think that graph would look like? _____

5. If you could win a prize for correctly predicting the outcome of one roll, which number would you choose? ____ Why? ____ _____

Note To The Teacher: Use these reproducibles with "Knock Out Nine!" on page 110.

Try For 100%!

Here's a test for you to take. "Where are the questions?" you might ask. There aren't any, but take the test anyway! Circle your best guess for each item.

1. a b c d	6. a b c d	11. a b c d	16. a b c d
2. a b c d	7. a b c d	12. a b c d	17. a b c d
3. a b c d	8. a b c d	13. a b c d	18. a b c d
4. a b c d	9. a b c d	14. a b c d	19. a b c d
5. a b c d	10. a b c d	15. a b c d	20. a b c d

a. What is the probability that you answered item 1 correctly? _____

b. What is the probability that you missed item 2? _____

c. What is the probability that the answer to item 3 is c? _____

d. The chances of each event above happening are based on theoretical probability. What do you think *theoretical probability* means? _____
_____

e. Now check your test.* What was the highest number of correct answers in your class?
_____

f. On another sheet of paper, make a graph to show your class's score.

Choices, Choices, Choices

To complete this activity, you'll need five different-colored cubes or chips. You'll also need colored markers or crayons.

1. How many ways can you arrange three different colors of cubes? Choose three colors and arrange them in as many ways as you can. Color each combination below:

2. What if you used four colors? How many different arrangements do you think you could make? _____ Use four colors and arrange them in as many ways as you can. Color each combination below:

3. What if you used five colors? Predict how many arrangements you could make. Then use another sheet of paper, your manipulatives, and your markers to check your prediction.

4. Suppose someone arranged four different colors—without you seeing them. What are the chances that you could guess the order in which the colors are arranged? _____

*Note To The Teacher: See page 310 for the "answer key" to 1–20 of the "Try For 100%!" activity.

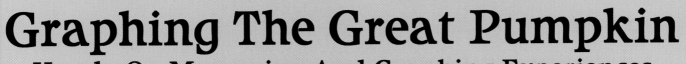

Graphing The Great Pumpkin
Hands-On Measuring And Graphing Experiences

Pumpkin patches everywhere are brimming with America's native vegetable. Invite pumpkins—and loads of math fun—into your classroom with the following hands-on learning experiences.

ideas contributed by Debbie Easterday

Pumpkin Graphing

Fall's here! And that means pumpkins will soon be ready for harvest. Set aside two or three days to complete the hands-on measuring and graphing activities in this math miniunit. Review with older students skills they've already learned, or use the activities as a fun project for younger children. Each teacher-directed activity is described in detail on page 114—including the basic attributes of the featured graphs. A ready-to-duplicate booklet in which students complete the activities follows on pages 115 and 116.

Get Ready...

About a week before beginning the unit, send a note home with each student requesting a donation of one pumpkin. Bring a few pumpkins yourself to ensure an adequate quantity for the activities. As pumpkins are brought to class, provide markers so that each student can label his pumpkin with its source: home garden, grocery store, produce stand, nearby farm, etc. Store the pumpkins in a central location until you're ready to begin the activities on page 114. Also see the materials list for each activity on pages 115 and 116.

Duplicate a class supply of pages 115 and 116. In addition, provide each student with a 9" x 12" sheet of orange construction paper. Have each student cut his two reproducibles in half and trim around the edges. Instruct the student to stack the half-pages in the correct order and then staple them inside the folded sheet of construction paper, stapling one time in the top left-hand corner (see the illustration below). Provide time for students to decorate the covers of their booklets.

Get Started...

When all materials are ready, divide students into cooperative teams of four or five students each. Provide each student with one pumpkin (not necessarily the one he brought). Have students arrange their seating so that each group's pumpkins are accessible to every child in that group. Then begin Activity 1 as described on page 114.

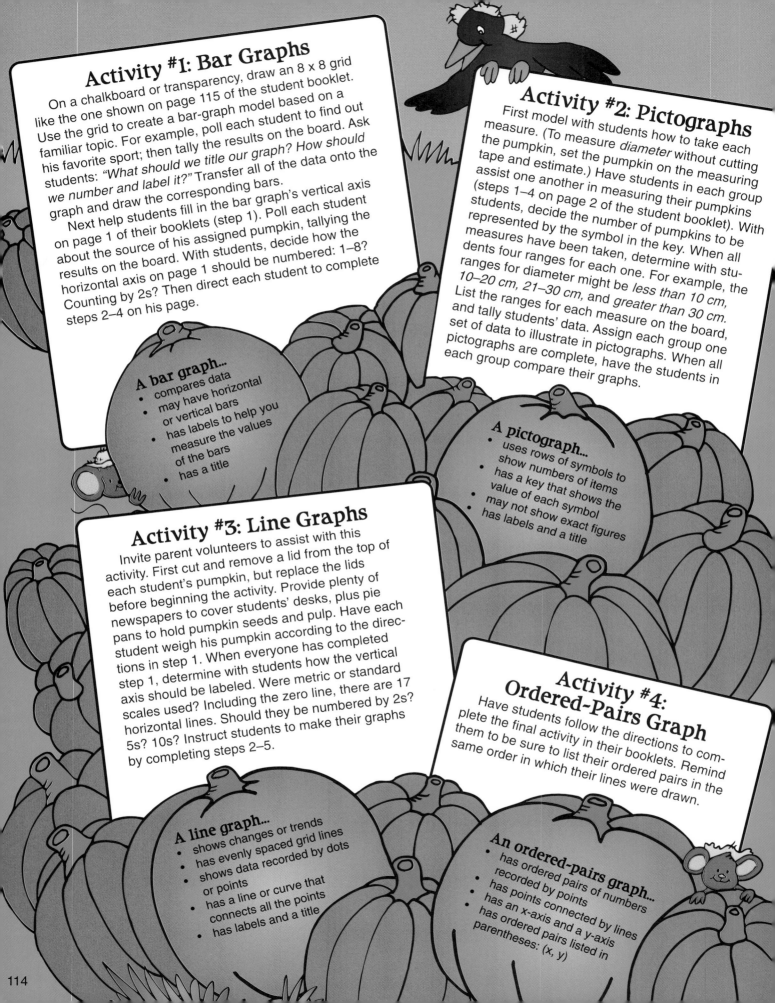

Activity #1: Bar Graphs

On a chalkboard or transparency, draw an 8 x 8 grid like the one shown on page 115 of the student booklet. Use the grid to create a bar-graph model based on a familiar topic. For example, poll each student to find out his favorite sport; then tally the results on the board. Ask students: *"What should we title our graph? How should we number and label it?"* Transfer all of the data onto the graph and draw the corresponding bars.

Next help students fill in the bar graph's vertical axis on page 1 of their booklets (step 1). Poll each student about the source of his assigned pumpkin, tallying the results on the board. With students, decide how the horizontal axis on page 1 should be numbered: 1–8? Counting by 2s? Then direct each student to complete steps 2–4 on his page.

A bar graph...
- compares data
- may have horizontal or vertical bars
- has labels to help you measure the values of the bars
- has a title

Activity #2: Pictographs

First model with students how to take each measure. (To measure *diameter* without cutting the pumpkin, set the pumpkin on the measuring tape and estimate.) Have students in each group assist one another in measuring their pumpkins (steps 1–4 on page 2 of the student booklet). With students, decide the number of pumpkins to be represented by the symbol in the key. When all measures have been taken, determine with students four ranges for each one. For example, the ranges for diameter might be *less than 10 cm, 10–20 cm, 21–30 cm,* and *greater than 30 cm.* List the ranges for each measure on the board, and tally students' data. Assign each group one set of data to illustrate in pictographs. When all pictographs are complete, have the students in each group compare their graphs.

A pictograph...
- uses rows of symbols to show numbers of items
- has a key that shows the value of each symbol
- may not show exact figures
- has labels and a title

Activity #3: Line Graphs

Invite parent volunteers to assist with this activity. First cut and remove a lid from the top of each student's pumpkin, but replace the lids before beginning the activity. Provide plenty of newspapers to cover students' desks, plus pie pans to hold pumpkin seeds and pulp. Have each student weigh his pumpkin according to the directions in step 1. When everyone has completed step 1, determine with students how the vertical axis should be labeled. Were metric or standard scales used? Including the zero line, there are 17 horizontal lines. Should they be numbered by 2s? 5s? 10s? Instruct students to make their graphs by completing steps 2–5.

A line graph...
- shows changes or trends
- has evenly spaced grid lines
- shows data recorded by dots or points
- has a line or curve that connects all the points
- has labels and a title

Activity #4: Ordered-Pairs Graph

Have students follow the directions to complete the final activity in their booklets. Remind them to be sure to list their ordered pairs in the same order in which their lines were drawn.

An ordered-pairs graph...
- has ordered pairs of numbers recorded by points
- has points connected by lines
- has an x-axis and a y-axis
- has ordered pairs listed in parentheses: (x, y)

Where Did You Get That Pumpkin?

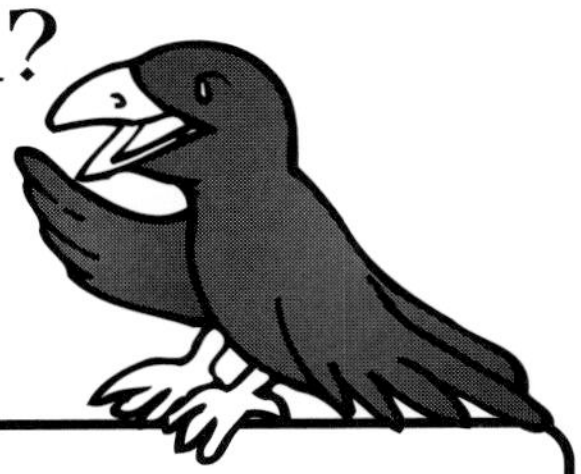

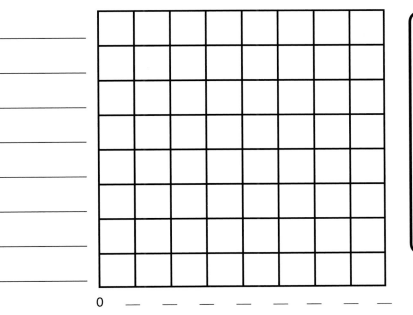

_____

_____

_____

_____

_____

_____

_____

_____

_____

0   —   —   —   —   —   —   —   —

Materials:
one pumpkin per student, pencils, colored pencils or markers

Directions:
1. Along the *vertical axis* (the left side of the graph), list all the sources of our pumpkins.
2. Label the *horizontal axis* with numerals.
3. Draw each matching bar. Use a different color for each one.
4. Give your graph a title.

You Oughta Be In Pictures!

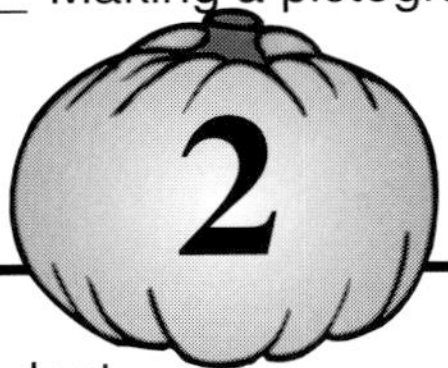

2

_____

_____

_____

_____

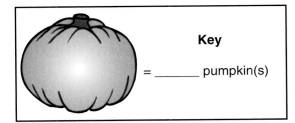

Key

= _____ pumpkin(s)

Materials:
one pumpkin per student, pencils, measuring tapes

Directions:
1. Measure your pumpkin's diameter:
   _____
2. Measure your pumpkin's circumference:
   _____
3. Measure your pumpkin's height:
   _____
4. Measure your pumpkin's stem length:
   _____
5. Complete the key by deciding how many pumpkins the symbol will represent.
6. Circle the data your group will illustrate in your pictographs: diameter, circumference, height, stem length.
7. Write the four ranges for your data along the vertical axis. Then complete the pictograph.
8. Give your graph a title.

My, You're Losing Weight!

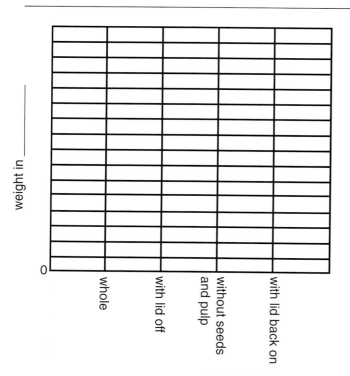

weight in _____

0

whole

with lid off

without seeds
and pulp

with lid back on

Materials: one pumpkin per student (with a precut lid), scale for each group, newspapers, metal spoons, rulers, pencils, pie pans

Directions:
1. Weigh the pumpkin...
   a. as a whole _____
   b. with its lid removed _____
   c. with its seeds and pulp
      (and lid) removed _____
   d. with its lid back on (no seeds
      or pulp) _____
2. Label the vertical axis.
3. Plot the points on your graph.
4. Connect the points, using a ruler to make sure your lines are straight.
5. Give your graph a title.

Plotting Your Great Pumpkin

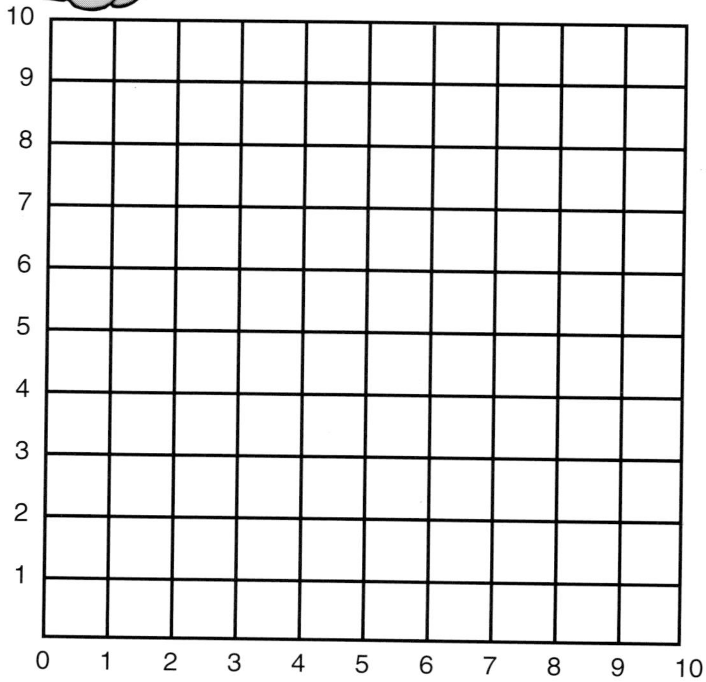

Materials: pencils, orange crayons

Directions:
1. Plot points on the graph to make a pumpkin shape.
2. Choose a point on the graph and write its ordered pair in the first blank below.
3. Draw a line from that point to a second point; record that point's ordered pair in the second blank.
4. Continue drawing lines and listing ordered pairs until you return to the first point.
5. Color your completed pumpkin.

(_____), (_____), (_____),

(_____), (_____), (_____), (_____),

(_____), (_____), (_____), (_____),

(_____), (_____), (_____), (_____),

(_____), (_____), (_____), (_____),

(_____), (_____), (_____), (_____)

Making Sense Of Percents
Teaching Strategies To Promote Real-Life Percent Skills

A 15% tip...a 6% sales tax...a 75% chance of rain...18% of the U.S. recommended daily allowance...a 12% sales commission. Just what exactly does each of these numbers mean? Help students gain a better understanding of percent concepts with the following creative teaching activities and reproducibles.

by Irving P. Crump

What's A Percent Anyway?

It's simply a fraction! Students have learned that decimals are fractions whose denominators are powers of ten. Percents are an even smaller set of fractions: fractions that have denominators of 100. The word *percent* comes from the Latin words *per centum*, meaning "per hundred." Discuss with students other familiar words that have the *cent* root, such as *century, centimeter, centennial, centigrade,* etc. Since percent means hundredths, any given percent can be expressed as a decimal fraction or as a common fraction.

We use percents in all areas of everyday life. Businesses use percent to determine profits, costs, and losses. Bankers use percent to compute interest on savings and loans. Taxes—on our incomes, property, and purchases—are determined in percents. In sports, statistics such as batting averages in baseball and shooting proficiency in basketball are based on percentages. And promotions such as "Big One-Day Sale! All Items 50% Off" will always grab the attention of consumers.

percent =
per
hundred

They're Everywhere!

From the early-morning weather report to the late-night sports statistics, it would be unusual to experience a day without seeing or hearing a percent-related fact. Begin a bulletin-board display of different uses of percents that you and your students encounter. Instruct students to be on the lookout in newspapers, magazines, and sales flyers for percents-off sales. See who can bring in a restaurant check that includes a computed tip. Share a credit-card statement that shows the rate by which interest on an outstanding balance is computed. Tell students to check out the sports sections of newspapers for different uses of percent in a variety of statistics. Challenge the class to find as many different uses of percents as possible for display on a board entitled "Making Sense Of Percents!"

80% of these flowers smell lovely!

Percent: The Main Idea

Percent is used so often in so many contexts, it's easy to forget the special meaning of this term. Before computing with percent, make sure that students understand the basics: that *percent* simply means "per hundred." To demonstrate this abstract idea to students, use concrete models that help them visualize percents. Make a class set of page 120. Rubber-cement each copy to a 9" x 12" sheet of colorful construction paper; then laminate the set. Provide students with overhead markers to use with these laminated pages. In addition, make three or four transparencies of page 120 to use with an overhead projector as you teach percent concepts. The laminated grids and teaching transparencies can be used over and over for years to come. Ask each student to bring an old sock from home to use as an eraser. Use the grids as you direct students in each activity on page 118.

Percent: The Basics

Have students shade their laminated grids to represent percents such as 10%, 25%, 40%, 7%, 95%, 1%, 50%, 80%, and 100%. Ask students to describe 100%. *(100% is represented by the entire square, or the unit square. 100% equals one whole.)* What about 1%? *(Guide students to see that 1% is represented by one small square, or 1/100th of the grid.)* Use the grids to represent something in real life that students can relate to, such as a one-dollar bill. Ask questions like, "What percent of a dollar is 12 cents? 75 cents? 50 cents? a quarter? a dime?" *(12%, 75%, 50%, 25%, and 10%, respectively)* For another example, tell students that the grid represents a 100-question test. Ask, "If you answer 95 items correctly, what percent is that? *(95%)* If you miss 12 items, what percent are correct? *(88%)* If you miss half of the items, how many is that? *(50)* What is your score if you miss half of the items?" *(50%)*

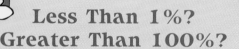

Less Than 1%? Greater Than 100%?

Extend the concepts of percent to represent amounts less than 1%, as well as those more than 100%. Have each student shade 1/2 of one small square in a grid. Ask what percent that represents *(1/2% or 0.5%)*. Instruct each student to shade 1/4 of one square in a grid. Then ask what percent that represents *(1/4% or 0.25%)*. Next have each student shade an entire grid plus 40 squares of a second one. Then ask what percent is represented. *(Since one whole grid means 100%, a whole plus 40% of another equals 140%.)* Ask students what amount is shown when two full grids are shaded. *(Two whole grids represent 200% or twice as much as one whole grid.)*

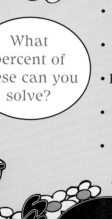

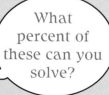
What percent of these can you solve?

Solving Percent Problems: Grids To The Rescue

The key to solving percent problems is knowing the value of one percent. Use the 10 x 10 grids on page 120 to guide students in solving the following percent problems:

—Let a grid represent 800, the number of kids in a school. Then ask the following:

- How many kids does each small square represent? *(Dividing 800 by 100 equals 8.)*
- How many kids does 10 small squares represent? *(10 x 8 = 80)*
- How many kids does 50 small squares represent? *(50 x 8 = 400)*
- What percent of the enrollment is 400 kids? *(50%)*
- How many kids does 1/2 of a small square represent? *(1/2 of 8 = 4)*
- How many kids would 8 1/2 squares represent? *(8 x 8 = 64; 64 + 4 = 68)*
- What percent of the enrollment is 200 students? *(By dividing 200 by 8, students will see that 25 squares represents 200 students. 25 squares equals 25%.)*

—Have students use another grid to represent the length of a school year, such as 180 days. Then ask the following:

- How many days does each small square represent? *(Dividing 180 by 100 equals 1.8. Review with students the dividing-by-100 shortcut: When dividing by 100, simply move the decimal point in the dividend two places to the left.)*
- How many days does 10 small squares represent? *(10 x 1.8 = 18)*
- How many days does 50 small squares represent? *(50 x 1.8 = 90)*
- What percentage of the school year is 90 days? *(50%)*
- How many days does 1/2 of a small square represent? *(1/2 of 1.8 = 0.9)*
- How many days would 8 1/2 squares represent? *(8 x 1.8 = 14.4; 14.4 + 0.9 = 15.3)*
- What part of the grid is 45 days? *(By dividing 45 by 1.8, students will see that 25 squares represents 45 days. 25 squares equals 25%.)*

Popular Percents Rummy

Using percent benchmarks *(50% means half as much)* and mental math, students can solve percent problems quickly and accurately. Make a classroom poster or a transparency of some of the most frequently used percents and their decimal/fractional equivalents (see the chart below). To provide practice with associating equivalent terms, divide students into pairs and give each pair 42 small index cards. Have each pair program its 42 cards—all in the same color—with the terms in the chart. After all sets of cards have been completed, review with students how to play the card game rummy. The object of rummy is to get rid of one's cards by forming equivalence sets. A set includes a percent and its fractional and decimal equivalents. To play:

1. Player 1 deals seven cards each to Player 2 and himself. Player 1 stacks the remaining cards facedown, then turns over the top card and lays it faceup beside the stack.
2. Both players check their hands to see if they have any matching sets. If so, each set is laid faceup between the two players.
3. Player 2 then begins the game by either selecting the faceup card or drawing the top card from the stack. If he can then form an equivalence set, he lays the set down. If not, he must then discard a card on the faceup stack. Then it's Player 1's turn.
4. Player 1 then takes a turn, repeating step 3.
5. If the facedown stack runs out, have players turn over the faceup stack, then turn over the top card and lay it faceup beside the stack.
6. Play continues until a player has no cards remaining in his hand.

Percent Concentration

Students may also use their percent card decks to play the memory game Concentration. Have each pair of students choose eight equivalence sets (24 cards altogether) and shuffle them. Next the pair places the cards facedown in a 4 x 6 array. In turn, students turn over three cards. If the three cards form an equivalence set, that player gets to keep the cards and take another turn. If the cards do not form a set, the player turns the cards facedown and his opponent then takes a turn. Play continues until all eight equivalence sets have been won. The player with the most sets wins.

Concentration Variations

Using their rummy card decks, have student pairs play each of the following variations of Concentration:

- Instruct each pair of students to remove all percent cards and their matching fractional equivalents from the deck. Have a student in each pair place these 28 cards facedown in a 4 x 7 array. Student pairs play Concentration as described in the preceding idea—except that instead of making equivalence sets of three elements, players make matches of percents and their fractional equivalents.
- Have each pair of students remove all percent cards and their matching decimal equivalents from the deck. Direct student pairs to play Concentration with these 28 cards.
- Finally, have each pair of students remove all fractions and their decimal equivalents from the deck. Have the students play Concentration with these 28 cards.

100% Guaranteed (Page 123)

Duplicate page 123 to use with your students as a culminating or challenge activity. When all students, or pairs of students, have completed the page, tell them that the 16 answers in the boxes form a magic square—the sum of the answers in each vertical, horizontal, and diagonal row should equal 100. Challenge students to find more ways that the square is magical. Refer to the answer key on page 310 for the solution for each individual box.

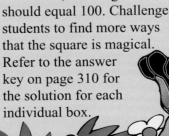

80%	=	$\frac{4}{5}$	=	0.80
40%	=	$\frac{2}{5}$	=	0.40
75%	=	$\frac{3}{4}$	=	0.75
25%	=	$\frac{1}{4}$	=	0.25
60%	=	$\frac{3}{5}$	=	0.60
20%	=	$\frac{1}{5}$	=	0.20
50%	=	$\frac{1}{2}$	=	0.50

$87\frac{1}{2}\%$	=	$\frac{7}{8}$	=	0.875
$37\frac{1}{2}\%$	=	$\frac{3}{8}$	=	0.375
$83\frac{1}{3}\%$	=	$\frac{5}{6}$	=	0.833
$33\frac{1}{3}\%$	=	$\frac{1}{3}$	=	0.333
$66\frac{2}{3}\%$	=	$\frac{2}{3}$	=	0.666
$12\frac{1}{2}\%$	=	$\frac{1}{8}$	=	0.125
$62\frac{1}{2}\%$	=	$\frac{5}{8}$	=	0.625

Name _____

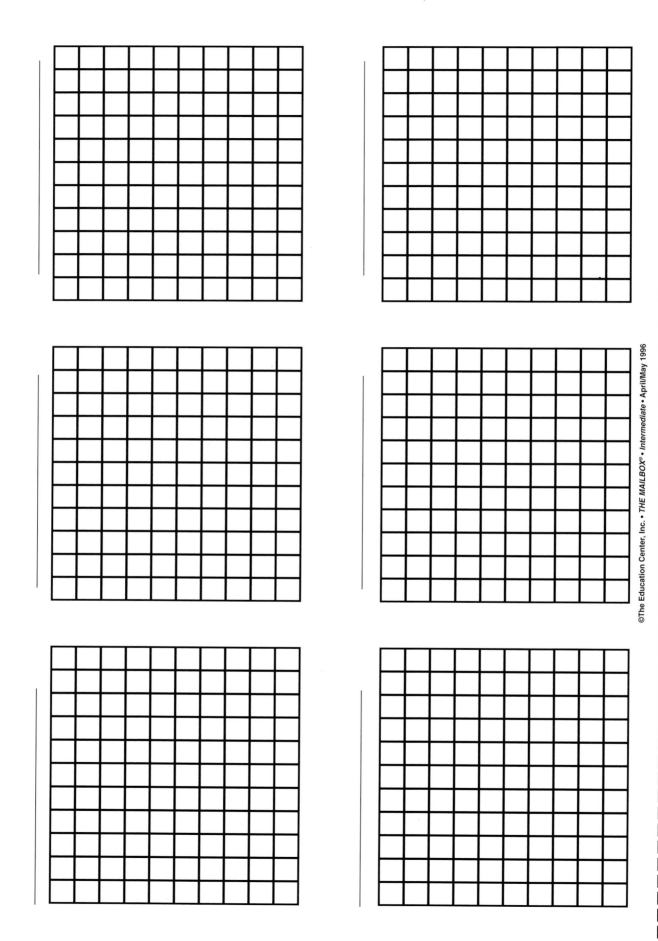

©The Education Center, Inc. • *THE MAILBOX®* • *Intermediate* • April/May 1996

Note To The Teacher: See pages 117 and 118 for activities using the grids on this page. Have students use the blanks above the grids for adding titles.

Pentagon Power

Looking for some easy percent shortcuts? Just study the information in the box below. Then use the information, the examples below the box, and mental math to help you solve the problems in the pentagon.

Percent	Means	What To Do
200%	twice as much	Multiply by 2.
100%	the same as the number	Write the number.
75%	3/4 as much	Multiply by 3/4 or 0.75.
50%	1/2 as much	Multiply by 1/2 or 0.5—or divide by 2.
25%	1/4 as much	Multiply by 1/4 or 0.25—or divide by 4.
10%	1/10 as much	Multiply by 1/10 or 0.1—or move the decimal one place to the left.
1%	1/100 as much	Multiply by 1/100 or 0.01—or move the decimal two places to the left.

Examples

50% of $18.50	=	$9.25	(Think: 1/2 of $18 is $9; 1/2 of 50¢ is 25¢; $9 + 25¢ = $9.25)
10% of 147	=	14.7	(Think: 147.0; then move the decimal one place to the left: 14.7)
200% of 85	=	170	(Think: 2 of 85; 2 x 85 = 170)
100% of $17.50	=	$17.50	(Think: 1 of $17.50 = $17.50)
25% of 28	=	7	(Think: 1/4 of 28 = 7)
1% of 25.84	=	0.2584	(Think: 25.84; move the decimal two places to the left: 0.2584)
75% of 60	=	45	(Think: 3/4 of 60; 3 x 60 = 180; 180 ÷ 4 = 45)

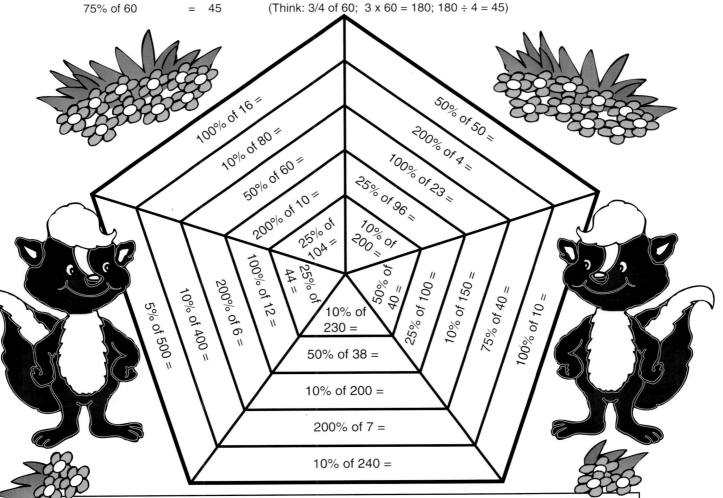

The pentagon contains the following problems:

100% of 16 =
10% of 80 =
50% of 60 =
200% of 10 =
50% of 50 =
200% of 4 =
100% of 23 =
25% of 96 =
25% of 104 =
10% of 200 =
5% of 500 =
10% of 400 =
200% of 6 =
100% of 12 =
25% of 44 =
10% of 230 =
50% of 40 =
25% of 100 =
10% of 150 =
75% of 40 =
100% of 10 =
50% of 38 =
10% of 200 =
200% of 7 =
10% of 240 =

Bonus Box: The pentagon is magical in two different ways. Can you figure out how it is magical? Write your answer on the back of this page.

Making The Connection

Play this game with a friend to learn fractions and their percent equivalents.

Materials: 2 dice, 2 different-colored pencils, 2 regular pencils, scratch paper, a calculator for checking

How to play:

1. Each player rolls the dice. The player with the larger roll is Player 1.
2. Player 1 rolls the dice and announces a fraction that can be made with the two numbers showing. For example: a roll of 3 and 4 = 3/4 or 4/3.
3. Player 1 then changes his fraction to a percent. For example: 3/4 = 75% or 4/3 = 133%. All percents are rounded to the nearest whole.
4. Using the calculator, Player 2 checks Player 1's percent by dividing the numerator of the fraction by its denominator. If it is correct, Player 1 writes (using his regular pencil) that percent in any box in the grid.

5. Player 2 then takes a turn.
6. The object of the game is to make rows—vertical, horizontal, or diagonal—of three percents each whose sum equals 2. See the two samples in the grid. When a player makes a row of percents whose sum is 2, he circles it with his colored pencil. A percent may be a part of two different rows, like 100% in the sample. To help you, some percents are already in the grid.
7. The winner is the player who circles the most rows.

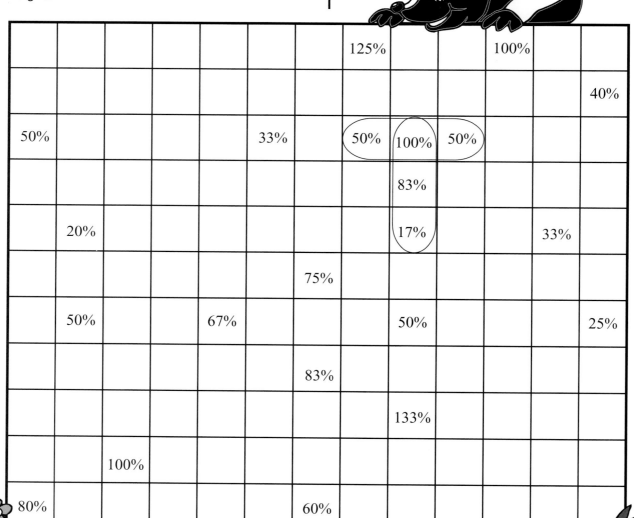

©The Education Center, Inc. • *THE MAILBOX® • Intermediate • April/May 1996*

122

Note To The Teacher: Before students play this game, they must know how to convert a fraction into a percent without using a calculator.

100% Guaranteed

Is a 100% guarantee really possible? With this puzzle, it is! We guarantee that you'll have fun answering the questions below. Just use your decimal/fraction/percent know-how and some research to solve each problem. When you've finished all 16 problems, go back and check over your work. Then wait for further instructions from your teacher.*

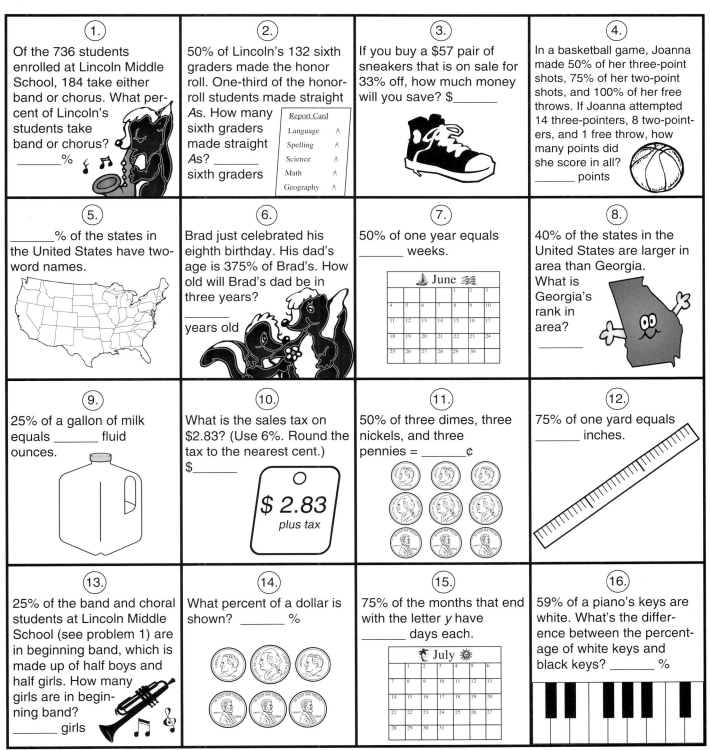

1.
Of the 736 students enrolled at Lincoln Middle School, 184 take either band or chorus. What percent of Lincoln's students take band or chorus? _____%

2.
50% of Lincoln's 132 sixth graders made the honor roll. One-third of the honor-roll students made straight As. How many sixth graders made straight As? _____ sixth graders

Report Card
Language .... A
Spelling .... A
Science .... A
Math .... A
Geography .... A

3.
If you buy a $57 pair of sneakers that is on sale for 33% off, how much money will you save? $_____

4.
In a basketball game, Joanna made 50% of her three-point shots, 75% of her two-point shots, and 100% of her free throws. If Joanna attempted 14 three-pointers, 8 two-pointers, and 1 free throw, how many points did she score in all? _____ points

5.
_____% of the states in the United States have two-word names.

6.
Brad just celebrated his eighth birthday. His dad's age is 375% of Brad's. How old will Brad's dad be in three years? _____ years old

7.
50% of one year equals _____ weeks.

June
1 2 3
4 5 6 7 8 9 10
11 12 13 14 15 16 17
18 19 20 21 22 23 24
25 26 27 28 29 30

8.
40% of the states in the United States are larger in area than Georgia. What is Georgia's rank in area? _____

9.
25% of a gallon of milk equals _____ fluid ounces.

10.
What is the sales tax on $2.83? (Use 6%. Round the tax to the nearest cent.) $_____

$ 2.83
plus tax

11.
50% of three dimes, three nickels, and three pennies = _____¢

12.
75% of one yard equals _____ inches.

13.
25% of the band and choral students at Lincoln Middle School (see problem 1) are in beginning band, which is made up of half boys and half girls. How many girls are in beginning band? _____ girls

14.
What percent of a dollar is shown? _____ %

15.
75% of the months that end with the letter y have _____ days each.

July
1 2 3 4 5 6
7 8 9 10 11 12 13
14 15 16 17 18 19 20
21 22 23 24 25 26 27
28 29 30 31

16.
59% of a piano's keys are white. What's the difference between the percentage of white keys and black keys? _____ %

©The Education Center, Inc. • THE MAILBOX® • Intermediate • April/May 1996 • Key p. 310

*Note To The Teacher: See "100% Guaranteed" on page 119 for information about this activity. You may wish to have students pair up to complete this page.

MMMM GOOD MATH!

Deliciously Fun Activities For Year-End Math Review

The long-awaited days of summer are just on the horizon. How do you keep kids tuned in to school? Try the following hands-on, creative math lessons using your students' favorite candies!

by Irving P. Crump

DONATIONS, PLEASE!

Enlist the help of parents to provide items for the activities in this unit. Duplicate a supply of the half-page request form on page 126. After reading over the materials lists on this page and pages 125, fill out copies of the form with the specific names, sizes, and quantities of the materials you need. Send home the requests about a week before the date of the scheduled activity. Don't be surprised if parents want to come and join in the fun!

DIVING INTO M&M'S®
Individual And Small-Group Activity

Materials per student: 1 bag (about 2 oz.) of M&M's® Plain Chocolate Candies, 1 deskmat (a 12" x 18" sheet of construction paper), 1 copy of page 127, a calculator

Just how does Mars, Inc., decide how many of each color of candy to include in a bag of M&M's®? Divide the class into small groups and provide each student with the materials listed above. Then invite students to take a closer look at what is undoubtedly one of their favorite treats: M&M's®. After each student completes the chart on his copy of page 127, have each group collaborate to complete the bonus box activity. When the project has been completed, invite students to reward themselves by eating their math! As students enjoy their treats, create a whole-class graph on a transparency by combining all of the groups' findings.

(A typical bag of M&M's® Plain Chocolate Candies consists of 30% brown candies, 20% each of yellow and red, and 10% each of green, orange, and blue. These percentages are determined by consumer feedback—what consumers want most!)

MAKE MINE REESE'S PIECES®
AND SKITTLES®
Individual And Small-Group Activity

Materials per student: 1 bag each of Reese's Pieces® and Skittles®, 1 deskmat (a 12" x 18" sheet of construction paper), a calculator

Have students follow the basic steps of the M&M's® activity above to investigate other similar candies. Divide the class into small groups. Provide each student with the materials listed above. Instruct each student to make a chart that includes the total number of Reese's Pieces® in his bag, the number of each color, and the percent of the total number represented by each color (see the example of this chart on page 127). Then have the students in each group collaborate to create a chart that combines all of their data. Next have students repeat the activity with their bags of Skittles®.

FROM MY PERSPECTIVE
Homework Assignment

Materials per student: one 6" x 18" sheet of white construction paper, any candy provided by the student

Give students visual-thinking practice with this homework/art activity. In class, instruct each student to turn his 6" x 18" sheet of white construction paper horizontally and divide it into four sections as shown. Then, for homework, have each student draw his favorite candy (unwrapped) from four different perspectives: the top, the bottom, the front, and a side. Draw the example shown on a chalkboard or on a transparency. Review the terms *perspective* and *proportion* with students. Remind them that perspective means observing a stationary object from different viewpoints—in this case, from four different sides. Being proportional means different parts of an object are properly related in size or other measurable characteristics. So if a piece of candy is twice as long as it is wide, its drawing should be similarly proportional.

Allow students two or three days to complete this assignment. When the drawings are brought to class, post them on a bulletin board titled "Yummy Any Way You Look At It!" Invite students to visit the board during free time and try to identify as many of the candies as possible.

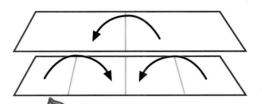

 front  bottom top side

GET YOUR LICKS IN!
Small-Group Activity

Materials for the class: 5–6 each of several kinds of lollipops and suckers (one per child)

How long does the average lollipop last? Divide students into small groups to complete this investigative estimation activity. Provide each group of students with similar lollipops or suckers. After students have examined their candies (size, weight, etc.), have each child estimate how long his sucker will last. Ask a recorder in each group to note each student's time estimate. Then, beginning at a set time, instruct the entire class to "start lickin'!" Be sure to tell students not to bite or chew their candies. As each student's candy completely dissolves, have him give the elapsed time to his group's recorder. After everyone's time has been recorded, find out which student's estimate in each group was closest. Also have each group find the average lasting power of its candies. For more lollipop fun, have students complete the reproducible lollipop logic puzzles on page 128.

SWEET SHAPES
Homework Scavenger Hunt

Materials: class copies of page 126 (bottom half only), a Reese's® Peanut Butter Cup

Candy comes in lots of interesting, three-dimensional shapes. Have students look more closely at some of these shapes with a homework challenge. First introduce several common three-dimensional shapes to students, such as the *sphere, cube, cone,* and *cylinder.* Discuss the attributes of these solids. Next provide each student with a copy of the bottom half of page 126. Discuss two key terms on the sheet before making the assignment:

- A *prism* is a solid figure with at least one pair of faces that are parallel and congruent. Its other faces are parallelograms. Have students examine the five prisms shown on the page. Since a prism can be named by the shape of the parallel and congruent faces, ask students why each prism was given its particular name.

- A *frustum* is a shape that results when a cut is made across a solid—a cut that is parallel to the base. Have students examine and determine the relationships of the square pyramid with its frustum, the cone with its frustum, and the cylinder with its frustum. Turn the Reese's® Peanut Butter Cup upside down and show it to the class. Ask them which frustum it resembles *(frustum of a cone).*

Instruct students to list types of candy on the back of the page that match the shapes. Students do not have to buy candies to complete the assignment.

HOW SWEET IT IS!

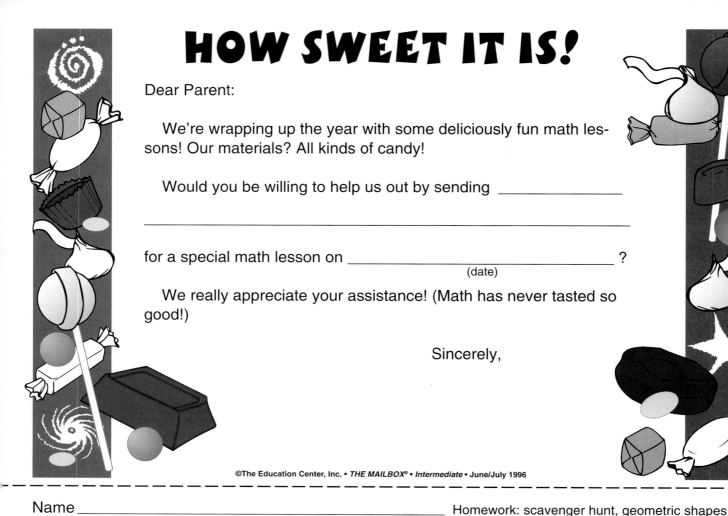

Dear Parent:

We're wrapping up the year with some deliciously fun math lessons! Our materials? All kinds of candy!

Would you be willing to help us out by sending _____

_____

for a special math lesson on _____ ?
(date)

We really appreciate your assistance! (Math has never tasted so good!)

Sincerely,

Name _____ Homework: scavenger hunt, geometric shapes

SWEET SHAPES

Below are pictures of some *three-dimensional solids.* An object that is three-dimensional has *length, width,* and *depth.* Examples: a marble is a *sphere* and a die is a *cube.*

Can you think of a candy that looks like each shape below? Number 1–14 on the back of this sheet. Write the name of a candy (or more than one) to match each shape.

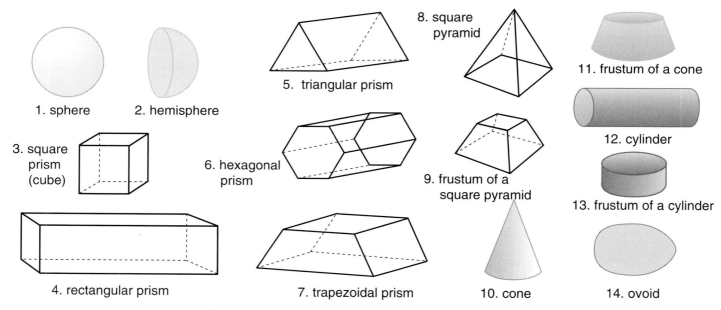

1. sphere
2. hemisphere
3. square prism (cube)
4. rectangular prism
5. triangular prism
6. hexagonal prism
7. trapezoidal prism
8. square pyramid
9. frustum of a square pyramid
10. cone
11. frustum of a cone
12. cylinder
13. frustum of a cylinder
14. ovoid

Note To The Teacher: Use the parent letter with "Donations, Please!" on page 124. Use "Sweet Shapes" with the activity on page 125.

Making a chart, determining percents, using a calculator

M&M's® ...MMMM GOOD!

1. How much does your bag of M&M's® weigh? _____ oz./ _____ g

2. Using a calculator, divide the number of grams by the number of ounces. About how many grams equal an ounce? _____ g

3. Take a look at the Nutrition Facts on the back of the package.
   a. How much is a serving size? _____
   b. How many calories are in one serving? _____
   c. Eating a bag of M&M's® candies would equal what part of a daily 2,000-calorie diet? Write a fraction and reduce it: _____

4. Open your bag of candy. Pour out the M&M's® and count them. Write the total in the last box of the chart. Then count the number of each color and record it in the chart.

green		orange		red		blue		yellow		brown		other?		Total
How many?	Percent of total?	How many?	Percent of total?	How many?	Percent of total?	How many?	Percent of total?	How many?	Percent of total?	How many?	Percent of total?	How many?	Percent of total?	

5. Check your work: Add all of the colors of M&M's®. Does the sum match the number you wrote in the "Total" box?

6. Use a calculator and its percent key (%) to find out what percent of the bag of M&M's® is represented by each color. To do this, divide the number of each color by the total number in the bag (see the examples). Write each percent in the chart.

Examples:

If 8 of 57 candies in a bag are blue,
press these keys: $\boxed{8}$ $\boxed{\div}$ $\boxed{57}$ $\boxed{\%}$ → $\boxed{14.035087}$

or

14% (rounded to the nearest whole percent)

If 17 of 57 candies in a bag are brown,
press these keys: $\boxed{17}$ $\boxed{\div}$ $\boxed{57}$ $\boxed{\%}$ → $\boxed{29.824561}$

or

30% (rounded to the nearest whole percent)

Bonus Box: Share your chart with the other students in your group. Work with one another to make a group chart of data. The chart should include the total number of candies in your group's bags, the number of each color of candy, and the percent of each color.

©The Education Center, Inc. • *THE MAILBOX®* • *Intermediate* • June/July 1996

Note To The Teacher: See "Diving Into M&M's®" on page 124 for information on how to use this reproducible.

DANDY CANDIES

Maggie, Megan, Mark, and Matthew are making candies to sell at their school's Spring Fling. They are making lollipops, mints, chocolate-covered pretzels, and caramel apples. They plan to package their items in tins, plastic bags, plastic wrap, and gift boxes.

Study the clues below to see who is making each item and the type of package in which it will be sold. Put a in a box in the grid to show a correct answer. Mark an X in a box to eliminate a choice.

Clues:

1. Matthew, the girl making mints, the boy using plastic bags, and the girl using plastic wrap hope to raise lots of money with their candy sales.

2. Maggie, her best friend who is making the pretzels, the boy making caramel apples, and the boy using gift boxes for his candies worked for hours preparing their recipes.

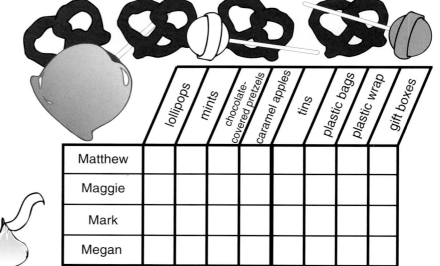

	lollipops	mints	chocolate-covered pretzels	caramel apples	tins	plastic bags	plastic wrap	gift boxes
Matthew								
Maggie								
Mark								
Megan								

- -

THE GREAT LOLLIPOP LICK-OFF

Which lollipop will last the longest? What is its color, and to whom does it belong? Use the diagram and the chart to help you organize the information in the clues. Fill in the chart and diagram with the students' names and the colors of their lollipops.

Clues:

1. Larry's lollipop was not green.
2. The red lollipop belonged to Linda, but it wasn't the shortest or longest lasting.
3. Laura's lollipop wasn't the shortest or longest lasting, nor was it orange.
4. Neither the first nor the second lollipop to be "licked away" was yellow.
5. Lane's lollipop wasn't orange and it was gone before Linda's.

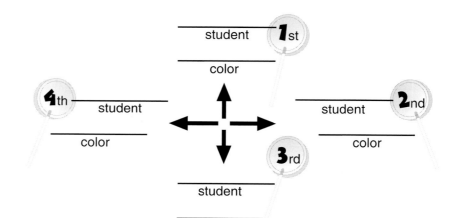

	1st (shortest-lasting)	2nd	3rd	4th (longest-lasting)
student				
color				

SOCIAL STUDIES UNITS

A Nation Torn

Thematic Activities For Studying The Civil War

It was a time when brother fought against brother, cities were razed, farms were ravaged, and more Americans lost their lives than during any other war in history. From the destruction of the Civil War rose a new Union, the abolition of slavery, and the promise of equality. Use the following ideas to introduce students to this tragic chapter in our nation's history.

with ideas by Becky Andrews and Liz Hagner

To Secede, Or Not To Secede

Historians agree that the Civil War was the result of complex economic, political, and social issues. One of those issues involved the right of a state to make its own decisions. *States' rights* was a popular position in the Southern states, as was a state's right to *secede* (withdraw) from the Union. In December of 1860, South Carolina became the first state to secede.

To help students understand secession, present the following scenario: One of your school's teachers has just announced that her class is seceding from your school. This means that the teacher and her students will be a part of the school in location only. Have small groups discuss the following questions: What problems will the seceded class create for the school? What problems might the seceded class face? How might this secession affect you as a student? After several minutes of discussion, meet as a class to share students' conclusions. Point out that President Abraham Lincoln believed that secession was illegal. When South Carolina seceded, Lincoln announced that he would hold all federal possessions. One such possession was Fort Sumter, which lay in the harbor of Charleston, South Carolina. Confederates fired on Fort Sumter and forced its federal troops to surrender. Lincoln then called for additional federal troops to enforce the nation's laws. Southerners saw this act as equivalent to a declaration of war. Other Southern states quickly joined the Confederacy, and the Civil War was born.

Extra! Extra! Point-Of-View Newspapers

Bring the Civil War period to life with an unusual writing project. Post the following list of topics:

slavery	states' rights	1860 presidential election
Robert E. Lee	abolitionist movement	Underground Railroad
the Dred Scott decision	Fugitive Slave Laws	Missouri Compromise
Harriet Tubman	Frederick Douglass	*Uncle Tom's Cabin*
Jefferson Davis	*Monitor* and the *Merrimack*	life on the home front
Fort Sumter	the economy in the South	the economy in the North
surrender at Appomattox	results of the Civil War	costs of the Civil War

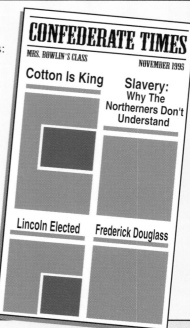

Have each student (or pair of students) choose a topic and write a newspaper article about it from the point of view of a Confederate sympathizer. (Provide research time as needed.) Have students compile their finished articles into a class "Confederate Times" newspaper, adding original illustrations. Next have students write newspaper articles on the same topics, but from a Northerner's point of view. Publish the finished articles in a class "Union Gazette" newspaper. Have small groups compare and contrast the different viewpoints presented in the newspapers.

Betty Bowlin, Henry Elementary, Ballwin, MO

The Music Of The Civil War

One of the most popular forms of entertainment in both the Union and Confederate armies was music. The war song of the South was "Dixie." Julia Ward Howe put new words to "John Brown's Body" to create "The Battle Hymn Of The Republic," the anthem of the Union army. Other popular tunes included "Yellow Rose Of Texas," "Eating Goober Peas," "Tenting To-night," and "When Johnny Comes Marching Home." Ask your music teacher to provide students with copies of these songs. Have students read the lyrics to find information about the Civil War. Let interested students perform the songs for the rest of the class.

American composer Aaron Copland wrote a composition called "Lincoln Portrait," an orchestral work with narration based on the famous words of Lincoln. This work employs parts of popular Civil War tunes. Check a public library for a recording of "Lincoln's Portrait." Listen to portions of the piece; then have each student write his reaction in a journal. *(See the ready-to-duplicate journal cover on page 135.)*

Civil War Correspondents

His photographs preserved forever the grim reality of the Civil War. Mathew Brady, famed Civil War photographer, felt compelled to go to war "to preserve the moment of experience for the future." That he did, with hundreds of photographs taken with the help of several photographic teams.

Tell students to pretend that they are members of one of Brady's photographic teams. A newspaper has asked each of them to keep a journal during the photographic trip. The journal will be reprinted in newspapers to give readers information about the war. Duplicate the journal cover pattern on page 135 on brown construction paper for each student. Have the student fold the pattern in half; then have him staple white paper cut to size between his covers. Give each student the list of writing topics on page 136 (or conserve paper by posting one copy at a center). Have students write in their journals during free time or writing workshop, using reference books as needed. Encourage students to add items such as sketches, diagrams, and poems in their journals. Let students read excerpts from their journals during a special sharing session. Later use the journals to assess your students' grasp of important concepts.

A Soldier's Life

Students may be surprised to learn that each Civil War soldier had to carry at least 40 pounds of equipment and personal items, including a nine-pound musket, a bayonet, a bowie knife, a canteen, a cartridge box, and a knapsack. To give students a better picture of the hard life of a soldier, label index cards with the following items (one per card): underwear, soap, towels, a comb, a brush, a looking glass, a toothbrush, paper and envelopes, pens, ink, pencils, shoe blacking, photographs, smoking and chewing tobaccos, pipes, twine, string, cotton strips for wounds, needles and thread, buttons, a knife, a fork, a spoon, two blankets, and a rubber ground cloth. Place the cards in a knapsack or large bookbag. Pull out each card, reading it aloud as you do. Place the cards in a chalk tray. When you've emptied the knapsack, point out that it was no fun carrying such a load on a hot day—and when it was soaked with rain, the knapsack became even heavier!

Follow up this activity by reading excerpts about a soldier's life from *Behind The Blue And Gray: The Soldier's Life In The Civil War* by Delia Ray (published by Lodestar Books). *The Boys' War: Confederate And Union Soldiers Talk About The Civil War* by Jim Murphy (published by Houghton Mifflin) is a spellbinding account of the war from the youngest soldiers' point of view, with excerpts from authentic diaries, letters, and journals of that time.

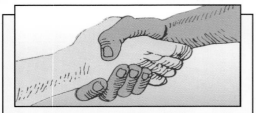

A Tale Of Two Soldiers

For an unforgettable reading experience, find a copy of Patricia Polacco's picture book, *Pink And Say* (Philomel Books). It tells the true story of two young Civil War soldiers: one a wounded boy left for dead in a battlefield, and the other a young black soldier who takes him to his mother's home to heal.

On the last page, Polacco tells readers, "This book serves as a written memory of Pinkus Aylee since there are no living descendants to do this for him." Discuss ways that famous people are remembered or memorialized today: statues, songs, poems, scholarships, buildings, highways, etc. Tell students to pretend that, like Polacco, they heard the story of Pinkus Aylee; but unlike Polacco, they have decided to remember Pinkus in a manner other than writing a book. Have each child describe his idea in a written proposal. Let students share their ideas; then post the ideas on a bulletin board.

Women And Minorities In The War

Women, African Americans, Native Americans, Hispanic Americans, European immigrants—all played important roles in the Civil War. For example, more than 440,000 European immigrants fought for the Union. Native Americans, treated harshly during the war, proved to be some of the Union's toughest soldiers. Introduce some of the brave women and minority heroes of the Civil War with the essay-writing reproducible on page 137. Publish finished essays in a class book entitled "A Brave Bunch."

For more information about women and minorities during the Civil War, look for *A Separate Battle: Women And The Civil War* by Ina Chang (Lodestar Books). Also look for *The Civil War To The Last Frontier: 1850–1880s* by William Loren Katz (part of the "A History Of Multicultural America" series published by Raintree Steck-Vaughn Publishers).

Civil War Flash Cards

Let your students make learning aids about the Civil War that you can use from year to year. Assign each of several small groups one of the categories listed below; then give each group a supply of large, unlined index cards. Have the students research each topic in its category. On one side of each card, have students write a topic and illustrate it. On the back of the card, have the students write a short description or definition. Place the cards at a center so students can drill each other during free time.

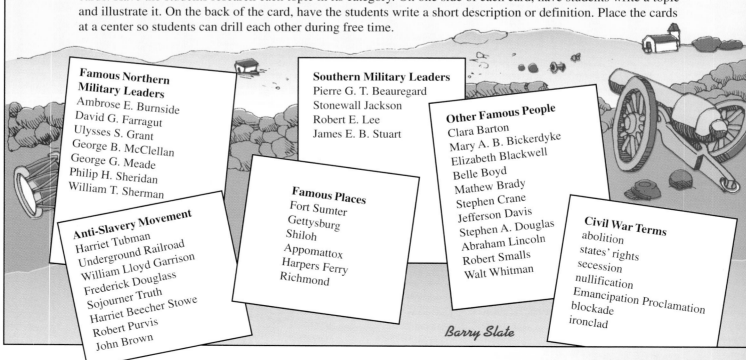

Famous Northern Military Leaders
Ambrose E. Burnside
David G. Farragut
Ulysses S. Grant
George B. McClellan
George G. Meade
Philip H. Sheridan
William T. Sherman

Anti-Slavery Movement
Harriet Tubman
Underground Railroad
William Lloyd Garrison
Frederick Douglass
Sojourner Truth
Harriet Beecher Stowe
Robert Purvis
John Brown

Southern Military Leaders
Pierre G. T. Beauregard
Stonewall Jackson
Robert E. Lee
James E. B. Stuart

Famous Places
Fort Sumter
Gettysburg
Shiloh
Appomattox
Harpers Ferry
Richmond

Other Famous People
Clara Barton
Mary A. B. Bickerdyke
Elizabeth Blackwell
Belle Boyd
Mathew Brady
Stephen Crane
Jefferson Davis
Stephen A. Douglas
Abraham Lincoln
Robert Smalls
Walt Whitman

Civil War Terms
abolition
states' rights
secession
nullification
Emancipation Proclamation
blockade
ironclad

Barry Slate

Civil War Literature

Incorporate these highly recommended books into your Civil War studies.

reviewed by Deborah Zink Roffino

Running For Our Lives

by Glennette Tilley Turner
illustrated by Samuel Byrd
published by Holiday House, 1994

Numerous books have attempted to tell the story of the Underground Railroad, but most are based on the life of Harriet Tubman. This dramatic chapter book tells the story of young Luther and his family as they escape from a Missouri plantation and head north to freedom. Enduring physical pain, biting cold, and the emotional assault of constant fear, Luther's family travels the Underground Railroad, meets abolitionists, and faces determined slave-holders. This enthralling book provides insight into the era just prior to the Civil War.

Christmas In The Big House, Christmas In The Quarters

by Patricia C. McKissack
and Fredrick L. McKissack
illustrated by John Thompson
published by Scholastic Inc., 1994

Magnificently woven, this well-researched book contrasts two distinctive Christmas celebrations held just before the Civil War: one in the big plantation house and the other in its slave quarters. Along with the chronicle of everyday life, the book holds a passel of recipes, rhymes, and riddles from the era. Full-page paintings add additional information on architecture, furnishings, and period clothing. Don't save this book for the holidays!

Barbara Frietchie

by John Greenleaf Whittier
illustrated by Nancy Winslow Parker
published by Greenwillow Books, 1992

During the second year of the Civil War, the battle at Antietam proved to be the bloodiest single day of the conflict. Whether or not Granny Frietchie waved her Union flag in the face of Stonewall Jackson as he marched through Frederick, Maryland, on his way to that conflict, this famous poem offers insight into the fever pitch of patriotism. Essential background details appear in the pictures, and on the introductory and concluding pages.

Escape From Slavery: The Boyhood Of Frederick Douglass In His Own Words

edited and illustrated by Michael McCurdy
published by Alfred A. Knopf, Inc.; 1994

Excerpted from his autobiography, this intimate account of Douglass's family, their separation, and the cruelty they endured personalizes the slavery experience for young-sters. The well-chosen text is laced with particulars on the food, responsibilities, housing, clothing, and punishment of a slave. It is a riveting story that covers Douglass's even-tual race to freedom and the beginning of his new life as an abolitionist.

Other Titles:
John Brown: One Man Against Slavery by Gwen Everett; published by Rizzoli International Publications, Inc.; 1993
Gentle Annie: The True Story Of A Civil War Nurse by Mary Francis Shura; published by Scholastic Inc., 1991
Lincoln: In His Own Words edited by Milton Melzer; published by Harcourt Brace & Company, 1993

A Related Book Unit

Take a look at pages 212–216, which feature a literature unit on *Who Comes With Cannons?* This grip-ping novel tells the story of a brave Quaker girl's involvement in the Underground Railroad.

A Nation Torn In Two

The Civil War was the result of years of disagreements between the states in the North and those in the South. When the war began, the North was clearly at an advantage. Use the chart and crayons or markers to fill in the bar graph.

INFORMATION CHART

Key:
*Color N bars **blue.***
*Color S bars **red.***

Population:
North—71%
South—29%

Wealth Produced:
North—75%
South—25%

Railroad Track:
North—72%
South—28%

Factories:
North—85%
South—15%

Bank Deposits:
North—81%
South—19%

Farms:
North—67%
South—33%

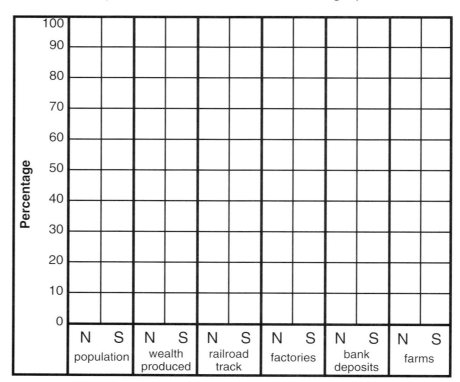

Write your answers to these questions on the back of this page.

1. Why do you think railroads were so important to both sides?
2. Compare the percentages of factories in the North and in the South. What problem would this create for southern cotton growers?
3. Which parts of the graph tell you that the South had trouble getting enough food during the war?
4. What difference do you think wealth and bank deposits made for the North in the war?
5. The one advantage that the South had during the war was that the South fought almost the entire war on its own soil. Why do you think this was an advantage?

Bonus Box: Look at a map of the United States. Take a close look at the eastern coastline. Which side of the war—the North or the South—do you think had the most shipyards and seaports? What difference do you think this made in the war?

My Civil War Journal

Fold.

Note To The Teacher: Use with "Civil War Correspondents" on page 131 and the reproducible on page 136. Duplicate on brown construction paper for each student. Have the student fold the pattern in the middle to make the front and back covers of a journal; then have him staple white paper cut to size inside the covers. Instruct the student to write his name at the bottom of the front cover.

Civil War Correspondent

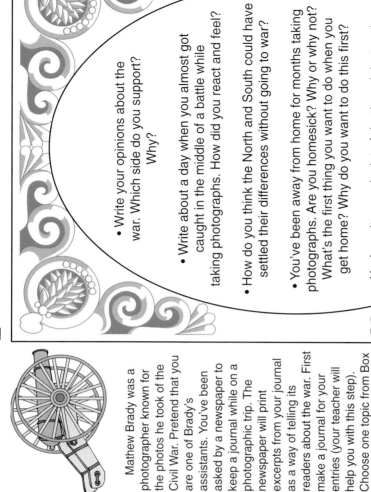

Mathew Brady was a photographer known for the photos he took of the Civil War. Pretend that you are one of Brady's assistants. You've been asked by a newspaper to keep a journal while on a photographic trip. The newspaper will print excerpts from your journal as a way of telling its readers about the war. First make a journal for your entries (your teacher will help you with this step). Choose one topic from Box A. Use research books or encyclopedias to help you write about this topic in your journal. Then choose three topics from Box B. Write about them in your journal.

Box B

- Write your opinions about the war. Which side do you support? Why?

- Write about a day when you almost got caught in the middle of a battle while taking photographs. How did you react and feel?

- How do you think the North and South could have settled their differences without going to war?

- You've been away from home for months taking photographs. Are you homesick? Why or why not? What's the first thing you want to do when you get home? Why do you want to do this first?

- You've witnessed a lot of death and destruction on this trip. Now that it's over, how do you feel about the war? Explain your answer.

Box A

- You've witnessed the battle of the *Monitor* and the *Merrimack*. Describe the ships and the battle that took place between them.

- You've just interviewed General Robert E. Lee at his headquarters. What did he say about the war and about leading the Confederate army? What was your impression of him?

- You've photographed a black soldier who has been in the Union army for a few months. What did he say about his time in the army? What hardships has he faced? Why did he join the army?

- You've just heard President Abraham Lincoln give the Gettysburg Address. What did you think of his speech? How did the rest of the audience react? Summarize what Lincoln said.

- You've arrived in Atlanta hours after the Union army has devastated the city. Describe what you see and experience there.

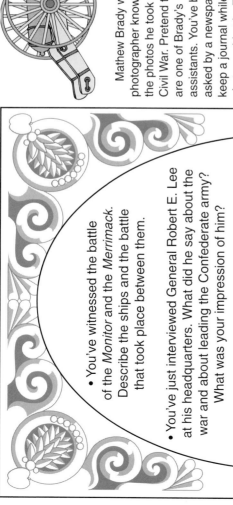

©The Education Center, Inc. • *THE MAILBOX®* • *Intermediate* • Oct/Nov 1995

Note To The Teacher: Use with "Civil War Correspondents" on page 131 and the reproducible journal cover on page 135. Provide students with reference books about the Civil War (see the suggestions mentioned on pages 131–132 and "Civil War Literature" on page 133).

A Brave Bunch

Women and minorities played a huge role in the Civil War. Below are the stories of six brave people who took part in this conflict. Read each story. With a crayon or marker, outline the box of the person you would nominate as "The Bravest Of The Bunch." On the back of this page, write a paragraph explaining why you chose this person.

Clara Barton

Collecting and delivering supplies to Northern troops was something that Clara Barton was very good at doing. A former schoolteacher, Barton once heard that injured Union soldiers who were her former students had arrived in Washington, D.C. These soldiers had no place to stay and no supplies. Immediately Barton found volunteers and supplies to care for the men. When other people who wanted to help the Union army heard about this, they began sending supplies to Barton. She loaded the supplies into wagons and took them straight to the camps and battlefields.

Robert Smalls

Robert Smalls grew up as a slave in South Carolina. He was trained to work as a sailor. Smalls was forced to work on a Confederate paddle steamer called the *Planter.* One night Smalls and the other slaves on the crew watched the white officers leave the ship for the evening. Then they brought their families aboard. Smalls secretly sailed the *Planter* out of the harbor until it met a Union ship. Smalls surrendered the Confederate ship to the Union captain. Later Smalls was made captain of the *Planter,* which became part of the Union navy.

Charlotte Forten

In 1861, the Union army invaded South Carolina's Sea Islands. The white plantation owners on the island fled. They left behind 10,000 slaves. When word got out that these slaves had been freed, other slaves flocked to the island. Charlotte Forten also went. She was a free black from the North who worked to end slavery. Forten went to the Sea Islands to teach the freed slaves. Many of these slaves didn't even know what a book was or how to hold one. Forten devoted her life to teaching and to working for civil rights.

Opothle Yahola

Life was hard for Native Americans during the Civil War. Many Native Americans were pressured to join the Confederacy. One Creek chief—Opothle Yahola—would not be pressured. He gathered African and Native Americans who either were *neutral* (did not take sides) or favored the North. Yahola asked President Lincoln to protect the group from the Confederates. When the Confederates heard of this, they attacked Yahola's group. Yahola escaped and led his people to safety across Union lines. Yahola's men who survived joined the Union army. They became some of its toughest soldiers.

Charles Zagony

Charles Zagony moved to America from the European country of Hungary. He became a major in the Union army. When the war started, Zagony organized trappers, hunters, and pioneers into three companies. He became famous for "Zagony's Death Ride." In this battle, Zagony and his 300 soldiers defeated a force of almost 2,000 Confederates!

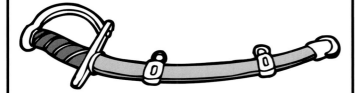

Mary Ann Bickerdyke

Conditions in Civil War hospitals were terrible. Mary Ann Bickerdyke had a cause—to improve the conditions in the Union army's hospitals. "Mother Bickerdyke" did everything she could to make sure her patients were clean, well fed, and warm. She even helped remove the wounded from battlefields. One night after rescue parties had gone to bed, an officer saw a light on the abandoned battlefield. It was Mother Bickerdyke, alone out looking for more survivors!

Bonus Box: On another piece of paper, design a certificate that you would like to have awarded to one of these brave people.

You Take The High Road And I'll Take The Low Road!
Creative Activities On Physical Geography

Hitch up your hiking boots, don your safari hat, and follow the not-so-very "Ruff Terrain" as he leads your students into the realms of physical geography.

by Christine A. Thuman

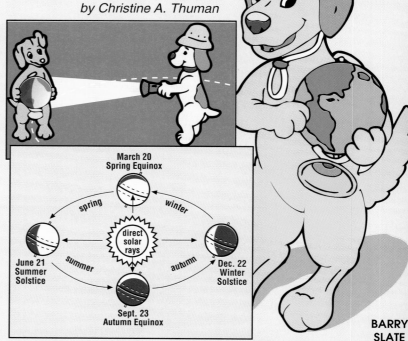

BARRY SLATE

As The World Tilts

Your students already know that the earth does not sit upright on its axis. But do they understand how this peculiar tilt affects the earth's climate? Demonstrate the earth's unique position and movement around the sun. First trace an ellipse on the floor with chalk or tape as shown in the diagram. Label the seasons, solstices, and equinoxes. As one student stands in the center of the ellipse holding a flashlight (the sun), instruct another child to carry a globe around the ellipse as shown, spinning the globe in a counterclockwise direction. Refer to the diagram to show the student the globe's position in relation to the sun. Turn out the lights and have the other students watch as the sun "shines" on the revolving, rotating earth. Occasionally pause the movement to discuss the changing angle of the sunlight and how the earth's climate is being affected. Which parts of the earth receive the most constant light? Which parts receive less light? Have students predict how this affects the climate of those regions.

Too Hot To Handle?

Do direct rays from the sun really make a difference in an area's climate? Demonstrate the effects of direct versus indirect sunlight on a location's climate with the following experiment. Take the flat disks of two canning jar lids and paint the top of each with black paint. Secure each disk to a table using a piece of clay. Point a desk lamp (with a 60-watt bulb) at the disks. Position one disk so that the painted side directly faces the light. Position the other disk with its painted side at an angle to the light as shown. Shine the light on the two disks for 15 minutes. Have a student take each disk and place the black side against the inside of his upper arm. Which disk is hotter? What does this tell your students about the effect of direct versus indirect sunlight?

Zoning Out

Here's a simple way for students to illustrate the diversity of geography and life in the three climate zones: polar, temperate, and tropic. Have each student fold a 12" x 18" sheet of paper into thirds. On the top third, have the student illustrate or create a collage of pictures depicting the diverse geography, people, plants, and animals of the polar zone. Instruct the student to repeat this procedure, illustrating the temperate region in the center and the tropics in the bottom third of the paper. Post the title "Zoning Out On Climates" at the top of a large bulletin board; then use masking tape to divide the board into three columns, one per zone. Have each student cut apart his three illustrations, then staple them to the correct section of the bulletin board collage-fashion to create a class montage for each zone.

Blowing In The Wind

As air near the equator heats up, it rises. As it cools, it falls back to earth. The earth—spinning at about a thousand miles per hour—circulates the air, resulting in a peculiar pattern of wind currents. Without these currents, certain areas of the earth would never be warm enough to support life. The following experiment demonstrates the movement of hot and cold liquids or gases.

Materials: one-quart jar with a large mouth, pitcher filled with ice water, baby-food jar, warm tap water, food coloring, spoon, four-inch square of aluminum foil, rubber band, pencil, timer

Directions:
1. Fill the baby-food jar to the brim with warm tap water. Stir in several drops of food coloring.
2. Seal the jar with foil and the rubber band.
3. Stand the baby-food jar inside the large jar.
4. Slowly pour ice water into the large jar until it is three-quarters full and the water level reaches above the top of the baby-food jar.
5. Using the pencil, carefully poke two holes into the foil on the baby-food jar as shown.
6. Observe and record results every five minutes for 20 minutes.

What Happens? *The cold water is heavier than the warm water. Heavy, cold water enters one of the holes, pushing the warm water out the other hole. The lighter (colored) warm water rises at first. After it cools it sinks. When liquids or gases rise and sink due to differences in temperature, we refer to these movements as* convection currents.

Same Latitude, Different Attitude

Climate zones enable us to make generalizations about sunlight's effect on climate. But many other factors play a role. Use the following activity to demonstrate the diversity of climates along a given latitude line. Divide your class into seven groups. Assign each of six groups one of the following latitudes and its listed cities. Have the seventh group research the latitude on which you live—locating four other cities worldwide that rest on approximately the same latitude. Have each group research its cities, noting average rainfall, temperature, outstanding landforms, plants, animals, and any interesting adaptations and problems humans living there have encountered; then have the group's members share its information on a 12" x 12' strip of paper. Post the completed strips in a hallway or along your classroom walls.

0° Latitude (The Equator)
Nairobi, Kenya
Singapore City, Singapore
Galápagos Islands, Ecuador
Quito, Ecuador

15° N Latitude
San'a, Yemen
Manila, Philippines
Tegucigalpa, Honduras
Dakar, Senegal

35° N Latitude
Kabul, Afghanistan
Tokyo, Japan
Los Angeles, California, USA
Atlanta, Georgia, USA

45° N Latitude
Bucharest, Romania
Harbin, China
Minneapolis, Minnesota, USA
Halifax, Nova Scotia, Canada

15° S Latitude
Lusaka, Zambia
Cooktown, Australia
La Paz, Bolivia
Brasília, Brazil

35° S Latitude
Cape Town, South Africa
Sydney, Australia
Santiago, Chile
Montevideo, Uruguay

NAIROBI KENYA — 3000-6000 ft. above sea level — unreliable rainfall — forested highland — population: 1,429,000 — wettest months: March, April, May

SINGAPORE CITY SINGAPORE — southern tip of low-lying island — warm, moist — Chinese, Malay, Indians — native vegetation replaced with high-density housing and industries — city's wealth comes through trade, banking, finance

GALÁPAGOS ISLANDS ECUADOR

Michelangelo's Guide To Geography

Sculpture and geography collide in this hands-on landform activity. Create a landform sheet for each student by gluing an irregular piece of brown paper onto a 12" x 9" sheet of blue paper. Laminate each sheet. Provide each student with a log of brown modeling clay. As you call out each of the landforms listed below, challenge each student to use the clay to construct that landform on his sheet. Then stand back and watch as your students get a grasp on geography!

bay	gulf	valley	mesa
island	mountain	volcano	peninsula
strait	basin	inlet	sound
isthmus	cape	delta	plateau

①

②

Getting It "Strait"

Does the mountain of geographic terms make your students feel like retreating into a cave? Duplicate page 141 for each student and review the directions. After students have completed the page, have each child translate her research into an informational pamphlet. Have her fold a rectangular sheet of white paper in half twice as shown. Opening the paper like a book will reveal two pages—one for each geographic term. Instruct the student to create cutouts on her pages using the pictures on the left as a guide. (You may want to provide art knives—to be used with supervision—for this step.) Then have her write and illustrate information about each term. Display these pamphlets on a table for students to check out.

Trade Books To The Rescue!

If you think well-written, colorfully illustrated geographic reference and trade books are as hard to come by as water in the desert, take a look at these titles!

Atlases
The Atlas Of Endangered Places by Steve Pollock (Belitha Press)
The Complete Atlas Of The World by Keith Lye (Raintree Steck-Vaughn Publishers)
The Earth Atlas by Susanna van Rose (Dorling Kindersley Publishing, Inc.)
The Kingfisher Reference Atlas: An A–Z Guide To Countries Of The World by Brian Williams (Kingfisher Books)

Series Books
People And Places series (Thomson Learning): Includes titles such as *The Alps And Their People, The Caribbean And Its People, The Mediterranean And Its People,* and *The Sahara And Its People.*
Wonders Of The World series (Raintree Steck-Vaughn Publishers): Includes such titles as *Grand Canyon, Great Barrier Reef, St. Lawrence River & Seaway,* and *Antarctica.*

Author Series
Jim Brandenburg (Walker Publishing Company, Inc.):
Titles include: *An American Safari: Adventures On the North American Prairie,* and *Sand And Fog: Adventures In Southern Africa*
Jan Reynolds' Vanishing Cultures series (Harcourt Brace & Company)
Titles include: *Amazon Basin, Down Under, Far North, Frozen Land, Himalaya, Mongolia,* and *Sahara*
Seymour Simon (Morrow Junior Books)
Titles include: *Deserts, Icebergs And Glaciers,* and *Volcanoes*

What's The Difference?

How do homes in the desert differ from homes in the tundra? Answer this and other ecological and geological questions using the chart below. Select two items from either the BIOMES or LANDFORMS lists below. Write your first item in box A and your second item in box B. Research each item; then compare the two by filling in the chart. If a category listed in the left-hand column is not appropriate for your items, replace it with a category of your choice.

BIOMES

tundra
boreal forest (taiga)
temperate coniferous forest
temperate deciduous forest
chaparral
desert
treeless grassland
savanna and woodland
tropical rain forest

LANDFORMS

bay   strait
gulf   lake
valley   isthmus
mesa   cape
island   delta
mountain   plateau
volcano   desert
river   cavern
waterfall   butte
peninsula   cave

Categories	A	B
 Animal Life		
 Plant Life		
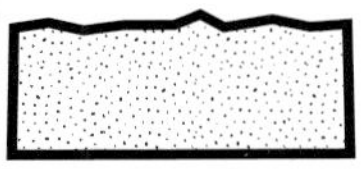 Soil		
 Average Rainfall		
 Average Temperature		
 How It Was Formed		
 Human Adaptations		

©The Education Center, Inc. • THE MAILBOX® • Intermediate • Aug/Sept 1995

Note To Teacher: Use this page with the "Getting It 'Strait'" activity on page 140.

141

Name _____

There's A Hole In The Bottom Of The Sea!

Did you know that the earth's ocean floor has mountains, volcanoes, and trenches just like the earth's land area does? Scientists map this undersea terrain using a sonar device that sends down high-frequency sound waves from a ship. Scientists record the time it takes for the waves to echo back to the ship. Simulate this ocean floor mapping process with the following experiment.

Materials per group:

12" piece of string
permanent marker
washer
2 or 3 rocks (no taller than 2")
transparent dish or tray (approximately the size of a cake pan and at least 3" deep)

18" ruler
paper towels
tap water
pencil

Directions:

1. Place the paper towels under the dish on a table. Place the rocks inside the dish.
2. Fill the dish with three inches of water. The water represents the ocean.
3. Tie the washer to one end of the string.
4. Using the ruler and marker, measure and mark a 1/2-inch scale along the string.
5. Lay the ruler lengthwise on the dish. The edges of the dish represent the shore.
6. Holding the free end of the string, position the string so that it is touching the edge of one side of the dish. Lower the string into the water until the washer lies down on a rock or on the bottom of the dish.
7. Counting the lines on the string's scale, determine the depth of the water. Round off the measurement to the nearest scale marking. Record the measurement on the chart on the right.
8. Continue measuring and recording the depth of water every 1/2 inch across the length of the dish.
9. Transfer the chart data to the graph on the right. The resulting outline will resemble the topography of the ocean floor.

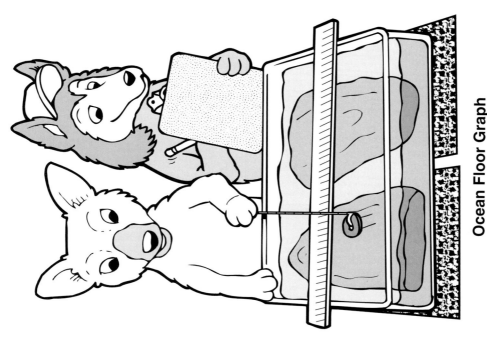

Ocean Floor Data Chart

Distance From The Shore	Depth
0.0 in.	
0.5	
1.0	
1.5	
2.0	
2.5	
3.0	
3.5	
4.0	
4.5	
5.0	
5.5	
6.0	
6.5	
7.0	
7.5	
8.0	
8.5	
9.0	
9.5	
10.0	
10.5	
11.0	
11.5	
12.0	

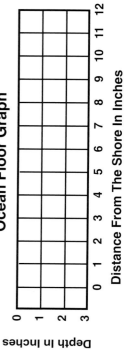

Ocean Floor Graph

Depth In Inches (0, 1, 2, 3)

Distance From The Shore In Inches (0 1 2 3 4 5 6 7 8 9 10 11 12)

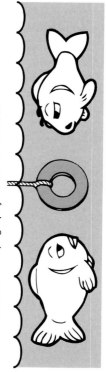

Final Summit

How many of these research challenges can you pack away in your traveling bag?

1. Choose one of the following Greek geographers to research. Tell how he contributed to human understanding of the earth's geography.

Aristotle	Ptolemy
Eratosthenes	Pythagoras
Strabo	

2. Geography is a mother lode of sciences. Define each of these scientific fields. Then tell how you think each relates to geography.

cartography	geology
climatology	oceanography
ecology	

3. The mythical lands of Atlantis and El Dorado hold a special place in the history of geography. Make a chart comparing and contrasting these two places.

4. How did the following places get their names?

Sandwich Islands	Red Sea
Greenland	Yellow Sea
Badlands	

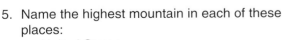

5. Name the highest mountain in each of these places:
   United States
   Canada
   Mexico
   South America
   Turkey

6. Name the major city that you would find on each of these rivers:
   Hudson
   Thames
   Seine
   Hooghly
   Parramatta

7. One way humans change the geographic features of an area is by building dams. Name the river that goes with each dam below:
   Hoover
   Shasta
   Pickwick
   Fort Peck
   Grand Coulee

8. What bodies of land do each of the following straits separate?
   Strait of Hormuz
   Strait of Gibraltar
   Strait of Dover
   Skagerrak
   Windward Passage

9. In which countries will you find the following bays?
   Table Bay
   Hudson Bay
   Guanabara Bay
   Bo Hai
   Kiel Bay

10. In which countries will you find the following deserts?
    Gibson Desert
    Kalahari Desert
    Arabian Desert
    Atacama Desert
    Mojave Desert

Note To Teacher: Duplicate this page for each student to work on independently. Or have students complete these activities as a research contract.

There's No Place Like Home!

Star-Spangled Ideas For Studying Your State

When we asked our subscribers to send us their favorite ideas on "studying your state," responses poured in from sea to shining sea! Add these star-spangled suggestions—all from creative teachers just like you—to your lesson plans. Then look for more ideas from this special collection in upcoming issues of *The* Intermediate *Mailbox®*.

(Many of the ideas that follow can also be used by students who are learning about United States regions, or studying states or countries other than their own. Adapt them to fit your teaching needs.)

Places To See

Here's a bright idea that sets its sights on your state's historical past! Duplicate the sunglasses pattern (page 148) on white construction paper for each student. In the left lens, have each child write two or three sentences describing one of your state's historical sites, making sure to explain its significance to your state's history. In the right lens, have the student illustrate the site. Instruct students to use colorful markers to decorate the frames of their sunglasses; then have them cut out the patterns and staple them to a bulletin board entitled "Places To See In _____ (name of your state)."

Pam Doerr—Substitute K–6
Lancaster County Schools
Mount Joy, PA

Digging Up Some Dirt

For an activity your students are sure to dig, try this! Before a student leaves on a trip that will take him to another state, give him a small baby-food jar (with a lid). Ask the student to fill the jar with a sample of soil from the state he visits; then have him bring the jar to school when he returns from his trip. Keep the labeled soil samples from year to year so that you can build a good collection. Have students compare soil samples from your state with those from the others in your collection. When you begin your U.S. regions unit, pull out the soil collection and have students look at samples from the particular states you're studying.

Jeri-Lyn Flowers
Cartersville Elementary
Cartersville, GA

Operation Alliteration

Help students remember important facts about your state with an exercise in alliteration. Begin by having each student list interesting facts about your state. Next have the student use a dictionary to list words that begin with the same letter as your state. As the final step, have the student use both lists—the state facts and the word list—to write an alliterative paragraph about your state. For a fun display idea, have students cut out samples of the letter they used from old magazines. Then have each child glue some of the letters around the edges of a sheet of construction paper. Finally have the student copy or paste her paragraph inside the frame of letters.

Kevin S. Spencer—Gr. 5
Raleigh Court Elementary
Roanoke, VA

Fort Niagara

Magnificent, Marvelous Minnesota

It's Curtains For You!

For an inexpensive state map, look no further than the bath section of your local department store. Enlarge an outline of your state on a white, plastic shower-curtain liner. Use a permanent marker to label items you wish to remain on the map, such as county lines, rivers, etc. Use a wipe-off marker for items you want students to add and then erase later. Let students use the giant map to play review games such as "County Twister," played like the popular color game.

Annette Smith—Gr. 4
Ward Elementary
Starkville, MS

Left hand, Jackson County.

Signed, Sealed, Delivered

With the help of the postal service, your class can be at the receiving end of a deluge of information about your state! I have my students write letters to other schools in our state, addressing each to "Any Sixth-Grade Student." In each letter, my students ask for information about the history, geography, famous people, natural resources, points of interest, and unusual features of the area in which that particular school is located. Long-distance peer teaching—how's that for a fun way to learn about your state?

Joy Horejsi—Gr. 6
Park Rapids Middle School
Park Rapids, MN

An Unforgettable Beginning

When I begin my unit on Kentucky, I let a famous person from our state's history do the talking for me! On the first day of the unit, I enter the classroom dressed as Rebecca Boone, wife of frontiersman Daniel Boone, who explored and settled in Kentucky. I talk about the various events of my and my husband's life in Kentucky. I also give students glimpses into what they will learn during our state study. My class is always spellbound by the performance and eager to begin learning about our state. Adapt this idea to your state by choosing a founding father (or mother!) to introduce your unit.

Mae Purrenhage—Grs. 4–5
Jackson Elementary
Ft. Campbell, KY

From Boonesboro, Kentucky, here he is... Daniel Boone!!!

Louisiana, Louisiana, What Do You See?

Picture books definitely aren't just for little readers—as this idea proves! After my students complete our unit on Louisiana, I spend a few minutes reading aloud the classic picture book *Brown Bear, Brown Bear, What Do You See?* by Bill Martin, Jr. After discussing the book's format, I challenge each student to create his own "Louisiana, Louisiana, What Do You See?" picture book using the same pattern Martin did (see the sample pages). Adapt this idea to make books about other states, U.S. regions, countries, or any unit of study.

Sue Calaway—Gr. 5
Jack Hayes School
Monroe, LA

Example

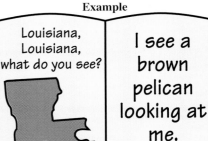

Louisiana, Louisiana, what do you see?

I see a brown pelican looking at me.

pages 1 and 2

Pelican, Pelican, what do you see?

I see pretty magnolias looking at me.

pages 3 and 4

145

Trek Across Our State

My students and I walked across the curriculum in style with this interdisciplinary activity. To start I posted a state map on a bulletin board entitled "Walk Around Washington." Then I challenged students to see how many miles they could walk. We calculated that eight trips around our playground equaled one mile. Each week we spent 10–15 minutes walking outside. Before each walking session, I assigned one child—the "Tour Guide"—to be in charge of recording each student's laps at the end of the walk. After the Tour Guide had totaled the number of laps walked by the entire class, we calculated our total mileage for the day. Then the Tour Guide used a highlighter pen to show our progress on the map. (Start your trek at your hometown or state capital.) As we trekked around our state, we discussed points of interest that we passed on our journey.

Lynn Marie Gilbertson—Gr. 4
James Sales Elementary
Tacoma, WA

County Countdown

Learn about your state one county at a time with a letter-writing campaign. As a class, have students write a letter to be sent to each county seat in your state. In the letter, ask for maps, information about places of interest, brochures, and any other items that might help the class learn about that county. While you're waiting for responses, use an overhead projector to make a large, cut-out shape of each county (making sure to keep the scale constant from county to county). After an information packet is received, have students fill in that county's outline with the facts and pictures contained in the packet. Let students show off the wealth of information they received by mounting the cut-out counties on a large wall space to make a giant state map.

Candy A. Enste—Gr. 4
St. Mary's Elementary
Rutherford, NJ

Good News In My State

What's black-and-white and "read" all over? All the newspapers in your state, that's what! And the information they contain makes them invaluable teaching tools. Write to several newspapers in your state to ask for complimentary copies. Or check with a local newsstand or bookstore to see if it will donate copies. Have students read through the papers to find inspiring, "good news" stories originating in your state. When a student finds such a story, have him write a paragraph reporting the date and location of the news. The student should also summarize the story and explain the types of people, community services, and materials that brought about the good news. Post the paragraphs on a "Good News In Our State" bulletin board.

Kevin S. Spencer—Gr. 5
Raleigh Court Elementary
Roanoke, VA

Happy Birthday To Our State!

Prior to our state's birthday, my students research to locate fascinating facts about Indiana. After the research has been discussed, we send teams of students to other classes in our school. The teams teach the students all about our state, from its symbols to important historical events and distinguishing physical features. At the end of the teaching sessions, all of the classes meet together in the gym where my students host a birthday party for our state. Set up around the gym are displays highlighting the projects we completed during our state study. After my students perform a skit about our state, everyone sings "Happy Birthday" and digs into a yummy birthday cake.

Julie Kaiser
Morgan Elementary
Palmyra, IN

Riddle Me This!

Whether your class is studying your state or researching other states, you'll love this fun bookmaking activity. After a student has researched his state, let him compose several riddles about it. Then have him type the riddles (one per page) on a classroom computer, using the fonts, styles, and sizes of his choice. Be sure the student types an answer key on a separate page. After printing the riddles and answer page, have the student staple them between two large paper covers cut in the shape of his state (with the answer key as the last page). Place the riddle books at a reading center for lots of free-time reading—and learning!

Marilyn Van De Venne—Gr. 5
Westwood Elementary
Portland, MI

Souvenir Shop

Students will shop 'til they drop with this fun culminating activity. At the conclusion of your state unit, distribute large pieces of art paper. Challenge each student to draw the inside of a souvenir shop that might be found in your state's capital city. Every aspect of the shop—from the signs to the items featured in the display cases and on the racks and shelves—should help visitors remember their trip to your state. Provide time for each shopkeeper to explain the items and tell why she chooses to stock her shop with them.

Jean Frigm—Gr. 4
Stewartstown Elementary
Stewartstown, PA

Barry Slate

State-In-A-Box

With this idea, a meaningful and fun assessment tool is in the bag—or, rather, the box! Ask each student to bring a large, unlidded box to school. After each child has a box, give him a copy of the "State-In-A-Box" project outline on page 149. Students follow the directions on the outline to transform their boxes into three-dimensional reports on your state. If desired, divide students into groups; then have each team create a boxed report on one aspect of your state, such as its geography, manufacturing, or history.

Maxine Pincott—Gr. 4
Oliver Ellsworth School
Windsor, CT

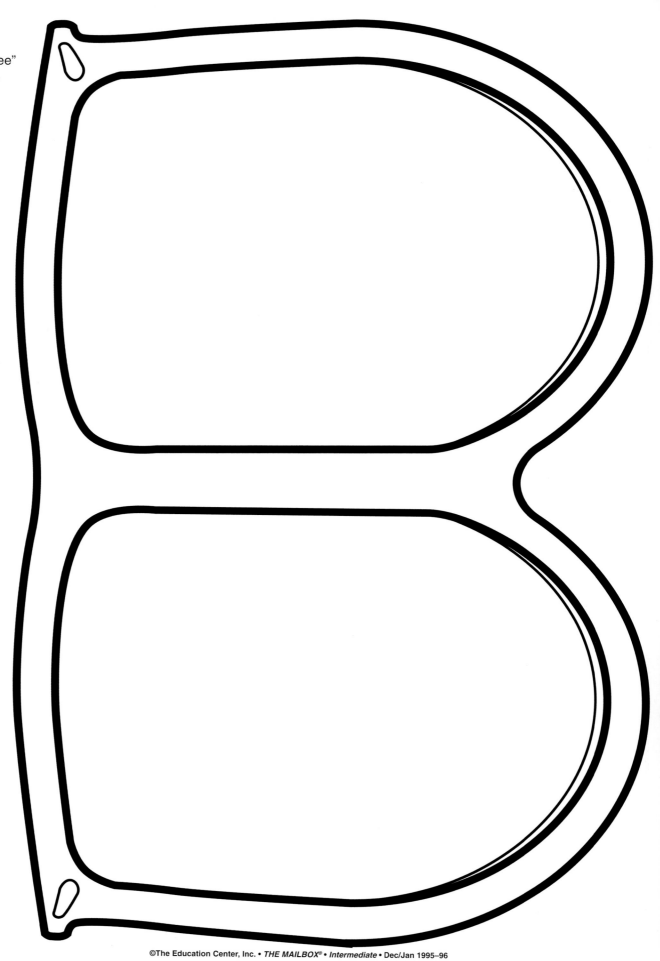

State-In-A-Box

Show everyone that you've got the facts on your state in the bag—or the box—by completing this unique project.

Materials you'll need: a large, unlidded box; glue or a stapler; paper to cover the box; art paper; scissors; crayons, markers, paints, or other art materials

Steps:
1. Read over this project outline; then jot down any questions you have in the box below. Be sure to ask your teacher these questions before you begin.
2. Fill in the due date that your teacher gives you.
   DUE DATE:_____
3. Cover the four sides and the inside of a large box with paper.
4. Store this sheet and any other papers in a folder for safe-keeping while you work.
5. Prepare the items in the "Must include..." list. Glue some of them on the outer sides of your box. Place other items inside your box. Put a check beside each item as you complete it.
6. If you want to earn extra points, include some or all of the items in the "Can include..." list.

Questions I Have About This Project

Must include on/in your box:
___ Illustration of your state's flag, including an explanation of the symbols on it
___ Map showing your state's natural resources (including a map key)
___ Illustration of the state bird, state tree, or state flower
___ Map showing some of your state's main tourist attractions (including a map key)
___ One-page report telling about two famous people who were born in your state
___ Three artifacts that represent your state

Can include on/in your box to earn extra points:
___ Written or tape-recorded interview with a famous contemporary state resident or a senior citizen who has lived in your state most of his/her life
___ Tape recording of your state's song
___ One-page report about a famous Native American from your state
___ Timeline showing at least five major historical events in your state's past
___ Additional illustrations and/or artifacts that give information about your state's geography, people, government, education, and industries
___ Anything else you think gives interesting information about your state

©The Education Center, Inc. • THE MAILBOX® • Intermediate • Dec/Jan 1995–96 • Idea by Maxine Pincott—Gr. 4, Oliver Ellsworth School, Windsor, CT

Note To The Teacher: Use this project outline with "State-In-A-Box" on page 147. Have each student bring in a large cardboard box (no lids needed). Provide each child with a file folder in which to store his work. If desired, fill in the due date (#2 in "Steps") before duplicating.

Plymouth Revisited

Creative Activities For Studying The Pilgrims

As our nation celebrates Thanksgiving Day this November, visions of a large gathering of happy Pilgrims and Native Americans breaking bread together will likely come to mind. But just how accurate are those images? Help your students fine-tune their knowledge about Thanksgiving's beginnings and the people of Plymouth with the following thought-provoking activities.

with activities by Terry Healy

How To Use These Activities

The approach of Thanksgiving provides a timely opportunity to involve your students in some fascinating investigative research, creative projects, and learning-packed experiences. Ask your media specialist to help you gather plenty of resources about the Pilgrims. As a class, complete one or more activities each week during the month of November. If you prefer a cooperative learning approach, divide students into investigative teams. Assign three to four of the activities to each team. Or form interest groups and let students choose their own activities. Have groups present their finished projects during a "Plymouth Revisited" forum, to which you've invited parents or other classes.

Ready-To-Use Gameboard

Introduce your students to even more fascinating facts about the Pilgrims with the ready-to-use gameboard on page 154. Give each of several cooperative groups copies of the question cards found on pages 152 and 153. Challenge the groups to use the library books mentioned in "How To Use These Activities" to answer the questions. After groups have had several days to research their answers, discuss them using the answer key on page 311. Then mount page 154 on a piece of construction paper. Copy pages 152 and 153 on construction paper. Cut out the cards and place them with the gameboard at a center, along with a copy of the answer key and a die.

ACTIVITIES

• While legend would have us believe that all Plymouth residents wore dull-colored clothing and tall black hats, the truth is much different. Wills left by citizens of Plymouth show estates that included scarlet-colored capes, yellow skirts, and other bright adornments. Have students research the clothing and other lifestyle elements of Plymouth's citizens. Then have each child pretend to be a Plymouth resident. Instruct the student to write a will listing his possessions and who is to receive them at his death. Remind students that their wills should reflect life as it *really* was in Plymouth.

• Even though they had some information about the New World—including maps from Jamestown and trading expeditions—the Pilgrims did not have an accurate picture of their destination. There were tales of miraculous plants, Indians who worshiped the white man, mountains of gold, and even fountains of youth! Have students research to find out what the Pilgrims thought about the New World before setting sail. Then have each child pretend to be William Bradford, the second governor of the colony. Instruct the student to write a journal entry—dated September 15, 1620 (the day before the *Mayflower* left England)—in which Bradford tells what he expects to find in America.

- Sailing to America on the *Mayflower* was not a thrilling adventure, but a perilous trial for the Pilgrims. Hundreds of pounds of cargo—together with 102 men, women, and children, and a menagerie of dogs, cats, birds, and livestock—were crammed into a very small ship. Challenge students to try this experiment to see what life was like on the *Mayflower*. First, tell students to imagine sitting on a single bed, the approximate amount of space each grown person had on the *Mayflower*. In this space, a Pilgrim adult had to cook all her meals, take care of her children, store her possessions, and spend most of her time. Now have students imagine sitting on their beds for an hour, unable to leave. (To help them envision an hour, have students imagine not leaving their beds until they had watched an entire episode of "Star Trek," including commercials.) Tell them to imagine the terrible odors that would be around because of the lack of sanitation. The *Mayflower* also encountered lots of bad storms. So have students imagine that every few minutes someone throws a bucket of icy water on them, and that the ship is pitching so violently that they have to be tied to their beds. At the end of the session, have each child write in his journal about the experience. How did he feel? How would he feel knowing that he had to live like this for many more weeks? How would he feel when land was finally sighted?

- In several famous paintings, the Pilgrims—including some women—are shown stepping triumphantly onto Plymouth Rock to begin their new lives. In reality, the *Mayflower* stayed anchored off the New England coast for about six weeks while an appropriate site for the settlement was chosen. When supplies—especially beer—began to run low, the exhausted Pilgrims decided on the Plymouth location. There were no triumphant speeches or celebrations—nor is there any evidence that women or Indians were present. The weary Pilgrims simply got to work unloading provisions and building a shelter from the freezing weather. Share some of the romanticized pictures of the Pilgrims; then have each student draw his own version of the Pilgrims' arrival at Plymouth.

- The first winter in Plymouth was anything but celebratory. Almost everyone got sick. Scarcely 50 people—only six of whom were women—survived that winter. Have students research the winter of 1620–1621. Then have each child pretend to be one of Plymouth's inhabitants and write a letter to a relative back in England. In the letter, have the student describe the conditions under which he/she lived during the winter of 1620–1621.

- The Plymouth colony was able to live peaceably with the nearby Native Americans for more than 50 years. The Indians—particularly two English-speaking natives named Samoset and Squanto—taught the Pilgrims many new skills that were vital to their survival. Have students research the relationship between the Plymouth colonists and their Native American neighbors; then have them research the colonist/ Indian relationship in Jamestown and the Massachusetts Bay Colony. Finally have students compare the three colonies by making large Venn diagrams.

- Many of the early citizens of Plymouth chose names for their children which today seem highly unusual. Share this list with students; then have them guess which individuals were male or female. Have students speculate about the reasons for some of the name choices.

Oceanus Hopkins (male; born on board the *Mayflower* as it was sailing to America)
Wrestling Brewster (male; named for "wrestling with the Devil")
Love Brewster (male)
Fear Brewster (female)
Patience Brewster (female)

Desire Minter (female)
Humility Cooper (female)
Peregrine White (male; name means "pilgrim"; lived to be 83 years old)
Resolved White (male)
Experience Mitchell (male)
Remember Allerton (female)
Constant Southworth (male)

Patterns

Use with "Ready-To-Use Gameboard" on page 150, the patterns on page 153, and the gameboard on page 154.

1. What was the name of the 60-ton ship that the Pilgrims bought along with the *Mayflower?*

2. How long did the Pilgrims live in Leyden, Holland?

3. What happened to the ship, the *Speedwell?*

4. To what other European country did the Pilgrims flee before seeking a home in the New World?

5. By what name were the Pilgrims called when they lived in England?

6. From what church did the Pilgrims "separate" while they lived in England?

7. What was the name of the company that gave the Pilgrims the right to establish an American settlement?

8. On what date did the *Mayflower* leave England?

9. How many people were on board the *Mayflower* when it left England in 1620?

10. From what English city did the *Mayflower* sail?

11. Approximately how many tons could the *Mayflower* hold?

12. In what city of Holland did most of the Pilgrims settle before deciding to go to the New World?

13. How long did the trip from England to the New World take?

14. How many people died on the trip to the New World?

15. What was the name of the child born during the Atlantic passage of the *Mayflower?*

16. Who was the captain of the *Mayflower?*

17. In what month of 1620 did the Pilgrims drop anchor near Plymouth?

18. In what month of 1620 did the Pilgrims make their historic landing at Plymouth?

19. What document did some of the *Mayflower's* passengers sign upon arriving in the New World?

20. Did any women sign the Mayflower Compact?

Note To The Teacher: Duplicate on construction paper. Use with "Ready-To-Use Gameboard" on page 150, the patterns on page 153, and the gameboard on page 154. Key on page 311.

21. Who was elected the first governor of the Plymouth colony?

22. What job did Miles Standish have in Plymouth?

23. Approximately what fraction of the Plymouth residents were alive after the first winter there?

24. Who was elected governor of Plymouth after John Carver died?

25. Why did the residents of Plymouth bury their dead at night?

26. What were the names of the two English-speaking Native Americans who helped the Pilgrims learn how to survive?

27. Who was the chief of the Wampanoag tribe that helped the Plymouth citizens?

28. What was the name of the child born while the *Mayflower* was anchored in the Plymouth harbor?

29. In April of 1621, what happened to the *Mayflower?*

30. In what year did the Pilgrims and Native American friends hold their first Thanksgiving feast?

31. For how long did the first Thanksgiving last?

32. How many times was William Bradford elected governor of the Plymouth Colony?

33. Were the women of Plymouth allowed to vote?

34. Were the Pilgrims familiar with corn before landing in the New World?

35. What English ruler gave the Pilgrims permission to leave England?

36. Were all of the passengers of the *Mayflower* Pilgrims?

37. What happened to William Bradford's wife, Dorothy?

38. Did the Pilgrim children attend school in Plymouth?

39. What president made Thanksgiving a legal holiday?

40. What was the name of the ship—holding 35 new settlers—that arrived at Plymouth in November of 1621?

Note To The Teacher: Duplicate on construction paper. Use with "Ready-To-Use Gameboard" on page 150, the patterns on page 152, and the gameboard on page 154. Key on page 311.

TALKIN' TURKEY!

1

2

3

4

5

PHONE BOOK

SOUP

Directions for 2–4 students:

1. Deal the cards facedown on the five spaces.
2. In turn, roll the die and take a card from the space indicated. If you roll a 6, skip your turn.
3. Give the answer. Have another player check the answer key.
4. If correct, you score the number of points rolled. If incorrect, return the card to the bottom of the pile on that space.
5. The game is over when all of the cards have been removed from the board or when time runs out. The player with the highest score wins!

Note To Teacher: Use with "Ready-To-Use Gameboard" on page 150.

The Commonwealth Of Independent States

Learning About The Former Soviet Union

Life hasn't been the same in the eastern half of the globe—or the world—since December 21, 1991. On that day, the Soviet Union ceased to exist. The collapse of this superpower forever changed the structure of world politics and reminded all peoples of the preciousness of freedom. Use the following ready-to-use activities and reproducibles to help your students learn about this intriguing region of the world.

by Simone Lepine

Background: The Collapse Of The Soviet Union

A thousand years ago, Russia was a small region in Europe. It gradually expanded its empire by conquering bordering nations. These conquered peoples clung to their ethnic heritage even as they lost hold of their countries. Monarchical rulers called *czars* ruled Russia for hundreds of years. A rebellion in 1917, led by Vladimir Lenin, overthrew this monarchical form of government and replaced it with a Communist regime. The Communist government controlled the economic structure by owning all factories and farms. To compensate for the lack of private ownership, all citizens would be provided with food, shelter, clothing, and jobs.

During the decades following Lenin's revolution, the people of the USSR experienced war, poverty, and an increasing lack of freedoms. When Mikhail Gorbachev came into power in 1985, the USSR—now a world superpower—was struggling domestically. Gorbachev's goal to restructure the USSR gave Soviet citizens a taste of democracy. When the Berlin Wall fell in 1989 with no interference from the Soviet Union, the world saw the beginning of the end for the USSR. An attempt by hard-line Communists to overthrow Gorbachev's government was quickly put down by popular demand, proving that the people of the USSR favored change. One by one, the republics of the Soviet Union began to declare their independence. On December 21, 1991, a confederation of 11 of the original 15 republics of the old USSR signed agreements to create the new Commonwealth of Independent States. *(For a list of CIS members and a map of the region, see pages 160 and 161.)*

The new Commonwealth of Independent States is a federation with more than 100 nationalities. Its various ethnic groups speak different languages, practice different religions, and observe different customs. There are still many problems to resolve as this region's people forge a new identity while tenaciously clinging to their ethnic heritage.

Sizing Up The CIS

The CIS is a huge region, taking up about one-sixth of all the land on earth! A flight across this vast area would take about 12 hours and would cross 11 time zones. Help students visualize the vastness of the CIS with an eye-opening measurement activity. Have each student use a ruler and pencil to draw a 6 1/2" x 3 1/2" box and a 2 1/2" x 1 1/2" box on a piece of paper. After students have cut out their boxes, lead them in a discussion about the United States and its different climates, landforms, and regions. Poll students to find out who has traveled across our country. Ask students to predict how long a cross-country trip like this might take by plane, car, etc. Your students should conclude that the United States is a large country with many different regions.

Next explain to students that the boxes they have created show the size difference between the United States and the CIS. Ask students to guess which box represents the United States. Are they surprised to learn that their large country is represented by the smaller box? Have students label their boxes; then have them estimate how many times larger the CIS is than the United States. Discuss with students what they think such a large confederation would be like in terms of landforms, climates, vegetation, people, customs, etc.

Pam Crane

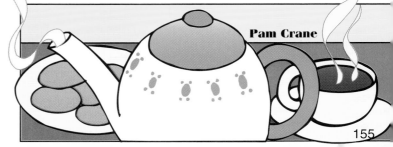

155

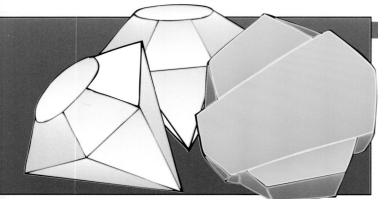

Paper Pysanky

Travel to the Ukraine and you're sure to be introduced to the rich tradition found in Ukrainian Easter eggs, or *pysanky.* These beautiful eggs are usually based on a geometrical design that contains symbols and colors of meaning to the artist. Pysanky is given to family and friends to convey one's love and best wishes during the Easter season. The process of making pysanky is based on the batik method of applying wax in several stages and dipping the eggs in dye. Let your students make their own paper versions of this lovely art form using the activity found on page 77.

CIS Fact Sheet

To help students learn some fast facts about the CIS, duplicate the Fact Sheet on page 161. Use this reproducible and the following activities to sharpen math, language, research, and analytical skills:

Activity 1: Focus on the effects climate and geography have on population with this activity. Have students list the countries according to population from greatest to least; then have them list the countries from greatest to least according to square miles. Ask students to compare the two lists to see if there is any correlation between population and area. Have students brainstorm why Turkmenistan—one of the largest CIS countries in area—has one of the lowest populations. Ask students what factors other than area might affect population *(climate, natural resources, landforms, etc.).* Have each cooperative group develop a theory as to why Turkmenistan's population is low. After groups have shared their ideas, explain that 80% of Turkmenistan is a desolate desert. Most of its population lives along the Caspian Sea, while the interior of this country is sparsely populated.

Activity 2: Many of your students are too young to remember or understand the significance of events that took place in Eastern Europe in the late 1980s. Discuss with students events that led up to the fall of the Berlin Wall in 1989 *(Gorbachev's policies of openness and change; the rise of nationalism in Eastern Europe; desperate economic conditions in many Communist countries; the fall of Communist governments in Hungary, Czechoslovakia, Poland, Romania, Bulgaria, and East Germany).* Explain how these events encouraged republics in the Soviet Union to declare their own independence. Using the Fact Sheet's "Date Declared Independence" column, have students create a timeline showing the order in which the former republics of the USSR broke away.

Activity 3: Add the names of the CIS member nations to your week's spelling list. Have students use their Fact Sheets to study the spellings.

Activity 4: Have students create symbols for the industries listed on the Fact Sheet. Give each child a copy of the map on page 160. Have students draw the symbols on the appropriate areas of the map.

Activity 5: List these topics on the board: Climate, Major Landforms, Bodies Of Water, Wildlife, Vegetation. Divide students into pairs and assign a CIS nation to each pair. For their country, have each pair research to find information about the topics on the board. Direct students to write each fact on an index card labeled with the pair's country. Post these on a bulletin board entitled "More Fabulous Facts About The CIS."

Nesting Boxes Research Project

The individuality of each commonwealth country can be seen in the folk art of these lands. One of the better-known crafts is the Russian nesting doll. This oval-shaped doll is hollow inside and detaches in the middle. Upon opening up the large doll, one finds a similar, smaller doll. This second doll, once opened, contains a smaller doll and so on. Use the steps below and the reproducible on page 162 to help students create nesting boxes that contain information about CIS countries. Display the finished boxes on a table with the poster described in "Getting Ready." During free time, let students visit the table and read each other's nesting box reports.

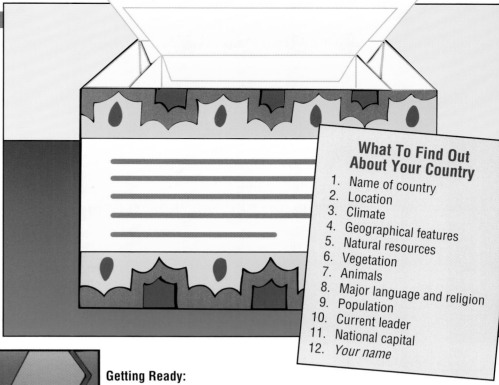

What To Find Out About Your Country
1. Name of country
2. Location
3. Climate
4. Geographical features
5. Natural resources
6. Vegetation
7. Animals
8. Major language and religion
9. Population
10. Current leader
11. National capital
12. *Your name*

Getting Ready:
1. Make a poster as shown. Discuss it with students; then display it for everyone to see.
2. Assign a CIS country to each student, pair, or group. Provide research time for students to locate the information on the poster.
3. Duplicate page 162 (three copies per student or group) on construction paper or another sturdy paper.

Making A Nesting Box:
1. Cut out one cross shape from each copy of page 162 so that you have three different sizes of crosses.
2. Place each cross number side up; then fold up and crease the four sides to make a box shape. *Do not attach the sides of the resulting three boxes until the entire project is completed.*
3. Unfold the boxes and turn each over to the back. Write a small number in the left-hand corner of each side as follows:
   - The sides of the large cross should be numbered 1–4.
   - The sides of the middle cross should be numbered 5–8.
   - The sides of the smallest cross should be numbered 9–12.

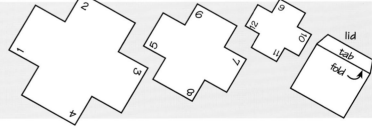

4. Write your research findings on the numbered panels to match the categories on the poster.
5. Decorate your boxes with fine-tipped markers, using traditional colors and designs from your country.
6. To make a lid for each box, trace the bottom of the box on paper, adding a tab as shown. Decorate the three lids before cutting them out.
7. Use clear tape to tape the sides of each box together.
8. Fold the tab of each lid where indicated. Tape the tab to the inside of its box.
9. Put your three boxes inside each other.

Environmental Woes In The CIS

In a hurry to modernize their country in a short time, Soviet leaders did not impose any laws to protect the environment. This legacy of pollution and rampant destruction of the environment concerns CIS citizens today. Share the information below about two of the region's main environmental problems. Review with students what happens in a food chain when one part of the chain is altered. For example, how would soil contaminated by the Chernobyl blast affect the food chain in those areas? What happens to Lake Baikal if the crustaceans that eat the lake's bacteria die from pollution? After the discussion, have students create posters that encourage CIS citizens to take care of their environment. Challenge students to do further research on Chernobyl and Lake Baikal to present to the class.

Chernobyl: On April 26, 1986, the Ukraine's Chernobyl nuclear reactor exploded, releasing over 11 tons of radiation into the air. A huge cloud of radiation contaminated a vast area of northwestern Europe. The devastation this explosion left behind can still be seen today. It is believed that more than four million people have been affected by the radiation. About 10,000 people have died from the initial effects, and predictions are that about 100,000 more will die prematurely from related diseases. The radiation also contaminated farmland and livestock. Due to desperate food shortages, some farmers are ignoring warnings, and are growing foods and feeding animals off contaminated soils.

Lake Baikal: Siberia's Lake Baikal is the world's oldest and deepest lake, holding one-fifth of the world's freshwater. The water in this lake is naturally pure due to a rare crustacean that eats bacteria. Lake Baikal is home to more than 2,000 species of plants and animals. At least 1,000 of these species are found nowhere else in the world. Over the past 40 years, Lake Baikal has become polluted from giant paper and pulp mills that pour chemical waste into the lake. These chemicals have killed off over 23 square miles of plant life on the lake's floor. Adding to the problem are the polluted rivers that run into Lake Baikal. If the pollution isn't stopped or reduced, the chemical balance of Lake Baikal may change and threaten the unique plants and animals that live there.

Diversity On The Dinner Table

The diversity of the CIS is reflected in the foods its people eat. In the Slavic countries of Belarus, the Ukraine, and Russia, bread is a staple food. Cabbage, potatoes, and a hearty beet soup called *borsch* are also favorites. The people who live in the Caucasus Mountain countries of Armenia and Azerbaijan are famous for living longer than most people in the world. Could that have something to do with the Middle Eastern flavorings they use? People in this area eat lots of lamb and rice dishes. In the central Asian countries of Kazakhstan, Uzbekistan, Turkmenistan, Kyrgyzstan, and Tajikistan, people eat lots of different fruits. In fact, over 1,000 different types of melons are grown in Uzbekistan!

Give students a taste of cooking from this region with a Russian apple pie named *pirog.* Let student groups make the recipe. (Depending on the number of students, prepare two or three pirogs.) While the pies cook, read the Russian folktales suggested on page 159 to students.

Pirog (Russian Apple Pie)

Ingredients:

4 small apples	1 cup flour	1 cup sugar
3 eggs	butter	

Directions:

1. Preheat an oven to 375°.
2. Cut cored, unpeeled apples into small pieces.
3. Mix the eggs, sugar, and flour in a bowl.
4. Spread a thin layer of butter inside a round, 8-inch cake pan.
5. Put the chopped apples in the pan; then pour the egg mixture over the apples.
6. Bake for 35–40 minutes or until golden brown. When cool and firm, cut into slices.

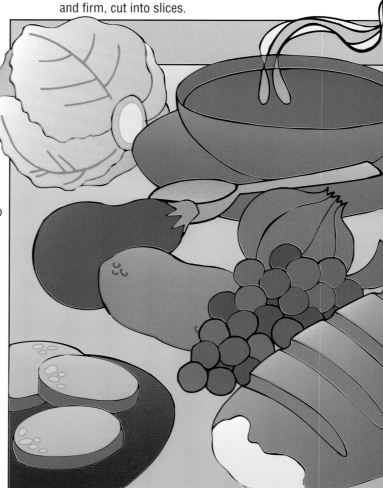

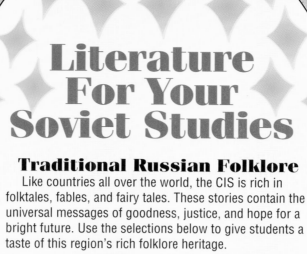

Literature For Your Soviet Studies

Traditional Russian Folklore

Like countries all over the world, the CIS is rich in folktales, fables, and fairy tales. These stories contain the universal messages of goodness, justice, and hope for a bright future. Use the selections below to give students a taste of this region's rich folklore heritage.

- *How The Moolah Was Taught A Lesson & Other Tales From Russia* adapted by Estelle Titiev and Lila Pargment (Doubleday, 1985)
- *The Firebird: A Russian Folktale* by Demi (Henry Holt & Company, 1994)
- *Koshka's Tales: Stories From Russia* by James Mayhew (Kingfisher Books, 1993)
- *I-Know-Not-What, I-Know-Not-Where: A Russian Tale* adapted by Eric A. Kimmel (Holiday House, Inc.; 1994)
- *Old Peter's Russian Tales* by Arthur Ransome (Viking Children's Books, 1975)

Nonfiction Titles

- *Russian Girl: Life In An Old Russian Town* by Russ Kendall (Scholastic, Inc.; 1994)

  Follow a young Russian girl named Olga as she goes to school, plays with friends, and lives her life in a traditional Russian village. The book's afterword contains information about Russia's history, language, alphabet, and foods.
- *Behind The Border* by Nina Kossman (Lothrop, Lee & Shepard Books; 1994)

  In poignant short stories, the author conveys the hardships and lost freedoms she experienced as a child living in the Soviet Union. This is an excellent book to illustrate the differences and similarities between life in the old USSR and the CIS today.
- *Sovietrek: A Journey By Bicycle Across Russia* by Dan Buettner (Lerner Publications, 1994)

  This fascinating book follows a team of bicyclists—two Americans and two Soviets—as they cycle across southern Russia. Although written just before the collapse of the Soviet Union, this book has many wonderful photographs and insights about the lifestyles of the region's people.

Pam Crane

Books By Patricia Polacco

Popular children's author and illustrator Patricia Polacco is a wonderful source of literature that subtly conveys Russian traditions. Ms. Polacco's parents are of Russian extraction, and she bases many of her stories on characters of Russian descent. Divide your students into groups. Have each group read one of the books below; then have group members list items or illustrations from the book that reflect traditional Russian customs.

- *The Keeping Quilt* (Simon and Schuster Books For Young Readers, 1988): Through the travels of an heirloom quilt, Polacco tells about Russian customs and how they've changed over time.
- *Rechenka's Eggs* (Philomel Books, 1988): This beautifully illustrated book highlights the Ukrainian/Russian tradition of decorating Easter eggs.
- *Babushka's Doll* (Simon and Schuster Books For Young Readers, 1990): A demanding grandchild is given a doll to play with by her patient *babushka* (grandmother). The doll comes to life and teaches the naughty girl a valuable lesson.
- *Babushka Baba Yaga* (Philomel Books, 1993): In Russian folklore, Baba Yaga is an evil witch who lives in the forest. Polacco gives this traditional character a new twist in a touching story about the danger of rumors.

The Commonwealth Of Independent States (CIS)

After the Soviet Union broke up, 11 of the 15 former republics agreed to join together and form the Commonwealth of Independent States. Look at a current atlas or world map. Add the items listed below to the CIS map.

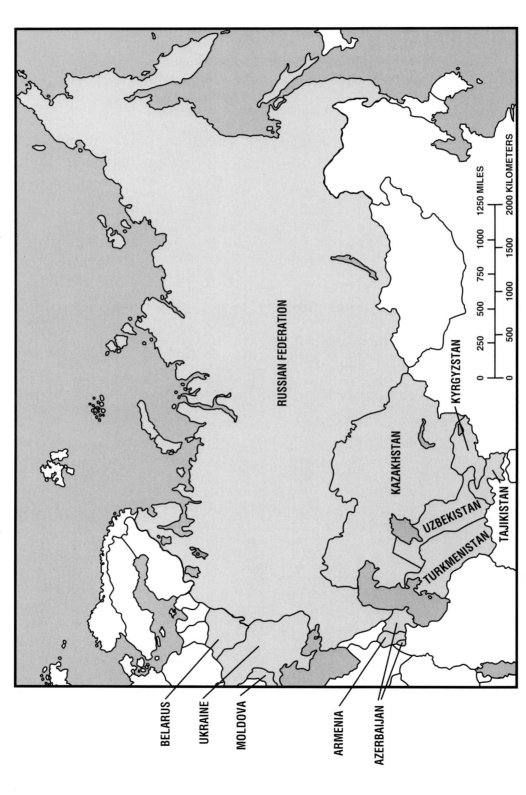

- **Label these bodies of water:** Aral Sea, Caspian Sea, Lake Baikal, Barents Sea, Sea of Okhotsk, Black Sea, Baltic Sea.

- **Label the four former republics of the USSR that did not join the CIS:** Estonia, Latvia, Lithuania, Georgia.

©The Education Center, Inc. • *THE MAILBOX*® • *Intermediate* • Feb/Mar 1996 • Key p. 312

Note To The Teacher: Use this map (current as of September 1995) to familiarize students with the locations, relative sizes, and other features of CIS countries.

Fast Facts About The CIS

The Commonwealth of Independent States (CIS) is a huge confederation of countries that used to be part of the old Soviet Union. Get your hands on some fast facts about these countries with the help of this chart.

Country	Population	Area In Square Miles	Capital City	Main Industries	Date Declared Independence
Armenia	3,293,000	11,500	Yerevan	agriculture, manufacturing	September 23, 1991
Azerbaijan	7,081,000	33,400	Baku	oil	August 30, 1991
Belarus	10,259,000	80,151	Minsk	dairy products, electrical appliances	August 25, 1991
Kazakhstan	16,691,000	1,049,155	Alma-Ata	livestock, mining	Did not formally declare
Kyrgyzstan	4,367,000	76,641	Bishkek	livestock, mining	August 31, 1991
Moldova	4,362,000	13,000	Kishinev	grapes	August 27, 1991
Russia	148,041,000	6,592,812	Moscow	mining, livestock, machinery, textiles, grains	Did not formally declare
Tajikistan	5,248,000	55,251	Dushanbe	cotton	September 9, 1991
Turkmenistan	3,622,000	188,456	Ashkhabad	livestock, cotton	October 27, 1991
Ukraine	51,839,000	233,089	Kiev	grains, dairy products, electrical goods	August 24, 1991
Uzbekistan	20,322,000	172,700	Tashkent	cotton	August 31, 1991

©The Education Center, Inc. • THE MAILBOX® • Intermediate • Feb/Mar 1996

Note To The Teacher: Use with "Background: The Collapse Of The Soviet Union" on page 155 and "CIS Fact Sheet" on page 156. (*Facts are current as of September 1995.*)

Patterns
Use with "Nesting Boxes Research Project" on page 157.

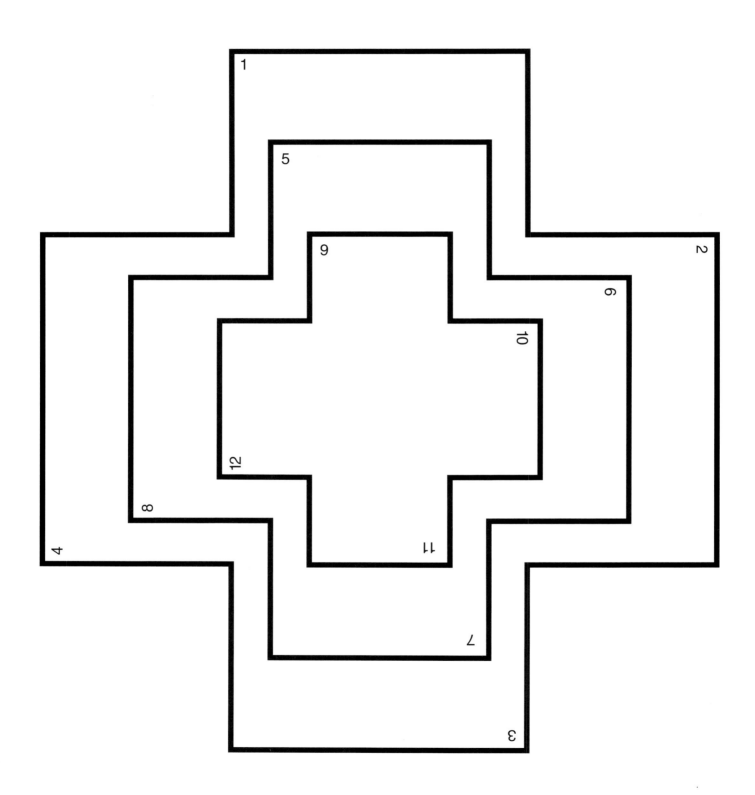

Getting A JUMP On Geography!

A Collection Of Our Subscribers' Favorite Geography Activities

Making and reading maps, identifying landforms, using latitude and longitude—all these skills and many more go together to make geography-smart students. The next time you're jumping to give your students a fun geography lesson, try one of the following teacher-tested ideas from our subscribers.

Globe Mobiles

Ask your local pizza parlor to help your students review geography basics by donating a supply of the cardboard circles used to line take-out boxes (one per student). Instruct the student to draw the Eastern Hemisphere of the earth on one side of his circle and the Western Hemisphere on the other. After the student has painted each side and let it dry, direct him to use fine-tipped permanent markers to add details to the hemispheres: continent borders, the equator, the two tropics, the oceans, the prime meridian, the international date line, the highest point on each continent, other major bodies of water, etc. Attach a length of heavy yarn to each circle. Then hang all the mobiles from your classroom ceiling for a colorful vista that's a reminder of basic geography facts. *Gloria Jean Stevens—Gr. 5, Frank Jewett Elementary, West Buxton, ME*

Take A Geography Cruise!

As part of our world geography study, I give each student a stamp from a foreign country and a copy of a cruise ship (see page 167). Each student adheres his stamp to the flag on his ship; then he researches his assigned country and fills out his ship pattern with the information. After cutting out his ship, the student mounts it around a world map posted on a large bulletin board. Then he uses a length of yarn to connect his ship to the country's location on the map. This is a great activity to do around National Stamp Collecting Day (November 2). *Kimberly Schwieren-VanHise—Grs. 4–6 Blended, Hines Elementary, Burns, OR*

Hometown Map

For a unique geography homework assignment, have each student choose one spot in your town. Direct the student to create a map that shows a visitor how to get from the student's house to that location. Inform students that the route must be the simplest and most direct way possible. Encourage students to add details that will help someone unfamiliar with your town to read their maps and find the special locations. Involve parents by asking them to help their child figure the mileage of his map's route. *Ruth Howell—Gr. 4, Carlisle Elementary, Spartanburg, SC*

163

Oui, Oui, mademoiselle! That is correct!

FRANCE
by
Simone Lepine

Country Wheels

Promote the sharing of newly learned information while your students travel the globe with this tactile research project. To begin, work together as a class to list ten questions that someone could research about a foreign country. Some suggestions include: "What type of government does this country have? In what continent is this country located? What are the major ethnic groups represented in this country? What is the size of the country in square miles?" List the questions on a piece of chart paper and display it in the classroom. Next have each student choose a country to research in order to answer the ten questions. Encourage students to write their answers as short, concise statements. After students have finished researching, give each a copy of the pattern on page 168. Provide stencils of the cover (see the directions for making them, below).

After students have made their wheels, let them swap and share them. Or put all the wheels in a special box at a center so that students can read them during free time. *Simone Lepine—Gr. 5, Syracuse, NY*

Making cover stencils:
1. Trace the inside circle of the wheel (page 168) on tracing paper. Trace only one pie-shaped piece.
2. Draw a line across the tip of the "pie wedge" right before the number so that the number will still show (see the illustration).
3. Cut out the tracing. Use this outline to make several cardboard stencils of the cover.
4. Place the stencils, a supply of tagboard, scissors, and brads (one per child) at a table. Let students visit the table when they're ready to make their wheel covers.

Latitude And Longitude Cards

When it's time to introduce latitude and longitude to your students, provide them with this handy tool. Have each child copy the diagram as shown on a small index card. Tape each student's card to his desktop as a ready reference to use during lessons on latitude and longitude. *Karen Bryant, Rosa Taylor Elementary, Macon, GA*

Latitude/Longitude Rhyme

Trying to keep latitude and longitude straight can frustrate even the most able student. Before a recent map skills test, one of my social-studies classes wrote the poem on the right to help everyone remember the basic facts about latitude and longitude. *Gaylin Black—Gr. 4, Frontier Elementary, Angleton, TX*

latitude
longitude

Latitude lines run east and west,
But measure north and south.
If you learn these parallels,
You'll know what they're about!

Longitude lines run north and south,
But measure east and west.
Learn all about meridians
And you will pass the test!

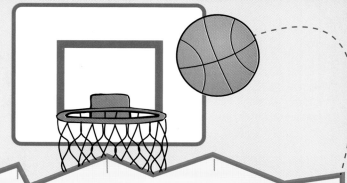

Pro Sports And Geography

During the fall, I type a list of all the professional football teams and give each student a copy. Students are challenged to locate each pro football city on a map and then write its latitude and longitude coordinates beside the city's name on the list. In the spring I repeat the activity as a review, using the names of professional basketball teams. What a great way to use a topic kids love to review map skills! *Dawn Carmack, Munford Middle School, Munford, TN*

Cookie Elevation Maps

Bet your students will take more than one bite of this yummy geography project! Purchase a U.S.-shaped cookie cutter. After studying about elevation, give each student a portion of refrigerated sugar-cookie dough (the amount will depend on the size of your cookie cutter). Have the student use a rolling pin to roll out the dough on waxed paper. Next have her cut the shape with the cookie cutter, and then use extra dough to add mountain ranges such as the Rockies and the Great Smoky Mountains. Prepare yellow, green, and orange edible paint using the recipe that follows; then have each student paint her cookie to indicate areas of low, medium, and high elevations. Sprinkle the cookies with a light dusting of sugar before baking them. *Karen Brown—Gr. 4, Hamilton-Parsons Elementary, Romeo, MI*

Egg Yolk Paint

Combine one egg yolk with 1/4 tsp. of water. Add food coloring to make the desired color. Paint on with a paintbrush.

Take Along A Travelmate!

All it took to get my students excited about geography was a collection of stuffed animals we called Travelmates. I placed each animal into a student-sized backpack, along with a supply of preprinted return labels and a logbook. Our Travelmates tag along with parents on business trips, students visiting Grandma's, and anywhere there is a traveler willing to let a Travelmate tag along. A Travelmate host is asked to complete a page in the logbook and send our class a postcard or photo showing where the Travelmate is vacationing. If a student is hosting a Travelmate, he gives an oral report about his trip when he returns. Our class keeps a Travelmates scrapbook that includes both world and U.S. maps. After receiving information about a Travelmate's trip, we color in the location on a map and add any souvenirs the stuffed critter brought back to the scrapbook. *Maxine Pincott—Gr. 4, Oliver Ellsworth School, Windsor, CT*

Log entry #1:
Tour Guide: Bruce Saunders
Occupation: Hotel Manager
Home Address: Summerfield, NC
Dates: April 6–April 10
Destination: Puerto Rico
Weather: Hot and humid
Transportation: Airplane and taxi
Experiences: Played golf, went scuba diving, toured old San Juan, saw a pirate ship

It's A Wonderful Day In The Neighborhood

To reinforce the concepts of cardinal directions, intermediate directions, and using a map key, draw a simple neighborhood map on a transparency or bulletin board. Mark the streets, stores, buildings, parks, and other elements on the map with labels that use the names of your students. Make sure each student is represented in this mythical neighborhood.

Once the map has been completed, create a set of question cards based on the map. For example: "Billy is going to Amy Walker Park to play basketball. If Billy leaves from Baxter's Shoe Store, in which direction will he travel to get to the park? Name the streets on which Billy will travel." Give each group several cards to answer. Or challenge students with a question anytime you have a few extra minutes to fill. *Jeffrey J. Kuntz—Gr. 4 Social Studies, West End Elementary, Punxsutawney, PA*

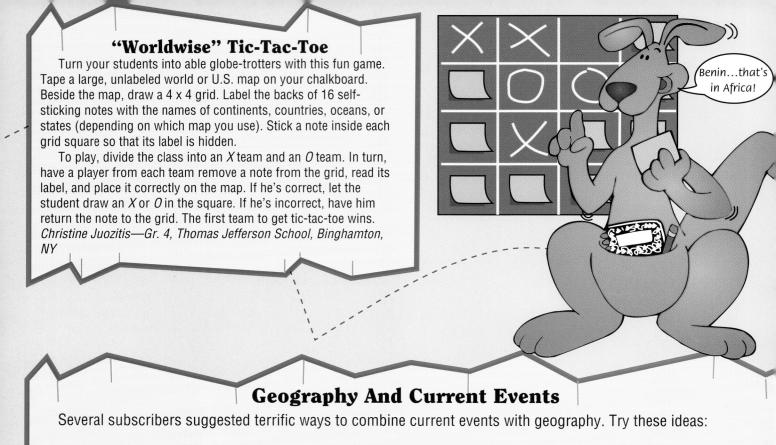

"Worldwise" Tic-Tac-Toe

Turn your students into able globe-trotters with this fun game. Tape a large, unlabeled world or U.S. map on your chalkboard. Beside the map, draw a 4 x 4 grid. Label the backs of 16 self-sticking notes with the names of continents, countries, oceans, or states (depending on which map you use). Stick a note inside each grid square so that its label is hidden.

To play, divide the class into an *X* team and an *O* team. In turn, have a player from each team remove a note from the grid, read its label, and place it correctly on the map. If he's correct, let the student draw an *X* or *O* in the square. If he's incorrect, have him return the note to the grid. The first team to get tic-tac-toe wins. *Christine Juozitis—Gr. 4, Thomas Jefferson School, Binghamton, NY*

Geography And Current Events

Several subscribers suggested terrific ways to combine current events with geography. Try these ideas:

Yearlong Current Events Maps

At the beginning of the year, I give each of my students a blank world map. Every Wednesday we meet in groups to discuss news articles. As one group member summarizes his article, each of his teammates uses a marker to draw a star on his map indicating where the event took place. At the beginning of a new marking period, we all change and use a different color of marker. By the end of the year, we've traveled the globe—and gained a new understanding of current events! *Karen Scro—Gr. 6, Washington Irving School, Garfield, NY*

Where In The USA?

For a terrific interactive display, mount a U.S. map in the middle of a bulletin board. Periodically have each student bring a news article to class along with a summary written on a small index card. Have students staple their articles and summaries around the map; then have them connect the articles to the correct locations on the map using lengths of yarn. Change the theme of the board every six weeks to cover different maps (Europe, Asia, Latin America, etc.) or types of articles (football news, world capitals, etc.). Award ten extra-credit points to each student who contributes to the display. *Dawn Carmack, Munford Middle School, Munford, TN*

Short Clips

Clip short (one- or two-paragraph) articles from the daily newspaper. Tape each article to a colorful index card; then give a card to each group. Direct the group to spend ten minutes reading the article, discussing it, and finding its location on a world map. After the ten minutes is up, have a representative from each group summarize the article for the class and point out its location on the map. Have each group label a sticky note with the name of the location, then place it on the map. *Beverly Sharpe—Gr. 5, Thornton Elementary, Littleton, CO*

Keeping Current

For one week, have students collect and read newspaper articles on events happening outside the United States. Direct students to summarize each article and then write a new headline for it. Have students post their new headlines around a world map mounted on a bulletin board. Then have them use yarn to connect the articles to the correct locations on the map. *Mary Gates, New Milford, CT*

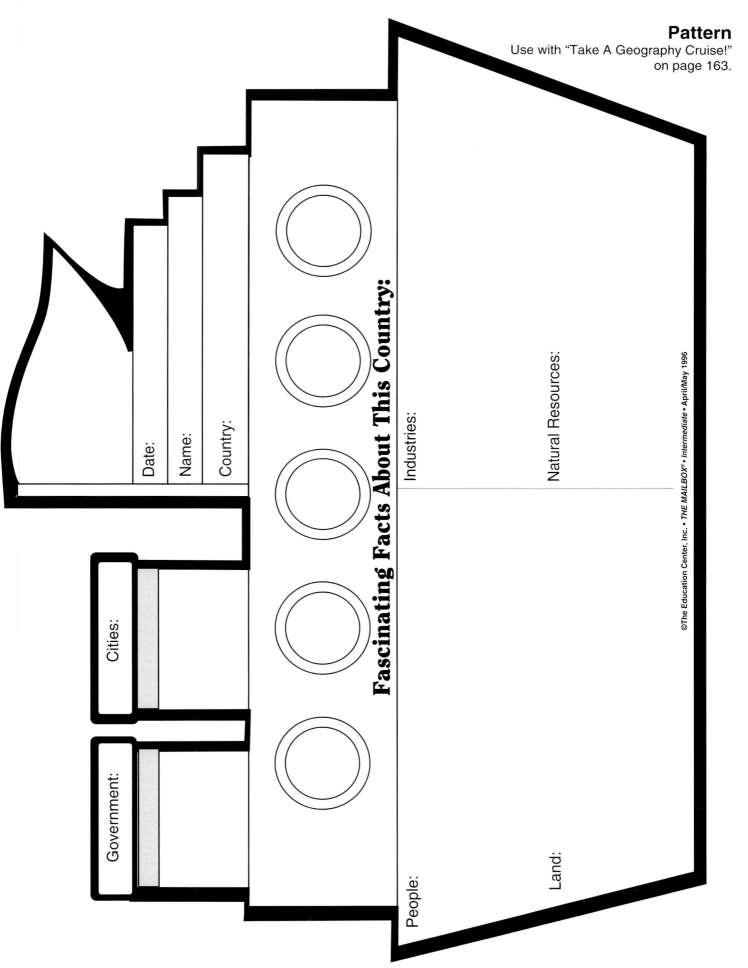

Date:

Name:

Country:

Cities:

Government:

Fascinating Facts About This Country:

Industries:

Natural Resources:

People:

Land:

©The Education Center, Inc. • *THE MAILBOX® • Intermediate •* April/May 1996

A Country Wheel

Directions:

1. Cut out the wheel and glue it to a piece of tagboard; then cut out the wheel again.
2. In the outer, smaller section labeled 1, write research question number 1.
3. In the pie-shaped section that is numbered 1, write the answer to question 1.
4. Continue writing questions and answers in this manner until the entire wheel is complete.
5. Use a stencil provided by your teacher to make a cover for your wheel.
6. Decorate the cover with the name of your country, your name, and small illustrations.
7. Place the cover on top of your wheel so that the centers are aligned. Use a straight pin to poke a hole in the center of the cover and wheel.
8. Push a brad through the pinholes to attach the cover to the wheel.
9. Swap your wheel with a partner, and get ready to learn about another country!

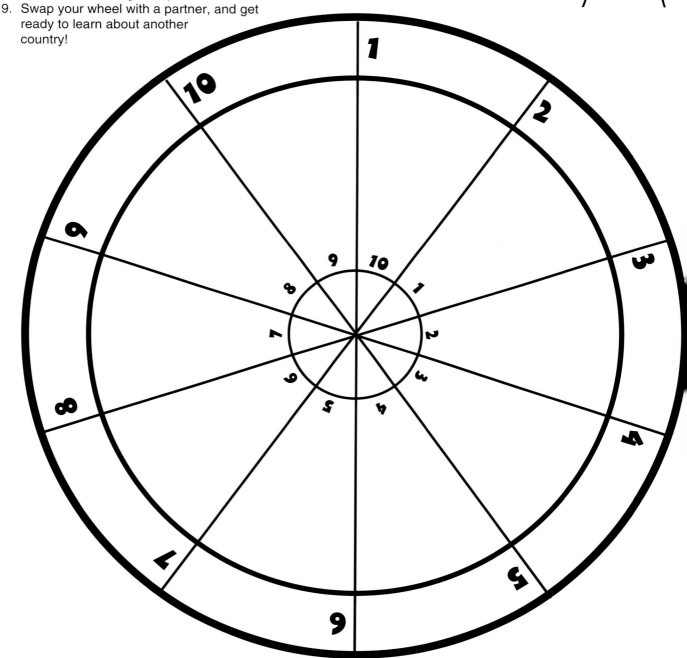

Note To The Teacher: Use with "Country Wheels" on page 164.

SCIENCE UNITS

Using Journals In Science

Leonardo da Vinci was one of the most gifted inventors and artists the world has ever known. Today we know about his ideas because he recorded much of what he saw and thought in his notebooks. His notebooks ranged from ones as large as wall posters to some that were small enough to carry on his belt. Some of Leonardo's notebooks have survived to this day. They're filled with lines and lines of neat print—written from right to left—along with numerous drawings and diagrams.

Journaling in science helps students reflect on skills they've learned, and creates orderly notes for later study. Use the suggestions below and the reproducible on page 171 to get your budding scientists into journaling.

by Irving P. Crump

Getting Started

Reproduce one copy of the journal cover (the top half of page 171) for each student. Have students color and decorate their covers; then have them cut lined paper the same size as the cover to make pages for their journals. Instruct each student to punch a hole in the top left corner of the cover and each journal page, then bind all of the pages behind the cover with a brad or ring. Make a journal for each major topic of study throughout the year.

Suggestions For Using Science Journals

Science Experiences:

Provide each student with a copy of the form on the bottom half of page 171 to complete after a science experiment or laboratory activity, a nature walk, or a field trip. Have the student follow the directions on the page, then add the completed page to his journal.

Free Writing:

Have students write about any aspect of a science or health topic of their choice. Let them express their opinions about a person, an event, or a thing. Anything goes!

Current Events:

Have students bring in magazine and newspaper articles dealing with science subjects. Share an article; then have students react to it in their journals.

Question Of The Day:

On the board write a question that relates to a topic you're studying, a news item, or a science-related subject. Examples: "Would you like to be a paleontologist? How would your family adjust if there were a gasoline shortage? What's the greatest environmental problem facing our community?" Have students respond to the question in their journals.

Vocabulary Words:

Have students write science words and their definitions in their journals.

Lists:

Have students list important facts, causes and effects of events, or statements comparing and contrasting the characteristics of objects or events. Examples: "List the characteristics of mammals. Compare and contrast tornadoes with hurricanes. List some of Leonardo da Vinci's ideas that have become realities in the past 300 years."

Observation Skills:

Have students observe an object or event over a period of time and record their observations. Examples: "Observe and record weather patterns for one month. Observe the growth of two plants: one that is fertilized and one that is not."

Writing From Another Perspective:

Have students write about an event from a different perspective. Examples: "Write about an oil spill from the perspective of a seal. How does a deer family feel about suburbs encroaching on its woodland home? How does a furniture manufacturer feel about a ban on the import of mahogany?"

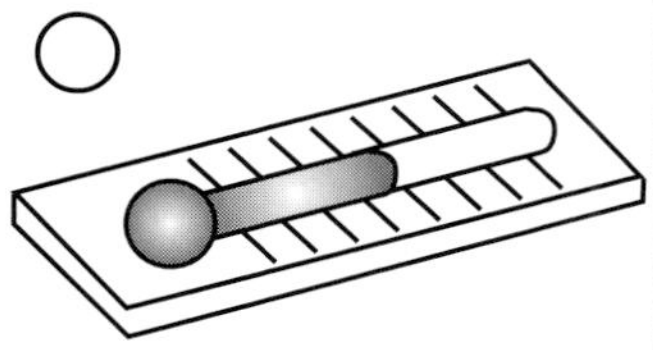
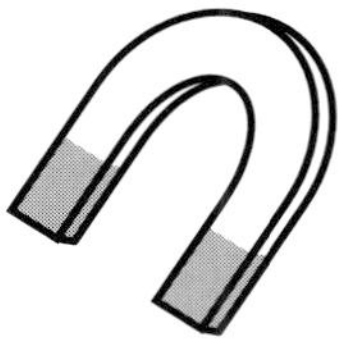
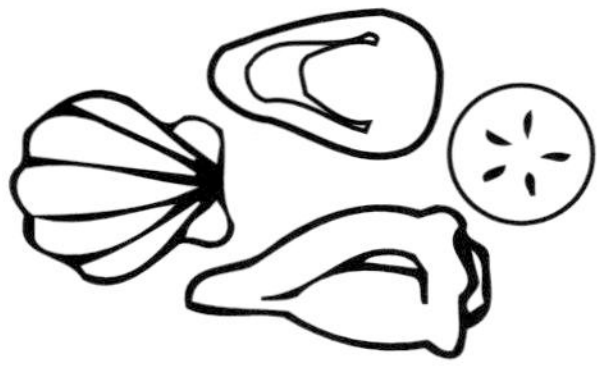
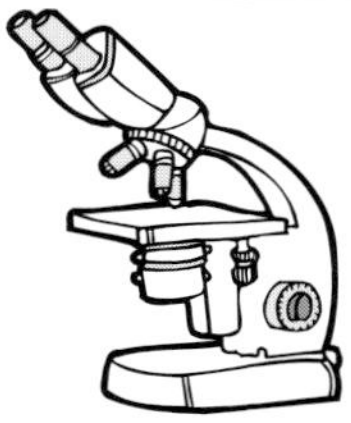
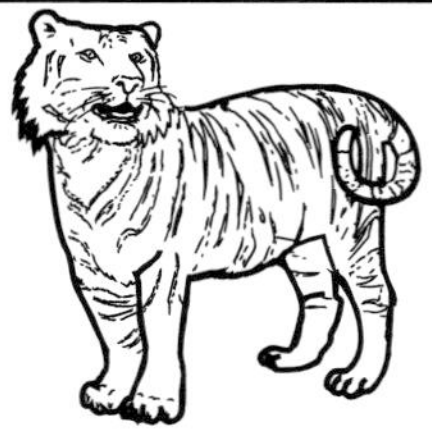

My Science Journal

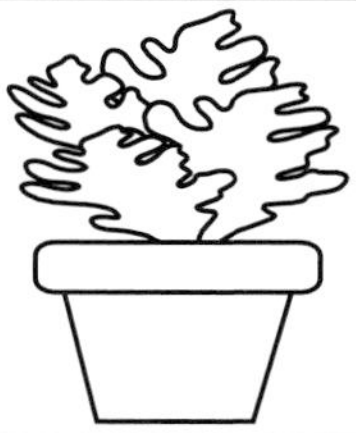
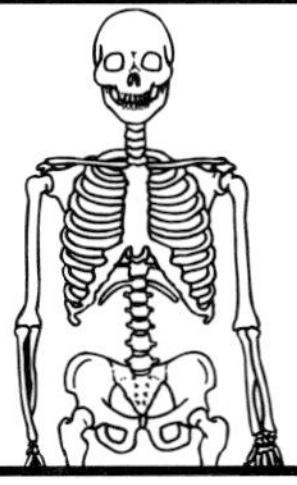
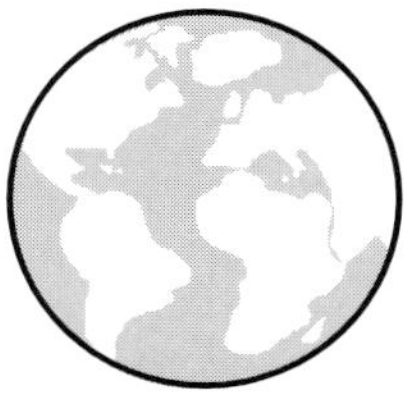

____

name

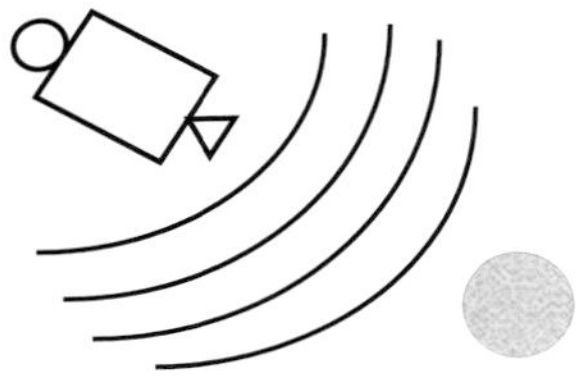
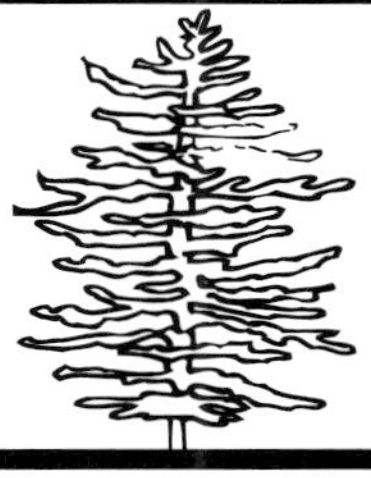
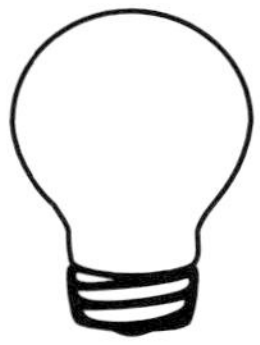
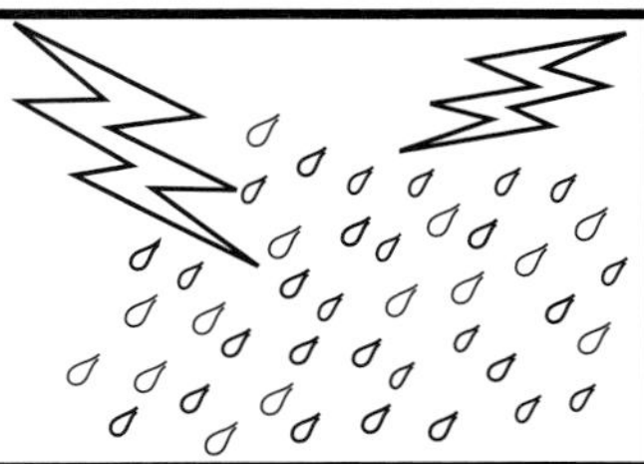

name ______________________________ date _______________

____

science experience

1. Briefly describe the experience: ______________________________

2. What special materials, if any, were used? ______________________________

3. Write a sentence describing something new you learned. ______________________________

4. In the space below, draw a diagram or picture that would help you describe this science experience to a friend.

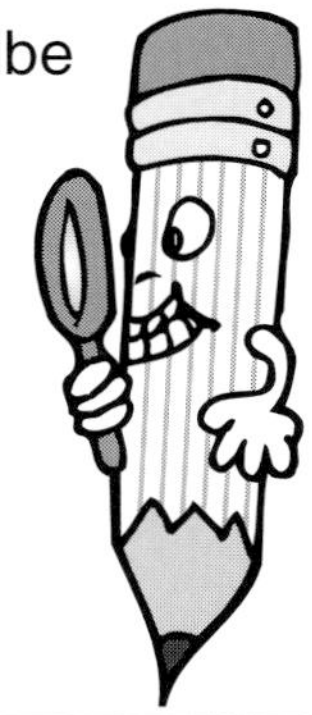

©The Education Center, Inc. • *THE MAILBOX*® • *Intermediate* • Aug/Sept 1995

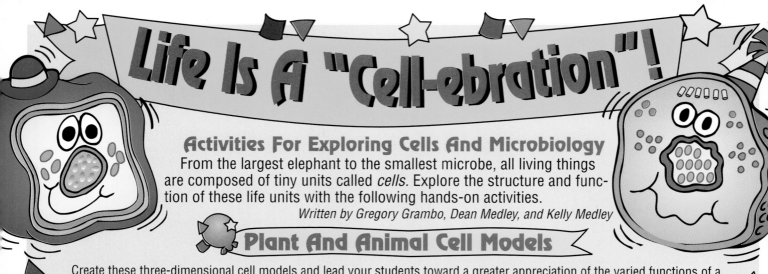

Life Is A "Cell-ebration"!

Activities For Exploring Cells And Microbiology

From the largest elephant to the smallest microbe, all living things are composed of tiny units called *cells*. Explore the structure and function of these life units with the following hands-on activities.

Written by Gregory Grambo, Dean Medley, and Kelly Medley

Plant And Animal Cell Models

Create these three-dimensional cell models and lead your students toward a greater appreciation of the varied functions of a single cell.

Materials:
- 1 shoebox, without lid
- 2 one-gallon zippered plastic bags
- 2 bunches green grapes
- 8 cups clear gelatin
- 30 jelly beans
- 2 Ping-Pong balls
- 2 tangerines
- 4 tablespoons candy sprinkles
- 2 plastic straws
- glue
- 2 paper plates
- scissors

Cell Structures Represented And Their Functions

cell wall: nonliving structure surrounding plant cell; provides shape and support
cell membrane: encloses the cell, controlling the inward and outward flow of materials
chloroplasts: contain chlorophyll, used by plants to make food
cytoplasm: jellylike material where chemical processes take place
mitochondria: rodlike structures that control the release of energy in cell processes
vacuoles: fluid-filled sacs that store different substances in liquid form
nucleus: contains DNA; stores information used to control cell activities
ribosomes: particles in cytoplasm that build the proteins needed by a cell
endoplasmic reticulum (ER): membranes that run throughout the cytoplasm; form tubes through which materials move to all cell parts

Before class: Construct the endoplasmic reticulum by putting glue in one paper plate and the sprinkles in another. Roll both straws in the glue and then in the sprinkles. After the straws dry, cut them into one-inch pieces.

Building the plant cell model:

1. Remind students that a plant cell has both a *cell wall* and a *cell membrane* (unlike the animal cell, which has only the cell membrane). These structures contain all the other parts of the cell. Line a shoebox with a plastic bag. Explain that the shoebox represents the rigid cell wall, while the plastic bag represents the cell membrane. Explain the function of each additional part (steps 2–7) as you add it to the model.
2. Add four cups of the gelatin *(cytoplasm)* to the bag.
3. Scatter 15 of the jelly beans *(mitochondria)* throughout the gelatin.
4. Place a Ping-Pong ball *(vacuole)* to one side in the gelatin.
5. Put a tangerine *(nucleus)* in the center of the bag.
6. Scatter half of the sprinkle-covered straw sections *(endoplasmic reticulum and ribosomes)* throughout the gelatin.
7. Position the grapes *(chloroplasts)* throughout the gelatin.

Building the animal cell model:

Use the same materials and steps as in the plant cell model with the following exceptions:

- Animal cells have no cell wall. Eliminate the shoebox.
- Animals do not produce their own food through photosynthesis. Do not include the chloroplasts (grapes).

After building the models: Have students compare the two models. Help them notice that the models are basically the same, except for the cell wall and chloroplasts.

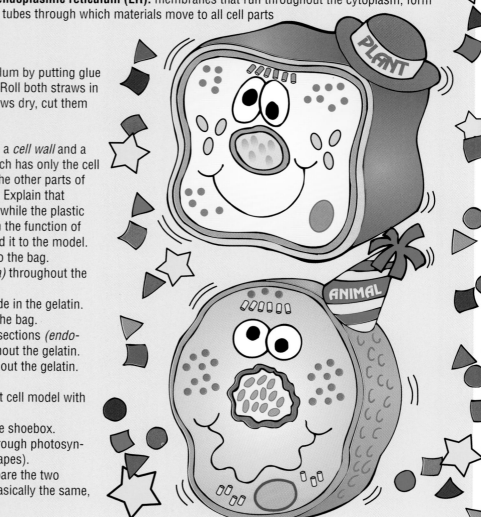

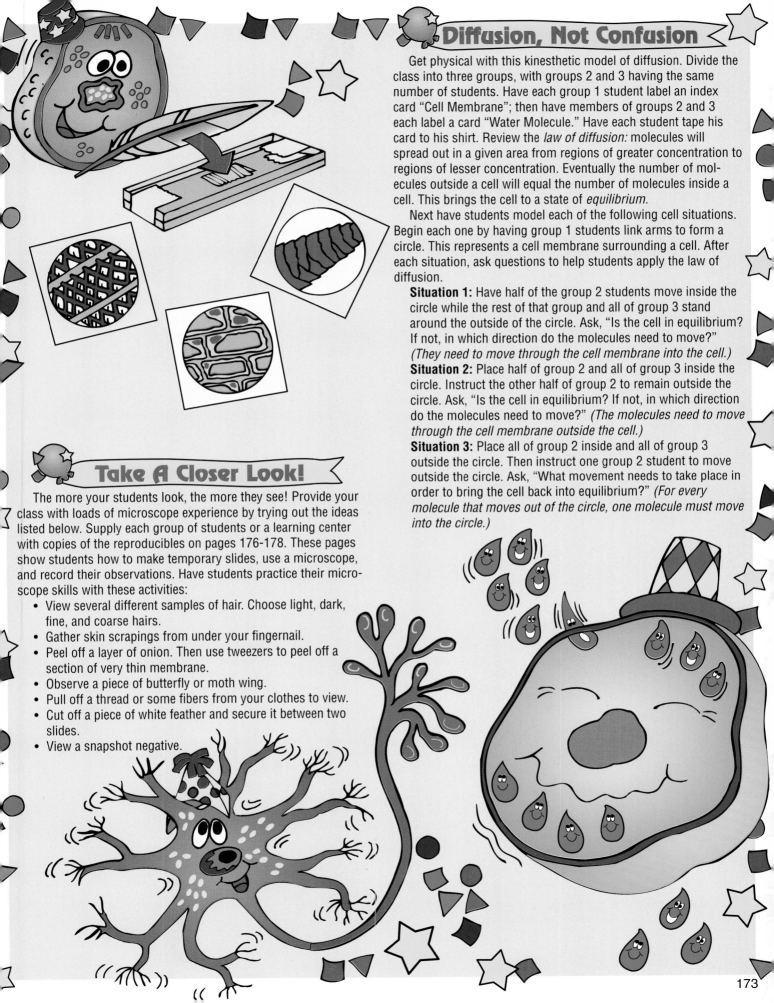

Diffusion, Not Confusion

Get physical with this kinesthetic model of diffusion. Divide the class into three groups, with groups 2 and 3 having the same number of students. Have each group 1 student label an index card "Cell Membrane"; then have members of groups 2 and 3 each label a card "Water Molecule." Have each student tape his card to his shirt. Review the *law of diffusion:* molecules will spread out in a given area from regions of greater concentration to regions of lesser concentration. Eventually the number of molecules outside a cell will equal the number of molecules inside a cell. This brings the cell to a state of *equilibrium.*

Next have students model each of the following cell situations. Begin each one by having group 1 students link arms to form a circle. This represents a cell membrane surrounding a cell. After each situation, ask questions to help students apply the law of diffusion.

Situation 1: Have half of the group 2 students move inside the circle while the rest of that group and all of group 3 stand around the outside of the circle. Ask, "Is the cell in equilibrium? If not, in which direction do the molecules need to move?" *(They need to move through the cell membrane into the cell.)*

Situation 2: Place half of group 2 and all of group 3 inside the circle. Instruct the other half of group 2 to remain outside the circle. Ask, "Is the cell in equilibrium? If not, in which direction do the molecules need to move?" *(The molecules need to move through the cell membrane outside the cell.)*

Situation 3: Place all of group 2 inside and all of group 3 outside the circle. Then instruct one group 2 student to move outside the circle. Ask, "What movement needs to take place in order to bring the cell back into equilibrium?" *(For every molecule that moves out of the circle, one molecule must move into the circle.)*

Take A Closer Look!

The more your students look, the more they see! Provide your class with loads of microscope experience by trying out the ideas listed below. Supply each group of students or a learning center with copies of the reproducibles on pages 176-178. These pages show students how to make temporary slides, use a microscope, and record their observations. Have students practice their microscope skills with these activities:

- View several different samples of hair. Choose light, dark, fine, and coarse hairs.
- Gather skin scrapings from under your fingernail.
- Peel off a layer of onion. Then use tweezers to peel off a section of very thin membrane.
- Observe a piece of butterfly or moth wing.
- Pull off a thread or some fibers from your clothes to view.
- Cut off a piece of white feather and secure it between two slides.
- View a snapshot negative.

Demonstrating Diffusion

Amaze your students with this demonstration of a cell membrane's ability to allow only certain molecules to enter the cell.

Materials:

test tube
water
index card
iodine
dialysis tubing (available from a science supply store)

eyedropper
empty jar
rubber band
scissors
soluble potato starch (1 g starch/100 ml water) —available from a science supply store

Directions:

1. Fill the jar with water.
2. Add a few drops of iodine to the water until the water is yellow in color.
3. Using the scissors, cut a small *x* in the center of the index card.

4. Fill the test tube with the starch solution.
5. Cover the opening of the test tube with the dialysis tubing; then secure the tubing with a rubber band.
6. Place the test tube through the opening in the index card as shown.

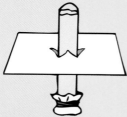

7. Place the test tube in the jar as shown.

8. Set the jar aside until the next day. Observe and discuss changes with students.

Diffusion is the spreading out of molecules in a given area from a region of greater concentration to a region of lesser concentration. Dialysis tubing is semipermeable like the cell membrane. Large particles, like starch, cannot pass through the tubing. However, small particles—like iodine—can. The iodine that passes through the dialysis tubing mixes with the starch in the tube, turning the liquid black. As more iodine enters the tube, the water in the jar will become clear.

Literature Connection

These books on cells and microbiology are worth a closer look.

The World Of The Microscope by Chris Oxlade and Corinne Stockley (Scholastic Inc.)
Atoms And Cells by Lionel Bender (Scholastic Inc.)
Cells Are Us and *Cell Wars* by Dr. Fran Balkwill (Carolrhoda Books, Inc.)
Mysterious Microbes by Steve Parker (Raintree Steck-Vaughn Publishers)
From the **DISCOVER HIDDEN WORLDS** series (Western Publishing Company, Inc.):
   The Home by Heather Amery and Jane Songi
   Nature by Heather Amery

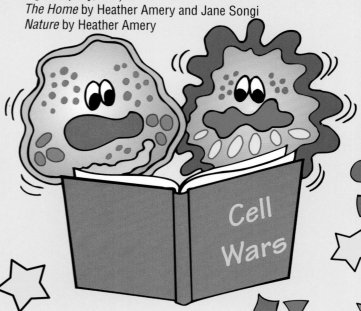

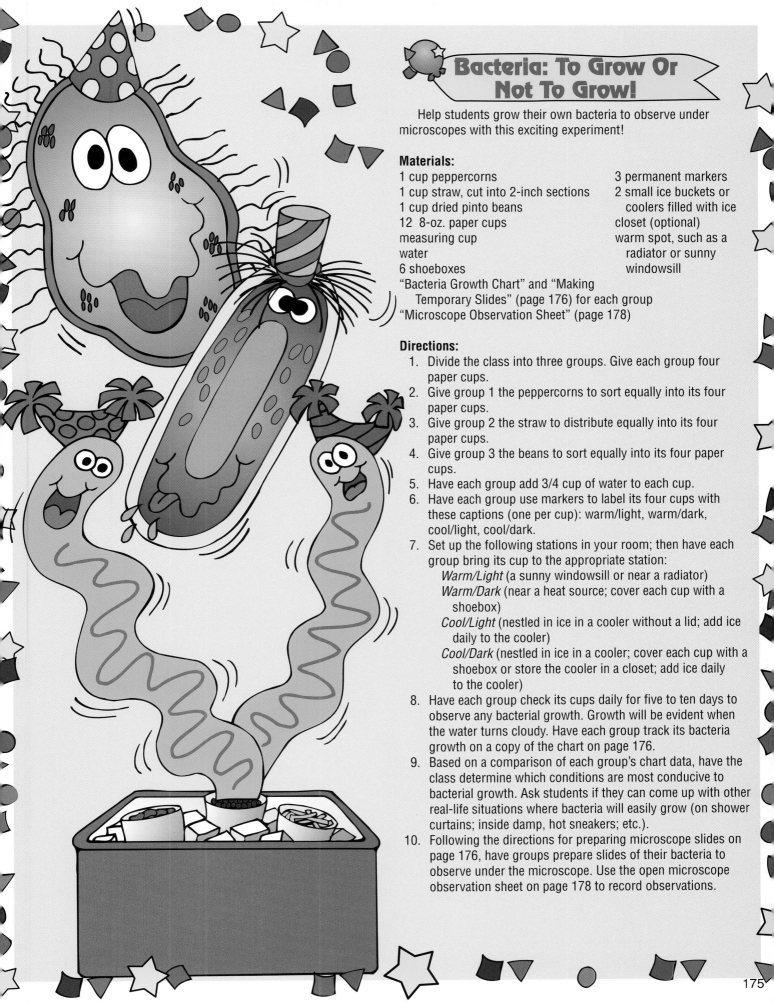

Bacteria: To Grow Or Not To Grow!

Help students grow their own bacteria to observe under microscopes with this exciting experiment!

Materials:

1 cup peppercorns
1 cup straw, cut into 2-inch sections
1 cup dried pinto beans
12 8-oz. paper cups
measuring cup
water
6 shoeboxes
"Bacteria Growth Chart" and "Making
   Temporary Slides" (page 176) for each group
"Microscope Observation Sheet" (page 178)

3 permanent markers
2 small ice buckets or
   coolers filled with ice
closet (optional)
warm spot, such as a
   radiator or sunny
   windowsill

Directions:

1. Divide the class into three groups. Give each group four paper cups.
2. Give group 1 the peppercorns to sort equally into its four paper cups.
3. Give group 2 the straw to distribute equally into its four paper cups.
4. Give group 3 the beans to sort equally into its four paper cups.
5. Have each group add 3/4 cup of water to each cup.
6. Have each group use markers to label its four cups with these captions (one per cup): warm/light, warm/dark, cool/light, cool/dark.
7. Set up the following stations in your room; then have each group bring its cup to the appropriate station:
   Warm/Light (a sunny windowsill or near a radiator)
   Warm/Dark (near a heat source; cover each cup with a shoebox)
   Cool/Light (nestled in ice in a cooler without a lid; add ice daily to the cooler)
   Cool/Dark (nestled in ice in a cooler; cover each cup with a shoebox or store the cooler in a closet; add ice daily to the cooler)
8. Have each group check its cups daily for five to ten days to observe any bacterial growth. Growth will be evident when the water turns cloudy. Have each group track its bacteria growth on a copy of the chart on page 176.
9. Based on a comparison of each group's chart data, have the class determine which conditions are most conducive to bacterial growth. Ask students if they can come up with other real-life situations where bacteria will easily grow (on shower curtains; inside damp, hot sneakers; etc.).
10. Following the directions for preparing microscope slides on page 176, have groups prepare slides of their bacteria to observe under the microscope. Use the open microscope observation sheet on page 178 to record observations.

Making Temporary Slides

Many specimens can be examined using temporary slides. These slides are considered temporary because after a while, the water used evaporates and the material decays.

Materials: slides and coverslips, tweezers, eyedropper, water, specimens

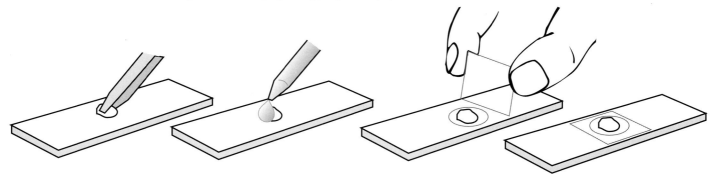

1. Place the specimen in the center of the slide.

2. Cover it with a drop of water.

3. Holding a coverslip by its side edges, place the bottom edge on the slide near the water drop.

4. Carefully lower the coverslip onto the specimen.

Clean slides and coverslips in warm water that contains a little dish detergent. Handle each slide by its sides. To dry a slide, stand it up at an angle on a dry paper towel. Let its upper end rest against a clean jar. Then soak the slide in rubbing alcohol to sterilize it. Allow the slide to dry completely before storing it.

Name(s) _____ Observation chart

Bacteria Growth Chart

Circle the specimen your group is observing: peppercorns   straw   pinto beans
Chart the growth of bacteria by noting whether the water is clear, cloudy, or colored. Also note any odors and/or other characteristics of the water.

	Day 1	Day 2	Day 3	Day 4	Day 5	Day 6	Day 7	Day 8	Day 9	Day 10
Warm/ Light										
Warm/ Dark										
Cool/ Light										
Cool/ Dark										

Based on your observations, which condition was best for growing bacteria? _____

_____

Note To The Teacher: Use "Making Temporary Slides" with "Take A Closer Look!" on page 173 and "Bacteria: To Grow Or Not To Grow!" on page 175. Use the "Bacteria Growth Chart" with "Bacteria: To Grow Or Not To Grow!" on page 175.

Name _____

How To Use A Simple Compound Microscope

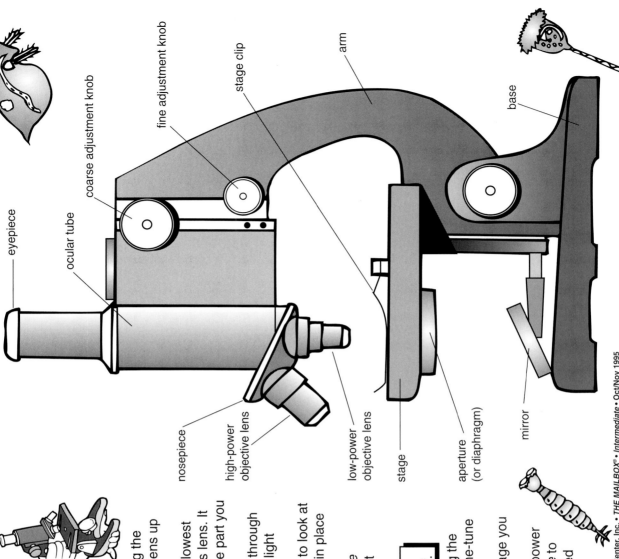

eyepiece

ocular tube

coarse adjustment knob

fine adjustment knob

stage clip

arm

base

nosepiece

high-power objective lens

low-power objective lens

stage

aperture (or diaphragm)

mirror

1. Handle with care! When carrying the microscope, grasp the *arm* with one hand while supporting the *base* with the other.

2. Position the microscope on a steady table near a good source of light. If possible, tilt the *ocular tube* so that you can get a clear view through the microscope without leaning over the *eyepiece.*

3. While looking at the microscope from the side, practice turning the *coarse* and *fine adjustment knobs* to see how they move the lens up and down. Raise the lens as far as possible.

4. Turn the *objective lenses* so that the microscope is set at the lowest power (probably 10X). Always start your observations with this lens. It allows you to see more of the object so that you can locate the part you want to observe more closely.

5. If the microscope has an *aperture,* open it fully. While looking through the eyepiece, tilt the *mirror* to reflect the maximum amount of light through the lens. You should see a white circle.

6. Place a prepared slide on the *stage* so that the part you want to look at is positioned over the hole and under the lens. Hold the slide in place with the *stage clips.*

7. While looking at the microscope from the side, turn the *coarse adjustment knob* to bring the lens down very close to—but not touching—the slide.

   **Never lower the lens while looking through the eyepiece. You could hit the slide, breaking it or breaking the lens itself.

8. Looking through the eyepiece, slowly raise the lens by turning the coarse adjustment knob. After the object comes into focus, fine-tune the picture by slowly turning the *fine adjustment knob.*

9. Slowly move the slide around until you find the part of the image you wish to observe.

10. To look at the image in more detail, change to a higher-power objective lens. First raise the lenses. Turn the *nosepiece* to select the higher-power lens. Lower the lens as explained in step 7, and refocus as in step 8.

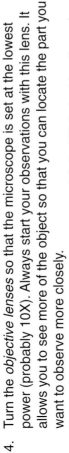

©The Education Center, Inc. • *THE MAILBOX®* • *Intermediate* • Oct/Nov 1995

Note To The Teacher: Use this page with "Take A Closer Look!" on page 173.

Microscope Observation Sheet

Draw the images you see through your microscope in the circles below. Don't forget to label each drawing with the name of the object, the date, and the lens power used.

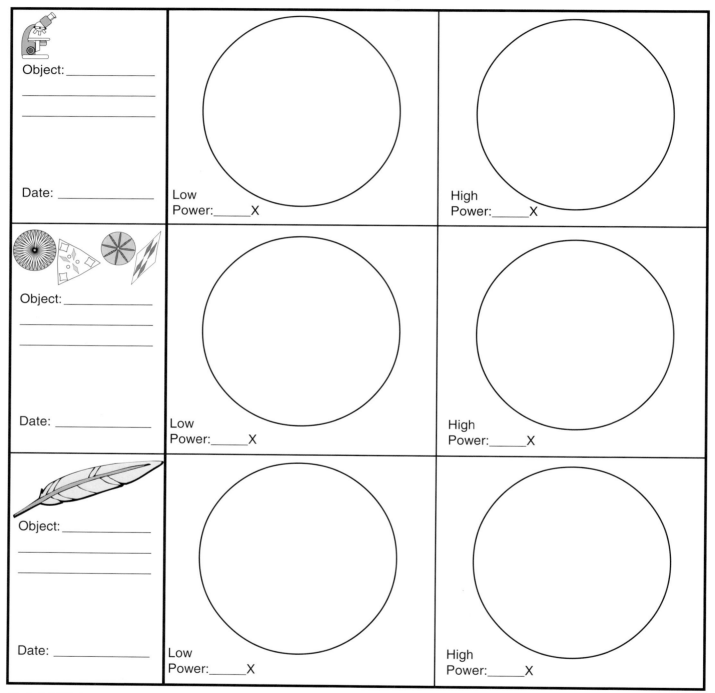

Helpful Hints:

- Look down the microscope with one eye and at your paper with the other.
- Use a sharp pencil when drawing. Give your drawing a title.
- Some objects are not transparent enough to be seen with bottom lighting (lighting reflected from the mirror under the stage). These objects need to be lit from above to see them in detail. To get the best top lighting, aim a lamp at the object on the stage. Move the lamp around to get the best lighting. Move the mirror so that no light comes up through the stage.

Note To The Teacher: Use this sheet with "Take A Closer Look!" on page 173, with "Bacteria: To Grow Or Not To Grow!" on page 175, or in other microscope experiences.

SPACE:

The Final "Fun-tier"

Thematic Activities On Space Exploration

Blast off into the study of space with the following
out-of-this-world activities!

by Christine A. Thuman

The Blue Planet

Although stars shine during the day, we have difficulty seeing them. Sunlight traveling to Earth reflects off the dust and water vapor in our atmosphere and prevents us from seeing all but the brightest planets at twilight. Simulate this effect with the following experiment.

Fill two identical glass jars with clear water. Dissolve a sliver of bar soap in one of the jars. Once the soap has dissolved, darken the room. Shine a flashlight horizontally through the jar filled with clean water. Note the color of the light as it passes through and out of the jar. Next shine the light through the soapy water. Again note the color of light as it passes through and out of the jar. What differences do you notice?

Light traveling through the soapy water bounces off the soap molecules. As a result, it is more difficult to see through the soapy water.

The Resource Connection

Enhance your space instruction with the following resource materials:

- **Literature:** Blast off to pages 186–187 for a review of outstanding books on space-related topics.
- **Solar System:** Check out the November/December/January 1995–96 issue of Grades 4–5 *Teacher's Helper*® magazine for an out-of-this-world unit on the solar system.
- **CD-ROM:** *Space Shuttle* (©1993) This interactive CD-ROM enables students to explore space-shuttle history, people, and missions. Macintosh® and Windows™ versions available. Contact: Mindscape, 60 Leveroni Court, Novato, CA 94949; 1-800-234-3088.
- **VHS:** *Astronomy 101* (©1994) An entertaining, 25-minute video that demonstrates how easy it is to study the night sky using binoculars, a telescope, and star charts. Contact: Mazon Productions, Inc.; P.O. Box 2427, Northbrook, IL 60065-2427; 1-800-332-4344.

Blast Off!

A rocket needs a lot of energy to leave Earth's atmosphere. The rocket's thrust of power comes from gases bursting from an exhaust opening at its base. Have student groups mimic this process using simple materials.

Materials for each group of students: long, skinny balloon; binder clip; tape; scissors; drinking straw; spool of thread; ruler
Directions:
1. Cut two 2-inch lengths of straw. String a long length of thread through the straw sections.
2. Blow up the balloon and close the end with the clip. Tape the straw sections to the balloon as shown.
3. Securely tape one end of the thread to a desk or heavy object near the floor.
4. Draw the thread taut and tape the other end securely to the top of a door frame.
5. After positioning the balloon so that it slopes upward, remove the clip and hold the end of the balloon tightly.
6. Let go of the balloon's end and watch your rocket fly!

binder clip

Star Twins

The next time you wish upon a star, you may actually be wishing on two stars! Some scientists believe that about half the stars in the universe may be double or *binary* stars. A binary star is actually a pair of stars that move around a common center. Binaries are usually so close together that you cannot see them as separate with the naked eye. Sometimes a small, brighter star is paired with a large, dimmer star. Viewed from Earth, this binary appears to blink or waver in brilliance depending upon which of the two stars is in front of, or *eclipsing,* the other. Demonstrate this concept using a tennis ball and a large, dark-colored beach ball. Tape each ball to the end of a different 12" piece of string. Tie the loose end of each string to an opposite end of a two-foot-long dowel. Tie another 12" length of string to the center of the dowel and balance the two balls like a mobile (see the illustration). As the class observes, rotate the two balls so that they take turns eclipsing each other. Discuss the following questions: When do you think the binary would appear the brightest? When would it appear the dimmest? What would this look like from Earth? What would it be like to live on a planet that revolves around a binary star system? Would you ever have a nighttime?

You Weigh How Much?

Looking for a quick weight loss program? Go live on the moon! Because the moon has less mass, its gravity is weaker than Earth's. As a result, objects on the moon weigh about one-sixth of what they weigh on Earth! Bite into this concept with the following tasty demonstration.

Materials for a class of 24 students: two packages of six presliced English muffins, 24 individually wrapped cheese slices, two 6-ounce jars of mild salsa, a bowl, two spoons, a toaster oven

Directions:

1. Before students arrive, remove five muffins from one package and set them aside. Close up this package. Next open one of the jars of salsa and spoon five-sixths of its contents into a bowl. Recap the jar.
2. Explain to students that objects on the moon weigh about one-sixth what they would on Earth. Invite a student to come to the front of the room and lift the opened muffin package in one hand while lifting the unopened package in the other hand. Have him compare the weight of the two packages and report his observations to the class.
3. Have two more students come up to the front of the classroom. Have one compare the weights of the opened and unopened jars of salsa. Have the other compare the weights of one cheese slice and six slices. Instruct both to report any observations.
4. Instruct every student to divide his own weight by six (rounding to the nearest pound) to discover how much he would weigh on the moon.
5. Finally celebrate this hypothetical weight loss by consuming man-on-the-moon muffins. Provide each student with a muffin half and a slice of cheese. Instruct each student to unwrap his cheese slice and carefully nibble off the corners to form it into a circle, and then place it on his muffin half. Pass around the salsa and spoons and have each student "shade" part of his moon muffin so that it resembles a particular stage of the moon (crescent, gibbous, half, or whole). If desired, have students toast their man-on-the-moon muffins before feasting on these lunar snacks!

Hey, you made crescent moons.

Pam Crane

How Far Is That Star?

Figuring out the distances of stars is as easy as a wink. The earth travels around the sun in an *elliptical,* or oval, path. When the earth is at one end of this ellipse, a scientist photographs the night sky. Six months later, when the earth reaches the other end of the ellipse, he photographs that same section of the sky. By comparing these two photographs, the scientist can spot any star that appears to have moved. The scientist measures this star's movement, or *parallax.* The closer a star is to Earth, the greater is its parallax.

To demonstrate this concept, paste 20 one-inch gold foil stars on different objects in the room; then have each student paste a star to the end of his right forefinger. Explain that the right eye represents the earth when it is at one end of its elliptical path, and the left eye represents the earth when it reaches the other end. Instruct each student to hold his star finger, pointing up, about a foot from his face. This placement of his finger represents a relatively close star. Closing his left eye, have him line up the star finger so that it covers one of the stars pasted around the room. Instruct him to open his left eye and close his right eye at the same time. His star finger will appear to move to the right. This movement represents the parallax of the star finger. Have him alternately wink his eyes several times to note the distance of the parallax.

Next have each student hold his star finger up at arm's length from his face. This represents a relatively distant star. Have him repeat the alternate winking procedure. Ask: "What differences did you notice in the movement of the star when it was held a foot away from your face and then at arm's length?" *(The student will notice that when the finger was held a foot from his face, its movement —or parallax—was greater than when the finger was held at arm's length. Stars that are closer to Earth have a larger parallax than more distant stars.)*

Death Star

What stellar spectacle inspires both dread and imagination? Why, a black hole, of course! Thought to be the result of a massive star's collapsed core, the gravitational pull of a black hole is so great that even light cannot travel fast enough to escape its clutches. Create a black hole model to demonstrate the pulling power of gravity. Stretch a piece of white, cottony material (like a piece of an old sheet) through a large embroidery hoop. Sprinkle a tablespoon of coffee granules in the center of the cloth. Turn on a vacuum cleaner; then hold its hose end under and near the very edge of the hoop. Making a small space between the vacuum cleaner hose and the fabric with your finger and thumb will cause the fabric to vibrate. The coffee granules will vibrate on the fabric and slowly be drawn toward the sucking vacuum hose. Similarly, a black hole attracts— but actually sucks up—nearby star fragments and gases. As a follow-up, have each student write a story describing what she thinks lies at the center of a black hole.

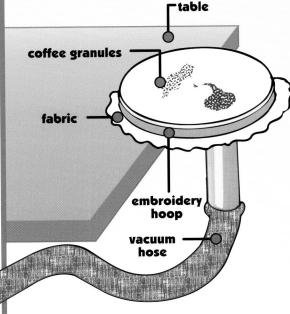

table

coffee granules

fabric

embroidery hoop

vacuum hose

Getting The Dirt On Mars

In the 1970s two unmanned space probes, called the *Viking* landers, were sent to the surface of Mars. These sophisticated machines tested Mars's soil to determine if life existed on that planet. They did this by feeding nutrients to the soil and observing the soil for signs of life. Conduct a similar experiment right here on Earth!

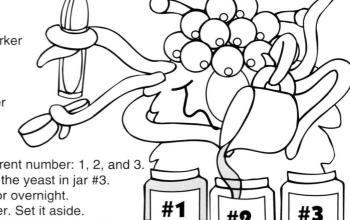

Materials per group of students:

three 12-ounce glass jars	3 labels and a marker
clean sand	large pitcher
long-handled teaspoon	measuring cup
2 teaspoons salt	1/2 cup sugar
2 teaspoons yeast	2 cups warm water
2 teaspoons baking powder	

Directions:

1. Fill each jar 1/3 full of sand. Label each jar with a different number: 1, 2, and 3.
2. Mix the salt in jar #1, the baking powder in jar #2, and the yeast in jar #3.
3. Mars is a cold place, so store the jars in the refrigerator overnight.
4. Meanwhile mix the sugar and warm water in the pitcher. Set it aside.
5. The next day, pour 2/3 cup of sugar water into each jar. Set the jars aside.
6. Record any reactions. Which jar do you think contains life?

Feeding the soil with nutrients will cause chemicals in the soil to react quickly. However, living cells, if present, will react slowly and will continue to react as they multiply.

- -

Note To The Teacher: Duplicate this experiment for a learning center or group activity. The jar containing salt will not react. The jar containing baking powder will react quickly, but then fizzle out. The jar containing yeast will react slowly and continuously because yeast contains living cells.

Why Does Mars Look Red?

By sending the two *Viking* landers to Mars, scientists discovered why that planet looks red from Earth. Conduct this experiment to find out why when we see Mars, we see red!

Aw, Mom!

Don't go tracking that red Mars mud into this house!

Materials for each group of students:

aluminum pie pan	heavy-duty scissors
sand	dishwashing gloves
steel wool pad	pitcher of water

Directions:

1. Half-fill the pan with sand.
2. While wearing the gloves, snip the steel wool into small pieces and mix them into the sand.
3. Carefully pour enough water into the pan to just cover the sand and steel wool mixture.
4. Set the pan in a safe place for several days. Replace any evaporated water daily.
5. Check the pan daily for any color changes. Record what you see. What does this tell you about the red soil of Mars?

When water mixes with iron, it creates rust. Although Mars is now desert dry, evidence exists that the planet once contained water. When this water mixed with iron compounds found in Mars's soil, the compounds rusted, making the soil look red.

- -

Note To The Teacher: Duplicate this experiment for a learning center or group activity. After sitting in water for several days, the steel wool will rust, giving the sand a red tint.

Name ______________________________ Space: division, calculators

Looking Good For Your Age!

Mercury, Venus, Earth, and Mars are called the *inner planets* because they are closest to the sun. How old would you be today if you had been born on an inner planet other than Earth? Use your division skills and a calculator to find out!

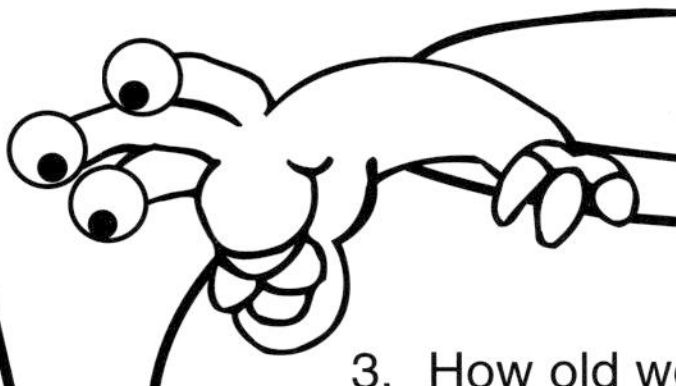

1. According to the chart, it takes 365.26 Earth days for Earth to make one trip, or *revolution,* around the sun. Each revolution is the same as a year. The chart shows that there are 88 Earth days in a Mercury year. How many Earth days are there in a Venus year? A Mars year?

   Number of Earth days in one Venus year: ______________

   Number of Earth days in one Mars year: ______________

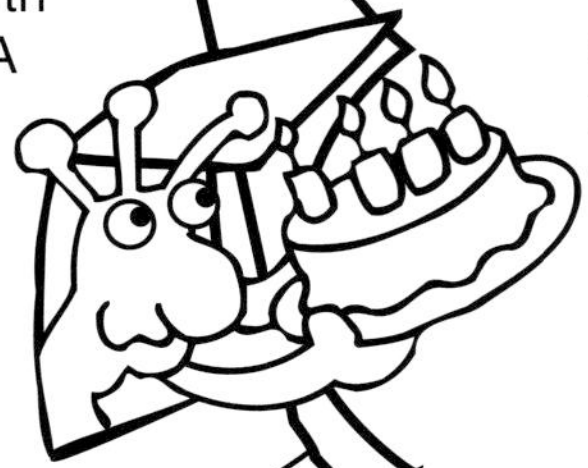

2. Write your age in years on the chart below. Then find your age in Earth days. To do this, multiply your age in years by 365; then add the number of days that have passed since your last birthday.

   Example: You are eight years old, and 28 days have passed since your birthday. Multiply 8 x 365; then add 28.

   (8 x 365) + 28 = days old
   2920 + 28 = days old
   2948 = days old

   Use the space below to calculate your age in Earth days.

   ________ x 365 + ____________ =
   (age in years) (days since birthday)

   *____________
   (age in Earth days)

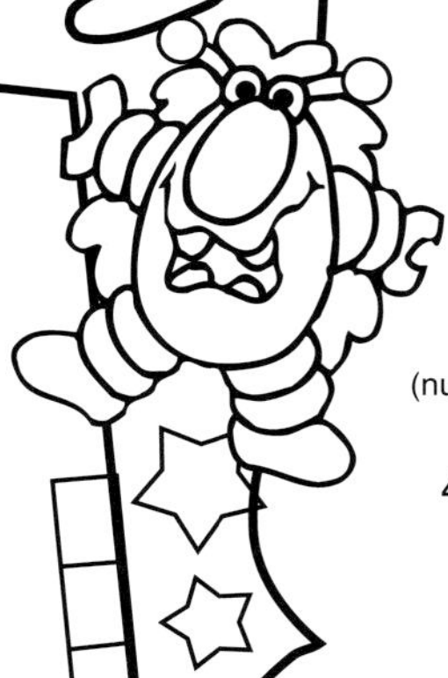

3. How old would you be if you had been born on Mercury? Here's how to find out. Take the number of Earth days in a Mercury year (88). Divide this number into your age in Earth days (the * answer from Step 2).

   Example: If you are 2948 days old, divide 2948 by 88 to determine your age on Mercury.

   $$88\,\overline{)\,2948.00}\quad = 33.50$$

   Wow! You'd be over 33 years old!

   Now find the answer using your age. Record the answer in the appropriate space on the chart below.

   (number of days in Mercury's year)) (your age in Earth days) = (your age on Mercury)

4. Calculate your age as if you'd been born on Venus. Record your answer on the chart.

5. Calculate your age as if you'd been born on Mars. Record your answer on the chart.

	MERCURY	VENUS	EARTH	MARS
Revolution around the sun in Earth days	88 days	224.7 days	365.26 days	687 days
My age in Earth years				

Note To The Teacher: Provide each student with a copy of this page and a calculator.

A Pixel Is Worth A Thousand Words

Everyone knows that there's no camera store in the sky. So how do we get those fantastic photos from the space probes? Computers on the probes convert the photographs into many tiny squares called *pixels,* which are then sent through space as radio signals. Simulate this transmission by playing the following graphic game.

Materials for two students:
two copies of this page; three different colored pencils or markers (they should be different shades of the same color—for instance, a light blue, a medium blue, and a dark blue); a book

Directions:

1. You are the *transmitter.* Your job is to record the picture and send it back—in pixels—to Earth. Using the colored pencils or markers, draw a simple design on the graph below. Use only one color in each square. Leave some squares blank.

2. Fill out the KEY above the graph. To do this, leave box 0 blank. Color box 1 with the lightest shade of marker, box 2 with the next lightest shade, and box 3 with the darkest shade.

3. Fill out the KEY on the other copy of this page in the same way as in step 2.

4. Give your partner the three pencils and the copy of this page with only the key filled in. (DO NOT show him your design!) Sit across from your partner. Set a book upright between you and your partner to create a screen so that he cannot see your design.

5. Your partner is the *receiver.* His job is to correctly record the incoming pixels. Instruct your partner to call out the coordinates (for example: A1, B3, etc.) for each box on the graph, calling out one box at a time in order beginning with box A1 (followed by A2, A3, and so on).

6. Each time your partner names a box, respond by telling him the key code number: "0" if the box on your graph is blank, "1" if the box is the lightest shade, and so on with "2" or "3." After he's called out the coordinates for the entire graph, compare your design with his to see how accurately the design was transmitted and received.

KEY

	0
	1
	2
	3

Note To The Teacher: If you would like each student to have the opportunity to play the roles of both transmitter and receiver, duplicate two copies per child. Give each student time to complete one graphic design and exchange it with a partner.

It's Greek To Me!

It may seem hard to believe, but the Greek philosopher Aristotle has traveled forward in time to the year 1996.

What to do: Research when and where Aristotle lived. Find out one of Aristotle's theories about space that was incorrect. Select one book from your school or classroom library that would explain space to Aristotle.

What to write: Write a story in which you meet Aristotle. Describe how you help him understand a modern truth about space.

Living In Space

You have been selected to live on a space station. Although you are excited about your upcoming adventure, you know that life on a space station has its advantages and disadvantages.

What to do: Using books and current magazines, research what it's like to live in space for a long period of time.

What to write: Write a letter to a friend describing one day in the life of a space station astronaut.

Where's Columbus?

Oh no! Sally Ride's space shuttle has been caught in a time warp. She has traveled back in time to Europe in 1492.

What to do: Research to find out what Christopher Columbus believed about Earth and space before he set sail for the New World. Select an astronomy book from your school or classroom library that Sally Ride might recommend that Columbus read before his journey.

What to write: Write an adventure in which Sally Ride meets with Christopher Columbus before his first trip to the New World.

To Boldly Go...

The year is 2050. Because you were born on a Martian space colony, you have never been to Earth.

What to do: Read about Mars's atmosphere and land. Find out what humans would need to do in order to build a livable colony on that planet.

What to write: Write a letter to your pen pal on Earth describing your colony. Tell how you and your family get food and oxygen, and how you dispose of waste. Describe your educational and entertaining activities too.

Close Encounters?

For two nights in a row, you have seen strange lights in the sky. You suspect that they may be UFOs. But you wonder if there is another explanation.

What to do: Research the theories that both support and argue against the existence of UFOs.

What to write: Write a story in which you either encounter beings from another planet, or find out that the lights you have been seeing have another, more logical explanation. Weave facts from your research into your story.

Led By The Light

During the 1800s, many slaves managed to escape to the North by following the constellation known as the Big Dipper. They called this constellation "the drinking gourd."

What to do: Read several stories explaining how constellations have helped to guide people in the past.

What to write: Write an original story in which one of the characters has an adventure or solves a mystery with the help of one of the constellations.

Note To The Teacher: Duplicate this page for a learning center, group work, or an individual research/writing activity. Cut the cards apart; then mount them on tagboard and laminate them for durability. Give one card to each group or individual.

Out-Of-This-World Space Books

Boldly go in search of the best children's books about space—but not before reading the recommendations that follow!

reviewed by Deborah Zink Roffino

One Giant Leap

written and illustrated by Mary Ann Fraser
published by Henry Holt and Company, 1993
Full of superb, realistic paintings and diagrams, this is an account of the expedition to the moon over 25 years ago. Readers are invited to join Neil Armstrong and his partners for a real insider's look into the Apollo 11 moon mission. Nice details from Mission Control and the Sea of Tranquility, too!

Exploring Space: Using Seymour Simon's Astronomy Books In The Classroom

written by Barbara Bourne and Wendy Saul
published by Morrow Junior Books, 1994
Recognizing the universal appeal of Seymour Simon's space books (see the review below), two educators collaborated to create this phenomenal full-color curriculum guide. Simon's books become even more valuable as learning tools when accompanied by this collection of projects, resources, bibliographies, and charts.

Space Books by Seymour Simon

published by William Morrow and Company, Inc.
There is an infectious sense of awe in these stunning books by renowned science writer Seymour Simon. Thin volumes, they never threaten to overwhelm; rather, they lure readers by their seeming simplicity. The photographs amaze, the sketches leave lasting impressions, and the simple text brims with fascinating data.

Mercury (1992)   *Galaxies* (1988)
Neptune (1991)   *Venus* (1992)
Mars (1990)   *Uranus* (1990)
Comets, Meteors, And Asteroids (1994)

The Space Atlas: A Pictorial Guide To Our Universe

written by Heather Couper and Nigel Henbest
published by Gulliver Books/Harcourt Brace & Company, 1992
Factoids and trivia bombard every square inch of this extralarge book on space. Each two-page spread explores a different heavenly body or galactic phenomenon with photos, graphs, charts, cutaways, and activities. A distance line atop each page indicates spatial relationships. A must-have book for any space study.

Pam Crane

How To Fly The Space Shuttle
written by Russell Shorto
published by John Muir Publications, 1992
In this exhilarating paperback—part of the "Masters of Motion" series—young readers are quantum-leaped into the shuttle just prior to takeoff. Every exciting detail of the experience is related in the first person, present tense with diagrams, photographs, and sketches packing the pages. Incidental lessons on gravity, rocket power, and acceleration flow through the book as naturally as air currents. You don't finish this book; you disembark from it!

Look Inside Cross-Sections: Space
written by Moira Butterfield
published by Dorling Kindersley, 1994
Intricate drawings reveal the insides of every spacecraft, from the early Mercury capsules to the multileveled shuttle and the problem-laden *Hubble* telescope. Clear labels, detailed cutaway approaches, and concisely packaged fact boxes encourage hours of mental grazing. Includes a glossary, a timeline, an index, and large illustrations of 11 different spacecrafts.

Our Universe: A Guide To What's Out There
written by Russell Stannard
published by Kingfisher, 1995
The physicist-author of this captivating edition clearly has a handle on his field of choice, but the book's allure lies in his ability to translate complex science—such as the big bang, neutron soup, and binary stars—into comprehensible ideas for young readers. Dynamic graphics balance friendly quizzes, and the chatty text is artfully placed without overpowering the page.

Insects From Outer Space
written by Vladimir Vagin and Frank Asch
published by Scholastic Inc., 1995
Don't overlook this bizarre picture book! The concept—a miniature world of surreal bugs that is suddenly invaded by aliens—and the humor reach way beyond most picture-book readers. Along with the outlandish art, students will find fresh ideas for the comic-book aliens they love to sketch and for some out-of-this-world creative writing.

ALSO RECOMMENDED:

Black Stars In Orbit: NASA's African-American Astronauts by Khephra Burns and William Miles; Harcourt Brace & Company, 1994

Space Camp: The Great Adventures For NASA Hopefuls by Anne Baird; Morrow Junior Books, 1992

How The Universe Works: 100 Ways Parents And Kids Can Share The Secrets Of The Universe by Heather Couper and Nigel Henbest; Reader's Digest Books, 1994

SIMPLE MACHINES... MADE SIMPLE!

Hands-on Activities For Exploring Basic Machines

Simple machines help us do work by trading force for distance. It's that simple! And no matter how complex a machine may be, it is based in some way on one or more of the six types of simple machines: the *lever, wheel and axle, pulley, inclined plane, wedge,* and *screw*. Help students discover how simple machines make things work with the following creative, hands-on activities.

by Dean and Kelly Medley

THE SIMPLICITY OF SIMPLE MACHINES

Simple machines came into being because they made work easier for early humans. Although a simple machine has few or no moving parts, it can help us maximize our strength and motion. The learning activities in this unit provide students with opportunities to work hands-on with everyday examples of simple machines.

Many of the activities and demonstrations are best suited for completing outside, using common playground equipment. However, the concepts can be presented just as effectively with alternative materials. Books are recommended as weights. Use comparable materials—or real weights—to complete the activities that require them.

A MACHINES MINIPOSTER

Provide each student with a copy of the miniposter on page 191. Use the poster in one of these ways:
- Have each student keep it in his science notebook as a ready reference.
- Have each student cut page 191 into six sections, then glue each section onto a separate page in his science journal.
- Have each student create an accordion book by folding a 6" x 24" piece of white construction paper into sixths. Then have him cut and paste each simple machine onto a section as shown. The student uses the blank sections of the book for his notes.

EASY DOES IT! (WARM-UP ACTIVITY)

Materials needed: 30 thick textbooks, 1 toy wagon, 2 jump ropes, 2 stopwatches

Directions:
1. Use the jump ropes to mark start and finish lines about 30 feet apart.
2. Divide the books into two equal stacks. Place the stacks a few feet apart behind the start line.
3. Place the toy wagon beside one of the stacks.
4. Choose a pair of students to stand behind each stack of books. Try to choose pairs that are fairly equal in strength. Also choose a timer for each pair.
5. Instruct each pair to move its stack of books across the finish line. For safety reasons, each pair may move only three books at a time. The pair with the wagon may load three books at a time into the wagon, then pull the wagon across the finish line. The other pair must carry three books at a time across the finish line, then return for more until all of the books have been moved.
6. When you signal, "Begin!", each timer times his team until all books have been moved across the finish line.

Discuss the results of this activity with your class. Allow other pairs to complete the race too. Students should see that using the wagon was quicker and required less physical energy than running back and forth carrying the books. Ask students how they could make the wagon an even better machine. (Answers might include adding a motor to the wagon or making the wheels bigger.)

PLAYGROUND PLANE (SMALL-GROUP ACTIVITY)

Materials needed: playground slide (or a board placed on an incline), 5 large books, 1 long jump rope

Directions:

1. Tie one end of the rope snugly around the stack of books.
2. Place the stack of books at the bottom of the slide's steps.
3. Have students take turns climbing to the top of the slide and pulling the books straight up by the opposite end of the rope.
4. Next place the stack of books at the bottom of the slide. Have each student pull the books up the slide to the top. Remind students to try to use the same amount of force when pulling the books up the slide as they did when pulling the books straight up in step 3.
5. Instruct each student to write a description of this activity. Ask students what adaptations they could make that would make the work even easier. Have students draw and describe their adaptations.

Students might consider spraying the slide with a cooking spray, wrapping the books in cloth, or using garbage bags to reduce friction. Or they may suggest placing the books in some type of smooth container.

VIEW THE SCREW (TEACHER DEMONSTRATION)

Materials needed: 2 pieces of 1/4-inch Plexiglas™, screw, screwdriver, drill

Directions: Predrill a small hole in the top of a piece of Plexiglas™. This hole is to help start the screw and should not go all the way through the Plexiglas™. Call a small group of students together to watch the demonstration. With the two pieces of Plexiglas™ held together, start the screw in the predrilled hole. Call on students in the group to use the screwdriver to screw the screw into the Plexiglas™. Students should observe the path of the screw through the Plexiglas™ and note how the screw works to cut through the glass. Continue to screw the two pieces together, but don't allow the screw to go completely through the bottom piece of Plexiglas™. Have students examine the tiny hole at the bottom where the screw is about to emerge. They should see how the screw, a simple machine based on the inclined plane, helps make work easier.

If the thread of a screw could be unwrapped and flattened, it would make an inclined plane. A screw is used to hold things together. The spiral motion of putting a screw into something actually requires less force and is less work for the builder. When a screw is put into an object, it moves material up and out of the hole it creates. A modern machine based on the design of a screw is a grain elevator.

MONKEY-BARS PULLEY (TEACHER DEMONSTRATION)

Materials needed: monkey bars (or a tall stepladder), pulley, strong string or twine, large book, spring scale

Directions: Have a student stand near the top of the monkey-bars ladder. Tie the string around the book; then hand the opposite end of the string up to the student. Instruct the student to pull the book straight up to the bars, which may be difficult. Next have the student come down from the monkey bars. Place the book on the ground under the bars and toss the opposite end of the string over any bar. Make sure the student can reach the end of the string. Now have the student pull on the string until the book reaches the bars. This task introduces the concept of a pulley.

Have students hypothesize why the second task was easier to complete. Show students how they can measure the amount of force needed to lift an object by using a spring scale. Repeat the steps above with a spring scale attached to the end of the string. Record the measurement on the scale for each lift. Next hang a pulley from a monkey bar and pass the string over the pulley's wheel. Repeat both lifts again, using the spring scale to measure the amount of force needed. Record each measurement on the scale.

Discuss with students that the pulley gives no mechanical advantage of lift, but changes the direction of the force applied to the load. This is especially important when it's difficult to reach the space underneath a load.

WONDER WEDGE (SMALL-GROUP ACTIVITY)

Materials needed for each group: box of heavy books; triangular, wooden doorstop; hammer

Directions:
1. The object of this activity is for students to understand the difference between an inclined plane and a wedge. Remind students of the playground slide activity (page 189). Ask them to describe an inclined plane.
2. Show students the doorstop. Discuss how an inclined plane and a wedge are alike *(similar shapes)*.
3. Divide students into small groups with the materials listed. Instruct each group to gently use the hammer and doorstop to lift an edge of the box of books off the ground. *The doorstop should be used as a wedge that students drive under the box with the hammer. The wedge will lift the box from the floor.*
4. Have students contrast the use and function of the inclined plane with the wedge.

   An inclined plane allows something to be moved to a higher level with less energy than lifting. A wedge is shaped like an inclined plane, but actually moves into a space, separating an object. This can also cause a type of lift. Other common wedges include knives, axes, and wood splitters.

BICYCLE BREAKDOWN (TEACHER DEMONSTRATION/ CULMINATING ACTIVITY)

Materials needed: 1 old, unused bicycle; tools (hammer, adjustable wrench, screwdriver); safety glasses

Directions: Several weeks before this activity, send a note home with students asking for the donation of an old, unused bicycle. Make it clear that the bike won't be returned. Provide each student with a copy of page 191 and a 6" x 24" piece of white construction paper. Have students make accordion books as described on page 188.

Discuss with students that a bicycle is a machine made up of many simple machines. These simple machines work together to make a very efficient machine that helps us move distances much faster than on foot. Have students examine the bike for several days; then direct each student to draw each type of simple machine he observes in the bike in his accordion book. Next use tools to begin dismantling the bike, being sure to wear safety glasses. Discuss with students the different parts of the bike that are simple machines.

Students should have several parts drawn as examples of simple machines. For example, the wheel and axle category may include gears, sprocket wheels, and the tires. The lever category may include the hand brake and the pedals, and students should note the many screws that hold various parts of the bike together.

BRICK SLIDE (SMALL-GROUP ACTIVITY)

Materials needed for each group: 1 brick, 3-foot-long piece of string, 10 round pencils

Introduction: Share several pictures of ancient structures with your students, such as the pyramids, Stonehenge, and the Greek Parthenon. Compare the types of machines we would use today to build these structures with the tools used by ancient builders. (Ask your librarian to locate resources that include pictures of ancient tools.) Have students brainstorm ways that ancient builders may have moved the huge stones used to build the pyramids. Then tell students they're going to experiment with one method.

Directions:
1. Divide students into small groups and provide each group with the materials listed.
2. Go outside to a hard-topped area. Instruct each group to first try to pull its brick across the ground by looping the string around it and pulling it. Also have each student try to push the brick along with just one finger.
3. Next have students duplicate the ancient method of using rollers. Instruct one student to lay the pencils side by side in front of the brick. Then, using the string still attached to the brick, instruct two or three students to gently pull the brick onto the pencils. (Other students in the group may need to hold some pencils in place.)
4. As the brick moves forward off a pencil, have a student pick up that pencil and place it in front of the rolling brick.

   After all groups have completed the activity, discuss their experiences. Students will note that it was much easier to move the brick using the pencils and that ancient builders may have moved large stones using rollers.

Lever

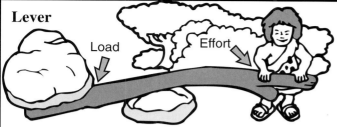

The lever is one of the earliest machines. A lever helps lift weights with less effort.

Examples:

Wheel and Axle

The wheel and axle can lift heavy weights for us with only a little effort on our part.

Examples:

Pulley

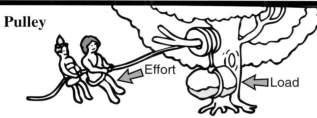

The pulley is a form of the wheel and axle. A pulley changes the direction of the force.

Examples:

Inclined Plane

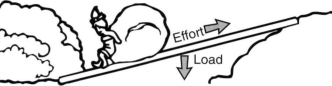

The inclined plane is so simple, it doesn't even look like a machine! An inclined plane makes it easier to slide a load upward than to lift it directly.

Example:

Wedge

The wedge is related to the inclined plane. It can be used to lift a heavy load over a short distance or to split a log.

Examples:

Screw

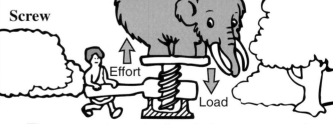

The screw is an inclined plane wrapped around a cylinder or a cone. Its main purpose is to raise a load over the *threads* (the spiral part of the screw) by applying a small force.

Examples:

©The Education Center, Inc. • *THE MAILBOX® • Intermediate •* Feb/Mar 1996

Note To The Teacher: Use with "A Machines Miniposter" on page 188 and "Bicycle Breakdown" on page 190.

SIMPLE MACHINES SCAVENGER HUNT

Do you realize that you're being surrounded—by machines, that is! Your school and its grounds are marvelous places to find examples of every type of simple machine. Work with your group to locate at least two examples of each simple machine listed in the chart. Draw the machine and label its parts. Also write where you found each example.

lever ▲		
wheel and axle		
pulley		
inclined plane		
wedge		
screw		

Note To The Teacher: After students have become familiar with the six simple machines, divide the class into groups to complete this activity.

CATAPULT SHOOTER

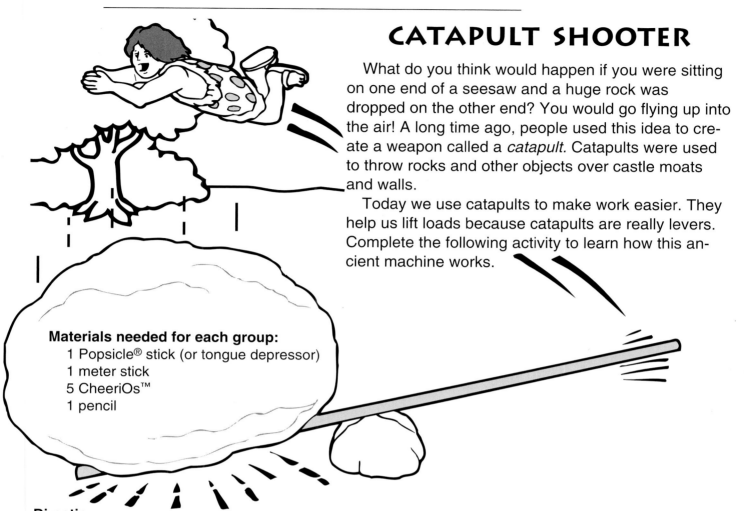

What do you think would happen if you were sitting on one end of a seesaw and a huge rock was dropped on the other end? You would go flying up into the air! A long time ago, people used this idea to create a weapon called a *catapult.* Catapults were used to throw rocks and other objects over castle moats and walls.

Today we use catapults to make work easier. They help us lift loads because catapults are really levers. Complete the following activity to learn how this ancient machine works.

Materials needed for each group:
1 Popsicle® stick (or tongue depressor)
1 meter stick
5 CheeriOs™
1 pencil

Directions:

1. Make a catapult on the floor by laying the Popsicle® stick across the pencil.
2. Place one piece of cereal on the end of the stick that is touching the floor.
3. Write "1" on the Popsicle® stick at the spot where it lies across the pencil (the *fulcrum*).
4. Flip the piece of cereal by hitting the end of the stick that is in the air.
5. Measure the distance the piece of cereal flew. Measure from the pencil.
6. Record the distance in the chart.
7. Change the location of the fulcrum—the spot where the Popsicle® stick crosses the pencil. Write "2" on the stick at the spot where it now crosses the pencil.
8. Repeat steps 2, 4, 5, and 6. Try to hit the end of the Popsicle® stick with the same force each time.
9. Complete steps 2–6 three more times, changing the location of the fulcrum each time (step 7).

How does the location of the fulcrum affect the distance the piece of cereal flies?

_____

_____

fulcrum number	distance
1	
2	
3	
4	
5	

Bonus Box: Extend the catapult activity by having an accuracy competition. Set a paper cup several feet from your group's catapult. Have each student in the group shoot a piece of cereal to see who can get it in the cup, or closest to the cup.

TOP SECRET

Classified Information

Activities To Introduce Budding Zoologists To Animal Classification

So many animals, so little time! How *do* scientists keep them all straight? It's no secret that they *classify,* or group, animals according to their common characteristics. Use the following activities to help your students uncover the hows and whys of animal classification.

by Gregory Grambo, Dean Medley, Kelly Medley, and Christine Thuman

Carl The Crocodile (Crocodylus porosus)

Alias: Crocodilly Willy

Info: 20 feet long Last seen in salty waters

Case Number: 103-28A

Agent: Polly Pye–Private Eye

SECRET

Sharky (Carcharodan carcharias)

Alias: Great White Shark, Jaws

Info: If he smiles, run!
Case Number: 56-224-5D
...lly Pye–Private Eye

Manty (Mantella aurantiaca)

Alias: Mantella

Info: Poisonous! Watch out for...

Twenty Questions

Play the familiar game Twenty Questions to demonstrate the thinking processes that take place during classification. Prior to class place a telephone book in a paper bag and hide it in a desk. When class begins, have students try to identify the book you are hiding by asking you 20 yes/no questions. Take note of the questions that your students ask. Do they inquire about color, size, number of pages, genre, or illustrations? All of these are categories by which we classify books. Afterward, point out how the types of questions students asked helped them to narrow down the possibilities. Tell students that this process is similar to what scientists go through when they are trying to *classify*, or group, a new species of animal.

The Flip Of A Coin

Scientists use observation to classify animals. How closely do your students observe the world around them? Test their observation acumen with the following demonstration. Quiz students about an object they probably see every day—a penny. Instruct students to write down the answers to the following questions on notebook paper. Warn them not to peek at a penny while answering these questions.

- We know that Lincoln's image is on the front, or *head*, of a penny. Who is pictured on the back of a penny? *(Lincoln. He can be seen sitting inside the Lincoln Memorial.)*
- What building appears on the back of a penny? *(the Lincoln Memorial in Washington, D.C.)*
- How many times does the phrase "one cent" appear on the coin? *(once, on the back)*
- Is the edge of a penny smooth or ridged? *(smooth)*
- What word appears to the left of Lincoln's head on the front of a penny? *("Liberty")*

Check to see how many students answered every question correctly. Point out that in order to distinguish between the thousands of species of animals, scientists must use careful, not casual, observation.

Observe And Draw

A picture is worth a thousand words. However, drawing pictures of animals is challenging when the animals move about. Scientists have learned to capture animal images in fast, simple drawings. They add the details later, after many repeated observations. The key to making animal drawings is to observe and draw as rapidly as possible.

If you don't have plans to visit the zoo, you can bring a live animal into the classroom for observation. The animal should be one that's used to being around large numbers of children. Set up a table where four to five students can sit around the animal. Place the animal in a large, see-through cage. Have small groups of students take turns drawing the animal using pencil and paper. Encourage students to use simple lines to capture the shape and movement of the animal's spine before adding the arms, legs, head, and tail. Help students focus their attention by posing the following questions: "What lines make up the animal's form?", "Which way does it bend or twist?", and "How can you capture that twist in a few strokes?" Afterward, place several how-to-draw-animals books in a center for students who wish to practice.

WANTED

Link The Skink
(Dasia smaragdina)

Last seen hiding among the leaves.

Spinning A Web Of Classification

Brainstorm a list of items that can be classified in our world such as stores, foods, furniture, transportation, school supplies, or musical instruments. Using *books* as an example, show students how to break down a category into its smaller classifications by modeling the webbing technique. Begin by writing *books* in an oval on the chalkboard. Explain to students that books can be divided into two main categories: fiction and nonfiction. Connect two other ovals to the center. Write *fiction* in one oval and *nonfiction* in the other. Have students help you name categories that would fit in each of these two divisions. Continue expanding the web by adding additional categories. See the diagram for ideas.

Next, divide the class into teams of three to four students. Supply each team with markers and a three-foot length of light-colored bulletin-board paper. Have each team select one of the topics you brainstormed at the beginning of the lesson; then have the team make a web that divides that category into more specific groups. Afterward, have each team share its web with two other teams.

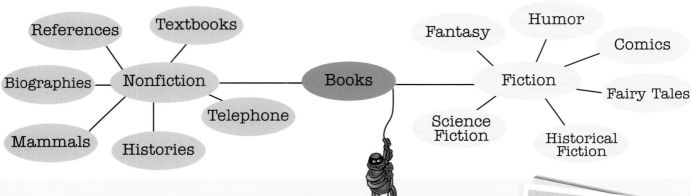

Toying With Taxonomy

Observing and classifying is child's play when your students examine their favorite toys. Instruct each student to bring in one toy or stuffed animal. Divide the class into teams of four to five students each. Instruct each group to sit in a circle with its toys placed in the center. Direct each team member to carefully examine each toy. Then have the team categorize its toys by grouping them according to similar characteristics. Give the group a copy of "Toying With Taxonomy" (page 197). Inform students that when they group some of their toys into one category, the remaining toys must then be grouped into an opposite category. For instance, if some of the toys are grouped under the heading "contain plastic parts," the remaining toys must fit into the category "contain no plastic parts." Encourage students to devise as many specific categories as they can for their toys.

After giving them about ten minutes with the first group of toys, have teams exchange toys with another team. Instruct teams to devise different categories for grouping this new set of toys. Have teams record their findings on the "Toying With Taxonomy" sheet.

The Hood
(Pitohui dichrous)

Alias: Hooded Pitohui

Info: Skin, feathers, and internal organs are poisonous.

☠

Case Number: 4770–3C

Agent: Polly Pye–Private Eye

TOP SECRET

I.D. Me!

No two people are exactly alike. Prove this statement to your students by creating a *dichotomous key* of your class. Explain that a dichotomous key allows you to make decisions between two choices until a specific organism is identified. Begin the key with the heading *Our Class* as shown in the diagram. Divide the class physically into two groups—*boys* and *girls*. Fill in the next two spaces on the key with these headings. Next divide each of these two groups further using the categories *brown eyes* and *blue/green eyes*. Record these categories on the key; then divide the students physically into these groups. Continue subdividing the class using one or more of the following categories: left-/right-handed; light/dark hair; can curl/can't curl tongue; attached/detached earlobes; can wink/can't wink one eye; can raise/can't raise one eyebrow; can touch/can't touch nose with tongue. The key is complete when each student is in an individual group by himself. Select one student and demonstrate how you can follow a pathway on the key to identify that student.

Next have students practice making their own dichotomous keys. Divide your class into groups of eight. Provide each group with a copy of "If The Shoe Fits" on page 198. Instruct groups to complete the reproducible according to the directions.

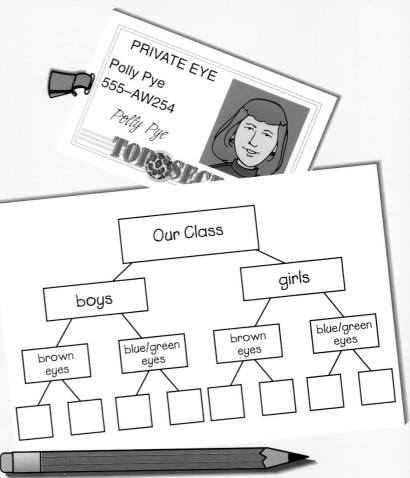

Arthropod Animation

While most students have a clear understanding of the backboned animals known as *vertebrates*—fish, birds, mammals, reptiles, and amphibians—they may not have extensive knowledge of the phylum of invertebrates (animals without backbones) known as *Arthropoda*. Use art to familiarize your students with a few of the millions of species in this phylum. Divide students into seven teams and give each team a copy of the "Arthropod Breakdown" on page 199. Assign each team a different class of arthropods to research. Instruct each team to research the body characteristics of its particular class of arthropod. Then have each team use craft materials to construct a three-dimensional model of an arthropod in that class. Provide craft materials such as paint, pipe cleaners, Styrofoam® balls, cardboard tubes, and glue. Have each team share its completed animal and describe the animal's body characteristics.

Literature/Software Connection

Big Bugs; written by Jerry Booth; Harcourt Brace & Company, 1994

Do You Know The Difference?; written by Andrea and Michael Bischhoff-Miersch; North-South Books Inc., 1995

Everything You Never Learned About Birds; written by Rebecca Rupp; Storey Communications, Inc.; 1995

Invertebrates; written by Bradford Burnham; Thomson Learning, 1995

The Kingfisher First Encyclopedia Of Animals; written by David Burnie and Linda Gamlin; Kingfisher, 1994

Tongues And Tails; written by Theresa Greenaway; Raintree Steck-Vaughn Publishers, 1995

A Wasp Is Not A Bee; written by Marilyn Singer; Henry Holt and Company, Inc.; 1995

How We Classify Animals: CD-Rom for Windows™ and Macintosh®; teaching module written by Helen Hansen; AIMS Media, 1995

Name(s) ____ Animal classification: taxonomy

____

Toying With Taxonomy

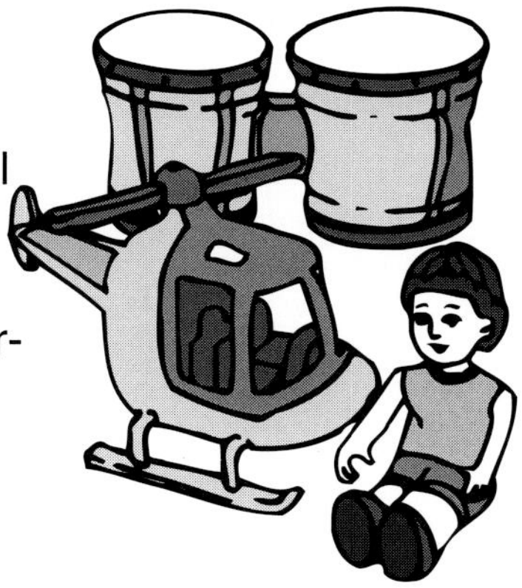

Here's your chance to play around in the name of science! In Part I, list the toys in your group. Then carefully examine each toy for details that will help you *classify,* or group, the toys. Divide the toys into two different groups. On the first set of lines under "B. Classifications," write the names of the two groups and the number of toys in each one. Try to list four different pairs of groups on the remaining lines. Repeat these steps in Part II using another team's set of toys.

Part I: Your Team's Toys

A. Write the name of each toy: ____________________ ____________________

____________________ ____________________ ____________________

B. Classifications

Group A	# of toys	Group B	# of toys
____________________	____	____________________	____
____________________	____	____________________	____
____________________	____	____________________	____
____________________	____	____________________	____
____________________	____	____________________	____

Part II: Another Team's Toys

A. Write the name of each toy: ____________________ ____________________

____________________ ____________________ ____________________

B. Classifications

Group A	# of toys	Group B	# of toys
____________________	____	____________________	____
____________________	____	____________________	____
____________________	____	____________________	____
____________________	____	____________________	____
____________________	____	____________________	____

Note To The Teacher: Use this reproducible with "Toying With Taxonomy" on page 195.

Animal classification: dichotomous key

If The Shoe Fits!

What makes your shoes unique? Find out by creating your own dichotomous key.

Directions for a group of six to eight students:

1. Have each member of your group remove one of his shoes and place it in the center of the table.

2. Carefully examine each shoe, noting its characteristics.

3. Have a group recorder write "Group Shoes" in the top box of the dichotomous key below.

4. Brainstorm to come up with two categories into which each shoe either fits or doesn't fit. No shoe should fit into *both* categories.

5. Physically divide the shoes into your two categories. Then write the names of these two categories in the next two boxes of the key.

6. Examine the two piles of shoes. For each pile, decide on another pair of categories into which each shoe either fits or doesn't fit. Write the names of these categories in the key.

7. Divide the shoes into additional categories, recording the names of the categories on the key, until each shoe stands alone.

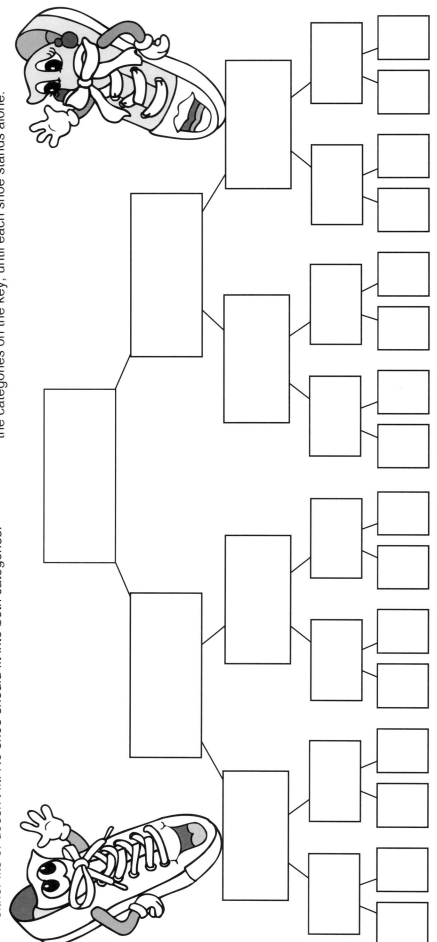

©The Education Center, Inc. • *THE MAILBOX® • Intermediate •* April/May 1996

Note To The Teacher: Use this page after completing "I. D. Me!" on page 196. Some possible categories for shoes are: left/right, fasten/slip-on, leather/not leather, or sneaker/not sneaker.

Arthropod Breakdown

There are a lot of arthropods out there!
In fact, this phylum contains the largest variety of creatures
in the animal kingdom. But as varied as they are, all arthropods do
have some common characteristics including a tough exoskeleton,
jointed limbs, and a nerve cord running the length of the body. Look over
the chart below to learn about some of the classes contained in the phylum
Arthropoda and its subphylum, Crustacea.

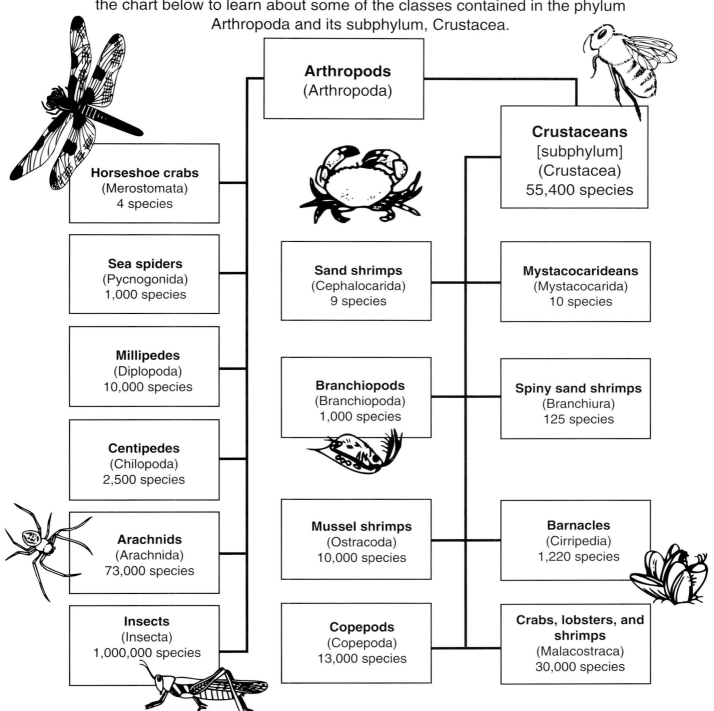

Arthropods
(Arthropoda)

Horseshoe crabs
(Merostomata)
4 species

Sea spiders
(Pycnogonida)
1,000 species

Millipedes
(Diplopoda)
10,000 species

Centipedes
(Chilopoda)
2,500 species

Arachnids
(Arachnida)
73,000 species

Insects
(Insecta)
1,000,000 species

Sand shrimps
(Cephalocarida)
9 species

Branchiopods
(Branchiopoda)
1,000 species

Mussel shrimps
(Ostracoda)
10,000 species

Copepods
(Copepoda)
13,000 species

Crustaceans
[subphylum]
(Crustacea)
55,400 species

Mystacocarideans
(Mystacocarida)
10 species

Spiny sand shrimps
(Branchiura)
125 species

Barnacles
(Cirripedia)
1,220 species

Crabs, lobsters, and shrimps
(Malacostraca)
30,000 species

©The Education Center, Inc. • *THE MAILBOX®* • *Intermediate* • **April/May 1996**

Note To The Teacher: Use this reproducible with the group research activity, "Arthropod Animation," on page 196.

Cycles Of Life
Interactive Games For Teaching The Food, Carbon, And Nitrogen Cycles

Energize your science curriculum by incorporating these three fun, outdoor activities into your ecology unit!

by Daniel Kriesberg

What's For Dinner?: A Food-Cycle Game

Care to munch on a nice, crunchy grasshopper or devour a juicy, green leaf? Maybe not, but students will see the problems caused by having too many or too few grasshoppers or leaves in the food cycle when they play this game!

To prepare students: Review the definitions of *producer, consumer,* and *decomposer.* Explain to students that during the game they will take the roles of producers, consumers, and decomposers by doing certain actions:

- Producers will reach for the sun and say, "Ahhhhh" (*to show that plants need sun, soil, air, and water to produce food*).
- Consumers will stretch out their arms in front of their bodies—opening and closing them like alligators' mouths—and say, "Chomp, chomp" (*to show that animals need to eat other living things because they can't make their own food*).
- Decomposers will wiggle their fingers and say, "Eeeeee" (*to show that decomposers live off dead plants and animals and thereby return nutrients to the soil*).

To play the game: Mark two starting lines about 15 feet from each other. Divide the class into two groups. Position one group at each starting line. Mark a home baseline about 20 yards behind each group. Direct each group to huddle together and decide whether the group will be producers, consumers, or decomposers. Have each group return to its starting line, stand shoulder to shoulder, and face the other team. At your signal, have each group act out its part. Depending on the roles chosen, one group will chase the other:

- Producers chase decomposers (*plants need good soil*).
- Decomposers chase consumers (*dead animals decay into the soil*).
- Consumers chase producers (*animals eat plants*).

If both groups choose the same role, ask students to rehuddle and pick again. During play, if a student is tagged before he crosses his home baseline, have him join the group of the student who tagged him. Play until all members of a group have been tagged or are safely across their home baseline.

As students rest, discuss how each part of the cycle needs the other parts. Ask whether students feel that having too many or too few of a group poses a problem. Also discuss how humans affect food cycles.

More Trees, Please: A Carbon-Cycle Game

Generate a newfound interest in planting carbon-eating trees by having students play this game about the carbon cycle. (You'll need a play area on which students can easily find fallen leaves.)

To prepare students: Begin by reviewing the carbon cycle with students. Carbon is one of the gases in our atmosphere that all living things need. Plants take carbon from the air and make food. Animals cannot take carbon from the air or make their own food, so they eat plants. When animals and plants die, carbon is returned to the soil by decomposers. Carbon is also returned to the atmosphere when animals breathe and when organic matter is burned.

To play the game: Divide the class into three groups: producers, consumers, and decomposers. Have each group member wear a sign that designates his group. Let fallen leaves represent carbon. At your signal, have the producers run about gathering leaves. Have the consumers chase the producers. When a producer is tagged by a consumer, have the producer give his leaves to that consumer and then sit down for 15 seconds before reentering the game. If a decomposer tags either a consumer or a producer, have the tagged player throw down his leaves and sit down for 15 seconds before reentering the game.

When the students are exhausted and are ready to sit and rest, review with them how carbon cycles through the environment. What happens to the cycle if large numbers of trees are cut down? What other ways do humans affect the carbon cycle? After this energetic game, expect students to have a newfound respect for trees and hardworking decomposers!

Metamorphosed Nitrogen: A Nitrogen-Cycle Game

Butterflies are not the only things that change form! Teach your students about the nitrogen cycle and the changes this important gas must go through with this fast-paced game.

To prepare students: Review the nitrogen cycle with students. Nitrogen is another one of the gases in our atmosphere that all living things need. But before it can be used, nitrogen has to be changed into a usable form by nitrogen-fixing bacteria that live in the roots of clover and in the soil. Producers use nitrogen to grow. Consumers get nitrogen by eating plants. Nitrogen is returned to the soil by decomposers.

To play the game: Scatter LEGOs®, Unifix® cubes, or other linking toys over the playing field to represent nitrogen. Divide the class into three groups: producers, consumers, and decomposers. Have each group member wear a sign that designates his group. Have the bacteria group run about collecting and connecting as many of the linking-toy pieces as possible. Direct the producers to chase the bacteria. When a member of the bacteria group gets tagged, have him give his nitrogen pieces to the producer who tagged him and then sit for 15 seconds before reentering the game. Have the consumers chase the producers. When a producer gets tagged, have him give his nitrogen pieces to the consumer who tagged him and sit down for 15 seconds before reentering the game. Have the decomposers chase consumers and producers. When a consumer or a producer is tagged by a decomposer, have him throw down his nitrogen pieces and sit for 15 seconds before reentering the game.

As students are resting, discuss with them the nitrogen cycle as well as problems caused by having either too much or not enough nitrogen. Then invite students to transform their tired bodies into reinvigorated ones by enjoying a healthy snack and drink!

The Peanut Man

Your students may know George Washington Carver as the peanut man. However, the following activities—just in time for Afro-American History Month in February—will take them in for a closer look at this skilled teacher and scientist who, despite the racially prejudiced attitudes of his time, devoted himself to helping a nation of farmers.

adapted from ideas by Jeri Ashford—Gr. 4, Jollyville Elementary, Austin, TX

Background For The Teacher

George Washington Carver was born about 1864 in Diamond Grove, Missouri (an exact birthdate is unknown). He became interested in plants and farming as a young child. Carver had his own garden where he cultivated different plants, carefully observing what made them grow and remain healthy. It wasn't long before he gained a reputation as the local plant doctor. Neighbors often called on young Carver to nurse their sickly plants back to health.

Carver completed high school in Minneapolis, Kansas. He then applied by mail for a scholarship to Highland College. Although he was accepted, when Carver arrived, Highland refused to admit him because of his race.

After his disappointing experience with Highland, Carver moved to Iowa, where he attended Simpson College and studied art. While enrolled at Simpson, he became friends with his teacher, Etta Budd. Noting Carver's interest in botany, she encouraged him to change his academic direction and pursue a scientific career. She then referred Carver to her father, a professor of horticulture at Iowa State College of Agricultural and Mechanical Arts. Carver transferred to Iowa State Agricultural College at Ames, where he graduated with a Bachelor of Agriculture degree in 1894.

Carver went to work at Tuskegee Institute in Alabama in 1896 at the request of Booker T. Washington. Despite his many administrative, teaching, and management responsibilities, Carver found time to experiment with plants. He also devoted himself to educating poor black farmers about crop diversification and rotation.

By the time he died on January 5, 1943, Carver had developed more than 300 uses for the peanut. His legacy is summed up on the inscription on his grave: "He could have added fortune to fame, but caring for neither, he found happiness and honor in being helpful to the world."

Meeting Hatred With Love

George Washington Carver was often the victim of racial prejudice. He responded with grace to each situation. In 1923 the National Association for the Advancement of Colored People (NAACP) awarded him the Spingarn Medal in recognition of his contributions to science and for his contribution to better understanding between the races. Inspiring others to meet hatred with love, Carver once said, "No man can drag me down so low as to make me hate him."

Discuss with students the meaning of Carver's quote. Have students describe situations where they've encountered prejudice or hatred. After sharing how they responded to such negative encounters, ask: "What actions can students in our school take to meet hatred with love?" Have each child write a letter to his school's student body describing ways students can meet hatred with love. Post these letters on a hallway bulletin board for all to read. Post Carver's quote at the top of the board as a title.

Peanut Potpourri

Create peanut-shaped templates using the pattern on page 204. Have each student trace the template on a sheet of 9" x 12" tan or white paper; then have her choose one of these activities to complete on her pattern:

- George Washington Carver found over 300 ways to use peanuts! Choose an ordinary object and invent a new way of using it. Describe your invention on your peanut.
- George Washington Carver was nuts about plants—so much so that he made a career out of studying them. What are you nuts about? On your cutout, write about something you like to spend lots of time doing.
- Why is a peanut considered a pea and not a nut? Research to find out. Then make two columns on your peanut pattern. In one column list how peanuts are similar to nuts. In the other column list how they are different.
- Read to find out more details about George Washington Carver's life. Write a summary of your findings on your peanut cutout.

Plant students' peanuts on a bulletin board entitled "We've Gone Nuts!"

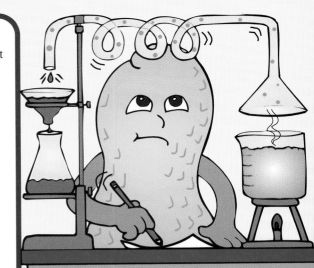

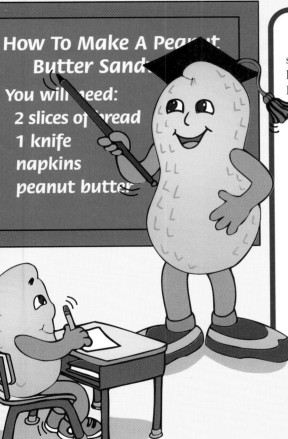

How To Make A Peanut Butter Sandwich

You will need:
2 slices of bread
1 knife
napkins
peanut butter

Sandwiching Directions

George Washington Carver was known as a talented teacher. His successful students probably knew how to follow directions! Introduce this peanut butter challenge to see how closely your students give and follow directions.

Directions:

1. Instruct students to write clear, concise directions for making a peanut butter sandwich. Have them reread their papers to check for missing steps before turning them in.
2. The next day, place the following items on a table at the front of the class: a jar of peanut butter, two loaves of sliced bread, napkins, and a table knife.
3. Have a student come to the table. Select one of the student papers from the previous day's activity.
4. Without revealing the name on the paper, read the directions for making a peanut butter sandwich. Instruct the student at the table to follow the directions exactly. For example, if the paper tells the student to "put the peanut butter on the bread," have the student place the entire jar of peanut butter on top of the bread. Since the student directions made no mention of using a knife, the knife is off-limits.
5. After several students have had an opportunity to make a sandwich, discuss the lessons learned about writing clear, concise directions.

Literature Connection

Crack open these books to find out more about Carver and other African-American scientists.

Extraordinary Black Americans From Colonial To Contemporary Times by Susan Altman (Childrens Press)
George Washington Carver by Gene Adair (Chelsea House Publishers)
I've Got An Idea: The Story Of Frederick McKinley Jones by Gloria M. Swanson (Runestone Press)
Make Me A Peanut Butter Sandwich And A Glass Of Milk by Ken Robbins (Scholastic, Inc.)
Outward Dreams: Black Inventors And Their Inventions by Jim Haskins (Walker and Company)
A Pocketful Of Goobers: A Story About George Washington Carver by Barbara Mitchell (Lerner Publications)

Yippee Skippee! Peanut Butter

Nuts About Science!

George Washington Carver was one of the most well-known African-American scientists in this century. However, others have been hard at work experimenting and inventing helpful products. Choose one of the following African-American scientists to research. Complete your research on the peanut pattern provided. Draw a picture of the invention in the box on the peanut.

George Alcorn
Benjamin Banneker
Henry Boyd
Otis Boykin
Benjamin Bradley
George E. Carruthers
James Forten
Frederick McKinley Jones
Percy Julian
Lewis Latimer
Garrett Morgan
Norbert Rillieux
Sarah Breedlowe Walker
Granville T. Woods

Bonus Box: Research to discover the names of the items that each of the following African-American women are credited with inventing: Sarah Goode, Sarah Boone, Julia Hammond, Archia Ross, and Claytonia Dorticus.

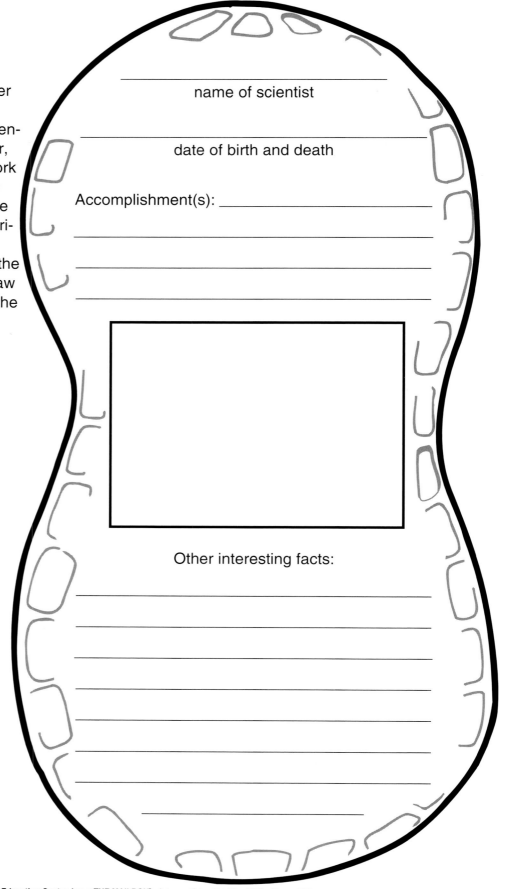

name of scientist

date of birth and death

Accomplishment(s): _____
_____
_____
_____

Other interesting facts:

_____
_____
_____
_____
_____
_____
_____
_____
_____

Note To The Teacher: Display your students' completed peanut patterns on a bulletin board entitled "They Were Nuts About Science!"

LITERATURE

SKINNYBONES

A Humorous Novel By Barbara Park

Alex "Skinnybones" Frankovitch has a major talent for wisecracking—a knack that gets him into major-league trouble! All it takes is one smart-alecky remark, and Alex lands himself in an embarrassing pitching contest with the best Little League pitcher in town. Winner of several children-selected awards, this hilarious novel is the perfect way to start your school year on a literary high note. Use these chapter-by-chapter activities and the accompanying reproducibles to introduce your class to the unforgettable Alex and the pure fun of reading.

with contributions by Lynn Greco

Chapter 1: The book begins with Alex's witty entry in the Kitty Fritters TV Contest. After reading chapter 1, challenge students to bring in items advertising contest offers (cereal boxes and other product containers, newspapers, magazines, advertising inserts, junk mail, etc.). After a week of gathering these items, have each cooperative group compare and contrast two or more examples, looking at elements such as the requirements for entering, restrictions, prizes promised, number of winners, format of the entry blank, etc. Have groups display their findings in charts drawn on large pieces of poster board.

Chapter 2: For wisecracking Alex, the perfect teacher would appreciate his sense of humor. For an exercise in descriptive writing, instruct students to close their eyes and imagine the perfect teacher. After several minutes, ask each child to open his eyes and list adjectives and phrases to describe his perfect teacher; then have him use his list to write a descriptive paragraph. Provide time for students to edit and revise their work. Bind the paragraphs in a class book entitled "The Perfect Teacher."

Chapter 3: Even though Alex tries to be friendly, T. J. Stoner wants nothing to do with him. Follow up this chapter by discussing with students how Alex received T. J.'s rejection. Did he handle the situation positively? How would students have handled T. J.? What can a person do when someone openly rejects him or her? Is it important that everyone be your friend and like you? Why or why not? After the discussion, have each student write reflections about the discussion in his journal.

Chapter 4: In Alex's opinion, the worst thing about belonging to Little League is the uniforms, which are always too big for him. At the conclusion of this chapter, have each student write the following sentence on a scrap piece of paper: "The worst thing about _____ is _____." Have the student fill in the blanks; then have her proofread her work with a partner's help and copy the revised sentence on a sentence strip. Mount the strips on a bulletin board entitled "What's The Worst?" Don't forget to add a sentence strip of your own!

Chapter 5: After T. J. brags about his pitching ability, Alex states, "My mother says that when people like T. J. Stoner brag, it's just because they're trying to get attention." Use this chapter as a springboard for a survey and graphing activity. Challenge each student to ask ten people this question: Why do you think people brag? Have students share the results of their surveys; then use the data to create bar or circle graphs. Does the majority of people surveyed agree with Mrs. Frankovitch?

Chapter 6: In this chapter, Alex goes head-to-head with T. J. Stoner in a pitching contest that ends in disaster. Use the reproducible on page 209 to give students practice in writing a news article about this calamitous event. Before students complete the activity, review the use of the *five Ws* (Who? What? Where? When? Why?) utilized by news reporters to gather their facts. This reproducible works equally well as a follow-up to chapter 10.

EVALUATION FORM

Group:

Editor:

I like

I like

I wonder

I wonder

Chapter 7: Alex's specialty might have been bunting, but his big dream was to hit a home run. Challenge cooperative groups to write a "dream" chapter in which Alex's fantasy comes true. Remind students to include some of the characters from *Skinnybones*, as well as new characters if needed. Hold a class conference during which each group shares its chapter. Give each student several copies of the evaluation form shown (one copy for each group except his own). After a group shares its chapter, have students in the other groups complete copies of the form. Collect the forms and give them to the appropriate group to use in revising its chapter. Bind the revised and recopied chapters into a class book.

Chapter 8: Dreading the pending humiliation of playing T. J.'s team, Alex drags himself into the kitchen, explaining in a preposterous lie why his legs no longer work. For fun, have students brainstorm a list of other "lame" excuses Alex could have used to avoid going to the game. Encourage students to share creative lame excuses they've used in the past with no success.

Chapter 9: Since *Skinnybones* is a first-person account written from Alex's point of view, we know what our hero is thinking and feeling on the eve of the big game. But what about the other characters? Choose five volunteers to come to the front of the room and take the roles of Mrs. Frankovitch, T. J. Stoner, Mr. Frankovitch, Brian, and Alex's coach. Tell the volunteers to pretend they are sitting in the bleachers waiting for the game to begin. One at a time, have each character "think out loud" and share his or her feelings about the pending game. Repeat the activity with different volunteers.

Chapter 10: This chapter includes the climactic ball game, an event that the entire book has led up to. Before reading the chapter, have students predict what might happen at the game. After reading the chapter, give each student a large index card. On one side of the card, have the student copy and finish this sentence: I was surprised when…. Have the student illustrate the sentence, then flip the card and complete the same activity with this sentence: I was not surprised when…. Collect the cards and read the sentences aloud, giving students time to respond.

Chapter 11: After the mortification of Saturday's ball game, the last thing Alex wants to do is face his classmates. What advice would your students give Alex at this point? Have each student write a letter to Alex advising him about how to handle his embarrassment. Let volunteers share their advice; then discuss positive ways to cope with embarrassment.

Chapter 12: Alex and his rival, T. J., may seem like polar opposites, but are they really? At the conclusion of this chapter, have pairs or small groups draw large Venn diagrams on chart paper, comparing and contrasting these two colorful characters.

At the conclusion of the book: When springtime rolled around each year, Alex had to face the problem of Little League and of being—in his own words—a "real stinky" ballplayer. Ask students to imagine that as the seasons change, so do Alex's problems. Give each child a 12" x 18" sheet of construction paper and four small index cards. Instruct the student to label each card with a season and a list of challenges that Alex might face during that particular time of the year. For example, on the Autumn card, the student might note that Alex would be too small to try out for the football team. Have students glue their cards onto the construction paper as shown, adding seasonal illustrations. Fold these mini-posters in half; then store them in your students' writing portfolios. When a story idea is needed, your students will know exactly where to turn! *(For another writing activity to be used at the conclusion of the book, see the reproducible on page 210.)*

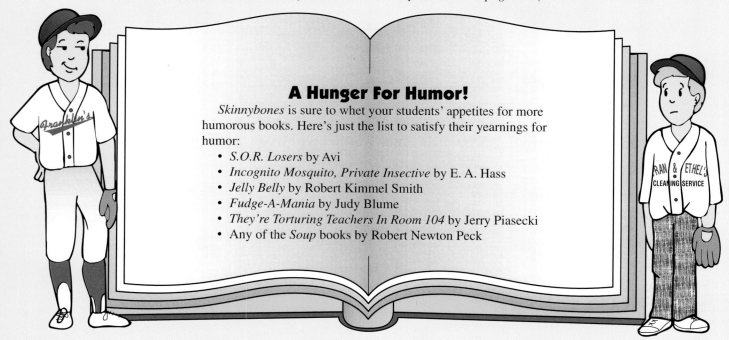

A Hunger For Humor!

Skinnybones is sure to whet your students' appetites for more humorous books. Here's just the list to satisfy their yearnings for humor:

- *S.O.R. Losers* by Avi
- *Incognito Mosquito, Private Insective* by E. A. Hass
- *Jelly Belly* by Robert Kimmel Smith
- *Fudge-A-Mania* by Judy Blume
- *They're Torturing Teachers In Room 104* by Jerry Piasecki
- Any of the *Soup* books by Robert Newton Peck

The Scoop On Skinnybones

Pretend that you are a reporter for the newspaper at Alex's school. You've just heard that a very unusual contest will be taking place after school between T. J. Stoner and some kid nicknamed "Skinnybones." Your editor has asked you to attend the contest and report on this newsworthy event.

Directions: Any good reporter knows that before writing a news article, he or she must answer a set of questions known as the *five Ws*. Think about the pitching contest between Alex and T. J.; then answer the five *Ws* below. Use the information to write a news story about the contest. Include an attention-grabbing headline and a picture.

Who was involved? _____

_____

What happened? _____

_____

Where did it happen? _____

_____

When did it happen? _____

_____

Why did it happen? _____

_____

GOSSIP GAZETTE

Vol. I, Issue 1	25 cents

Bonus Box: On the back of this page, write a headline and draw a picture for a news article that you would love to see on the front page of tomorrow's newspaper.

Note To The Teacher: Use after students have read chapter 6.

Mending The Ending

Skinnybones ends happily for Alex, who's on his way to New York City to star in a Kitty Fritters commercial. Suppose you could "mend the ending" and change the story's conclusion.

Read the baseballs below. Choose one to help you write a new ending for the book. Color and cut out the ball. Glue it onto the top of a sheet of writing paper; then rewrite the ending to *Skinnybones*.

After the big game, T. J. decides that he's been too tough on Alex and asks him to be his friend.

Alex hits a home run during the big game.

Mr. and Mrs. Frankovitch decide not to make Alex play in the ball game.

After the big game, a reporter and camera crew from the local television station show up at Alex's house. The reporter wants to do a special story on "the booga booga kid" to be shown on the evening news.

When Alex arrives at school after the big game, he discovers that T. J. and his family have moved back to San Diego.

An Eventful Story

Skinnybones by Barbara Park is packed with one hilarious scene after another. Choose three different memorable events from the book. For each event, do the following:

1. Describe the setting.
2. List the characters involved.
3. Describe the conflict.

4. Explain how the conflict was resolved.
5. Summarize the lesson learned by the character(s).

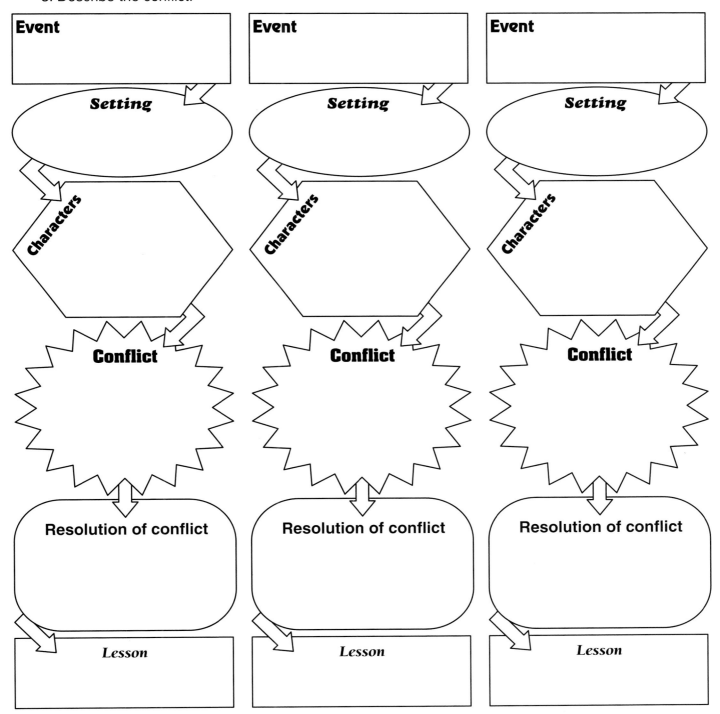

Bonus Box: What event from your own life is very memorable? On the back of this page, complete a story map like the ones above to describe this unforgettable experience.

Who Comes With Cannons?
A Civil War Novel
By Patricia Beatty

When Truth Hopkins is sent to live with relatives in North Carolina, little does the young Quaker girl know that she will soon find herself helping runaway slaves escape on the Underground Railroad. This gripping novel about one family's commitment to stand against slavery is the perfect complement to a Civil War unit. Use the following activities and reproducibles to help share Patricia Beatty's thrilling story with your students.

Before Reading: For a book-long character development project, ask parents to donate five rolls of paper towels. Run a broad piece of ribbon through each roll of towels; then tie the two ends of the ribbon together. Staple the ribbon of each roll to a bulletin board so that the roll hangs and the towels can be pulled down. Pull down about a foot of each roll; then use a pushpin to attach the towel end to the board. Above each roll, staple a nametag for one of these characters: Truth, Aunt Elizabeth, Uncle Matthew, Robert, Todd. As students read the book, let them label slips of colored paper with traits exhibited by these characters. Have students tape each slip to the appropriate roll of towels, pulling down a roll as more space is needed.

Chapters 1 and 2: Like Truth, the Bardwell family are Quakers. Their unique beliefs are central to the plot of *Who Comes With Cannons?* After students have read the first two chapters, have them brainstorm a list of things they learned about the Quaker faith from reading these chapters. List student responses on a large piece of chart paper. As students read the book, have them relate how a particular Quaker belief listed on the chart affected the story's plot.

Chapters 3 and 4: Truth soon learns that the Bardwell's home is actually a secret station on the Underground Railroad. The Bardwells regularly risk their lives to help fugitive slaves. Discuss with students times when they took a risk to help someone else (such as speaking up for a friend who was being teased or spending an allowance to help a needy neighbor).

Who Comes With Cannons? is published by Morrow Junior Books, 1350 Avenue of the Americas, New York, NY 10019.

Chapters 5 and 6: Robert and Todd head to Canada to escape conscription into the Confederate army. Write the term *civil disobedience* on the board and ask students what they think it means. Explain that civil disobedience is the deliberate and public refusal to obey a law, and that it is usually nonviolent. The Quakers and other abolitionists practiced civil disobedience when they helped slaves escape. Other examples of nonviolent civil disobedience include:

- Susan B. Anthony (also a Quaker) protesting the lack of women's rights by illegally voting in an election.
- Rosa Parks refusing to give up her bus seat to protest racial segregation.
- Opponents of the U.S. involvement in the Vietnam War refusing to register for the draft.

Many people would say that it is never right to break a law deliberately. Divide students into groups and have them discuss this statement, giving reasons for their opinions.

Chapters 7 and 8: In chapter 7, an injured Todd returns to North Carolina after having survived the first battle at Bull Run in Manassas, Virginia. In chapter 8 and in other chapters, several major battles are mentioned. Assign each of several small groups one of the following battles to research. Have groups share their information using posters, overhead transparencies, or other visual aids.

Battles to research:
- first Bull Run (Manassas), Virginia—July 21, 1861
- Shiloh, Tennessee—April 6–7, 1862
- second Bull Run (Manassas), Virginia—August 29–30, 1862
- Sharpsburg (Antietam), Maryland—September 17, 1862
- Fredericksburg, Virginia—December 13, 1862
- Gettysburg, Pennsylvania—July 1–3, 1863

Chapters 9 and 10: Truth makes an extraordinary trip on the Underground Railroad to win the release of Robert from a Union prison. Tell students to pretend that it is years later. Truth is going to be interviewed by a local paper that wants to print the story of her extraordinary trip. Have each pair of students write a list of interview questions that answer the five *Ws*: *Who? What? Where? When?* and *Why?* Then have each pair write answers as Truth might have given them. Let students record their interviews on cassette tapes to place at a listening center.

Chapters 11 and 12: Truth finished her dangerous rescue mission the same way she began it: on the Underground Railroad. At the finish of these chapters, use the reproducible on page 215 to introduce students to a famous conductor on the Underground Railroad. Mentioned in the notes at the back of Beatty's book, Levi Coffin— the unofficial president of the Underground Railroad—was a courageous Quaker who dedicated his life to the principle of equality. After students have completed the reproducible, encourage them to find out about other famous Quaker abolitionists such as Susan B. Anthony, John Greenleaf Whittier, and Lucretia Mott.

Chapters 13 and 14: To culminate the reading of this exciting novel, have students create a mural highlighting character traits illustrated throughout the book. Divide a large piece of butcher paper into six puzzle-piece-shaped sections. Cut out the puzzle pieces; then number each on the back for easy reassembly later. Assign one of these character traits to each of six groups: bravery, honesty, ingenuity, trustworthiness, teamwork, determination. Have each group write its trait in bold letters on its puzzle piece. Then have the group label and decorate the piece with examples of the characteristic as found in the story. When students are finished, reassemble the giant puzzle and review the important events in the book. (For another activity on character traits, see the reproducible on page 216.)

Word Wise

With your partner, complete the following vocabulary activity:

1. Circle one word in each chapter list below. Make sure that the words you circle are different from the ones your partner circles.

2. Write each circled word on an index card. On the back of the card, write the word's definition and a sentence of your own using the word. Use a dictionary to help you.

3. Store your cards in a small manila envelope. Decorate the outside of the envelope with your name and a favorite scene from *Who Comes With Cannons?*

4. During practice sessions, use your cards to teach your partner the meanings of your words.

5. After two practice sessions, create a quiz that will test your partner's knowledge of your words. Provide an answer key.

6. On a day designated by your teacher, give your partner the test; then score the test. With your partner, evaluate how you did as a teacher. Answer these questions on the back of this page:
   - How did my partner do on the test?
   - Was it easier or harder than I thought to teach someone?
   - How could I have improved my cards, my test, and/or my teaching methods?

Chapter 1: stocky, knead, sanatorium, stifle, lanky, bodice, frank, eavesdrop, anticipate, scuttle, dapple

Chapter 2: meditating, curse, stoke, mused, doff, flaxen, ruddy, fugitive, remnant

Chapter 3: astounded, levelly, gravely, prime, retrieve, compose, vile, strained

Chapter 4: towheaded, abolitionist, somberly, glazier, secede

Chapter 5: sorrel, spiteful, locket, militia, conscription

Chapter 6: whitewash, cultivated, grim, fodder, rout

Chapter 7: bleary, trussed, cleft, cavern, crude, deserter, astride, gelding, prosperous, clapboard, veranda, corncrib, portly, gallant

Chapter 8: staunch, telltale, buffeted, scoffed, disheartening, sultry

Chapter 9: nimble, engrossed, privy, hearse, confinement, seizure

Chapter 10: crinoline, barrage, contempt, sect, scaffolding, vendor, brackish, gilded, flounce, silhouette, damask

Chapter 11: baritone, sallow, authorization, malaria, sentry

Chapter 12: depot, courteously, fitful, faltered, basin

Chapter 13: chafe, confiscated, plundered, courier, urgent, midwife

Chapter 14: point-blank, clamor, buoyant

Note To The Teacher: This activity is to be completed after reading *Who Comes With Cannons?* Provide each student with a small manila envelope and 14 index cards. Divide students into pairs. After students have completed steps 1–3, schedule three or four practice sessions during which partners can teach each other their words. Use the chapter word lists with other vocabulary activities.

Levi and Catherine Coffin: A Courageous Couple

At the conclusion of *Who Comes With Cannons?* author Patricia Beatty mentions a famous Quaker who was involved in operating the Underground Railroad. Levi Coffin, with his wife Catherine, operated one of the most successful stations in the underground system. The story of the Coffins—like the story of Truth and the Bardwells—is one of inspiring dedication to the principles of love and equality.

As a young boy living in North Carolina, Levi Coffin was introduced to slavery at an early age. One day he saw a runaway slave being mistreated by the slave's master. The master put a chain around the slave's neck and attached the chain to his wagon. Then he got in the wagon and took off at full speed. The slave was forced to run behind the wagon so that he wouldn't be dragged by his neck. This scene sickened young Levi. He decided that he would dedicate his life to helping slaves and ending slavery.

On his twenty-sixth birthday, Levi married a childhood friend named Catherine (Kate) White. He and Kate moved north to Indiana. There Levi opened a successful store. But his real business was helping runaway slaves escape to freedom in Canada. Levi and Kate's home became an important station on the Underground Railroad. Almost every week, the Coffins would hear a soft rap at their door. When they opened the door, they found a wagon loaded with fugitives—men, women, and children. Levi and Kate would silently escort the fugitives into their home. Once inside, they closed the thick curtains and made a fire. Kate would prepare food for the hungry runaways. Clothes and food were distributed; then the slaves would sleep in front of the fire. In the morning, the runaways were either sent to the next station or hidden for a day or two longer.

This work went on for more than 20 years. During this time, Levi became known as the president of the Underground Railroad. He was once quoted as saying:

"Both my parents and grandparents were opposed to slavery, and none of either of the families ever owned slaves; and all were friends of the oppressed, so I claim that I inherited my antislavery principles."

Levi and Kate provided food, clothing, safety, encouragement, and safe passage on the Underground Railroad north to Canada for about 100 slaves a year. Each time they helped a runaway, they risked arrest and the loss of their property. The Coffins lived lives that were true to their beliefs and principles. A courageous couple indeed!

Staple a sheet of notebook paper to the back of this page. Choose three of these activities. Complete the activities on the back of this page and on the notebook paper.

---

1. In a paragraph, write your reaction to the cruel treatment of the slave described in the second paragraph above.

2. Reread the quote at the end of the article. In it, Levi talks about his family being "friends of the oppressed." What does *oppressed* mean? (Use a dictionary if needed.) Who do you think is oppressed in America today? How could you be a friend of the oppressed? Write your answers in a paragraph.

3. Levi and Catherine Coffin were a courageous couple. So were Matthew and Elizabeth Bardwell. List ways in which the couples are alike. Then list ways in which they are different.

4. One woman that the Coffins helped was a runaway slave named Eliza Harris. Eliza crossed a frozen river with her small child in order to reach the Coffin's station. Years later the Coffins met Eliza and her child enjoying a life of freedom in Canada. Write the conversation you think the Coffins and Eliza had during their reunion.

5. Levi and Kate Coffin took many risks to do what they believed was right. For what belief or principle would you be willing to take such risks? Why is this issue so important to you? Write your answer in a letter to Levi or Catherine.

A Collage Of Characteristics

With a partner, choose one of the topics below and discuss the questions. Then work with your partner to create a collage that illustrates the topic. Follow the directions below for making your collage. Be prepared to explain your collage to the rest of the class.

★ ★ Honesty ★ ★

The main character in *Who Comes With Cannons?* is named Tabitha Ruth. But her nickname—Truth—is much more suitable for the young Quaker girl.

- Truth stays true to her name. List incidents in the book when Truth—instead of lying to make peace or save embarrassment—is honest.
- Describe a time when you told the truth even though someone made fun of you or got angry with you.
- Describe a time when you didn't tell the truth but later wished that you had.

★ ★ ★ ★ ★ Trustworthiness ★ ★ ★ ★ ★

Both Robert and Martha mistrust Truth when they first meet her. Their judgments are based on the fear that Truth will find out about their involvement in the Underground Railroad. Later they find out that Truth is worthy of their trust.

- How does Truth respond to Robert's distrust of her? How would you have responded if you had been Truth?
- Have you ever made a judgment about someone only to find out later that your first impression was entirely wrong? What did you learn from this experience?
- Who is someone you would trust with your life? How has this person proven his/her trustworthiness?

★ ★ ★ Courage ★ ★ ★

Bravery, boldness, daring, valor—all are synonyms for courage. And all describe many of the characters in *Who Comes With Cannons?*

- Name at least three incidents in the book when courage is exhibited by a character.
- When the Gibsons make the second threatening visit to the Bardwells at night, Truth angrily shouts at them from her bedroom window. Do you think Truth was courageous or foolish? Explain your answer.
- What do you wish you had the courage to do?

★ ★ ★ ★ Pacifism ★ ★ ★ ★

Pacifism is an opposition to war or violence as a way to settle arguments. Many of the characters in *Who Comes With Cannons?* practice pacifism.

- How does the Bardwell family respond to the rock-throwing Gibson family? How would you have responded if you had been Mr. or Mrs. Bardwell?
- If the Bardwells lived today, how do you think they would respond to the violence on television and in movies?
- What can you do to promote peace in our classroom? In our community?

Directions for making the collage:
Cut out magazine pictures, letters, and words to illustrate your topic. Glue them collage-fashion to a large sheet of construction paper.

©The Education Center, Inc. • *THE MAILBOX®* • *Intermediate* • Oct/Nov 1995

Note To The Teacher: Complete this project at the conclusion of the book. Divide students into pairs. Give each pair a copy of this page, two sheets of construction paper, two pairs of scissors, and glue. Provide students with a supply of old magazines. Display the collages—grouped by topic—on a bulletin board.

GRADE-A READING MOTIVATION

Book-Sharing Activities From Our Subscribers

How do you motivate your students to read and even share about the books they're reading? When we asked you—our subscribers—to send in your ideas, the response was terrific! Together they make a "grade-A" collection of practical and fun book-sharing activities.

Reading "Hooks"

My students earn "Acerra Bucks"—our class incentive/reward—by "hooking" their classmates into books they have read. A student who wants to earn an Acerra Buck gives a brief introduction to his book; then he reads a portion he thinks will "hook" others into wanting to read his book. Since starting this program, my students' oral reading skills have improved. Their eyes have also been opened to a variety of authors and writing techniques.

Janet M. Acerra—Gr. 5
Forest Lakes Elementary
Oldsmar, FL

Sneak Peeks

To encourage my older intermediate students to read for pleasure—not just for a grade—I created "Sneak Peeks." Each Friday I preview an award-winning book selected from our media center. We note the title and author; then I read the first chapter aloud. I keep several copies of the book on hand for interested students to check out. My kids ask all week about the book that will be featured on "Sneak Peek," and this interest leads to avid readers.

Martha Ennis
Arnold Middle School
Columbus, GA

A Poppin' Good Idea!

Our class makes reading a feature presentation with this poppin' good idea. For each student, I mount a popcorn box on a bulletin board entitled "And Now For Our Feature Presentation: Reading!" Each time a student finishes a book, she writes a brief summary and evaluation on a popcorn-shaped cutout; then she places the cutout in her box. When each student has read four books, we have a popcorn party. While we enjoy the buttery treat, each pupil shares her book reports.

Neva J. Doerr—Gr. 4
Creighton Community Schools
Creighton, NE

Catherine, Called Birdy
by Karen Cushman

Walk

POPCORN

RIP INTO READING

Rip Into Reading

Here's how I get my class to literally rip into reading. Each time one of my students reads a book, he and I conference so that he can tell me about it. Then he records the title, author, and his name on a piece of paper selected from the scrap box. After ripping around the edges of the paper, the student tapes it onto the wall under the banner "Rip Into Reading!" Before long my classroom is wallpapered with colorful evidence that students are ripping into reading!

Jodi Larsen
Laura B. Anderson School
Sioux Falls, SD

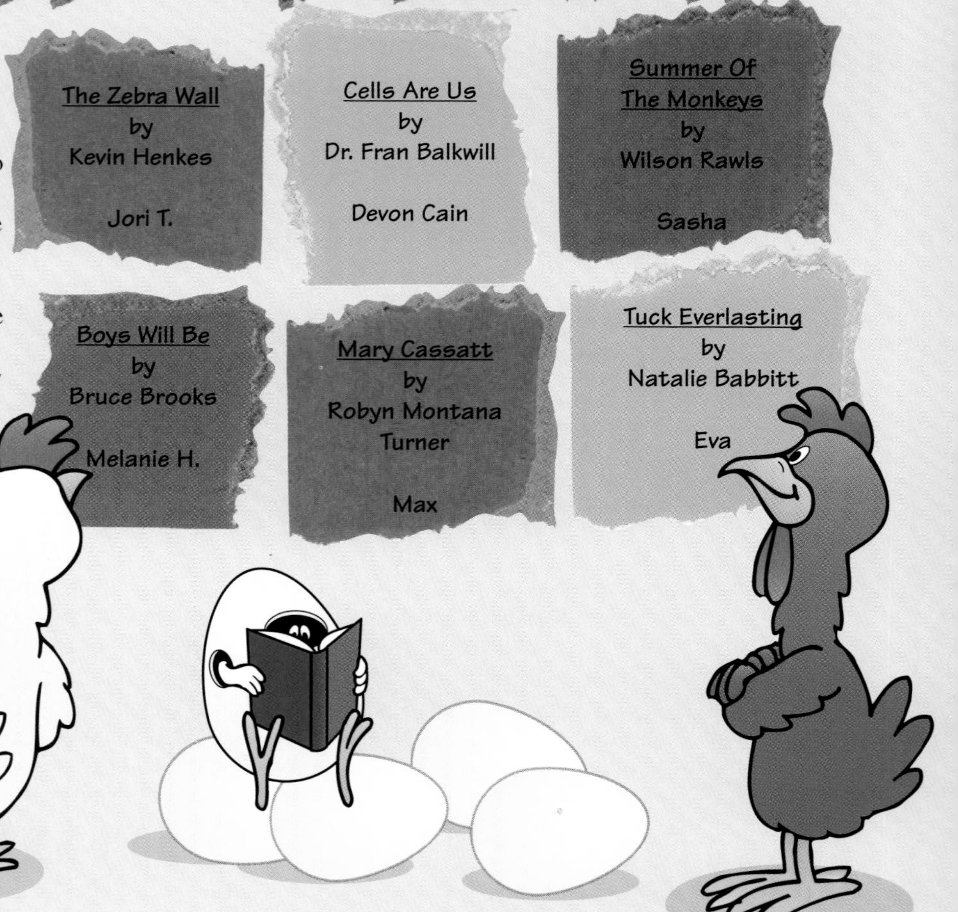

<u>The Zebra Wall</u>
by
Kevin Henkes

Jori T.

<u>Cells Are Us</u>
by
Dr. Fran Balkwill

Devon Cain

<u>Summer Of
The Monkeys</u>
by
Wilson Rawls

Sasha

<u>Boys Will Be</u>
by
Bruce Brooks

Melanie H.

<u>Mary Cassatt</u>
by
Robyn Montana
Turner

Max

<u>Tuck Everlasting</u>
by
Natalie Babbitt

Eva

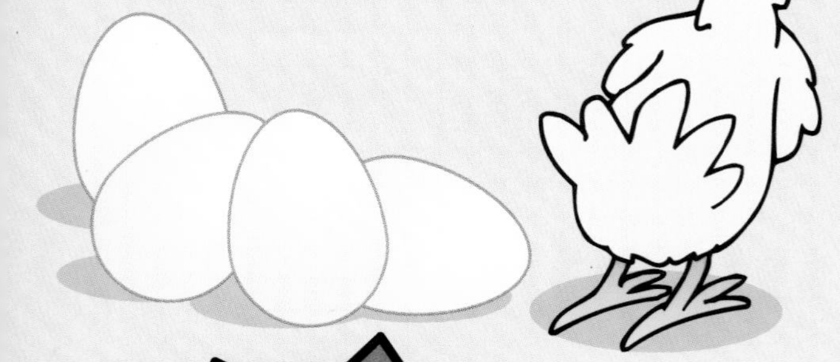

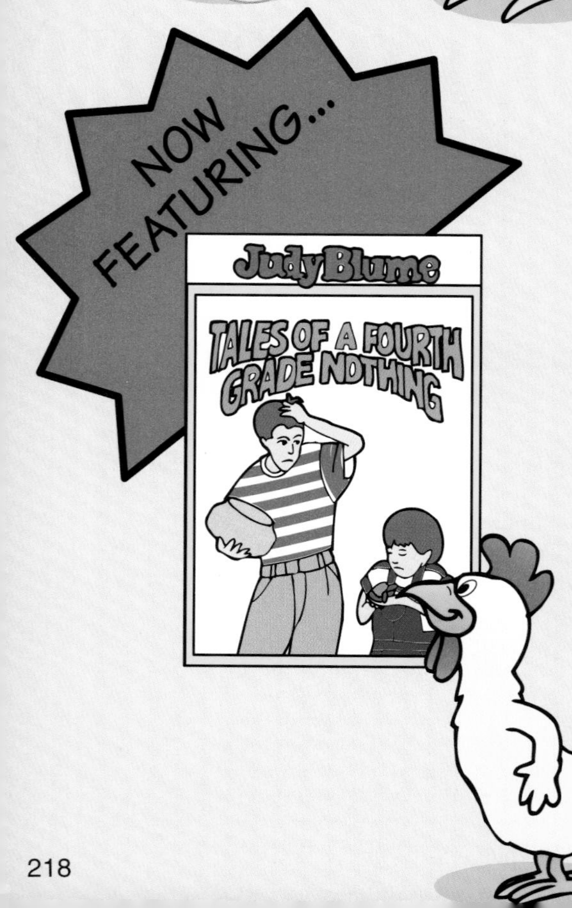

Now Featuring...

In my class we alternate between reading a novel together and having groups read different books from the same genre, such as "mystery." To interest my students in the upcoming novel, I create and display a replica of the book's cover. First I copy the cover onto a transparency. Using an overhead projector, I project the image onto poster board that has been taped to the wall. After tracing the image, I add color and mount the poster on the wall under the title "Now Featuring…." It's surprising how easily this simple display motivates my students to start the new novel.

Mary T. Spina—Gr. 4
Bee Meadow School
Whippany, NJ

A Student Newscast

As a culminating activity to reading *Maniac Magee,* I guide my students in writing a news story covering the events in the novel. We begin the newscast by taping a scene in the "newsroom"; then we move outdoors where one student (acting as a news reporter) interviews other students who role-play characters from the book. After the outside filming, the reporter directs the camera back to the newsroom where two anchorpersons follow up the report for the television audience. We share the edited version of our newscast with parents during Open House. For fun, I introduce the tape by acknowledging that, although the parents may have missed the news on TV that night, the class has a special report that is sure to interest them.

Debra Harris Knick—Gr. 5 Gifted
Chinchuba Middle School
Mandeville, LA

The Mark Of A Great Book

Capture the unique qualities of great books by creating these illustrative bookmarks. Provide each student with a bookmark pattern—either oversized to display on a wall or small enough to tuck into a favorite book. On the front of the bookmark, have the student draw an important scene from the book, and then add the book's title, its author, and her name. On the back, instruct the student to write a poem about a feeling the book evoked in her, including the event(s) in the story that produced this feeling. Laminate each bookmark; then punch a hole in the top for adding a yarn tassel.

Julia Alarie—Gr. 6
Essex Middle School
Essex, VT

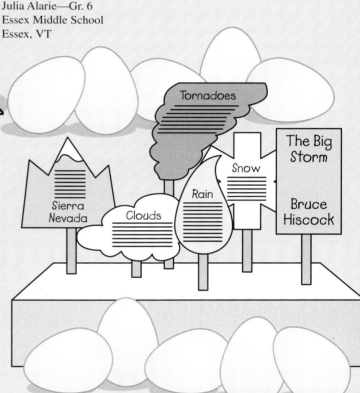

Stabile Book Reports

Every teacher is familiar with the moving displays called mobiles. But have you heard of *stabiles?* Have students share their favorite books by creating these nonmoving displays. Each student needs a block of stiff Styrofoam® (the kind used in packages) and seven sticks (chopsticks, Popsicle® sticks, or wooden skewers). Have the student mount an illustrated portion of her book report onto the end of each stick; then have her insert each stick into the Styrofoam, securing it with a drop of glue. Instruct the student to include the following information on her stabile: the book's title and author, her name, the main characters, the setting, three main events in the plot, a rating for the book, and something she learned from reading the book. Display the finished stabiles on a table in your school's media center or foyer.

Julia Alarie—Gr. 6

Apron Art

To model the joy of reading for our students, each staff member at our school chose a favorite book to illustrate on the front of an apron. (As principal, I provided the pocketed aprons.) Using paint, markers, glitter, and even battery-operated lights, we brought the aprons to life. Props—such as finger puppets and items found in the story—were stored in the apron pockets to enhance the book sharing. We debuted the completed aprons at our school's "Reading Lock-In Party." Thereafter, the school celebrated "Apron Days" twice a month. On these special days, staff members visited classrooms to share their apron stories. Students were impressed by the talent, creativity, and dedication to reading exhibited by their school's staff.

Donna Neel—Principal
Lincoln Elementary
Norman, OK

Centered On Book Reports

This year-round center will keep your students turning the pages of their favorite books. Post a variety of creative book-report ideas in the center along with examples of completed projects. As a student completes a book, have her visit the center to choose a book-sharing method. As each student hands in her project, display it at the center. You'll enjoy grading a variety of reports rather than 25 identical ones. And students will appreciate the freedom of choosing their own book-sharing method and seeing their classmates' completed projects.

Pamela Doerr
Elizabethtown School District
Elizabethtown, PA

Picture-Book Critiques

Motivate your lower-level readers by having them critique picture books for younger students. Over a small display table covered with Halloween fabric, hang a pumpkin-shaped sign that reads, "You're Never Too Old For Picture Books!" On the tabletop, display 20 or more picture books relating to the autumn/Halloween theme. Instruct each student to read eight or more books. For each book read, have the student fill out a critique form shaped like a ghost (see the example). Hang the completed ghosts around the display. By changing the theme of the display, this challenge can continue throughout the year.

Beth Meyer—Gr. 6 Learning Disabled
Marshall Middle School
Marshall, MI

Let's Discuss This!

Ignite reading comprehension and interest by holding weekly book discussion groups. In groups of four to five, have students discuss the latest books they've been reading. Generate and guide discussion by supplying each group with a few general questions selected from the list below. Select group leaders to initiate talk and keep track of time.

- Who was your favorite character? Why?
- How would the book be different if boys and girls in the story were switched?
- What surprised you about the story?
- Predict what will happen in the next chapter.
- What is something in this book that you can use in YOUR writing?
- Describe the main character.
- Does the main character remind you of any character in another book you've read? How so? If not, what makes this character unique?
- What clues did the author give for you to predict the ending?
- What, if anything, would you change in the story?

Susan Barnett—Gr. 6
Northwest Elementary
Ft. Wayne, IN

Title: _____
Author: _____
Illustrator: _____
Awards: _____
_____
Main characters: _____
Tell what the story was about: _____
_____
Approximate age level of this book: _____
Would a younger child like this book? Why or why not? _____

Talk Show Interview

A talk show format—like Oprah's—is a great way to encourage book sharing. The student who has read a book is the guest, while a classmate acts as the show's host. (You can even name the show after the host student.) The host walks around the classroom taking questions from the audience. I give the guest student a book-report grade, while the host and those in the audience receive credit for participation. My students really get involved with this fun way of sharing books.

Cindy Schooler—Grs. 5–7
Rayland, OH

Caldecott Gameboards

My sixth graders recently read about the origin and purpose of the Caldecott and Newbery awards. After reading the selection, each student was instructed to choose a book from the Caldecott Award list and design a children's game about it. (We chose Caldecott books since they could be read in one sitting.) Before the designing began, students determined the criteria for the games: clear directions, a specific number of illustrations, a logical way to advance play, and overall neatness. Since they would share the gameboards with their second-grade buddies, students also decided to include some comprehension questions to ask before playing the game. Not only was this a motivational activity for my students, it also helped our second-grade buddies practice listening and following directions. Most of all, everyone now knows a lot about the Caldecott books!

Julie Plowman—Gr. 6, Adair-Casey Elementary, Adair, IA

I Wonder...

This simple trick never fails to produce lively book sharing. At the end of a read-aloud session or a period of silent reading, I raise my hand and simply say, "I wonder...." Students' hands immediately go up, each wanting to share what he's wondering about. This five-minute activity sharpens listening skills, fosters critical thinking, and gives opportunities for predicting.

Nona Helsing—Gr. 5
Eagle Elementary
Eagle, NE

Marvelous Minimobiles

Turn book reporting into a fanciful art project! Ask each student to bring a clean, two-liter, plastic soda bottle to class. Cut off the top of each bottle; then have the student punch seven holes along the bottom edge. Instruct each student to label paper cutouts related to the book with the following:

- student's name
- the book's title and author
- an illustration or description of the main character
- an important object from the book
- a picture of the setting (drawn or cut out from a magazine)
- a rating of the book
- new or interesting words from the book

Have students punch a hole in each cutout and tie it to a piece of yarn; then have students tie the yarn through the holes on the bottle top as shown. Punch two additional holes at the top of each mobile and add yarn for hanging. Hang the completed mobiles in your classroom for everyone to enjoy.

Julie Alarie—Gr. 6
Essex Middle School
Essex, VT

Cooperative Book Mural

When several students read the same book, suggest that they create a chapter-by-chapter mural. Cover a bulletin board or wall space with white background paper. Have the group members draw a rough sketch of their mural before transferring their drawings to the larger paper. Or provide a group with 9" x 12" sheets of white construction paper. After each chapter has been illustrated on a sheet, instruct students to tape all of the sheets together to make a mural.

adapted from an idea by Pamela M. Szegedy
Erieview Elementary
Avon Lake, OH

The Joy Of Storytelling

Storytelling gives students an opportunity to be creative and brings them closer to their audience. It also results in an immediate response from listeners and motivates students to read. Provide each student or pair of students with a copy of the reproducible storytelling guidelines on page 224. Then gear up for some better-than-ever book reports as students share what they've read through the magic of storytelling.

Jeannie Maier—Gr. 5
Allen W. Roberts Elementary
New Providence, NJ

Story Maps

Help students present the plots or main events of books that they read with story maps. Have each student choose a book from a genre that takes him on a journey, such as fantasy or science fiction. After students have read their books, instruct them to think about the places mentioned in the story, plus each character's actions. Direct each student to list the most important events in his book; then give him a large sheet of drawing paper on which to draw a map that illustrates or summarizes his book. The map should include symbols and pictures related to the story, plus labels for places and objects along the route. Let students use quotes from the book, as well as their own words. Display the story maps on a bulletin board entitled "On The Road: Our Reading Adventures."

Jeannie Maier—Gr. 5

Comparing And Contrasting Settings

Focus on setting by having students compare and contrast their books' communities with their own. Provide each student with a 12" x 18" sheet of white construction paper. Instruct the student to divide the sheet into two halves; then have him illustrate the setting of his book on one half and his own community on the other half. Finally have the student label two index cards with ways the two settings are alike and different. Have him tape the cards to his drawing before displaying the project on a bulletin board.

Pamela M. Szegedy
Erieview Elementary
Avon Lake, OH

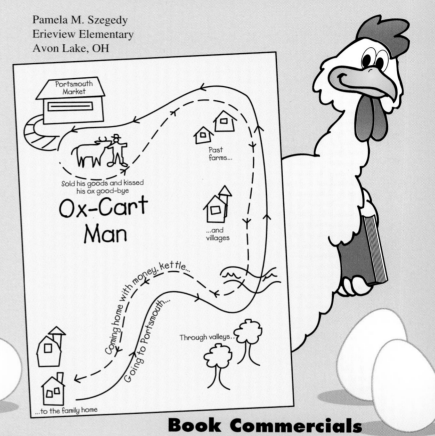

Book Commercials

Creating and presenting book commercials is a fun way for students to share their books. After students have read their books, have each child write a commercial that will convince others to "buy" her book. Suggest that students use puppets, dolls, and other props when performing their commercials. For an extraspecial effect, check with a local television repair shop and ask for a discarded television set. Remove the TV's insides so that students can use the TV cabinet for presenting their commercials. Persuasive writing, summarizing, and paraphrasing are just some of the important skills that are reinforced with this fun book-report format.

Donna S. Railing—Gr. 4, Quarryville Elementary, Quarryville, PA
Tammie Boone—Gr. 5, Sheldon Middle School, Sheldon, IA

For a reproducible form to use when evaluating book-sharing projects, see page 224.

Coupons For A Character

Which character in your book needed help during his/her adventures? Design some coupons for this character to use. Create a product that would have come in handy as the character dealt with his/her problem. Or design your coupons to provide opportunities or abilities that would have made a difference in the outcome of the adventure. Add colorful illustrations in the spaces provided.

This Coupon Is Good For:

_____

_____

_____

Presented To:

_____

(character's name)

From The Book:

_____

This Coupon Is Good For:

_____

_____

_____

Presented To:

_____

(character's name)

From The Book:

_____

This Coupon Is Good For:

_____

_____

_____

Presented To:

_____

(character's name)

From The Book:

_____

This Coupon Is Good For:

_____

_____

_____

Presented To:

_____

(character's name)

From The Book:

_____

©The Education Center, Inc. • THE MAILBOX® • Intermediate • Oct/Nov 1995 • idea by Julia Alarie—Gr. 6, Essex Middle School, Essex, VT

Book-Sharing Project Evaluation Form

Name: _____ (2 pts.)

Date: _____ (2 pts.)

Title of book: _____ (2 pts.)

Author's name: _____ (2 pts.)

Illustrator's name: _____ (2 pts.)

Favorite character .... (5 pts.)

Description of character .... (10 pts.)

Plot (including the setting) .... (10 pts.)

Favorite part .... (10 pts.)

Recommendation .... (10 pts.)

Promptness .... (5 pts.)

Neatness .... (10 pts.)

Organization .... (10 pts.)

Creativity .... (10 pts.)

Presentation .... (10 pts.)

total

©The Education Center, Inc. • THE MAILBOX® • Intermediate • Dec/Jan 1995–96

Note To The Teacher: Provide each student with a copy of this evaluation form before beginning a book-sharing project. Use the form to help you and your students evaluate their book-sharing projects. *Christine L. Juozitis—Gr. 4, Thomas Jefferson School, Binghamton, NY*

Name _____

Storytelling guidelines

The Joy Of Storytelling

Where To Find A Good Story

Use the school or local library to find a good story to share. Or ask your teacher for suggestions. Folktales, picture books, short-story books, and anthologies are great sources.

Simple Rules To Remember

1. Be sure you know the story well, but don't memorize it.
2. Use any phrases or quotes that are important parts of the story.
3. Use expression in your presentation—but don't be too dramatic. That can detract from your story.
4. Look directly at your audience.
5. Practice telling your story before presenting it.

Practice Makes Perfect...Better!

1. Tell your story to yourself in front of a mirror.
2. Tape-record your story as you practice it.
3. Present your story to your family.
4. Don't try to remember every single word. Tell the story in your own words.

It's Show Time!

- You don't need experience to dramatize a story. Try one or more of the following props:

  puppets   a flannelboard   vests   hats
  stuffed animals   masks   a chalkboard   photos
  sound effects   music

- Stories can be dramatized without props by using accents. Or consider singing or background music. Audience participation can also be a lot of fun!

And Finally...

Be original! Be creative! But most of all—HAVE FUN!

©The Education Center, Inc. • THE MAILBOX® • Intermediate • Dec/Jan 1995–96
• Jeannie Maier—Gr. 5, Allen W. Roberts Elementary, New Providence, NJ

Note To The Teacher: Use with "The Joy Of Storytelling" on page 222.

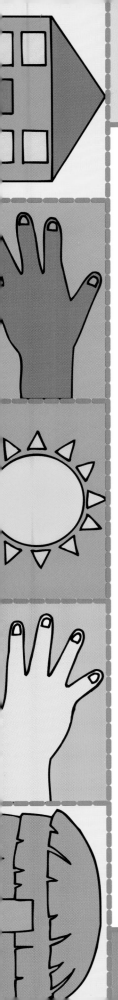

A Patchwork Of Poetry

Multicultural Poetry Activities And Collections

Poetry—it's a universal language spoken in every culture and country of the world. Introduce students to the rich treasure found in poems from different cultures, backgrounds, and lands with the following activities and recommended poetry collections.

A Great Place To Start

Give students their first taste of multicultural poetry with *This Same Sky: A Collection Of Poems From Around The World* (selected by Naomi Shihab Nye; published by Four Winds Press/Macmillan Publishing Company, 1992). Available in both hardback and paperback editions, this eloquent anthology features poems by 129 poets from 68 countries. It's a great tool to introduce students to poems written by people who live in different lands and cultures. Try these activities to introduce and extend this exciting book:

- To introduce the book, copy three favorite poems from it on separate sheets of chart paper. After you and several students have read each poem aloud at least twice, divide the class into cooperative groups. Give the groups several minutes to list information each poem gives about the poet and his or her homeland. After groups have shared their lists, help students conclude that they can catch glimpses of different people, cultures, and lands through poetry. Each morning, share one or two poems from the book. After several days, let students volunteer to select poems to read aloud.

- During the Gulf War of 1991, the compiler of this anthology searched for poems by Iraqi poets. She wanted to show students that there were "real people living inside those headlines." Extend this idea with a thought-provoking display. On a bulletin board, post a world map and a newspaper story (including the headline) that describes an event taking place in another part of the globe. Discuss the event with students; then challenge them to look in poetry collections (see the suggested books on pages 226–228) to find poems from the country or region mentioned in the news story. When a student has found an appropriate poem, have him copy it onto a sheet of paper and staple it beside the news report. Have him also copy the poem onto an overhead transparency. Display the poem on the overhead and have the student read it aloud. As a class, discuss what the poem has to say about the people who are living that particular news story. As a follow-up, have students respond in their journals about how the news story and/or poem made them feel.

- When Naomi Shihab Nye decided to compile a collection of multicultural poems, she sent out a call for poems from poets around the globe. Send your students on a similar mission to collect poems for a class anthology. Duplicate the form letter on page 229. Have students distribute the forms to other classes, staff members, neighbors, family members, pen pals, area writers, etc. After the poems have been collected, let students group them into several chapters (adding some of their own original poems to the collection). Have each student illustrate his favorite poem; then bind the poems and illustrations between two tagboard covers. When asking for entries to her collection, Nye asked poets to send their signatures. These signatures appear on the endpapers of the book, along with a selection of the envelopes and stamps that were used. To further pattern your class anthology after *This Same Sky*, each poet is asked to write his or her name on the bottom of the reproducible letter. Have students cut out these signatures and glue them onto the inside front and back covers of your anthology. Don't forget to have students add their own signatures as well.

Multicultural Poetry For Your Students

On the next three pages, you'll find suggestions for outstanding poetry collections that feature poems from various cultural backgrounds and lands. For a quick poetry activity to use with any of these books, see the "Poetry Lesson Plan" on each page.

reviewed by Deborah Zink Roffino

Celebrate America In Poetry And Art
edited by Nora Panzer
Hyperion Books For Children, 1994

This reverent compilation honors a multitude of cultures, eras, and people of the United States. Paintings, sculptures, and photographs from the Smithsonian Institution's National Museum Of American Art are thoughtfully matched with the works of poets to form complete expressions of the American experience. If a classroom could have only one anthology, this unforgettable volume would be the perfect choice.

The Dream Keeper And Other Poems
written by Langston Hughes and illustrated by Brian Pinkney
Alfred A. Knopf, Inc.; 1994

This 1932 compilation lauding the African American experience demonstrates its timeless charm in a new version decorated with precise pen-and-ink sketches. Words and pictures interlock, offering exuberant images of seasons past, grand characters, rolling rivers, and joyous songs. Upbeat, powerful, and hopeful—the works of Langston Hughes stand ready for a whole new generation of Americans to celebrate.

Neighborhood Odes
written by Gary Soto and illustrated by David Diaz
Harcourt Brace Jovanovich, 1992

Take a walk through this fiesta of poems and you'll catch a glimpse of the vitality and exuberance of a Mexican American neighborhood. The author writes of the pleasures of simple things such as snow cones, tennis shoes, tortillas, and the library. Dramatic black-and-white prints add to the book's spirit and impact.

Poetry Lesson Plan
Share with students one of your favorite memories; then give them opportunities to describe some of theirs. Read examples of poems about memories that you've gleaned from collections such as those on this page and on pages 227–228. Then have each child write a poem about a favorite memory. To generate ideas, ask questions such as, "How did this memorable event make you feel? What did you taste, see, smell, touch, and hear during this event? What color is this memory? What is its shape? How does this memory make you feel today?" Encourage students to create specific details they can't remember. Have each child copy and illustrate his completed poem on a sheet of art paper to bind inside a class book.

Poets not only see things objectively; they also see them subjectively. For example, a poet might look at a picture and see a broken vase. On another level, he might also see an argument with a friend. To give students practice in seeing things objectively and subjectively, display a magazine picture of a simple object or scene. Have each student write a detailed description of what he sees with his eyes; then have him describe what he sees at another level. After you've done this exercise with several pictures, have volunteers read one of their descriptions (either objective or subjective) without naming the picture. Have classmates try to guess which picture is being described.

A Caribbean Dozen: Poems From Caribbean Poets

edited by John Agard and Grace Nichols; illustrated by Cathie Felstead
Candlewick Press, 1994

This spicy collection of poetry is the work of 13 Caribbean poets who spread their memories across the scorching colors of the festive pages. Adding to the interest of this anthology, each set of poems is introduced with a first-person account from the poet. Vigorous patterns, collages, and colors dance off the pages to a reggae beat.

My Song Is Beautiful: Poems And Pictures In Many Voices

selected by Mary Ann Hoberman
Little, Brown and Company; 1994

Fourteen simple poems reflect images of childhood from the perspectives of many diverse cultures. Illustrated by a variety of renowned children's artists, this multicultural anthology features a variety of poetry styles and illustration techniques. Readers will find a poem by a child and a piece of original artwork by a class of elementary-school students tucked inside the pages.

The Kingfisher Book Of Children's Poetry

selected by Michael Rosen and illustrated by Alice Englander
Kingfisher Books, 1993

This very special collection—part of English poet Michael Rosen's efforts to rekindle enthusiasm for poetry in children—features poems from around the world, including translations from Chinese, Chilean, French, and Russian. From Auden all the way to Yeats, these entertaining poems tell stories, breathe nonsense, rant and rave, amuse, and make youngsters pause and think.

Pierced By A Ray Of Sun: Poems About The Times We Feel Alone

selected by Ruth Gordon
HarperCollins Children's Books, 1995

Loneliness, as these stirring poems illustrate, has no regard for race, creed, or background. In a book that tackles the question, "Am I the only such person on Earth?", advanced readers will find a collection of poems that speak of the universality of loneliness.

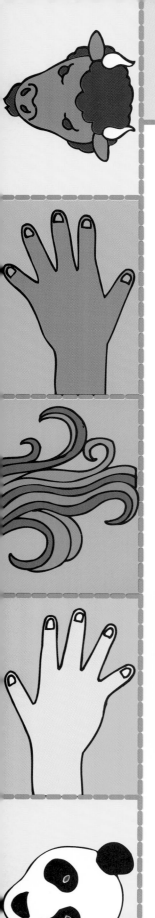

In The Eyes Of The Cat:
Japanese Poetry For All Seasons
selected and illustrated by Demi
Henry Holt And Company, 1992

Classic Japanese poetry fills the pages of this lovely collection. Organized by seasons, these poems comment on both the familiar and unusual in nature. Simple, yet evocative, paintings add to the enchanting quality of this little book. Students who are overwhelmed with the idea of writing lengthy poems will be pleasantly surprised and motivated by these short, yet powerful, verses.

Soul Looks Back In Wonder
compiled and illustrated by Tom Feelings
Dial Books, 1993

After completing the stunning artwork, Tom Feelings asked several poets to contribute poems for this memorable picture book. Fourteen renowned writers—including such talents as Maya Angelou, Walter Dean Myers, and Langston Hughes—responded with verses that speak boldly and eloquently of the African American experience. The resulting collaboration is a must-read for young and old poets alike.

On The Road Of Stars:
Native American Night Poems And Sleep Charms
selected by John Bierhorst and illustrated by Judy Pedersen
Macmillan Publishing Company, 1994

Gentle lullabies and sleep songs drawn from over 20 Native American tribes lull readers and listeners to sleep in this unusual collection. Illustrated with remarkable artwork, the more than 50 poems in this book are sure to uncover the magic of nighttime and the people who understood its significance.

Poetry Lesson Plan

Have students bring in objects that are special to them: things that they treasure or that have interesting textures, smells, colors, shapes, uses, etc. As a class, examine and discuss each object. Then have each student choose one item and spend time studying it. After the student has listed details and thoughts about the object, have her write a poem about it. If desired, have students write *persona poems* in which they take on the personalities of their objects. Ask questions such as, "How do you feel and smell? What does your shape remind you of? Where have you lived or traveled? What are your dreams? How have you changed?" Have students copy their poems on poster-board cutouts of their shapes.

Other Outstanding Collections:
Festival In My Heart: Poems By Japanese Children
selected and translated by Bruno Navasky; Harry N. Abrams, Inc.; 1993

I Have A News: Rhymes From The Caribbean
collected by Walter Jekyll; Lothrop, Lee & Shepard Books; 1994

Pass It On: African-American Poetry For Children
selected by Wade Hudson; Scholastic Inc., 1993

broccoli · loneliness · vacations · noises · faces · being stranded · pizza · my best friend

embarrassment · water · school · a promise · a storm · a fear · joy · prejudice · shoes · a distant land · nighttime

my favorite memory · the best holiday ever · a pet peeve · the elderly · homelessness · clouds · my room · springtime · dreams

Be A Poetry Partner!

Dear ______________________________,

My class is positively pumped up about poetry! We are so excited that we are planning to compile a class book of poems. Some of the poems in the book will be written by us students. But we want the rest of the poems to be contributed by other people we know—like you!

So how do you become one of our "poetry partners"? It's simple! Just write a short, original poem in the space below (use the back of this page if you need more space). You can write a poem about any topic you want. If you need help with an idea, choose one of the topics listed around the border of this letter.

After you've written your poem, please complete the information in the box below. I will collect your poem on ______________.

Thanks for being one of our poetry partners. Happy writing!

Signed: ______________________________

____

____

____

____

____

____

____

____

____

____

____

Please sign your name on the line below.
Add small illustrations around your name if you like.

____

Note To The Teacher: Use this reproducible with the idea on page 225. Before duplicating the letter, write the due date in the blank. Give each student one or more copies of the letter. Have each student sign his copy(s) before giving it to a family member, friend, neighbor, etc. Or duplicate a supply for a neighboring class. Have each student sign one copy; then have two students deliver and distribute them to the neighboring class. Have two other students collect the finished poems on the due date.

Make Mine A Mystery!
Spine-Tingling Whodunits Your Super Sleuths Will Love!

It's no mystery why mystery books are so popular. Teachers know that this genre sharpens powers of reasoning and deductive skills. Intermediate students plow through these books (often under the covers, with their flashlights on) for one reason: mysteries are just plain fun! The following excellent mysteries give students the thrill of solving a puzzle and one chill after another—what more could a reader ask for?

reviewed by Deborah Zink Roffino

Following are three sections: individual titles, serials, and novelty books. The books in each of these sections are listed in order from least difficult to more challenging.

Individual Titles

The Birthday Wish Mystery
written by Faye Couch Reeves and illustrated by Marilyn Mets
Little Rainbow®/Troll Associates, Inc.; 1994

Take easy text; short chapters; believable kids; and a strange, empty box that appears on the front doorstep—the result is this perfect first mystery book. Clues tumble across the pages, challenging readers to identify the enigmatic Annabelle Dupree before young Wynnie does. A host of characters send Wynnie on a series of searches. On the way she makes a friend, solves the puzzle, and learns just how much she is loved.

Mysteries Of Sherlock Holmes
written by Sir Arthur Conan Doyle and adapted by Judith Conaway
Bullseye Step Into Classics™/Random House, 1994

This reprinted classic is a terrific way for young readers to get hooked on one of the most famous detectives in literature. Three short mysteries—with an abundance of clipped, typical Holmes dialogue—offer the facts. Can you solve the mystery before Holmes? Large print and detailed black-and-white drawings make this edition less overwhelming than most versions.

The Seven Treasure Hunts
written by Betsy Byars and illustrated by Jennifer Barrett
HarperCollins Children's Books, 1991

Newbery-winner Betsy Byars appeals to reluctant readers in this hilarious chapter book. Two best friends spend every spare minute hiding treasure just for the sheer pleasure of unearthing it. When a delicious portion of the hoard truly disappears, the boys suspect sibling shenanigans and must apply all of their detective prowess to solve the mystery. Told engagingly in the first person, this book is peppered with clever black-and-white sketches that ably augment the story.

Marvelous Marvin And The Wolfman Mystery

written by Bonnie Pryor and illustrated by Melissa Sweet
Morrow Junior Books, 1994

Something *verrrry* weird is happening next door at Mr. Wolfe's house! The curious and suspicious Marvin Fremont begins some delightful detective work in this chapter book for medium-level readers. The believable plot draws on clues, secret cryptograms, and reasoning to build to a Halloween climax. Readers pleased with this adventure can check out the follow-up mystery, *Marvelous Marvin And The Pioneer Ghost* (1995), featuring the same crew of amateur sleuths.

The Bones In The Cliff

written by James Stevenson
Greenwillow Books, 1995

Pete's abusive father is terrified of a big, mysterious stranger who smells like cigars. For moderately accomplished readers, this captivating story in first person carries the reader on a dramatic search for truth. On the way, the battered and weary Pete finds a lasting friendship and a better life.

Panther Glade

written by Helen Cavanagh
Simon & Schuster Books For Young Readers, 1993

Mystery stalkers are lured by this sort of dark and menacing adventure in the wilderness. Young Bill accompanies his archaeologist aunt on a dig to a Calusa burial mound in Florida. His discovery of a small artifact believed to have great powers sends him on a solitary journey to learn the foundation of its legend. For stronger readers, this story features rich characters, heart-pounding tension, and a satisfying resolution.

The Missing 'Gator Of Gumbo Limbo: An Ecological Mystery

written by Jean Craighead George
HarperCollins Children's Books, 1992

One of the first environmental writers for youngsters is still one of the best. Jean Craighead George lures more accomplished readers into the Gumbo Limbo section of the Everglades. When an official tries to do away with Dajun, an enormous alligator, Liza K. must find the missing 'gator with careful detective work and an ability to read environmental clues. It's botany, ecology, biology, and mystery all in one terrific book!

The Sluggers Club: A Sports Mystery
written by Paul Robert Walker
Harcourt Brace Jovanovich, Publishers; 1993
Competent readers are rewarded in this baseball/detective novel with fully developed characters, more twists than a triple play, lessons on vicious prejudice, and a full-blown puzzler. Baseball aficionados will follow the Matt Christopher-style play-by-play better than the uninformed, but even nonfans can get hooked as equipment vanishes, questions multiply, and suspicious characters surface.

Super Serials For Super Sleuths

The Boxcar Children® Special #3: The Mystery At Snowflake Inn
created by Gertrude Chandler Warner and illustrated by Charles Tang
Albert Whitman & Company, 1994
For those unfamiliar with this popular series, four children are found living alone in a box-car and are taken in by their grandfather. The adventures the children encounter while learning to be a family provide the framework for the simple mysteries they solve. The text offers strong context clues for new vocabulary and mixes history lessons in the story line. Several books in the series—including this one about a puzzling holiday trip to an old-fashioned New England inn—end with several pages of puzzles, games, and recipes that reflect the plot.

The Kerry Hill Casecrackers #4: The Case Of The Mysterious Codes
written by Peggy Nicholson and John F. Warner
Lerner Publications Company, 1995
The mystery starts instantly with the arrival of coded messages, and some ominous and unwelcome gifts. The Casecrackers—sharp, young detectives from New England—use logical deductions and powers of observation to get to the resolution of their cases. Like Nancy Drew and the Hardy Boys, these kids from Kerry Hill start to feel like old friends after one book. And, delightfully, there are four books in this fine, new series.

Welcome Inn #3: The Skeleton Key
written by E. L. Flood
Rainbow Bridge®/Troll Associates, Inc.; 1994
Don't be scared off by the cover images of haunted houses and grave digging; this is good, tense fun without any gore or supernatural villains. Plodding, old-fashioned detective work solves this mystery for moderately strong readers. Close calls, dark encounters, and foreboding disappearances engage the reader from page one to the satisfying and reasonable conclusion.

Novelty Books

Puzzle Island
devised, written, and illustrated by Paul Adshead
Child's Play (International) Limited, 1995

For individual or group detective work, this creative puzzle/book challenges youngsters to read a diary, decipher the clues, make inferences, and then identify and help rescue an endangered species. Lush tropical paintings give this paperback the tone of a picture book. But don't be too quick to jump to conclusions; traces of evidence are hidden with great skill in the detailed jungle scenes. Amateur sleuths will compete to solve this fascinating mystery.

Whodunit: Science Solves The Crime
written by Steven Otfinoski and illustrated by Betsy Scheld
Scientific American Books For Young Readers/W. H. Freeman and Company, 1995

Ten fascinating chapters, each featuring a real criminal case, demonstrate the science of forensics. Dating back to the 1800s, the cases touch each new technology—including fingerprinting, DNA, tissue analysis, ballistics, and the detection of poison—that leads to resolution of a mysterious crime. Vibrant art provides an interruption of the text, making the information less intimidating and more storylike. This slim compendium offers an intriguing link between technology and mysteries, and between the science curriculum and reading.

More Marvelous Mysteries

The Disappearing Bike Shop
by Elvira Woodruff; Holiday House, Inc.; 1992

Spider Kane And The Mystery At Jumbo Nightcrawler's
by Mary Pope Osborne; Random House Books For Young Readers, 1994

Skateboard Tough
by Matt Christopher; Little, Brown and Company; 1991

The Man Who Was Poe
by Avi; Avon Books, 1991

The View From The Cherry Tree
by Willo Davis Roberts; Aladdin/Macmillan Children's Book Group, 1994

The Court Of The Stone Children
by Eleanor Cameron; Puffin Books, 1990

The Cay
A Powerful Novel Of Survival

Use the following activities and reproducibles to extend Theodore Taylor's story of two unlikely friends and their struggle for survival on a tiny Caribbean island.

with ideas by Lynn Greco

Book summary: Eleven-year-old Phillip Enright is in a struggle for survival. The freighter on which he and his mother are traveling from the Dutch island of Curacao to the United States is torpedoed by the Germans during World War II. Phillip awakens to find himself floating on a raft with an elderly West Indian named Timothy. After a crack on the head leaves Phillip blind, the castaways land on a tiny barren island, or *cay*. How these two mismatched companions build a friendship and challenge nature's elements makes for an unforgettable story.

Before reading: Place a class set of page 236 (duplicated on white construction paper) at a center. Before you begin reading, have each student select a chapter from the book (which has 19 chapters). After a chapter has been read, direct the student who selected that chapter to get a copy of page 236 and complete the mini-mural activity about his chapter. Display the completed mini-murals on a large table or windowsill. By the end of the book, you'll have a visual summary of the story.

After reading Chapter 3: All Phillip notices are the differences between himself and his raft mate. One of those differences is Timothy's calypso-like dialect. Discuss dialect with students; then have them find examples of Timothy's speech from Chapter 3. List these examples on the board for students or pairs of students to translate. Provide more examples of Caribbean dialect with *A Caribbean Dozen: Poems From Caribbean Poets* (Candlewick Press, 1994). Edited by John Agard and Grace Nichols, this rich volume recalls the childhood memories of 13 Caribbean poets, and includes many poems written in the distinctive dialect of the region.

After reading Chapter 5: After reading this chapter, give students two minutes to list things they would do with a good friend if they could spend three days with him or her. After students have shared their lists, review Phillip and Timothy's situation: adrift on the open sea, little to eat or drink, scorched by a blazing sun, surrounded by unfriendly waters. Set a timer for another two minutes; then have pairs of students list things they might do to pass the time while adrift. After this exercise, let students pretend to be Phillip or Timothy and write in their journals about the days in the raft.

After reading Chapter 7: The two castaways find themselves on a small Caribbean island in what Timothy calls the "Devil's Mouth"—a U-shaped group of islands with sharp coral banks on either side. After briefly reviewing map skills, give each student a sheet of art paper and challenge him to draw a bird's-eye view of the cay. Remind students to reread portions of the chapter to help them locate information about the island. Provide time for students to compare their finished maps. At the conclusion of the book, take a second look at the maps and discuss how the students' views changed as they read further.

After reading Chapter 10: Phillip began his adventure with racial prejudices inherited from his mother. When he asks Timothy why there are different colors of skin, Timothy replies that he thinks "...beneath d'skin is all d'same." Let students communicate their own ideas about this statement in original collages. Begin by brainstorming with students reasons why people have prejudices about others who are different from them. Then give each student a sheet of construction paper, scissors, and a glue stick. Have the student cut out pictures, words, and phrases from old magazines to illustrate "beneath d'skin is all d'same." After students have glued their cutouts collage-fashion to the paper, provide time for them to share their thought-provoking creations.

After reading Chapter 12: In this chapter, Timothy contracts malaria and is nursed back to health by Phillip. Write the last line of the chapter on the board: "He never really regained his strength." Without reading any further, have students or student groups list their predictions as to how this statement might be a foreshadow of upcoming events. Let students share their predictions as you list them on chart paper. Post the list so students can compare their ideas to actual events as the story continues to unfold.

After reading Chapter 15: A massive hurricane has just swept over the island with devastating results. Depending on where you live, it's likely that you and your students have never experienced a hurricane. Invite a meteorologist to speak to your class about hurricanes and their effects. Perhaps he/she can bring news videotapes taken before, during, or after a hurricane. Have students compare the information gathered from this talk with the author's description of Timothy and Phillip's ordeal.

After reading Chapter 16: It isn't until after Timothy dies that Phillip realizes the love behind the old man's stubbornness. Discuss the qualities Phillip found in Timothy that made the gentle sailor such a good friend. What qualities do your students look for in a friend? After this discussion, give each child a copy of page 237. Tell students that their mission is to find out what other people look for in a friend. Go over the directions on the reproducible so that each child understands how to complete the survey. After the surveys have been completed, let students compare them and graph the results, noting the most frequently mentioned qualities.

Culminating activity: Ask your librarian for a copy of *If Once You Have Slept On An Island* by Rachel Field (Boyds Mills Press, Inc.; 1993). In this enchanting picture book, a simple 14-line poem about life on an island is illustrated with descriptive watercolors. Share the book with students, and discuss how both the author and Phillip felt about their islands. Then challenge your class to write a version of the poem as it might have been written by Phillip a few months after his rescue. Copy the lines of the poem on chart paper to post in the classroom as a reference. Work with students to create a class-written poem that follows Field's pattern. After the poem is polished, assign two or more lines to each cooperative group. Instruct the groups to write each line at the top of a separate piece of art paper, and then illustrate it with scenes from the book. Bind the finished pages together into a class book that honors a memorable story.

Name _____

Make A Mini-Mural

Before you begin reading the book: Select a chapter from *The Cay*.

After reading your chapter: Follow the directions in each panel. Then cut out the three panels along the heavy lines only. Write your name on the back of the panels. Then fold on the two dotted lines to make a standing mini-mural.

Fill in the blanks to write an "If... Then..." statement about the chapter.

If....

_____
_____
_____
_____
_____

Then...

_____
_____
_____
_____

Write some thoughts you had while reading the chapter.

Chapter _____

Draw a scene from the chapter.

Note To The Teacher: Before you begin the book, have each student select a chapter on which to complete this activity. Duplicate student copies on white construction paper. Use with the "Before reading" activity on page 234.

Finding A Friend

Timothy and Phillip—at first sight, they seemed unlikely to ever become friends! Phillip didn't understand Timothy's stubborn insistence that he learn to take care of himself despite being blind. It wasn't until after Timothy's death that Phillip realized his friend had been so strict because he wanted young Phillip to learn how to survive on his own. Timothy proved to be the best friend Phillip had ever had.

What qualities do people look for in a friend? Interview ten people to find the answer to that question. Write the name of each person and his/her relationship to you (relative, friend, teacher, neighbor, etc.) in the chart below. Then check off the qualities that person looks for in a friend. If necessary, add qualities to the chart by writing them in the starred blank boxes.

Information About Interviewees			Friendship Qualities									
Name of interviewee	Relationship to interviewer	M = Male F = Female	Fun to be with	Something in common with me	Easy to talk to; listens	Caring	Clever/smart	Sense of humor	Helpful	★	★	★
1.												
2.												
3.												
4.												
5.												
6.												
7.												
8.												
9.												
10.												

Note To The Teacher: Use after reading Chapter 16 in *The Cay*. See the activity on page 235.

Dis B'Dat Outrageous New Chapter!

At the end of *The Cay*, Phillip says that one day he'll charter a schooner out of Panama, explore the Devil's Mouth, and find the cay on which he and Timothy lived. Suppose you could add a chapter about this trip to *The Cay*. What would you write?

Directions: Decide on six key events that you would include in your new chapter. Illustrate each event in a box on the storyboard below. Under the box, write a brief summary of the scene.

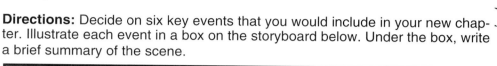

_____   _____
_____   _____
_____   _____

_____   _____
_____   _____
_____   _____

_____   _____
_____   _____
_____   _____

Bonus Box: On another piece of paper, write your chapter using the ideas included in the storyboard above.

THE WESTING GAME

An Intriguing Whodunit

Who killed Sam Westing? Is he really dead? Tantalize your students with this clever Newbery Medal-winning mystery by Ellen Raskin.

by Beth Gress

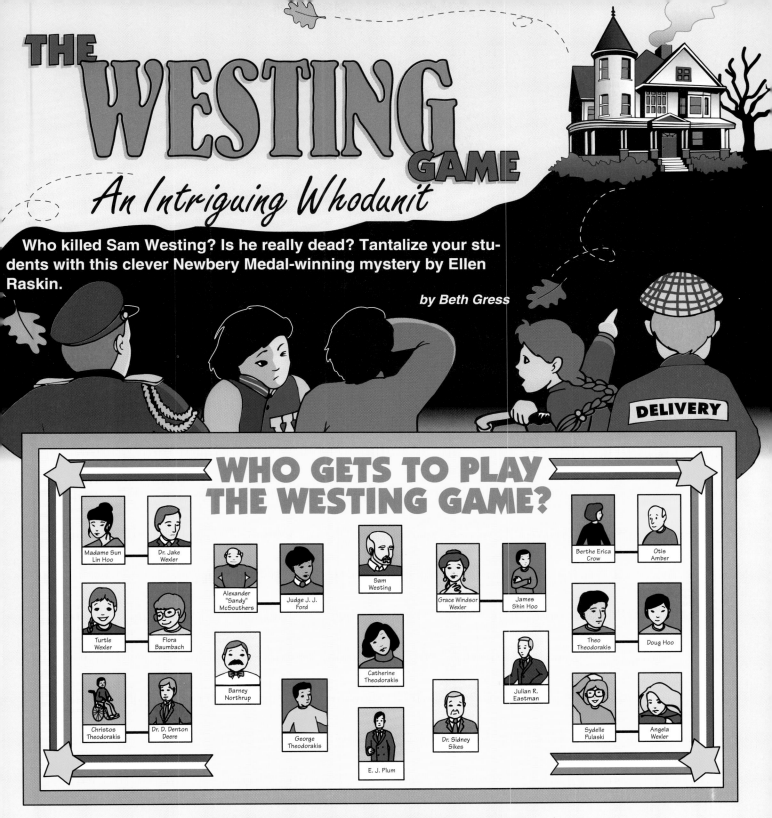

WHO GETS TO PLAY THE WESTING GAME?

Madame Sun Lin Hoo — Dr. Jake Wexler

Alexander "Sandy" McSouthers — Judge J. J. Ford

Sam Westing

Grace Windsor Wexler — James Shin Hoo

Berthe Erica Crow — Otis Amber

Turtle Wexler — Flora Baumbach

Barney Northrup

Catherine Theodorakis

Theo Theodorakis — Doug Hoo

Christos Theodorakis — Dr. D. Denton Deere

George Theodorakis

E. J. Plum

Dr. Sidney Sikes

Julian R. Eastman

Sydelle Pulaski — Angela Wexler

Who Gets To Play The Westing Game?

Keeping up with all the different characters in *The Westing Game* is loads of fun, but can be a bit confusing. Have your students make a display that keeps readers straight on who's who. Collect magazines that contain photos of people. After your class has read the first seven chapters, pass out piles of magazines to small groups of students. Instruct groups to use the story clues to select photos that could represent the story characters. Once every group has selected a photo for each character, have the class vote on the picture they think best represents each character. Arrange the pictures on a bulletin board with the portraits grouped according to their Westing Game partnerships (see the illustration).

Keeping Case Notes

Tracking clues in *The Westing Game* will be easier—and even more fun—if students work together in groups. Supply each group with one copy of the book and two copies of the "Case Notes" reproducible on page 242. As you or the students read the book, instruct groups to record each character's name and information about him/her on the reproducible. (Refer students to the bulletin board described on page 239 to help them list the characters.) Give each group a folder in which to store its case notes.

How will you keep curious students from reading ahead and spoiling the fun for more patient readers? Each day—before handing out the books to each group—secure the pages you don't want students to read by putting a rubber band around them from top to bottom. Discourage students from peeking ahead by telling them that they may not remove the rubber bands from their books.

Who's The Quicker Picker-Upper?

Which of your students will figure out the clues first? Help your student groups search for the solution to the mystery in the same way that the characters do. In the story, the Westing Game clues are written on squares cut from paper towels. Cut several paper towels into two-inch squares. Give each group six to eight of the squares and one whole paper-towel sheet. As they read, have students use felt-tipped markers to write the clue words given in the story onto the squares. Post the clue word squares on the bulletin board (page 239) next to the game partners. As clue words are added to the display, have groups try to figure out the meaning of the clues. Prior to reading chapter 17, have each group submit the solution (written on the whole paper towel) it thinks is most likely. After completing the book, compare the actual solution to the students' predictions.

Journal Topics And More!

Chapter titles often give clues to upcoming events, and those in *The Westing Game* are no exception. At the beginning of each chapter, have students predict what will occur according to the chapter title. After reading the chapter, discuss how the title related to the events in the chapter.

In addition to looking at the titles, encourage students to reflect on and react to each section of the story by responding to the following thought-provoking journal questions:

Ch. 2: What would it take for you to volunteer to do what Turtle did?

Ch. 4: What would you do if you had found the body like Turtle did?

Ch. 7: Who is your favorite character so far? Why?

Ch. 8: What would you do with the $10,000?

Ch. 9: What notice might you put up in the elevator?

Ch. 11: Choose one pair of game partners and explain why they make perfect partners.

Ch. 13: Choose three characters and give reasons why each might have set off the bomb.

Ch. 22: Write the words to "America, The Beautiful" or some other patriotic song. Explain what the words mean to you.

Ch. 25: Do you think Berthe Erica Crow is guilty or innocent? What evidence can you give to support your view?

End: Who would you say is the hero of *The Westing Game?* Why? Is there a villain in the story? If so, who is it?

Who Am I?

I don't go by my real name most of the story.

I have a small room.

I play the stock market.

I kick shins.

I have a long braid.

Answer: Turtle Wexler

Who Am I?

Use the many characters of *The Westing Game* to make up a Who Am I? game. Write each character's name on a slip of paper. (See the bulletin board on page 239 for a complete listing of characters.) Then have each student draw one name. Instruct the student to write five clues about the identity of his character on an index card, listing them from the hardest clue to the easiest clue. Collect and shuffle the clue cards; then divide the class into four teams. Read the top clue from a card to the first team. After the team has collaborated, instruct a spokesman to tell you the team's guess. Award points based on the number of clues needed to guess the solution. For example, if the team guesses correctly after only one clue, it wins five points. If only two clues are read, the team wins four points, and so on. After one team has guessed from a card, move to the next team using a new card. After all the cards have been read, tally the points to determine the winning team.

Follow The Stocks

Turtle Wexler convinced Flora Baumbach that the best way to invest their $10,000 was to play the stock market. Explore the stock market with your class by having cooperative groups select three well-known stocks to follow for the duration of the unit. Divide the class into five groups. Give each group a copy of stock quotes from the business section of the daily newspaper and a copy of "Staking Out The Stocks" on page 244. (Two well-known places which register and list stocks are the New York Stock Exchange [NYSE] and the American Stock Exchange [AMEX].) Help students locate some of the better-known stocks. Then have them use the information in "Staking Out The Stocks" to help them determine the price of their chosen stocks and how to keep track of daily changes in price.

If desired, make a class poster tracking each of the groups' stocks. Then have each group create a line graph plotting the rise or fall of its stocks during the unit. Post these line graphs with the stock report poster.

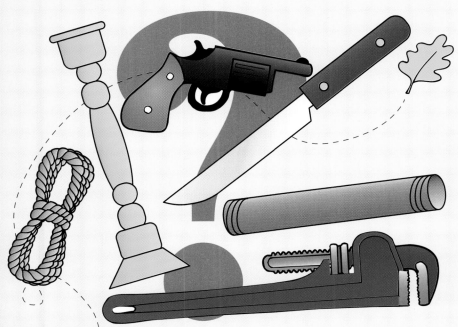

Have A Clue?

Teach your students the board game Clue®, and you'll teach them note-taking, organization, and logical-thinking skills. Have students compare Clue® to *The Westing Game* story. Which characters from Clue® do *The Westing Game* characters resemble? Discuss the similarities between the clue cards in the game and the paper-towel squares in the story. Expand this connection by having student groups create their own mystery board games using Clue® and *The Westing Game* as models. Provide pizza boxes for gameboards. Instruct students to include a background story, a cast of characters, game cards, playing pieces, and directions. Trade the completed games among the groups for playing.

Name(s) _____

Case Notes

Can you figure out who killed Sam Westing? Record what you discover about each character on two copies of this sheet. Then put together the clues to solve the mystery. Perhaps *you'll* be the winner of The Westing Game!

Character	Family	Occupation	Westing Game Partner	Other Information	Paper-Towel Clues

©The Education Center, Inc. • *THE MAILBOX*® • *Intermediate* • April/May 1996

Note To The Teacher: Duplicate two copies for each group or individual student. Use with "Keeping Case Notes" on page 240.

Money-Making Quotes

As you read *The Westing Game,* look for the following quotations. You'll find the speakers' names written on the stock market ticker tape around the page. As you figure out a quotation, cross off the portions of the name that are on the tape. Then rearrange the remaining letters to uncover a revealing message. Write the message in the box.

Gra   outhers   ber   ge   row   He   Wex   Jud   gela   ler   ca

1. _____ "Hi, Sandy, I won!"

2. _____ "I am the answer and I am the winner. I give half of my inheritance to Otis Amber, to be used for the Good Salvation Soup Kitchen. I give the rest of the money to Angela."

3. _____ "My mother was a servant in the Westing household, my father worked for the railroad and was the gardener on his days off."

4. _____ "I'm no fool, you know. I knew I couldn't trust any one of you. You can't read my shorthand because I wrote in Polish."

5. _____ "But Crow still needs me, and I'll stick by her no matter what. I've grown fond of the woman; we've been together such a long time."

6. _____ "I'll hem your witch's costume, Turtle."

7. _____ "What a lovely living room, so practically furnished. Our apartments are identical in layout, but mine looks so different. You must come see what I've done with it. I'm a decorator, you know."

8. _____ "I can take some credit for those paper innersoles. My feet were killing me, standing at the door all day, so I said to Jimmy: 'Jimmy, if only somebody would invent a good innersole that didn't take up so much room like those foam-rubber things.' And sure enough, he did it. They're great, I got a pair in my shoes now, wanna see?"

C laski is An J. J. no Ber delle dy Ford We Otis Eri

Bonus Box: Find three other important quotes in the book. Write each quote on a separate piece of paper (without identifying the speaker). Write your name on the back of each slip; then give the slips to your teacher to read aloud to the class. How many of your classmates can identify the speakers of your quotes?

Sy t xler Am de the McS Wex ad tle San Pu

The hidden message:
_____

ce Tur ler

Note To The Teacher: Use this reproducible after students have read the book.

243

The Last Word

Now that you've finished reading *The Westing Game,* choose one list of words below. On your own paper, define each word. Then use the words to write a paragraph about the topic described below that list.

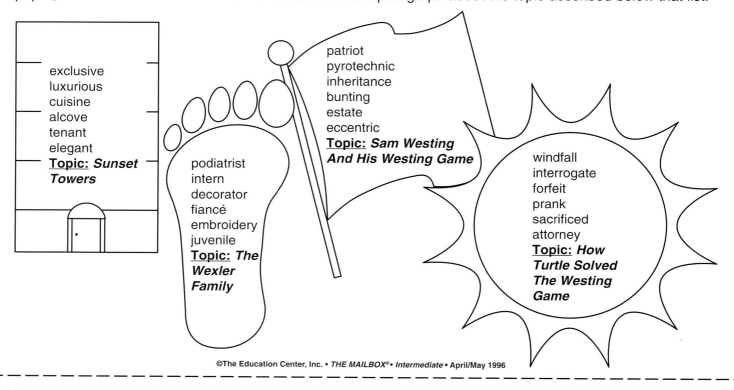

exclusive
luxurious
cuisine
alcove
tenant
elegant
Topic: *Sunset Towers*

patriot
pyrotechnic
inheritance
bunting
estate
eccentric
Topic: *Sam Westing And His Westing Game*

podiatrist
intern
decorator
fiancé
embroidery
juvenile
Topic: *The Wexler Family*

windfall
interrogate
forfeit
prank
sacrificed
attorney
Topic: *How Turtle Solved The Westing Game*

©The Education Center, Inc. • *THE MAILBOX®• Intermediate • April/May 1996*

Staking Out The Stocks

Turtle and Baba successfully invested their $10,000 in the stock market. How well do you think you can do? Use the chart below to help you read the stock listings. Then keep a ten-day account of three of your favorite stocks to see how well you might have done if you had played the Westing Game.

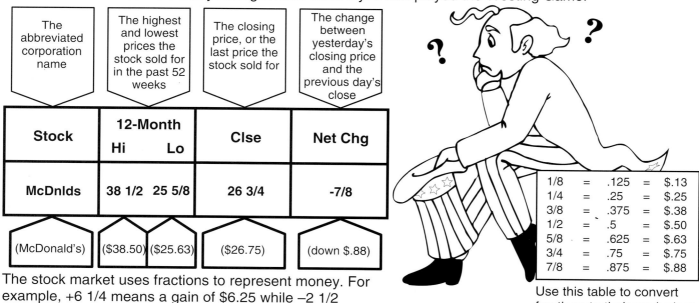

| The abbreviated corporation name | The highest and lowest prices the stock sold for in the past 52 weeks | The closing price, or the last price the stock sold for | The change between yesterday's closing price and the previous day's close |

Stock	12-Month Hi Lo	Clse	Net Chg
McDnlds	38 1/2 25 5/8	26 3/4	-7/8
(McDonald's)	($38.50) ($25.63)	($26.75)	(down $.88)

The stock market uses fractions to represent money. For example, +6 1/4 means a gain of $6.25 while −2 1/2 means a loss of $2.50.

1/8	=	.125	=	$.13
1/4	=	.25	=	$.25
3/8	=	.375	=	$.38
1/2	=	.5	=	$.50
5/8	=	.625	=	$.63
3/4	=	.75	=	$.75
7/8	=	.875	=	$.88

Use this table to convert fractions to their equivalent money amounts.

©The Education Center, Inc. • *THE MAILBOX®• Intermediate • April/May 1996*

Getting Kids Into Books

Cupboard Book Reports

After reading *The Indian In The Cupboard* by Lynne Reid Banks, have each student bring a cereal box from home and cover it with brown bulletin-board paper. Help the student cut along three of the box's front edges to make a door; then have the student cover his door with aluminum foil so that it resembles a mirror. Provide the student with poster board to make the cupboard's shelves and a brad for a doorknob. Give the student an inexpensive plastic cowboy, Indian, and horse to glue to his shelves. Then direct the student to glue his book report inside the cupboard's door.

Anne H. Warnke—Grs. 4–5, Sandston Elementary, Sandston, VA

From Architects To Sculptors

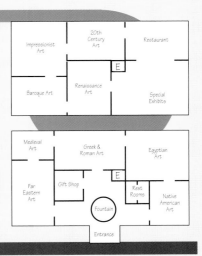

Follow up the reading of E. L. Konigsburg's book, *From The Mixed-Up Files Of Mrs. Basil E. Frankweiler,* with a creative, two-part project. First provide each student with a copy of the Metropolitan Museum of Art's floor plan (given in the book). Have the student use this copy to design a floor plan for his own museum. Require that the design consist of two floors and that each floor be divided into labeled rooms. Explain that the plan should also include restrooms, elevators, a gift shop, and a map key. Have the student color and label his floor plan, including the name of his museum somewhere in the plan.

Next have each student make a small model of a statue (similar to the angel statue in the book). Require that the statue be made from recyclable materials and have a unique name. Have each student attach a brief paragraph describing his work of art to his statue. Display the completed projects in the library for others to admire!

Elise Nash—Gr. 5, Delaware Academy, Delhi, NY

Main-Character Photo Albums

Photographs promise to capture a moment forever—so why not capture the life of a favorite book character by creating a unique photo album? After a book has been read, have each student draw and color at least ten "photographs" that could have belonged to the main character. Have the student cut out each photo, mount it on construction paper (either singly or in groups), and write a caption beneath it. Provide the student with materials for making front and back covers. Have him staple his photo pages inside. Then have him write the title of his book on the front cover and illustrate it. Direct him to write his name on the back cover.

Anna Bordlee—Gr. 5, Boudreaux Elementary, Harvey, LA

New Names

If you're looking for a great book to finish the year, try Virginia Hamilton's novel, *Zeely.* Then follow up the book with a fun activity based on names. Discuss why the children in *Zeely* chose to call themselves Geeder and Toeboy for the summer. Then allow students to choose new names for themselves. Stress to students that each name they choose must have a meaning. To help students, provide a few books that give the meanings and origins of names. Let the students make nameplates for their desks and use their new names for a week!

Diana West, Main Elementary, Rome, GA

Getting Kids Into Books

Novel Tablecloths

When reading a novel that doesn't have any chapter titles, my students create a novel tablecloth. First I cover a tabletop with white bulletin-board paper. Next I divide the paper into squares (one for each chapter of the book). After reading the first chapter, students divide into small groups and brainstorm possible chapter titles. I list their ideas on a chalkboard; then students vote for their favorite. The winning group writes its title at the top of the first square on the tablecloth, then illustrates a scene that best represents the chapter. It's a lot of fun to see our tabletop art develop as each chapter is read. By the end of the book, we have a colorful tablecloth representing the major events of our book.

Julie Plowman—Gr. 6, Adair-Casey Elementary, Adair, IA

Spotlight On Reading

As a fun way to share books my students have read, I decorate a bulletin board to resemble a movie theater marquee, adding the title "Now Playing." Every two weeks I ask several students (selected on a rotating basis) to write book reviews of books they've read independently. I mount one of the books and its review on an artist's easel located to the side of the bulletin board. This motivating, easy-to-make display has encouraged my students—who love to "show and tell"—to read even more.

Judith Brinckerhoff—Gr. 6, Hanaford School, East Greenwich, RI

Biography Boxes

After completing a study of biographies, have students create these unique book reports. On a large sheet of tagboard, have each student draw a pattern like the one shown. Have students illustrate the six squares in the pattern with the following: 1) the title and author of the book, a drawing of the biography's person, and the student's name; 2) the person's greatest accomplishment; 3) a sequential list of seven important events in the person's life; 4) any weakness, failure, or disappointment that the person had or experienced; 5) important people in the person's life; and 6) the student's choice of something important about this person. To complete the cube, instruct each student to fold on the dotted lines and tape the sides together. Display these boxed reviews in your media center for others to enjoy.

Julia Alarie—Gr. 6, Essex Middle School, Essex, VT

Thumbprint Story Maps

For a fun art project that doubles as a book review, try thumbprint story maps. First have each student draw a squiggly line from one edge of a piece of art paper to the other. Next direct the student to use an ink pad to make thumbprints strategically across this route. As he reads the book, have the student decorate each thumbprint to represent a character or an important item from each chapter read. Your students are sure to give these novel summaries a big thumbs up!

Debbie Patrick—Gr. 5, Park Forest Elementary, State College, PA

Journal Topics Just For This Month

JOURNAL TOPICS

Looking for original and thought-provoking journal topics for students to write about during the first weeks of a new school year? Look no further than the following topics created just for August and September. Use the reproducible journal covers on page 258 to help students make their very own personal journals for these busy months.

by Paula Holdren

Tips For Using Journals And These Topics

- Duplicate a class supply of this page and page 249. Have each student store his copies and journal in a pocket folder. During journal time, students can select the ideas that interest them.
- Duplicate one copy each of this page and page 249. At the beginning of the month, cut the individual ideas apart and place them in a basket. Each morning let a volunteer select the day's writing topic by drawing a slip from the basket.
- Model journal writing so that it doesn't become just another form of busywork. When students are writing in their journals, be sure to write in yours. Be ready to share your writings with students.
- No teacher has time to read all of her students' journals every day. To save time, purchase five colors of self-sticking dots. Put a dot on the outside cover of each journal. Read and respond to only one colored set of journals each day or week.
- Cut apart the individual ideas and glue each to an index card. File the cards in a box by month; then place the box at a writing center. When a student gets stuck for a writing idea during writing workshop, let him browse through the ideas for that month.

August Journal Suggestions

- Vacation has come to an end, and it's back-to-school time! What are you going to pack in your keepsake box labeled "Summer 1995"?

- August is Foot Health Month. What does the idiom "He really put his foot in his mouth" mean? Write about a time when you put your foot in your mouth.

- August marks the beginning of the school year in many parts of the country. What do you think your teacher should know about you to help you have a successful school year?

- National Mustard Day is observed by condiment lovers on August 5. Are you more like plain mustard or the bold and spicy variety? Explain.

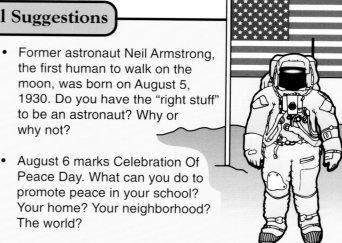
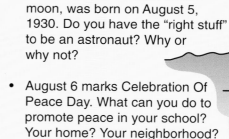

- Former astronaut Neil Armstrong, the first human to walk on the moon, was born on August 5, 1930. Do you have the "right stuff" to be an astronaut? Why or why not?

- August 6 marks Celebration Of Peace Day. What can you do to promote peace in your school? Your home? Your neighborhood? The world?

- August 19 is President Bill Clinton's birthday. After he blows out the 49 candles on his birthday cake, what would you like to sit down and chat with him about?

- August 22 is Be An Angel Day. Describe one angelic thing you could do for someone today. (Then do it!)

- Oscar-winning actress Marlee Matlin was born on August 24, 1965. Have you ever given an "award-winning" performance? Explain.

September Journal Suggestions

- September is National Chicken Month. Is there anything that you are "chicken" to do? Has anyone ever called you a chicken? How did the remark make you feel?

- September is National Courtesy Month. If someone is rude to you, how do you handle it?

- Since September is Self-Improvement Month, what would you most like to improve about yourself? Write a plan for achieving your goal.

- Cartoonist Cathy Lee Guisewite (creator and writer of "Cathy") celebrates her birthday on September 5. Which cartoon character are you most like? Explain.

- Be Late For Something Day is September 5. What's your best, most creative excuse for turning in homework late? Did it work?

- September 6 is National Do It! Day. What have you been putting off that you are going to finish (or at least start) today?

- On September 8, 1921, the first Miss America was crowned. Do you think beauty pageants should still be held? Explain.

- California became the 31st state on September 9, 1850. Would the threat of a possible earthquake affect your feelings about living in California? Explain.

- Citizenship Day is September 17. In your opinion, what are the responsibilities of a good citizen?

- International Priorities Week is September 17–23. What activity is a top priority in your life? Why is it so important to you?

- The birth of Chinese philosopher Confucius is observed on September 21. What's the wisest thing you have ever done?

- World Gratitude Day is September 21. For whom or what are you most grateful?

- It's football time again! From whose vantage point would you prefer to view a game: as a cheerleader on the sidelines, as a field-goal kicker, or as a reporter covering the game?

- On September 25, 1877, the first cream separator was patented. What do you think of separate schools for boys and girls? Would you like to attend such a school? Why or why not?

- National One-Hit Wonder Day (September 25) salutes rock-and-roll stars who had only one big hit song. What's the one thing for which you'd most like to be remembered?

- National Food Service Employees Week is September 25–29. What's your opinion of school lunch programs that are catered by fast-food restaurants?

JOURNAL TOPICS

Searching for original, fun, and thought-provoking journal topics for students to write about this month? Look no further than the following ideas created just for the fall months. Use the reproducible covers on page 259 to help students make personal journals for October and November.

by Irving P. Crump

October Journal Suggestions

- October is National Communicate With Your Kid Month. Its purpose is to promote better communication between teenagers and their parents. In your opinion, which is tougher: being a teenager or being the parent of a teenager? Explain.

- Family History Month is observed in October. Describe an event in the life of your family that you would definitely include in a book entitled *My Family History.*

- October is National Youth Against Tobacco Month. Write a letter to a friend (young person or adult) encouraging him or her to stop smoking.

- October 8–14 is Fire Prevention Week. What's something that really makes you "hot under the collar" (angry)?

- Cornelius Crane celebrates his birthday on October 8. You know him better as actor/comedian Chevy Chase. Why do you think so many entertainers change their names? If you could change your name, what would you change it to? Why?

- October 13 is the second of two Fridays in 1995 that fall on the 13th day. Some people have a fear of the number 13, which is called *triskaidekaphobia.* What is your biggest fear? How do you deal with this fear?

- Martin Luther King, Jr., received the Nobel Peace Prize on October 14, 1964. If you could work for peace between two people, two groups of people, or two nations, who would they be? Explain.

- October 14 marks the 35th anniversary of the day that soon-to-be President John F. Kennedy first spoke about the Peace Corps. Would you be willing to leave your home and family for two years to volunteer in a foreign land? Why or why not?

- Dictionary Day (October 16) honors the birthday of Noah Webster. If you could put in a good word about yourself to your teacher, what would you say?

- October 23 is Michael Crichton's birthday. Crichton wrote the book *Jurassic Park,* on which the popular movie was based. What do you think of the idea of re-creating creatures of long ago, such as dinosaurs?

- October 24 is the birth anniversary of Belva A. Lockwood. In 1884 she became the first woman formally nominated to be president of the United States. Do you think the United States will soon have a woman president? Why or why not?

- The Mount Rushmore National Memorial was completed on October 31, 1941. Suppose one more face were added to this monument. Who do you think deserves such an honor? Why?

- November is Aviation History Month. Which do you think is the more important invention: the automobile or the airplane? Explain the reasons for your choice.

- Project Red Ribbon (November 1–January 1) is a national effort to encourage Americans not to drink and drive. Each participant attaches a red ribbon to his vehicle as a sign that he is committed to this effort. Write about why you support Project Red Ribbon. Copy your paragraph on an index card and attach a red ribbon to it. Give the card to someone who drives.

- Comedienne/actress Roseanne turns 42 on November 3. Do you think her show "Roseanne" depicts the typical American family? Explain.

- November 6 marks the birth anniversary of Adolphe Sax. He was a Belgian musician who invented—you guessed it!—the saxophone. Which would you rather be: a world-renowned pianist, a drummer in a rock-and-roll band, or a jazz saxophonist? Explain.

- November 7 (at 5:15 A.M. EDT) marks the halfway point of autumn. If you could choose one of the four seasons to last all year long, which would you choose? Why?

It's an on-line superconductive chocolate fabricator!

- On November 8, 1895, German physicist Wilhelm C. Roentgen discovered X rays. He called them *X rays* because he didn't understand what they were at first! Now, 100 years later, what great scientific discovery would you wish for? Why?

- The song "God Bless America" was first performed on radio on November 11, 1938. Some people think "God Bless America" would be a better national anthem for our country than "The Star-Spangled Banner." What do you think?

- November 12–18 is American Education Week. Describe one important life lesson that you learned from a past teacher. Why do you remember this lesson so well?

- Robert Fulton, inventor of the steamboat, was born November 14, 1765. Some people called his ship "Fulton's Folly" because they thought it would never work. Describe an invention of the 1990s that would have amazed people of the 19th century.

It'll never work.

- November 17–23 is National Farm-City Week. Would you rather live on a farm or in a large city? Give several reasons for your choice.

- Mickey Mouse first appeared November 18, 1928, on the screen of the Colony Theatre in New York City. This Walt Disney film, *Steamboat Willie,* was the first animated cartoon talking picture. Why do you think Mickey Mouse has remained popular for so many years?

- National Game And Puzzle Week (November 24–30) has two purposes: to increase appreciation of games and puzzles, and to promote spending time with family and friends. What game do you and your family (or you and your friends) enjoy playing together? Why is it so much fun?

HAPPY THANKSGIVING!

Psst.... pass the turkey!

- On November 26, 1789, President George Washington proclaimed the first U.S. holiday: Thanksgiving Day. It was a day for our entire nation to give thanks. What do you think our nation should be thankful for today?

- Singer Tina Turner will be 57 years old on November 26. Mick Jagger of the Rolling Stones celebrated his 52nd birthday this past summer. What do you think of these "senior" rock stars? Should they retire or keep on rockin'?

- Madeleine L'Engle, author of *A Wrinkle In Time,* turns 77 on November 29. Do you like science fiction books and movies? What's your favorite science fiction book (or movie)? Why?

JOURNAL TOPICS

Take time during the busy months of December and January for students to reflect on these thought-provoking journal topics. Use the reproducible journal covers on page 260 to help students make personal journals for these months.

by Paula Holdren

December Journal Suggestions

- The game of bingo was born this month in 1929. What is your favorite game? What changes would you make to improve the rules of this game?

- It's no coincidence that December, with its many holidays, is also Safe Toys And Gifts Month. What toys on the market do you think are unsafe? What would you do to improve the safety level of one of these toys?

- National Stress-Free Family Holidays Month will be observed in December. What are three things you can do to help make your family's holiday celebrations less stressful this year?

To relieve stress during the holidays, would send my little brother to live with another family.

Amber

- December 1 is Becky Thatcher Day. It marks the birthday of Laura Hawkins, the girlfriend of young Sam Clemens (Mark Twain). Hawkins inspired Twain to create the character of Becky Thatcher. This day honors girls and women who have written or inspired great literature. Would you rather write a great American novel or be the hero or heroine of it? Why?

- On December 1, 1955, Rosa Parks refused to move to the back of a city bus in Montgomery, Alabama. Her arrest and the resulting bus boycott have often been called the birth of the modern civil rights movement. Is it ever appropriate to disobey a law? Explain your answer.

- The American Federation of Labor and the Congress for Industrial Organizations joined together to become the AFL-CIO on December 5, 1955. Should public employees—workers such as teachers and firefighters, who are paid with tax dollars—be allowed to go on strike? Why or why not?

- The annual meeting of Keep America Beautiful will be held December 6–9 in Washington, D.C. In your opinion, what would be a fair punishment for someone who was caught littering, polluting, or vandalizing a city park?

America The Beautiful— *please!*

- During the first week of each December, New York City begins the holiday season by lighting the giant Christmas tree at Rockefeller Center. What event marks the beginning of the holiday season for you?

- On December 11, the eleventh annual list of the most boring celebrities will be announced. Who would you nominate for the "Most Boring Celebrity" award this year? Why?

This year the award goes to....

MOST BORING

- On December 14, 1798, David Wilkinson of Rhode Island received a patent for the first nut-and-bolt machine. What's one thing that really drives you nuts? Explain.

- Eat What You Want Day is observed on December 16. What would be on your menu for breakfast, lunch, and dinner that day?

BREAKFAST

LUNCH

DINNER

- December 17–23 is Tell Someone They're Doing A Good Job Week. Who are you going to encourage each day this week? Why?

- The first crossword puzzle was published in the *New York World* newspaper on December 21, 1913. If you could write a weekly newspaper column entitled "Just For Kids," what topics would you include and why?

- Former First Lady Claudia Alta "Lady Bird" Johnson will celebrate her 83rd birthday on December 22. What would be the advantages of being married to a world leader? What would be the disadvantages?

- You're All Done Day on December 31 is a day to celebrate the past year's accomplishments and the satisfaction of a job well done. What personal accomplishment of this year are you most proud of? Why?

- On January 1, 1924, Frank Buckley Cooney of Minnesota invented the first "ink paste," or crayon. Which color best describes you? Explain.

- Each January, newspapers and magazines review the top news stories of the previous year. In your opinion, what were the top five news events of 1995?

- January 1996 is year number seven in the Decade Of The Brain. Use your brain to figure out the best way to stick to your New Year's resolution. Explain your plan—then stick to it!

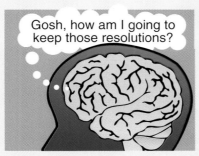

- January is Diet Month. How could you help an overweight friend feel good about him- or herself?

- American seamstress Betsy Ross, who is often credited with sewing the first American flag, was born in Philadelphia on January 1, 1752. In your opinion, is the design of the American flag still a good one? Why? How would you redesign it?

- Martin Luther King's birthday will be observed with a federal holiday on Monday, January 15. In your opinion, what can students in your school do to improve relationships between people of different races?

- January 15 is Elementary School Teacher Day. Which of your teachers has influenced you the most? Explain.

- Answer Your Cat's Question Day is observed on January 22. If your pet could talk, what do you think it would say to you?

- Gold was discovered in California on January 24, 1848. The secret of this discovery leaked out to the public and the gold rush began. Have you ever told a secret? What were the consequences of telling it?

- Mark Goodson—creator of popular television game shows like "The Price Is Right" and "Family Feud"—was born on January 24, 1915. Why do you think game shows are so popular?

- The first nationally televised presidential news conference was held on January 25, 1961. In this election year, what questions would you most like to ask the major presidential candidates?

- It's Backwards Day on January 26. Looking backwards, describe how you have changed since school started last fall.

- Wolfgang Amadeus Mozart was born on January 27, 1756. He began performing at age three and composing at age five. What sacrifices do you think a *prodigy* (an extremely talented child or youth) would have to make in order to be successful? Do you think it would be worth it? Explain.

- On January 31, 1919, Jackie Robinson was born. He was the first black major-league baseball player. Would you rather be a "first," or follow in someone else's footsteps? Explain.

- Many people vacation in January after the holidays. What souvenir would you design for tourists to take home as a reminder of their visit to your town? Why?

JOURNAL TOPICS

Need a journal topic in a snap? Then take a look at the following inventive, fun, and thought-provoking journal ideas to carry your students through February and March. Use the reproducible journal covers on page 261 to help students make their own personal journals for these busy months.

by Paula Holdren

February Suggestions

- February is American Heart Month. What do you wish for most, from the bottom of your heart?

- February 1, Robinson Crusoe Day, is the anniversary of the 1709 rescue of Scottish sailor Alexander Selkirk. His adventures formed the basis for Daniel Defoe's famous book, *Robinson Crusoe.* If you were stranded on a remote island, what three things would you miss most about your life back home?

- Be An Encourager® Day is observed annually on February 1. Who has given YOU the most encouragement in your life so far? Explain your answer.

- On February 2, 1936, Babe Ruth was voted into the Baseball Hall of Fame in Cooperstown, New York. Who would you include in your personal Hall of Fame? Explain each choice.

- On February 3, 1690, the first American paper money was printed in Massachusetts. If you had to name ten things that money can't buy, what would you list? Write your list in the order of importance to you, with number one being the most important item.

- On February 4, 1861, the Confederate States of America was organized in Montgomery, Alabama. How might your life be different if the South had won the Civil War?

- February means the cold and flu season is upon us. What's the quickest way to help you feel better when you are sick? What's the quickest way to make you feel worse?

- During summer hot spells, merchants often advertise cool drinks and other items to remind you of the frosty, blizzardy days of winter. What could you invent that would get everyone in the mood for a midwinter heat wave? Explain your invention. Include a labeled drawing if you like.

- One of America's first weather forecasters, John Jeffries, was born on February 5, 1744. What weather term best describes how you feel today: sunny, stormy, cloudy, misty, foggy, breezy, or partly cloudy? Explain your answer.

- On February 12, 1870, women in the Territory of Utah were given the right to vote. In your opinion, what should be the legal voting age in this country? Give reasons for your opinion.

- On February 13, 1635, America's first public school—the Boston Latin School—was established. Do you think a college degree is a necessity these days? Give reasons for your answer.

- February is the birth month of "Honest Abe" Lincoln and George "I-cannot-tell-a-lie" Washington. If your best friend asked you an embarrassing question, would you tell the truth even if it was unpleasant or difficult to do so? Why or why not?

- Presidents' Day is observed this year on February 19. In today's political campaigns, candidates often say unkind things about their opponents. They are also often criticized and watched closely by the media. Do you think that running for public office is worth going through these types of hassles? Explain your answer.

- On February 23, 1633, Samuel Pepys—author of a world-famous diary—was born in Cambridge, England. How would you feel if someone read your diary? What famous person's diary would you REALLY like to sneak a peek at?

My compliments to the chef...

- National Pig Day is March 1. If you could go to any restaurant and "pig out" for free, what restaurant would you visit? What exactly makes this restaurant so "pig-errific"?

- March is Youth Art Month. Would you rather be recognized for outstanding artistic, writing, or athletic ability? Explain your answer.

- Movie director Ron Howard (who directed *Apollo 13*) was born on March 1, 1954. He started his career in show business as a child playing Opie on "The Andy Griffith Show." Would you like to be on a national television show? Give reasons for your answer.

- Dr. Seuss—whose real name was Theodor Geisel—was born March 2, 1904. His first book, *And To Think That I Saw It On Mulberry Street,* was rejected by 27 publishers before finally selling. Dr. Seuss succeeded because he was persistent! Write about a time when you were persistent and it paid off.

- March is National Frozen Food Month. Have you ever been "frozen" with fear? Describe what caused your fright and how you dealt with it.

- March 1–7 is Return The Borrowed Books Week. Do you agree with the old saying, "Neither a borrower nor a lender be"? Explain.

- Samuel Colt, inventor of the first pistol with a revolving cylinder, incorporated his Patent Arms Manufacturing Company on March 5, 1836. How do you feel about gun control?

- National Save Your Vision Week is observed March 3–9. What do you see more clearly now than you used to see?

- When he played for the Philadelphia Warriors, basketball star Wilt Chamberlain scored 32 points in a game against Detroit on March 10, 1961. This made him the first basketball player to score more than 3,000 points in a season. How would you feel if you held a world record like Wilt Chamberlain? How would you feel if someone else broke your record?

- TV Turn-Off Week is observed annually the second week in March. Why do you think people watch so much television these days?

WHIIIRRRR **Mom!**
Make her quit it!!
Somebody come in here and clean up this mess!
meow
woof woof woof

- On March 13, 1877, Chester Greenwood received a patent for his invention called "earmufflers." What sounds would you like your earmuffs to drown out?

- Albert Einstein—who was born March 14, 1879—once said, "Imagination is more important than knowledge." Do you agree or disagree? Explain your answer.

- Pocahontas (Rebecca Rolfe) died March 21, 1617. How do you think she would feel about the recent cartoon movie made about her? Explain.

"Scream and Stomp" by Snake Sydney and The Grinning Reptiles. The rich lyrics and melodic imagery are just sublime....

- Composer Stephen Sondheim was born March 22, 1930. Annually his birthday is declared National Sing-Out Day. In your opinion, what's the best song ever written? Why is it your favorite?

- Liberty Day is March 23. It marks the 221st anniversary of Patrick Henry's famous "give me liberty or give me death" speech. Exactly what liberties are kids your age entitled to these days? Why do you think these freedoms are important?

JOURNAL TOPICS

Usher spring-fever-inspired writing into your classroom with these seasonal journal topics. Then use the reproducible journal covers on page 262 to help students make personal journals for these months.

by Paula Holdren

April Journal Suggestions

- April is the month known for its spring showers. For this reason, people often say it's "raining cats and dogs." What do you wish would pour down from the skies?

- April Fools' Day is observed on April 1. Do you have a good sense of humor? What's the best joke you ever played on someone?

- A former slave named Robert became a very famous American hermit. He died on April 1, 1832, at his hermitage in Seekonk, Massachusetts. What do you think would be the advantages and disadvantages of a solitary life? Do you ever feel like becoming a hermit? Explain.

- April 2 is International Children's Book Day. It marks the birthday of Hans Christian Andersen. If you could trade places with a famous book character, who would you select and why?

- Walter Hunt received a patent for inventing the safety pin on April 10, 1849. "Pin" your thinking cap on and explain four new uses for the safety pin.

- The ill-fated *Apollo 13* spacecraft was launched on April 11, 1970. After experiencing a problem with a ruptured oxygen tank, this flight's planned moon landing was cancelled. The crew successfully splashed down on April 17, 1970. Describe the qualities you think a person with a life-threatening job should possess.

- In addition to being an inventor and U.S. president, Thomas Jefferson—whose birthday was April 13, 1743—was also an architect. Architects design buildings. What features would you include in your design of an ideal school, home, or room?

- April 16 is observed annually as National Stress Awareness Day. What things are stressful for you? Describe several different ways you could handle these pressure-causing incidents.

- Look-Alike Day (April 16) recognizes people who look like famous people. What famous person do you think you resemble? Does this make you happy? Explain. Would you like to trade places with this person? Why or why not?

Well, personally I think I possess a certain Brad Pitt quality.

- On April 24, 1800, the Library of Congress was established. Sir Richard Steele once said, "Reading is to the mind what exercise is to the body." What type of literature do you most often use to exercise your mind? Elaborate on the types of books you almost always choose to read.

- The annual Take Our Daughters To Work Day will be recognized in April. What occupation do you foresee yourself performing when you take *your* daughter to work in a few years? Explain.

- Gideon Sundback patented the zipper on April 29, 1913. Can you keep your lips zipped when someone confides in you, or do you always manage to spill the beans? Explain.

- May is Revise Your Work Schedule Month. Describe your plans to work smarter, not harder, at your schoolwork.

- Older Americans Month is celebrated in May. What is the most important thing an older person has taught you? Explain how it has benefited you.

Turn that rattle-trap DOWN for Pete's sake!!

My grandfather has taught me to appreciate quiet music. Tony

- May is National High Blood Pressure Education Month. What causes your blood pressure to rise? Why?

- May is Better Hearing Month. Describe in detail three things you are most likely to "tune out" and not hear.

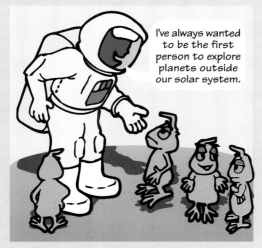

I've always wanted to be the first person to explore planets outside our solar system.

- Jockey Diane Crump became the first woman to ride in the Kentucky Derby in May of 1970. What "first" would you like to become noted for and why?

- May 3 is International Tuba Day. Do you think all kids should be required to take music lessons? Justify your reasons.

- Horace Mann, who became the "Father of the Public School System," was born on May 4, 1796. Explain how you would change your school if you could.

- In Japan, Children's Day is celebrated on May 5. Do you support the observance of this day in the United States? List and clarify your reasons.

- People are encouraged to collect and send picture postcards during National Postcard Week, held May 5–11. Describe the location in your town that would make the best picture-postcard photograph.

Visit Our Beautiful
WATER PURIFICATION SYSTEM

Your home for "TIP-TOP-TAP" water!

- National Teacher Day will be observed on May 7. Describe an ideal teacher. Do you think you have those qualities? Do you think teachers should be replaced by computers or TVs? Explain your answer.

- May 8 is No Socks Day. What other stuff would you like to omit, skip, or ignore for a day?

my little brother

- Mother's Day will be celebrated on May 12. Think of a famous mom you would like to adopt for a week. Describe how you would spend your time together.

- Gabriel Fahrenheit, the inventor of the mercury thermometer, was born on May 14, 1686. Are you usually a cool cucumber or a hothead? Explain.

- On May 16, 1868, the impeachment of President Andrew Johnson failed by one vote. What would you say to a person who told you he has never voted in a presidential election and never will?

- May 16 is Biographers Day. Whose biography would you most like to write? Why?

Patterns

Use the journal cover art with the ideas on pages 248 and 249.

Make Good Writing

YOUR GOAL!

My September Journal

Name _____

©The Education Center, Inc. • THE MAILBOX® • Intermediate • Aug/Sept 1995

WELCOME BACK...

To Writing!

My August Journal

Name _____

©The Education Center, Inc. • THE MAILBOX® • Intermediate • Aug/Sept 1995

Note To Teacher: Duplicate this page on white construction paper for each student. Instruct students to cut their copies in half on the dividing line. Have students decorate their August covers; then have each child staple several sheets of lined paper (cut to size) behind his cover. Save the September covers to use for September journals.

WRITING TALKING TURKEY

My November Journal

Name

©The Education Center, Inc. • *THE MAILBOX®* • *Intermediate* • Oct/Nov 1995

My October Journal

Name

©The Education Center, Inc. • *THE MAILBOX®* • *Intermediate* • Oct/Nov 1995

Note To The Teacher: Duplicate this page on white construction paper for each student. Instruct students to cut their copies in half on the dividing line. Have students decorate their October covers; then have each child staple several sheets of lined paper (cut to size) behind his cover. Save the November covers to use for November journals.

Patterns

Use the journal cover art with the ideas on pages 252 and 253.

Celebrate New Beginnings!

HAPPY NEW YEAR!

My January Journal

Name _____

©The Education Center, Inc. • THE MAILBOX® • Intermediate • Dec/Jan 1995–96

Write Upon A Star!

My December Journal

Name _____

©The Education Center, Inc. • THE MAILBOX® • Intermediate • Dec/Jan 1995–96

Note To The Teacher: Duplicate this page on white construction paper for each student. Instruct students to cut their copies in half on the dividing line. Have students decorate their December covers; then have each child staple several sheets of lined paper (cut to size) behind his cover. Save the January covers to use for January journals.

Writing—
Writing
HOW SWEET IT IS!

Candy Hearts

My February Journal

Name _____

©The Education Center, Inc. • THE MAILBOX® • Intermediate • Feb/Mar 1996

My Writing Is As Good As Gold!

My March Journal

Name _____

©The Education Center, Inc. • THE MAILBOX® • Intermediate • Feb/Mar 1996

Note To The Teacher: Duplicate this page on white construction paper for each student. Instruct students to cut their copies in half on the dividing line. Have students decorate their February covers; then have each child staple several sheets of lined paper (cut to size) behind his cover. Save the March covers to use for March journals.

Patterns

Use the journal cover art with the ideas on pages 256 and 257.

NEVER TOO BUSY TO WRITE

My May Journal

Name _____

Showers Of Thoughts

My April Journal

Name _____

Note To The Teacher: Duplicate this page on white construction paper for each student. Instruct students to cut their copies in half on the dividing line. Have students decorate their April covers; then have each child staple several sheets of lined paper (cut to size) behind his cover. Save the May covers to use for May journals.

OUR READERS WRITE

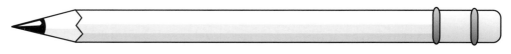

OUR READERS WRITE

The Right Combination

Do your students have the locker blues? Ease their anxiety by constructing these easy-to-make practice locks. Enlarge the pattern shown; then duplicate a class set. Cut out each pattern and attach it to a tagboard square using a brad fastener. Draw a zero line on each square as shown. Have students practice turning right to the first number, left past the first number to the second number, then right again to the third number. In no time your students will be opening their lockers with confidence.

Laurie Bailey—Gr. 5
Central Grade School
Washington, IL

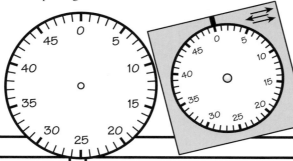

Bye-bye, Birthday Blues!

Beat the belated birthday blues by purchasing a box of cards at the beginning of the year. For each student, write a message on a card and insert it into an envelope labeled with the student's name and birthday. Then tape the envelopes in order on a birthday bulletin board or wall. As each student's special day arrives, present him with his card, a birthday pencil, and a treat. Your students will enjoy seeing whose birthday is coming up next.

Laurie Bailey—Gr. 5

Delightful Door Display

Welcome your new students with this foot-stomping door display! Write the name of each student on a construction-paper footprint. Mount the prints on the door with a cutout of a magnifying glass. Top off your display with the caption "The Mystery Is Solved! Here's Who's In _____'s Room!"

Marion Young—Gr. 4
Weigelstown Elementary
Dover, PA

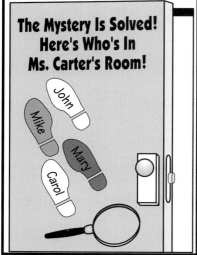

Computer Guidelines

Start the year with this handy computer station tip. After instructing students on computer routines such as loading/removing diskettes, turning on/shutting down the system, and using the printer, post a step-by-step chart near the computer. With the basics outlined and at your students' fingertips, you can focus your attention on more complicated computer instruction.

Julie Granchelli, Lockport, NY

Guest Lessons

Combine the talents of your grade-level teachers by exchanging classes once a week for "guest lessons." First decide on a subject area you wish to teach (for example, punctuation). Then have each teacher develop a fun lesson on that subject. If you choose punctuation skills, one teacher could teach a lesson on ending punctuation, another on using commas, and another on quotation marks. On Friday morning, have teachers rotate through the classrooms to share their lessons. The students' anticipation of a new face and a different teaching style will make for a lively and productive morning!

Debbie Patrick—Gr. 5
Park Forest Elementary, State College, PA

Classroom Rules Mobile

Let your students create an eye-catching classroom rules display. Begin by brainstorming a set of rules for the classroom with your students. Present a large poster-board ruler labeled "CLASS RULES" along with several smaller poster-board rulers. Draw names to see which students get to write the classroom rules on the small rulers. Attach each small ruler to the bottom edge of the large ruler using varying lengths of yarn; then suspend the large ruler mobile-fashion from the ceiling.

Debbie Patrick—Gr. 5

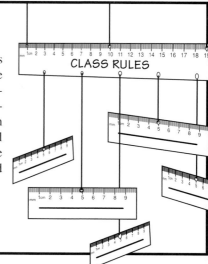

Basket Of Birthday Wishes

Recycle plastic berry baskets into colorful birthday gifts. Ask a local grocery store to donate a basket for each student in your class. Weave a ribbon through the slots of each basket and tie it in a bow. After sending the birthday boy or girl on an errand, have each student write a birthday greeting on a seasonal cutout. Place these wishes in the basket with a balloon, stickers, and a birthday pencil. When the student returns, present her with the basket while singing "Happy Birthday!"

Lisa Hoffman—Gr. 5
M. M. Pierce Elementary
Remington, VA

Circle The Wagons

One Friday a month, my class invites parents, friends, and school-board members to join us for an hour's worth of informative entertainment that we call "Circle The Wagons." One student—the "wagonmaster"—welcomes the visitors and introduces new guests. Servers offer up coffee, while registrars obtain signatures and comments from the guests. Students are selected from a random drawing to give impromptu reports on the activities occurring in our classroom that month. I solicit help for any upcoming field trips and answer questions about plans and curriculum. The session closes with a choral reading, skit, or song. Students benefit from planning and carrying out these monthly sessions. Parents enjoy being informed of classroom events in such an entertaining fashion.

Jan Ayles—Gr. 4
Cannon Beach Elementary, Cannon Beach, OR

WANTED

9-27-95

Betsy Clark

Helping others.
Finishing work on time.
Using time wisely.
Playing soccer.
Baby-sitting my brother.

Self-Esteem "Wanted" Posters

Everyone wants to be wanted! Let your students know how much you value them by writing "WANTED" across the top of a piece of poster board. Leave space for a photo and a sheet of writing paper. Each week select a student to appear on the poster. Photograph her holding a sign labeled with the date as shown. Post this mug shot in the photo space. Then add a sheet on which the student has listed five positive behaviors or accomplishments for which she's "wanted."

Amy Olswang—Gr. 4
Bernard Zell Ansche Emet Day
  School
Chicago, IL

Positive Postcards

At the beginning of the year, purchase a class set of stamped postcards. Have each student address a card to his parents or someone else whom he would like to receive some good news about his progress. Collect the cards; then take time during the next month to jot a positive note about each student on his card. Mail the cards, and watch as happy faces arrive in a few days after their positive postcards have been delivered.

Michele Wells
Redmond, WA

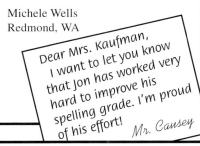

Dear Mrs. Kaufman,
I want to let you know that Jon has worked very hard to improve his spelling grade. I'm proud of his effort!
Mr. Causey

Give 'Em An Inch...

When it comes to using standard rulers, do your students measure up? Introduce or review parts of an inch by creating a magnified ruler section on a bulletin board. Mark off and label each fraction of an inch as shown. If students are familiar with fractions, practice reducing the fractions shown on the model.

Karen A. Jones—Gr. 4
Oxhead Road Elementary
Smithtown, NY

Made In The Shade!

Here's a bright idea for this year's hall passes. Take advantage of summer sales by purchasing two pairs of inexpensive sunglasses. Write "Pass" and your name on the earpieces of each pair. Students will enjoy wearing these cool shades as they perform duties that require traveling from the classroom and back.

Stella Bizzio—Gr. 5
LeRosen Elementary, Lafayette, LA

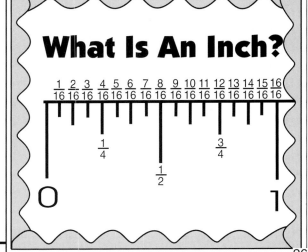

What Is An Inch?

Business-Card Awards

If you're into computer-generated incentives, here's an idea for you! Using a business-card program (I use Print Shop Deluxe Companion®), you can make awards and incentives quickly and economically with your computer. Each printed page contains ten cards, big enough for students' names to be written on them. I make several copies of each page of awards to use throughout the year.

Virginia H. Kotok—Gr. 4
St. Margaret School
Pittsburgh, PA

Awesome Award!
This award is presented to

for an outstanding score on the ____ test!

Valid as one question pass for the 95-96 SMS school year. Must present pass at time of test.

Signed:
Mrs. Crane

Student Of The Week

Sometime during the school year, each child in my class is named "Student Of The Week." I trace each weekly winner's body on bulletin-board paper. After the student cuts out his tracing, he adds facial features or invites friends to help him create a look-alike figure. I display the cutout and invite each classmate to write a positive comment on it. This activity builds self-esteem for every*body*!

Edie Dege—Gr. 4
Pulaski Elementary
Wilmington, DE

Joe is a terrific speller.

Joe is my best friend.

Joe is kind.

Joe always tries his best.

Joe has good manners.

Note It With A Sticky

I ask my students to bring Post-It™ Brand notes in the fall as one of their back-to-school supplies. During peer writing conferences, students write positive comments and suggestions on the notes; then they stick them directly to their partners' papers. I use the notes to add further recommendations or to mark spelling errors on final drafts. Since I don't write directly on a student's paper, she doesn't have to recopy the whole page.

Denise Amos—Gr. 4
Crestwood Elementary
Crestwood, KY

The Three Rs

To my class, the three Rs stand for respect, responsibility, and the right to learn. Early in the year, my students brainstorm class rules and classify them into three categories: respect for each other, respect for each other's property, and responsibility for everything they say and do. Everyone agrees to these Rs because everybody has the right to learn.

Susan M. Reed—Gr. 4
Ebenezer Elementary
Lebanon, PA

Bulletin-Board Magic

Tired of putting up and then removing background paper from your bulletin boards all year long? Cover each board with an inexpensive, colorful plastic shower liner. Then tape any items to the plastic with Scotch® Removable Magic Tape. Your bulletin boards will look great all year long—with no pins or staples to remove!

Joy Ann Tweedt—Gr. 6, Northwood Elementary, Ames, IA

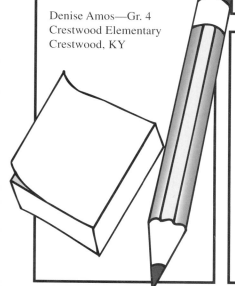

On A (Penny) Roll!

Each year our team of students chooses a community-service project, such as raising money to help a seriously ill child. We've found an easy way to raise money: a "Penny Roll." For several weeks, students collect pennies from home, their friends, and neighbors. Then on Penny Roll Day, we spend our math class counting and wrapping pennies. A local bank provides us with plenty of wrappers. Each year we raise several hundred dollars for someone who needs assistance!

Martha Ennis
Arnold Middle School, Columbus, GA

Welcome To Our School!

It's a stressful time when a child enters a new school at mid-year. To ease the anxiety for new students, my fourth graders created "Welcome To Whiteley School" booklets. First we brainstormed and listed important information, plus our classroom and school routines. Each student chose an item from the list and created a booklet page to explain it. A personal introduction and photo was also included on each page to help a new classmate match faces with names. What a worthwhile writing project!

Barbara Benton—Gr. 4
Frank C. Whiteley School
Hoffman Estates, IL

Honoring Our Veterans

After reading the book *The Wall* by Eve Bunting (published by Houghton Mifflin), I have my students pretend they work for a greeting-card company. I encourage them to design cards to honor and thank our veterans. We bundle all of the cards together and deliver them to a veterans' home or hospital on Veterans Day.

Kerry L. Simmons—Gr. 4
Golden Hills Elementary
Omaha, NE

Let's Watch "Jeopardy!"

I encourage my fifth graders to watch the TV game show "Jeopardy!" which often includes many topics we cover in social studies. If a student hears something that we have discussed in class on a show, she tells me the next day; then I let her choose a small prize from my grab bag. This is a fun way to reinforce topics learned in class!

Theresa O'Connell—Gr. 5
Our Lady of Grace School
Greensboro, NC

Mystery Objects

Sharpen describing skills with this fun activity. Have each student take an empty film canister home and fill it with a small, unbreakable object. Students should keep secret the identities of their objects. When all the containers are returned to school, secretly number each one; then make a list of numbers and matching owners. Place the containers on a table for students to examine (no peeking allowed). Challenge each child to find his canister, write its number on a slip of paper, then give the slip to you. If a student finds his canister, have him describe its object to the class, using clues that are as descriptive as possible. If the object is guessed, the student takes it home. Those students who didn't find their canisters initially can then try again. Continue this activity over several days and watch word power grow!

Debra Orr, Sidney, IL

Reinforcing Rounding Rules

To help children visualize the rounding process, I created a learning device out of ordinary notebooks and index cards. Each binder ring holds 11 hole-punched index cards: ten labeled with the digits 0–9, plus one with a decimal point. I place the notebooks side by side, creating a number with the cards. Students name each digit's place value and round the number to a given place value. We then flip the cards to the right of the rounded place to zero. Because each notebook represents a whole-number "family" (ones, thousands, millions, etc.), students can easily recognize where commas belong. This easy-to-make teaching tool has been invaluable in helping my students learn rounding skills.

Lauri A. Shoup—Grs. 3–6 Mathematics
Homer-Center Elementary
Homer City, PA

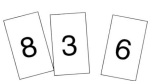

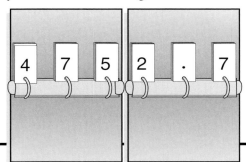

Theme Doorway

After seeing some unique shower-curtain designs, I decided to buy several to enhance our thematic studies. I hang a curtain in our classroom doorway, depending on the theme we are studying. I have a jungle curtain for our study of tropical forests and a curtain covered with fish that's perfect for oceanography. Students love entering and exiting through our theme doorway!

Maura Hendrickson—Grs. K–6
Hall County District 5
Wood River, NE

Easy Birthday Display

Here's a simple birthday display that's a snap to make. List each month—along with students who have birthdays in that month—on a sticky label attached to a paper birthday-party plate. Attach the plates to a bulletin board, door, or wall space. The result—a birthday display that's colorful, eye-catching, and doesn't require tons of time to make!

Sharon Wilkens—Gr. 4
Imbler School District
Summerville, OR

NOVEMBER
Lucas = 7th
Stephanie = 21st

Parts-of-Speech Transparencies

When introducing a part of speech such as nouns, I give each student a blank transparency and a wipe-off marker. I instruct each student to write a paragraph that includes lots of nouns on his transparency. After completing the paragraph, the student counts the nouns and writes the total at the bottom of his transparency. At the beginning of each language period, I put one of the transparencies on the overhead and invite its owner to "teach" his lesson. He underlines the designated part of speech as his classmates identify each one. When all the words are found, the "teacher" counts them. If the total matches his total, the class earns a point; if not, I earn a point. When all of the transparencies have been shared, the students receive an award if they have more points than I do.

Julie Plowman—Gr. 6, Adair-Casey Elementary, Adair, IA

Math Bake Sale

To reinforce measuring skills, my class held a bake sale. But first we had to have products to sell! Each student—with the help of a parent—completed these steps:
1. Choose a dessert recipe.
2. Shop for the necessary ingredients.
3. Determine the total cost of the dessert.
4. Follow the recipe's directions to make the dessert.

Our various cookies, brownies, and cupcakes were wrapped in plastic bags. Students planned their sale, determining prices and creating an advertising campaign. After the sale, we graphed all of our data and used our profits to purchase math computer software.

Kimberlee Collins—Gr. 5
Johnston Elementary
Woodstock, GA

25¢

Student Mailboxes

I obtained a large quantity of empty, clear tennis-ball containers. After removing all of the labels, I used a hot-glue gun to attach 25 of the containers together in a squarelike shape. These containers now serve as our classroom mailboxes. I encourage students to write notes to each other in the morning before school starts and at the end of the day. Student mail carriers take turns each week delivering the mail.

Janet Moody—Gr. 4, Truman Elementary, Lafayette, LA

Writing Word Problems

Make writing and solving math word problems more fun for your students with this activity. Provide each child with a 12-inch strip of adding-machine tape. Instruct him to write and illustrate a multistep math story problem on the strip. When all of the strips are complete, have students swap them and solve each other's problems. Collect the tapes and laminate them—then you've got an instant math center to use year after year!

Barbara Gerow—Grs. 3–4, Neil Armstrong Elementary, Port Charlotte, FL

Bingo Tip

Provide students with blank bingo sheets to program with spelling words or multiplication facts. In addition, give each student a clear plastic sleeve in which to place his sheet, a wipe-off marker, and a small rag. When your class plays bingo, students can write directly on the plastic sleeves, then clean them off when beginning a new game. Collect the plastic sleeves, markers, and rags for future games.

Mary M. Perunko
Donora, PA

B I N G O

8	9	16	25	6
12	15	20	10	18
14	21	FREE SPACE	35	30
16	27	28	45	54
18	6	36	30	48

Student Teacher Farewell

Provide your student teacher with a bagful of wonderful memories! Purchase a large, white tote bag. Have each student press his hand into fabric paint and then onto the tote to leave a print. After the bag dries, write each student's name above his handprint. Next have each student place a note of farewell or a small gift in the tote. Present this special gift to your student teacher at his/her farewell party.

Beverly Langland—Gr. 5
Trinity Christian Academy
Jacksonville, FL

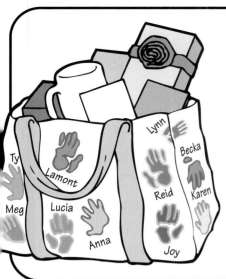

Thematic Pencil Toppers

To help my students get excited about our next thematic unit, I enlarge several clip-art patterns related to that theme. Before duplicating the patterns (one per student), I draw two slits on each one. I instruct students to color their patterns, cut them out, and carefully cut along the slits. Student can then slip the pencil toppers on their pencils as constant reminders of the unit we're studying.

Lydia Montgomery—Gr. 6
Lincoln Middle School
Indianapolis, IN

You CAN Make Money

Money doesn't grow on trees, but it does come in cans! My sixth-grade students and I recycle aluminum cans. The money we raise helps to purchase supplies, games, treats, and materials for classroom projects. Not only does this project relieve my piggy bank, it also gives my students a chance to make a difference in the world.

Emily Lambert—Gr. 6
Wilson Elementary
Brooksville, MS

Beating The New-Year Rush

If the thought of taking time to put up a January bulletin board right after the holiday party doesn't appeal to you, try this snappy solution. First put up January's board; then cover it with a December holiday display. When students leave after the holiday party, peel off the top layer to reveal the January board!

Charlene Starcher—Gr. 5
Rushwood Elementary
Sagamore Hills, OH

Big Bands

Stacks of stuff scattered all over your desk and work area? Try this storage tip. To make a giant stretchable band, cut the waistband from a pair of old, cleaned pantyhose. Use the band to bundle together file folders, class sets of magazines, or stacks of paperback novels.

Patricia Dancho—Gr. 6
Apollo-Ridge Middle School
Spring Church, PA

Holiday Friendship Chain

Instead of focusing on what we *want* during the holidays, try focusing on what we *have*. Provide each student with several 1" x 6" strips of red, green, and white paper. After discussing friendship, have students describe the different people—classmates, neighbors, relatives, etc.—they consider their friends. Instruct each student to write the name of a friend on a strip of paper using a marker. (Allow students to label as many strips as they want.) Tape each strip into a loop, connecting it with the next strip to form a chain. Each time a student sees the decorative chain hanging in your classroom, he'll be reminded of the chain of friendship that connects all of us!

Elsie B. McGill—Grs. 6–8
College Park Middle School
Hickory, NC

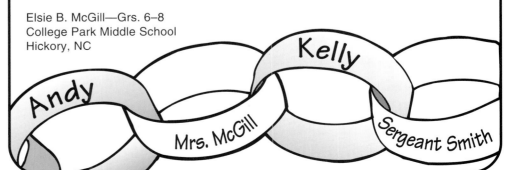

We're "Tree-ific"!

What could be a better holiday gift than a word of encouragement from your peers? Provide each student with a six-inch circle cut from colorful construction paper. After writing her name on the top, have the student pass her ornament around the room so that each classmate can write a brief note of encouragement. Hang the completed ornaments on a large paper tree mounted on a bulletin board. Embellish the board with tinsel and a border of blinking lights.

Adapted from an idea by Susan Daniel—
Chapter I, Gr. 6
Goliad Middle School
Big Spring, TX

Stacey
Helps with math.
Makes me laugh.
Plays soccer well.
Is a good friend.

"Soup-er" Bowl Week

Celebrate Super Bowl week in January in a uniquely "soup-er" way! Prior to the Super Bowl, have students read the story *Stone Soup.* Use this work as a springboard to a community service project. Have parents join students in preparing a large batch of homemade soup. After the soup has been cooked and cooled, pour it into containers and deliver it to area shut-ins. What a "souper" way to help students become super caring kids!

Pat Madden—Gr. 4
Blessed Katharine Drexel School
Chester, PA

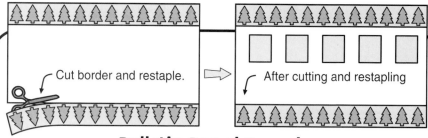

Cut border and restaple. → After cutting and restapling

Bulletin-Board Bargain

For a ready-to-use holiday bulletin board, here's a real bargain! Purchase a seasonal paper tablecloth that has a border design and is blank in the middle. (Save money by buying several on sale after the holidays.) The blank center is perfect for displaying student work. If the bottom border is upside down when you pin the tablecloth to the board, simply cut it off, flip it, and restaple it right side up.

Doreen Placko, Antioch School System, Antioch, IL

A Rhyming Reminder

When it comes to metric conversions, many students have trouble remembering which way to move the decimal. To help them out, I teach my students a simple rhyme:

Large to small,
Heavy to light,
Move the decimal
To the right.

This reminds students that the decimal must move to the right when converting from a large measurement to a smaller one, such as meters to centimeters or kilograms to grams. Any other time, the decimal moves left.

Michelle Bauml—Gr. 5
Gladys Polk Elementary
Richwood, TX

Holiday Calendar

Count down the days until your holiday break by having students create a special calendar. First have students draw a winter mural on butcher paper. Cut small doors in the scene—one for each day until the holiday break. Glue the mural onto another sheet of butcher paper, being careful not to glue the doors shut. Behind each door, write an activity that students can complete in a day. For example, read *The Snowy Day* by Ezra Jack Keats, sing a holiday song over the office intercom, make hot cocoa, etc. Tape the doors shut; then number them according to the days in the countdown. Let students open one door each day and complete the activity.

Sarah Gray—Grs. 5–6
Fairhaven Elementary
Klamath Falls, OR

Celebrity Stockings

Here's a holiday activity that's stuffed with creative- and critical-thinking practice! With students, brainstorm a list of famous people—both living and deceased—from all walks of life: sports, politics, television, science, etc. Have each group of three students select one celebrity and design items that would go in that person's stocking. Instruct each group to mount its items on the outside of a stocking (an inexpensive fabric stocking or a large paper one), being careful not to identify the celebrity anywhere on the stocking. Display the stockings on a wall in the hallway; then invite other classes to guess the identity of each stocking's celebrity.

Susan Robinson—Gr. 5, Kings Park, NY

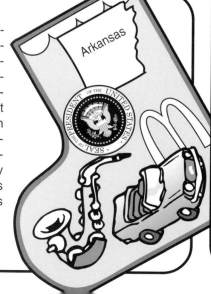

Arkansas

The Switch Game

Try this simple activity to reinforce mental math skills. Write mental math problems on index cards (one per card), preparing enough so that each student will have a card. Distribute the cards; then give each student 15 seconds to complete the problem on his card and record an answer on paper. When time is up, call out, "Switch!" At this signal, students exchange cards in a predetermined order. Have students continue exchanging cards until everyone has seen each card. Call on volunteers to share their answers.

Georgia A. Moonis—Gr. 4
St. Joseph's School
Cockeysville, MD

40
x40

6 children
4 dogs
How many legs in all?

Upholstery Lettering

This idea has saved me countless hours, since I'll never again have to make and laminate bulletin-board letters. I went to a local upholstery shop and asked for scraps of heavy-duty, nylon-backed upholstery fabric similar to that used on lunch counter seats. I placed each of my capital-letter patterns facedown on the back of the fabric and traced around it with a ballpoint pen. (Ink or felt pens smear.) I made 15–20 tracings of each vowel and 10–12 tracings of each consonant, plus tracings of numerals and punctuation marks. After cutting out the tracings, I stored them in an accordion file. These indestructible letters can quickly be removed from a bulletin board just by carefully pulling them off and removing the staples.

Beth E. Berg
Yorkton, Saskatchewan
Canada

Journals Organizer

Try this tip to help you keep your student journals organized. Purchase an inexpensive dish rack at a department store or garage sale. Space journals evenly in the rack's plate dividers. If desired, write your students' names on tabs near the side of the rack so they'll always know which journal slots are theirs.

Maura Hendrickson—Grs. K–6
Hall County District #5
Wood River, NE

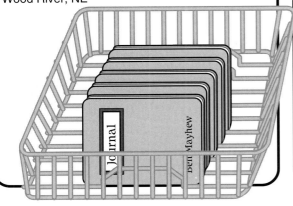

Journal Idea

Each Friday for their journal assignment, my students write to me and tell about the books they're currently reading. I write a brief response to each student in his journal, asking questions that encourage him to focus on character traits, setting, predictions, etc. My students are much more eager to read their books, knowing that they can write to me in their journals and I will respond.

Susan Barnett—Gr. 6
Northwest Elementary
Ft. Wayne, IN

Fact And Opinion Fun

After teaching the skill of identifying facts and opinions, I have the class read a literature selection. I then give each child a sentence strip and an index card labeled *fact* or *opinion*. Each student reads the word on his card without revealing it; then he writes a fact from the story or an opinion on his sentence strip, depending on what is written on his card. Next I divide the chalkboard into two columns labeled "Fact" and "Opinion." As the student reads his sentence aloud, his classmates decide whether the statement is a fact or an opinion. The reader calls on a student to classify the statement. Once a statement has been classified, the reader tapes his strip to the board in the correct column and calls on another volunteer. We continue until all students have shared their statements and placed them on the chalkboard.

Michelle Bauml—Gr. 5
Gladys Polk Elementary
Richwood, TX

Flowers In Bloom

No matter what the weather is outside, these flower boxes are sure to brighten up your classroom. Have students create brightly colored flowers (about 12–15 inches tall) from construction paper. To make the flower boxes, cut lengths of construction paper that are as wide as your windows and about six inches tall. Place two of these sheets on top of each other and staple the sides and bottom. Have students glue their flowers between the sheets of each flower box so that the tops and leaves stick out. Mount the boxes in your windows.

Sharon Sealts—Substitute Teacher
Columbus Grove, OH

Message Mailbox

In my classroom, I have a standard-sized mailbox that is mounted on a pole anchored in a bucket of plaster of paris. I discuss with students the importance of mailboxes and the rules and regulations regarding them. We also talk about the consequences of going into another person's mailbox. I emphasize that each memo, letter, or note returned to school should be placed in the mailbox. Our class mailbox is labeled with the school address and our classroom number. We discuss the importance of addresses, and students are encouraged to learn and remember their own. In addition to our class mailbox, each student has his own personal mailbox made from a half-gallon-size milk carton.

Cynthia Acierto—Grs. 3–5
Ka'elepulu Elementary
Honolulu, HI

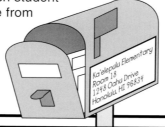

Ka'elepulu Elementary
Room 18
1248 Oahu Drive
Honolulu, HI 96834

Review Sheet Signatures

My students take home a unit review sheet two days before a unit test. At the bottom of the sheet are two lines for a parent's signature. If the student studies with a parent two nights in a row and gets the parent's signature for each night, I add bonus points to that child's test grade.

Eleanor Maxwell—Gr. 4
Thornton Elementary
San Antonio, TX

Review Sheet:
The Civil War

Beautiful Banners

To decorate my classroom for the holidays or a theme unit, I create huge, colorful banners. First I roll up newspaper into two small cylinders. Then I fold each end of a large sheet of bulletin-board paper over a cylinder and tape it down. (The bottom cylinder serves as a weight to keep the bottom of the banner from rolling up). Next I tape a clothes hanger to the top of the banner. I program the banner with theme illustrations, vocabulary, or relevant quotes; then I hang the banner from the ceiling. I often have my students make banners and program them with grammar rules, science facts, etc. Kids study and use the banners because they made them!

Paula Kear—Gr. 4
St. Mary's Grade School
Ellis, KS

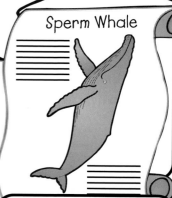

Sperm Whale

Octopus

Put-Ups Instead Of Put-Downs

To promote self-esteem, positive behavior, and school pride, our students are encouraged to earn "put-ups" (compliments). If a teacher or student notices a class exhibiting outstanding behavior—such as walking down a hall quietly or lining up in an orderly fashion—he writes a put-up and delivers it to the office. All put-ups are read the next day during the morning announcements. Each classroom has a put-up board on which to display its compliments after they have been read. For an even greater incentive, there is an end-of-the-year, schoolwide competition for the most put-ups earned. No matter what grade level, a put-up is better than a put-down anytime!

Debbie Cohn—Gr. 5
Desert Sage Elementary
Glendale, AZ

"Pop" Quiz

Before reviewing for an upcoming test, I bring an inexpensive, two-liter bottle of pop and small paper cups to class. I distribute the cups to students before I begin quizzing them. If a student correctly answers a question, she gets a cupful of pop. What a fun and tasty way to review!

Julie Leingang—Gr. 6
Grimsrud Elementary
Bismarck, ND

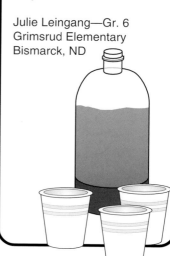

Find A Pencil? Leave A Pencil!

It seems students are always finding pencils and turning them in, or losing pencils and trying to find them. To avoid such interruptions, I borrowed an idea that convenience stores often use with pennies. Simply label a cup with "Find a pencil? Leave a pencil. Need a pencil? Take a pencil." Begin by putting a dozen pencils in the cup. Then students know where to put pencils that they find, or where to borrow pencils if they lose theirs.

Find a pencil?
Leave a pencil.
Need a pencil?
Take a pencil.

Jonathan S. Cohen—Gr. 4 Student Teacher
Maple Shade, NJ

Less Than, Greater Than

Do your students need help with placing the inequality symbol? If so, direct their attention to the space between the two numbers being compared. Have them place one dot next to the number that is less and two dots next to the number that is greater. Then have them simply draw lines to connect the dots and complete the symbol.

Warren Caldwell—Gr. 5
Cage Elementary
Houston, TX

Step One:	417 · : 471
	861 : · 816
Step Two:	417 < 471
	861 > 816

Reading Challenge

Sometimes a simple motivational scheme works better than an elaborate one. To motivate your class to read, establish a goal with each student for reading a set number of pages or books. Tell him that when the goal is reached, he will earn 15 minutes of after-school, fun time with you doing an activity of his choice (playing computer games, shooting some hoops, etc.). This easy idea creates one-on-one time that allows you to praise the student for reaching his goal.

Maura Hendrickson—Grs. K–6
Kenesaw Elementary
Kenesaw, NE

Positive Behavior Grids

Interested in a monthly or thematic method for reinforcing positive behavior? Duplicate for each team a simple, seasonal picture on which you've drawn a grid. Display the grids on a bulletin board in the classroom. Whenever a group is observed following directions, working cooperatively, or staying on task, allow one square on the group's shape to be colored. When all of the shape's squares are colored, award a homework pass or other reward to each member of the group. When every group successfully colors in all squares, hold a class popcorn party to celebrate.

Julie Bliss—Grs. 4–5
Holy Family School
Des Moines, IA

Lights! Camera! Action!

While preparing for a class Parent Night presentation, I discovered that the needed spotlight would not work properly. To ensure that the proper mood would still be created for the children's speeches and performances, I devised a construction-paper template to cover the classroom overhead projector (see the illustration). The substitute spotlight worked even better than the original one because it was not as blinding nor as hot.

Sharon Schweitz—Grs. 3–4
Devinny Elementary
Lakewood, CO

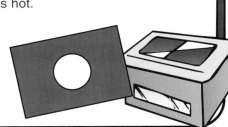

Latched-Onto-Reading Rug

A cozy, new look was given to our reading corner after I taught my fifth graders to latch-hook rugs. From a craft shop, I purchased latch-hook canvas, several skeins of rug yarn, and five latch hooks. Using primary-colored, permanent markers, I drew block-style letters in the center of the canvas grid to spell the word READ. The background was filled in with a fifth color. The students then went to work measuring and cutting the yarn. Groups of five worked on the project before school, as a reward for good work, or as a free-time activity. Girls and boys alike enjoyed creating this great addition to our room!

Marilyn Davison—Grs. 4–5
River Oaks School
Monroe, LA

Just One Look

Here's an easy way to help a student catch up on a literature-based book after being absent. Assist your class in completing sentence strips that document and illustrate each important event in the book as it is read. Display the completed sentence strips in order on a wall of the classroom. When the absent student returns, he finds that catching up isn't so difficult after all.

Andrea McMahan
Munford Middle School
Munford, TN

Something Old— Something New

Recycle those old poster catalogs into brand-new bookmarks your students will love. Cut pictures of posters from old catalogs such as *Argus*. Glue the cut-out pictures onto construction-paper strips; then laminate them. Use these fun bookmarks as motivators or rewards.

Jennifer Cooper—Gr. 4
Park Hills Elementary
Hanover, PA

Some of my best friends are books.

Jenny

Mom's Favorite Recipes

Need a memorable Mother's Day gift idea for your class? Try integrating this book-making activity into your math lesson on customary measurement. Ask each student to bring in his mother's favorite recipe(s). After you compile and duplicate them, allow each student time to organize the recipes into his own special book for his mother. Have the student include a dedication page before binding his recipes inside an original, student-designed cover.

Kay Pahl—Gr. 6
Challenger 7 Elementary
Melbourne, FL

Favorite Recipes For Mom

Know Your "Writes"

Add some spice to those humdrum, business-letter lessons by choosing a hot political topic from your local paper. Have your students write to one of their state representatives, offering their views on the topic as well as possible solutions. This is a terrific way to teach business letters—and incorporate reading, citizenship, and problem-solving lessons at the same time!

Andrea McMahan
Munford Middle School
Munford, TN

Good Punctuation Pays!

Here's an activity designed to motivate students to use good punctuation. Request that each student bring in a favorite candy bar. Divide students into groups of two. Give one student ten sentences that contain punctuation errors and a pack of play money (in $1, $5, and $10 amounts). Assign the other student the role of editor and present him with the answer sheet. Instruct student number one to mark all the errors he can find and then give the sentences to his editor for correction. Tell the editor he is to charge the student $1 for every missed comma or period; $5 for every missed question mark, exclamation mark, apostrophe, or colon; and $10 for every missed pair of quotation marks. (Be sure that the amount of play money given to the student at the beginning of the activity is equal to the amount needed to cover the errors in the sentences.) If the student has enough money remaining, he may purchase a candy bar. If he does not have enough money left over to buy a candy bar, the student can try again with a different set of sentences.

Donna Frazier—Gr. 6
Immaculate Conception School
Jefferson City, MO

Fraction Cookies

Here's a scrumptious way to have your students practice fractions at home and earn extra credit! Simply provide sheets outlining the directions below:

1. Choose a cookie recipe.
2. Decide whether to halve the recipe's ingredients or to double them. (You'll want to have enough to share with your classmates.)
3. Prepare the recipe and bring the baked cookies to class to share.
4. Ask your parent to sign this sheet and return it.

I baked these cookies by myself and did the math calculations on my own.

Signed _____

              Student   Parent

Marcia Lehrman—Gr. 5
Maple Elementary
Avon, IN

Jewel's Cookies
2 cups flour
2 sticks margarine, softened
1/2 cup sugar
2 egg yolks
1 bag Hershey's Kisses®

Preheat oven to 350 degrees. Mix all the ingredients together. Lightly grease a cookie sheet linear off walnut-sized pieces and roll them into balls. Flatten each ball. Bake for 25 minutes. Cool on a wire rack. Makes 35 cookies. (For variety, press a chocolate Kiss into the center of each cookie after removing from the oven.)

Book Bag Lunches

Our school's Field Day lunches will never be the same again! Prior to this event, my class rewrote favorite book reports saved from throughout the year onto one side of white lunch bags. A picture illustrating the book was drawn on the other side. We then gave the bags to our cafeteria staff, and they served bag lunches in them to our fourth and fifth graders on Field Day. Everyone had a great time eating the lunches and reading their friends' bags!

Cathy Ogg—Gr. 4, Happy Valley Elementary, Johnson City, TN

Number The Stars is a great book by Lois Lowry. It takes place during World War II. The ...

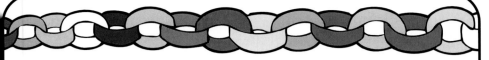

Chain Border

Looking for an inexpensive, yet jazzy bulletin-board border? Give groups of students a supply of two-inch strips of construction paper, and glue or staplers. Have students use the materials to make long paper chains. Staple the resulting 3-D, student-created border onto your bulletin board.

Marilyn Davison—Grs. 4–5, River Oaks School, Monroe, LA

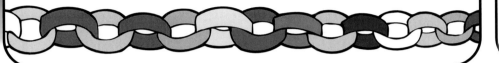

Recycled Posters

Do you have lots of old, out-of-date posters lying around? Give an old poster to a cooperative group. Direct the group to turn the poster over on its back, and then design and color a new poster that correlates with a unit of study. Each old poster now has a fresh, new look and use!

Paula Kear—Gr. 4
St. Mary's Grade School
Ellis, KS

Typing Treat

After buying a home computer, I took my old typewriter to my classroom. On each student's birthday, I allow the honored child to type her work instead of pushing a pencil! My kids love this simple birthday treat.

Brandi Lampl—Gr. 4
W. A. Fountain Elementary
Forest Park, GA

Fraction Garden

Here's a creative way to teach fractional parts of a whole! Divide your math class into groups. Give each group a total number of flowers and a fraction to represent each flower's color. For example, tell students they have 30 flowers, and that three-fifths are yellow, one-third are red, and one-fifteenth are purple. Have each student group determine how many flowers there are of each color. Then challenge the group to design a flower garden that shows the correct number of flowers by color on a piece of art paper. The completed flower gardens make a terrific math bulletin board!

Mary Spina—Gr. 4, Bee Meadow School
Whippany, NJ

My Fraction Garden

Famous-People Baseball Cards

Help students remember the historical figures they study by having them make famous-people baseball cards. Cut tagboard into rectangles, each the size of a baseball card. After the class has researched famous people, give each student a card. Direct the student to label the front of his card with his person's name and an illustration of him/her. On the back of the card, the student writes his person's "stats"—birthdate, birthplace, occupation, reason for his/her fame, etc. Punch a hole in the corner of each card; then bind all of the cards together to make a class set.

Jennifer Bruce—Gr. 5
East Sparta Elementary
Canton, OH

Clara Barton

Birthdate: December 25, 1821

Place Of Birth: Oxford, Massachusetts

Occupation: Nurse

Reason For Fame: Founded the American Red Cross in 1881

Staying Organized

Looking for a decorative way to organize the odds and ends on your desk? Purchase some inexpensive kitchen canisters. They are the perfect size to hold your supplies!

Sharon Zacharda—Gr. 4
West View Elementary
Pittsburgh, PA

Write To Us!

Whenever a popular student moves away, remedy the feelings of loss with a letter-writing campaign! Bring in a class supply of letter-sized envelopes and stamps. Review the form for addressing envelopes with students; then direct each student to address an envelope to himself, stamp it, and place it in a large manila envelope. Have a group of students make a large poster that says "Write To Us!" Let each student write a short message on the poster. Fold the poster, put it inside the large envelope, and mail it to the student who moved. The next day have each student write a letter to the child who moved away. Mail these letters inside another large envelope. The student who moved will have the terrific treat of receiving two special packages—and your students will have the fun of waiting for a reply!

Julia Alarie—Gr. 6, Essex Middle School, Essex, VT

Dear Jenny,
Wish you were still here at Mi... Elementary. W... hope that yo... enjoying your... school.

Write To Us

I miss you!
-Sarah

It's not the sam... without you.
-Matt

Your desk is still empty.
-Scott

What is your new school like?
-Megan

Wallpaper Book Covers

Try this idea to keep books looking new for a longer period of time. Obtain a discarded book of wallpaper samples. Use the sheets of wallpaper to make sturdy, colorful, and economical book covers. You'll discover that one book of samples will cover lots of books!

Colleen Dabney—Gr. 6
Williamsburg Christian Academy
Williamsburg, VA

Velcro® Magic

Every teacher knows how difficult it is to hang charts and posters on the walls. Try using self-adhesive Velcro® dots and strips. Attach the hooks to the wall and the loops to the back of each poster or chart. Even when not in use, the Velcro® hooks do not detract from the room's appearance. Charts and posters become easy to change—and never fall off the wall!

Ginger Pope—Gr. 5, Brooklyn Springs School, Lancaster, SC

Paper Suncatchers

Decorate your classroom windows every month with this easy art activity. Give each student a piece of thin tracing paper. Have the student place it on top of a coloring book picture and trace it with a dark-colored marker (or have students draw their own pictures on the tracing paper). After students have cut out their tracings, stick the each picture onto a classroom window using Tack A Note® adhesive. The sun's rays will beam right through the thin tracing paper for beautiful decorations that will make students shine with pride!

Antoinette Parry—Gr. 5
Wellwood International School
Baltimore, MD

Salt-Dough Relief Maps

Here's a hint to use when mixing ingredients for salt-dough relief maps in your classroom. Put all of the necessary ingredients—flour, salt, and water—into a large Ziploc® bag. Then just knead the bag until everything is mixed!

Susan Deprez, St. Mel School, Woodland Hills, CA

Absentminded Scientist Folders

To help my students organize materials for each science unit we study, I give each child a folder, a straight pin, and four brads. The student uses the straight pin to make two holes at the top of a small stack of paper. He also makes two small holes at the top of the left side of the opened folder. Then he uses two brads to attach the paper to the folder as shown. After repeating these steps on the other side of the folder, the student decorates the front of the folder. During the unit, the student can write his notes on the folder's paper. It's also easy to add handouts to the folder. The result is a science folder that keeps my absentminded scientists from misplacing important papers.

Frances Beloin—Gr. 6
Jewett Street School
Manchester, NH

Traveling The USA

Each year my fifth graders have great fun playing the computer geography game, Where in the USA is Carmen San Diego?® To build on this game's popularity, I obtained an assortment of U.S. travel books, road atlases, and brochures from travel agencies and local libraries. Cooperative groups used these resources to design their own Carmen games. Each student was responsible for finding and listing at least three facts each about 15 different cities and 15 points of interest. Next each group drew an outline of the United States on oaktag; then the group labeled the cities and points of interest that its members had researched. Finally groups devised game rules, wrote clues, named characters, etc. Imaginations soared and so did retention of facts!

Judy Bas—Grs. 3–5
Lower Saucon Elementary
Hellertown, PA

Open-Ended Mystery Calendar

It is always challenging to think of closing-day activities that require little teacher-preparation time yet are stimulating for students. After purchasing some Crayola® Mystery Writer Markers, I decided to make a mystery calendar. At the beginning of each month, I use a mystery writer marker to write an open-ended statement in each school day's calendar space. (For example: I was so happy when..., I was frightened when..., etc.). Then, at the close of each day, I choose a student to reveal the statement of the day by coloring that day's space with the decoder marker. The student reads the statement aloud to the class, completes it, and asks volunteers to suggest their endings.

Maura Hendrickson—Grs. K–6
Kenesaw Elementary
Kenesaw, NE

Teacher Appreciation Week

Roll out the red carpet for your teachers! That's exactly what we did at our school. The celebration kicked off on Monday with our teachers being declared kings and queens for the week. Our student council even made crowns for them to wear. On Tuesday each teacher was given a tissue-paper flower. Wednesday teachers were presented with Hershey's Kisses® to recognize their sweetness. On Thursday a bulletin board featured photos taken on Monday showing each teacher being crowned. Each teacher's photo was accompanied by students' quotes about him or her. To culminate the celebration, gifts were presented to the teachers on Friday. These practical gifts were hand-sanded, wooden stir sticks that the students had painted, decorated, and labeled "Hall Pass." A royally good time was had by all!

Gina L. Mojica-Rasmussen—Gr. 5
McKee Intermediate
Bakersfield, CA

Mrs. Hayes

- "...a super math teacher!"

- "...always encourages me to do my best."

- "...willing to help her students."

- "...makes learning fun!"

Classroom Author Chair

Once a week my class highlights the week's student authors. Each author is allowed to sit in a special chair in front of the room to share his composition(s) with the class. I purchased an inexpensive, white, plastic-form chair. Using puff paint and brushes, students were allowed to design the outside back and sides of our author chair. Because the decorations are their own, my students are much more eager to write and then share their published work, seated in this chair of honor.

Maura Hendrickson—Grs. K–6

Surf's Up!

It was a bit difficult to find ideas for a reading corner that my sixth graders truly enjoyed, but here is one idea that received a thumb's up! I concocted a mock beach for their reading pleasure complete with a lounge chair and umbrella, a beach towel, seashells, an air mattress, sunglasses, sand toys, and small containers of sand from beaches across the country. By following a rotating list, students could "go to the beach" during silent reading time.

Valerie Hornbaker—Gr. 6, Elreka Grade School, Hutchinson, KS

RIDE THE WAVE!

Rounding Hive

Rounding numbers can "bee-come" a snap with this clever idea! Make a class supply of laminated paper hives like the one shown. Give a hive and a wipe-off marker to each student. Call out a number; then have each child write the number in the door of his hive. Have students underline the digit of the place value to which the number should be rounded. Direct each student to use the numbers on the sides of the hive to help him decide whether to round the door's number up or down. After the correct answer has been discussed, have students wipe the hives clean and get ready for round two!

Katherine Gegner—Grs. 3–4
Linkhorne Elementary, Lynchburg, VA

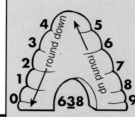

Milk-Cap Math

Recycle plastic milk caps to create a game that provides plenty of place-value practice. Have each student fold a sentence strip into fourths and label the sections from left to right: thousands, hundreds, tens, and ones. Next give the student a paper lunch bag that contains ten plastic milk caps numbered 0–9. Pair each student with a partner. Explain that the object of the game is to build the largest possible number. Have each player reach into his bag, pull out a milk cap, and place it somewhere on his sentence strip. Repeat this step three times; then have the pair compare their two numbers. The student with the higher number earns one point. At the end of ten rounds, have students total their points to determine the game's winner.

Brandi Lampl—Gr. 4, W. A. Fountain Elementary, Forest Park, GA

The Reward Wreath

Who says wreaths are only for Christmas? Use staples, pins, or a hot glue gun to attach an assortment of hard candies to an inexpensive straw wreath. Then hang the wreath in your classroom. When a student exhibits exemplary behavior, let her pull a candy from the wreath. Positive reinforcement—how sweet it is!

Tracy L. Smith
Gr. 5
Heritage
  Christian School
Owensboro, KY

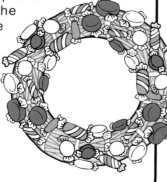

Magnetic U.S. Map

If you have a wall map that will no longer roll up, recycle it as a magnetic, portable puzzle! Cut out each state; then glue a couple of magnetic strips to the back of the cutout. Let students work together to reassemble the map on the chalkboard. This handy cutout map is also a great tool for reviewing U.S. regions, states, and capitals.

Valerie Johnson—Gr. 5
Hagerstown Elementary
Hagerstown, IN

A Poem To Learn By

My students seem to remember facts more easily when the information is presented in a fun format. To teach the five kinds of living organisms, I created a simple poem (see the illustration). Everyone got an *A* on this science test!

Carol Neisen
Westside Catholic
  Consolidated School
Evansville, IN

Bacteria has
Just one cell.
It makes you sick
Or makes you well

Protist cells are
Wet and green—
Slimiest things
You've ever seen!

Fungus grows on
Something dead.
The mushroom
Even has a head!

Plants can grow, b
Don't move much.
You can eat some
With your lunch.

An animal can
Move about.
Its many cells can
Scream and shout!

Brainteaser M&M's®

Generate high interest in problem solving by pairing a brainteaser with a popular snack! Form a triangle on the overhead projector as shown, using ten pennies. Give each student ten M&M's® candies and ask him to duplicate the triangle on his desk. Challenge students to invert the triangle by moving only three candies. Once the puzzle is solved (see the solution shown), let students munch on their manipulatives!

Michelle Kasmiske—Gr. 4
Monroe Elementary
Janesville, WI

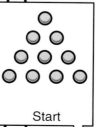
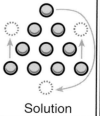

Start   Solution   Finish

GET IT TOGETHER

Get It Together!

Teacher-tested Ideas For Cooperative Learning

Team Effort

Promote cooperative learning with this easy-to-manage system. Begin by arranging student desks into cooperative groups of five. Place a small paper cup on each group's table. Keep a jar filled with dried beans or unpopped popcorn on a shelf. Inform students that groups or individual group members can earn a bean for every instance of cooperative or responsible behavior. Post a list like the one below in your classroom. At the end of the day, reward the team that has earned the most beans.

Earn A Bean For:
- scoring 100% on a test
- running an errand
- keeping your desk tidy
- working quietly
- completing an assignment
- honoring guests with polite behavior
- completing extra-credit work
- demonstrating sportsmanship
- lining up in an orderly fashion
- bringing in parent notes, permission slips, etc.
- demonstrating responsible behavior during special classes

Kathy Green—Gr. 4
Anna Jarvis Elementary
Grafton, WV

Higher Expectations

Who says students won't live up to expectations if given a chance?! At the beginning of the school year, inform students that they may earn ten extra minutes of recess time by bringing the class test average up to 70%. As the school year progresses, increase the expected average to 80%. At the end of the school year, push it up to 90%. Then watch as students take studying more seriously, parents express their pleasure at student progress, and students meet the toughest tests with confidence.

Denell Hilgendorf—Grs. 4–6
Osaka International School
Osaka, Japan

Why Work Together?

Point out to your students the importance of cooperative work by having them role-play real-life group activities. Divide students into groups of four or five. Assign each group one of the situations below; then have each group present a skit to demonstrate its situation. Afterwards discuss how important cooperation was to each activity. Ask students to consider reasons why it is important to work together as classmates this year.

Role-Playing Situations:
Group #1— as fire safety officers at the scene of a fire.
Group #2— as doctors performing surgery.
Group #3— as a football team who wants to win the Super Bowl.
Group #4— as a family planning a surprise birthday party.
Group #5— as a track team running a relay race.

Donna Hupe
Evans City, PA

Team Spelling Game

Cooperation is the name of the game here! Divide your class into two teams. Give each team a set of large index cards that have been labeled with the letters of the alphabet (one letter per card). Call out a word that does not have any duplicated letters in it. Then challenge each team to come up with a strategy for coordinating the group's spelling of the word. Some teams will give each student two or three letters; others will put all the letters on the floor or table, or seem to have no strategy at all! If one team wins the contest two or three times, let it demonstrate its strategy while the other team watches. Then scramble the teams and start a new round. Reward teams for working together quietly as well as spelling accurately.

Elsie B. McGill—Grs. 6–8
College Park Middle School
Hickory, NC

Get It Together!

Teacher-tested Ideas For Cooperative Learning

Cooperative Spelling Lessons

Cooperative teamwork really motivates my students to learn weekly spelling lists. On Monday, I give a pretest. Students then correct their own words and make take-home lists to study. From Tuesday through Thursday, students study and write their spelling words within cooperative groups. Then on Friday, students are given a posttest. Individual accountability is encouraged because each student must score at least 80% on his Friday test. Teamwork is also reinforced in the following ways:

- If a whole group scores 80% or better, each group member earns an extra sticker.
- If each member of a group scores 100%, that group earns an extra five minutes of recess.
- If every student scores at least 80%, the entire class is rewarded with no spelling homework the following week.
- If the entire class scores 100%, students are rewarded with a party, five extra minutes of recess, and no homework the following week. (We're still working on this goal!)

Julie Foster—Gr. 4
Prospect Hill School
Burlington, IA

Reading Buddies

My classroom book collection has grown so much that I now have duplicate copies of several titles. For a cooperative-learning activity, I divide my class into pairs and provide students in each pair with like books. Each pair also makes a literature journal. The couple decides how many chapters of its book to read each night. That night, one student takes home the journal and creates questions about those chapters. The next day the pairs meet and discuss the questions. They also decide how much to read that night. Students then exchange roles for the next day's question-and-answer session. After finishing its book, each pair gives a short book talk. This cooperative activity ensures that students are reading and discussing good books.

Laura Vazquez—Gr. 5
Charles R. Hadley Elementary
Miami Springs, FL

Meals For A Day

As a wrap-up project for a unit on nutrition, my students use the Food Guide Pyramid to plan meals and a snack for an entire day. First I divide the class into groups of four. Each group is provided with four paper plates, old magazines, grocery ads, scissors, paste, and a copy of the Food Pyramid. Following the guidelines of the Food Guide Pyramid, each group cuts out food pictures to create menus for breakfast, lunch, dinner, and a snack. The cutouts for each meal and the snack are arranged and then pasted onto the paper plates. What a fun way to encourage healthful eating habits!

Kathleen Channell—Gr. 6
Berry Middle School
Lebanon, OH

Team Interviews

I use real-life techniques to help my students learn how to conduct good interviews. Students are divided into five groups, with each group consisting of two interviewers, one recorder, and a photographer. Students select five school employees—other than teachers—whom they want to interview. Each group then develops six questions that it wants to ask its interviewee and writes a letter to set up an appointment. At the agreed-upon time, the group conducts its interview and takes an instant photo. After the interviews are completed, each group organizes its information into paragraphs, edits the article, and prepares a final draft. All of the final articles and photos are combined into a class booklet to share with parents and other visitors.

Dolores A. Davis—Gr. 5
Hungerford Elementary
Eatonville, FL

Get It Together!

Teacher-tested Ideas For Cooperative Learning

Awesome Adventures

Use this exciting activity to trigger students' thinking toward making plans for summer outings. Provide brochures from resort areas, theme and amusement parks, hands-on science museums, or even advertisements for zany adventures like hot-air balloon rides. Also include playing schedules from sports teams or arrival/ departure schedules for trains, cruise lines, etc. Allow students time to peruse the material and form groups according to interest. Group work should include the following:

- Selecting a destination
- Deciding on a method of transportation
- Calculating expenses for the activity itself, round-trip transportation, meals, and lodging (as applicable)
- Dressing appropriately for the adventure and presenting findings to the class

Variations for this activity include having the groups work within an assigned budget or time limit.

Barbara J. Wissink—Gr. 5
St. Croix Catholic School
Stillwater, MN

ORLANDO, FLORIDA

UP, UP, & AWAY

Adventures In Hot-Air Ballooning

Roll-The-Dice Review

Tired of taking turns and calling on cooperative groups to answer review questions for a test? Try this new way of challenging *everyone* to be ready with an answer. Divide the class into six groups. Number the groups one through six; then number each student. Pose the question and give a short amount of time for the group to discuss the answer. Then roll two dice. The left die indicates which group will answer the question. The right die tells which group member will answer the question. (If a group has less than five or six members, let any member answer when a five or six is rolled.) When a member answers a question correctly, he earns a point for his team. Students are much more excited about reviewing for a test when this method is used. Also, members take more responsibility for helping everyone on the team know the answers.

Therese Durhman—Gr. 5
Mountain View School
Hickory, NC

Forming Cooperative Groups

Try this fun and innovative method for forming groups. Decide how many groups need to be formed. Select the same number of old greeting cards. Cut off the front of each card. Then cut each front into three or four different-sized pieces (depending on how many students you desire in each group). Mix up the pieces and then pass them out. Direct the students to match the pieces and reconstruct the front of a card. This will form mixed groups of three or four for your particular activity.

Barbara Lozier—Gr. 4
Westbrook School
West Islip, NY

A Microphone For Quiet

When students are working in groups and you want to control the noise level, simply reach for the "mike." Duplicate a microphone pattern onto construction paper (see the illustration). Cut the pattern out, glue it onto heavy paper, and then laminate it. Give each group of students one microphone. Make sure it is understood that the only time it is permissible to speak is when the mike is in hand. If another member of the group wishes to speak, he must extend his hand and the holder of the mike must pass it. This means, of course, that only one student at a time should be speaking. The other members should listen without interrupting. The result is a dramatic reduction of noise without stifling discussion. Suggested modifications include:

- The student with the mike may say only one or two sentences.
- The mike must always be passed to the left (this avoids domination by one or two students).
- When the mike is passed to a student, he <u>must</u> add to the discussion (this involves all students).
- Give mikes to those students you want to separate. Build groups around them.

William J. Porter
Monroe, WI

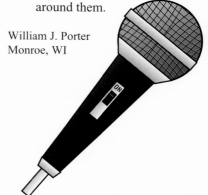

GAME PLANS

GAME PLANS

Fictionary

Creative thinking and vocabulary skills go hand in hand with this challenging word game. Divide the class into groups of four to six students each. One student—the Reader—finds a word in the dictionary that he hopes nobody in the group knows. He pronounces and spells the word for the group. Each group member then makes up a definition for the word and writes it on a slip of paper. The Reader copies the dictionary definition on a slip of paper, gathers all the slips, and shuffles them. He then reads each definition aloud. After hearing all of the definitions, each person—except the Reader—votes for the definition he thinks is the correct one. The Reader tallies the votes for each definition; then he reveals the true definition and awards points as follows:

> Each vote for a false definition earns the author of that definition 1 point.
>
> Each vote for the correct definition earns the voter 1 point.
>
> If no one votes for the correct definition, the Reader earns 10 points.

Caroline Jensen and Janice Holsteen—Gr. 5
American School in Aberdeen
Scotland, UK

> hebephrenic—
> a condition of
> adolescent silliness

> dibble—
> to drink like a duck, lift-
> ing up the head after
> each sip

Multiplication Tic-Tac-Toe

Tic-tac-toe your way to reinforcing two-digit multiplication skills. Draw a large tic-tac-toe grid on the board. Divide the class into an X team and an O team; then give each team a pair of dice labeled with assorted numbers from 1 to 9. To play, have each team roll both dice and place the resulting two numbers in a two-digit multiplication sentence—either in the tens or the ones place. The team rolls again, filling in the remaining two spaces with the numbers rolled. Then each team member solves the multiplication sentence, double-checking with fellow members to ensure that the answer is correct. The team with the highest answer gets to place its X or O on the tic-tac-toe grid. The first team to complete a tic-tac-toe wins!

Meg Tessitore—Gr. 4
Timothy Christian School
Piscataway, NJ

Technical Trivia

Reinforce a current unit by having students make a trivia game. Divide the class into groups; then give each group 30 colored cards (a different color for each group). Have each group create at least 20 questions from the unit you've been studying, gathering information both from their notes and the text. Instruct each group to write a question on the front and the correct answer on the back of each card. Since incorrect answers cost the team one point each, encourage students to double-check their work before turning in the cards to you.

To play, ask one group member a question from an opposing team's cards. If she cannot answer the question by herself in 30 seconds, let her call on a teammate for help. After 30 more seconds, the student must pass or give an answer. Award points accordingly:

> 2 points for giving an answer without help.
>
> 1 point for a team answer.
>
> 0 points for a pass or an incorrect answer.

The team with the most points at the end of the game wins.

Donna Lewis—Gr. 4, Country Club Elementary, Farmington, NM

GAME PLANS

Compound Connections

Make the connection between compound words and fun with this lively game! On each of 70–80 index cards, write a word that is part of a compound. Place the cards facedown on a table. After students are divided into teams of four or five each, ask one player from each team to choose ten cards from the table and take them back to his team. Each team then works cooperatively to make as many compound words as possible from the words on the cards. (A word can be used more than once.) A recorder on each team lists the words his team makes. After about five minutes, call time and direct students to return all cards to the table. After mixing up the cards, begin round two by having a second player from each team choose ten cards. After several rounds, meet together as a class and use dictionaries to check all of the compound words. The team that lists the most words wins.

Gloria Jean Stevens—Gr. 5, Frank Jewett School
West Buxton, ME

Fraction Dice Game

Wrap up a study of fractions with a roll of the die! Divide students into teams of three to five each and provide each team with a die. Instruct students on each team to take turns rolling the die two times: the first number rolled is the numerator for a fraction, while the second is the denominator. After everyone has rolled the die and recorded his fraction, students on each team compare their fractions with each other. The player with the greatest fraction—in its simplest terms—earns a point. Continue play until a student earns ten points. For a variation, provide each team with two dice or with 12-sided dice.

Sherri Kaiser—Gr. 4, Walnut Grove Elementary
Suwanee, GA

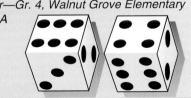

26-Square Wipeout

My students love this game that provides plenty of basic math practice. I made a laminated gameboard with the numbers 1–26 on it (see the illustration). Students are divided into two teams. To begin play, I give Team 1 three numbers. That team then has one minute to come up with as many equations that will result in answers of 1–26 as possible. Students may multiply, divide, add, or subtract—or use any combinations of the operations. As players call out their equations and answers to me, I cross out each correct answer on the gameboard with a wipeoff marker. At the end of one minute, I count the numbers marked off. I then clean the gameboard and give the opposing team three numbers. After several rounds, the team that earns the most marked-off numbers gets to choose a math game to play on the following Friday.

Debbie Patrick—Gr. 5
Park Forest Elementary
State College, PA

+	1	2	3	4	−
5	6	7	8	9	10
11	12	13	14	15	16
17	18	19	20	21	22
×	23	24	25	26	÷

$$\frac{6}{4} = \frac{3}{2} = 1\frac{1}{2}$$

GAME PLANS

Build-A-Word

Increase vocabulary and thinking skills with this fun word-building game. Give each student a grid of 36 squares. To begin play, ask a student to call out a letter. Have each child write that letter in a square on his grid. Continue having students call out letters and write them in their grids. Challenge students to form words of three or more letters horizontally, vertically, or diagonally. Explain that once a letter is written in a square, it cannot be erased, moved to another square, or changed. Have students circle their words as they build them. When all of the squares have been filled, declare the student with the most words the winner.

Joyceann Dreibelbis—Gr. 4
Kean Elementary
Wooster, OH

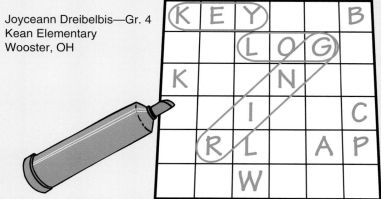

Ticktacktoe Board

Here's a nifty idea for making ticktacktoe boards that are durable and easy to store! Simply use a permanent black marker to draw a 3 x 3 grid on a square of thin, colorful foam (available at craft stores). Store each square inside a plastic Ziploc® bag. Also include ten fun-shaped erasers (five each of two different colors) to use as markers. Presto—a ready-to-use game that's perfect for a center or free-time review!

Colleen Dabney—Gr. 5
Williamsburg Christian Academy
Williamsburg, VA

Grammar Review Game

Spice up an end-of-the-chapter review with a grammar game your students are sure to love! Divide your class into teams of four to six students each. Give each team a number; then list those numbers on a scorecard you've drawn on the chalkboard. Have each team select a recorder. Give each recorder a small chalkboard, a piece of chalk, and an eraser.

Begin the review by asking each team to listen for all of the nouns (or whatever skill you're reviewing) in a sentence you will read aloud. Have each team discuss the sentence; then have the team recorder write the sentence's nouns on the team's chalkboard. Ask each recorder to hold up his chalkboard. Award one point to each team that answers correctly. At the end of the game, total the points and give each winning team member a small prize.

Donna Vaden—Gr. 5
Santa Rita Elementary
Midland, TX

word
pencil
paper

Three Steps

Need a quick and fun math game? Then try this! Call two students to the front of the class. Show a flash card to them. Have the first student to answer correctly take a step forward. Continue play until one of the students has taken three steps. Declare that student the winner and allow him to face another opponent. Permit the other student to hold the cards for the next game.

Jane Dvorscak—Gr. 5
Merrillville, IN

LIFESAVERS

The Job Squad

Every classroom can at times become cluttered, disorganized, and just plain trashed out! Create a classroom cleanup kit containing a feather duster, a whisk broom, cleaning rags, paper towels, glass cleaner, a sponge, dishwashing liquid, a pail for water, and disinfectant spray. Post a sign-up list for students that includes a job for everyone, such as erasing chalkboards, watering plants, emptying trash, dusting shelves, picking up paper, and alphabetizing encyclopedias. Then schedule a regular cleaning time in your classroom. Friday afternoons are ideal so that you can begin the week on the following Monday with a truly tidy classroom!

Penny Parchem—Grs. 4–8
Dallas, TX

Magnetic Management

Here's a really "attractive" way to help students who, no matter how hard they try, consistently misplace their worksheets. Use refrigerator magnets to hang an extra worksheet from a filing cabinet. When a student loses a reproducible, let him copy (but not remove) the hanging sheet. You won't have to scramble to make an extra copy, and the student gets a chance to make up his work.

Judith Brinckerhoff—Gr. 6, Hanaford School, East Greenwich, RI

Simple Storage For Seasonal Essentials

Organize those monthly and seasonal bulletin boards and activities with these sturdy pockets. Use either extra large, bulletin-board oaktag folded in half, or two sheets of poster board. Staple together all but the top sides to create a large pocket. Label the contents on the outside of the pocket. For smaller items and monthly masters/handouts, staple the sides of a legal-size manila folder, leaving the top open. Store the smaller folders in the larger monthly pockets. Place all items together in a sturdy box that's been decorated by your students.

Theresa Azzolino—Gr. 6
Washington School
Lodi, NJ

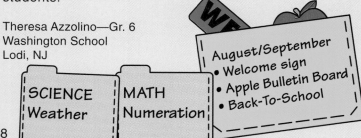

SCIENCE Weather | MATH Numeration

August/September
• Welcome sign
• Apple Bulletin Board
• Back-To-School

Teacher's Assistant

Here's a great way to teach responsibility and give yourself a helping hand in the classroom. At the beginning of the year, select a different student each day to be the Teacher's Assistant. Give the assistant such tasks as taking attendance to the office, escorting ill or injured students to the clinic, returning library books to the media center, giving make-up spelling tests, collecting papers, and greeting visitors to the classroom. Allow the assistant to sit at your desk (since you probably never get to sit down anyway!). After each student has had a chance to serve as assistant, use the position as a reward for responsible behavior. Since everyone has served as assistant and knows how much fun the job is, students work extra hard to earn the privilege.

Susan Keller—Gr. 5 Reading and Language Arts
Plumb Elementary
Clearwater, FL

Pick A Pupil

Keep a little suspense in the selection of pupil volunteers by choosing names randomly from a basket at your desk. At the beginning of each year, write each child's name in permanent marker on a clothespin (not the kind that pinches). When you need a student volunteer, pick a name out of the basket. Or draw names during review sessions. Since no one knows who will be called upon, everyone stays alert.

Susan Ely—Gr. 4
Churchville Elementary
Newtown, PA

No Substitute For Preparation

As you prepare your substitute folder for the new year, be sure to include a special class pictorial. Duplicate your students' photos from last year's yearbook. Cut out each photo and paste it next to the student's name on a class chart. When it comes to acquainting a substitute with your students, what a difference a picture makes!

Pamela J. Fox—Gr. 4
Brassfield Elementary
Bixby, OK

Jackson Crane | Janet Anthony | Graham Bell

LIFESAVERS...management tips for teachers

Double-Duty Nametags

These sturdy nametags also serve as handy pencil holders. For each nametag, fold a sheet of heavy paper twice to form four sections. Open the sheet; then overlap the two end sections and glue them together to make a base for the resulting triangular tube. Write the student's name on both sides of the nametag. Punch a hole for holding a pencil at the top of the nametag as shown. Helpful for substitutes too!

Cynthia E. Britton
Longley Way School
Arcadia, CA

Race The Clock

Draw a clock face on poster board; then laminate it. For each day that no one is placed in time-out or is sent to the office, place a sticker on one of the clock face numbers. When all 12 numbers are covered by stickers, reward the entire class with extra recess or a video party.

Beverly Langland—Gr. 5
Trinity Christian Academy
Jacksonville, FL

The Dog Ate It!

Accountability is key! The next time a student comes to class without his homework, have him write his reason on a sheet such as the one shown. (Duplicate these sheets on brightly colored paper so parents are sure to notice them.) Send the sheet home to inform the parent about her child's homework record. Store returned forms in a special folder to use during parent conferences.

Marcia Lehrman—Gr. 5, Maple Elementary, Indianapolis, IN

HOMEWORK NOTICE

Name: _____
Date: _____
Assignment: _____
Date due: _____
I did not bring / complete / do (circle one)
my homework because _____
_____
_____
Parent signature: _____

HOMEWORK

Inexpensive Mailbox System

Simplify your system of distributing student papers by creating stacking storage shelves. Purchase an inexpensive cardboard magazine box for each student. Label each box with a student's name; then stack the boxes as shown. Rather than handing papers back to students, just stick each paper in its appropriate box. At the end of the day, students know right where to go to get the papers they need to take home.

Jennifer Overend—Gr. 6
Aprende Middle School
Chandler, AZ

Taking Turns

Here's the key to giving your students equal opportunity to write on the chalkboard or perform popular classroom jobs. Obtain two boxes, including one that easily fits inside the other. Write each student's name on a slip of paper; then place these slips in the larger box. Whenever you need a student volunteer, draw a name from the larger box. After choosing a student, place her name slip in the smaller box. Once every student has had a turn, empty the smaller box into the larger one and begin again.

Faye Wells
Marion County Elementary
Buena Vista, GA

Munch Money

Save yourself the time and aggravation of dealing with forgotten lunch money by keeping a "Munch Money" jar in your classroom. At the beginning of the year, fill this jar with $10.00 to $15.00 in change. Allow students who have forgotten or lost their breakfast or lunch money to take out a loan from the jar. Since this is an honor system, students are responsible for paying back any money they've borrowed. As an end-of-the-year treat, use the leftover "Munch Money" to pay for an ice-cream-sundae extravaganza.

Phil Forsythe
Northeastern Elementary
Bellefontaine, OH

Mac To The Rescue!

Keeping track of all the books in your growing classroom library can be a daunting task! With the help of your Macintosh® computer and a Microsoft® Works database, you'll get organized in no time. Create four alphabetically arranged categories on the database: title, author, code, and student name. Once the program is in place and all the books have been cataloged, have several capable students keep the catalog current. With this tool it's easy to add new books or locate those already in the library.

Antoinette Parry—Gr. 5
Wellwood International School
Baltimore, MD

A Simple Reminder

Are you sitting down? If so, you don't need to look far for a simple reminder to send home important papers and school notes. Whenever you have important papers to send home, place these items on your chair. When you return to sit at your desk, you'll be reminded to pass out the papers. Even your students will remind you to look at your chair before they leave for the day.

Deena Block—Gr. 4
George B. Fine Elementary
Pennsauken, NJ

Fast-Food Calculator Caddies

If you love french fries, you'll love gathering materials for this calculator storage idea! Collect a fast-food french-fry container for each calculator. Cover each container's logo with a hamburger cutout. Write a student name or number on each cutout. Arrange the calculator caddies on a bulletin board using thumbtacks.

Melissa Kienzl
Eldred Elementary
Kunkletown, PA

A Little Tape Will Do It!

Don't throw away those old duplicating masters that have answers on them. Instead, cover the answers using Post-It™ Brand 1-Line Correction & Cover-Up Tape. After covering the answers with the tape, duplicate the page to create a new master. Then remove the tape to reveal a ready-made answer key.

Marcia Lehrman
Maple Elementary
Avon, IN

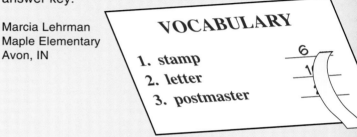

VOCABULARY

1. stamp
2. letter
3. postmaster

Handy Red Pens

What one tool has made more corrections than any other? The red pen, of course! Provide each student with his own pen for making corrections. Attach the rough side of sticky-back Velcro® to the front of each student's desk; then attach the soft side to a red pen. When it's time to correct papers, students will always have marking pens right at their fingertips.

Lorri Burton—Gr. 5
Huddleston Elementary
Huddleston, VA

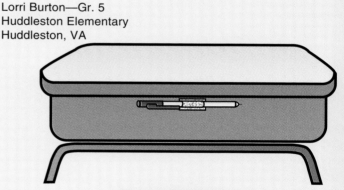

Novel Solution

Need a source of teaching ideas for your next novel? Create your own teacher's edition. Purchase a personal copy of the novel. As you preview the book, underline important vocabulary words and significant phrases or figures of speech. Make notations in the margins next to sections that illustrate predictions, character personalities, cause and effect, and other skills. At the end of each chapter, jot down any writing activities that occur to you. This handy tool will prove useful year after year.

Laura Vazquez—Gr. 5
Charles R. Hadley Elementary
Miami Springs, FL

LIFESAVERS...management tips for teachers

Restroom Traffic Control

"May I go to the restroom?" can be an annoying question to a teacher, especially in the middle of a lesson. I've solved this problem by making two signs—one each for my boys and girls—with the words STOP and GO on opposite sides. Each laminated sign has a magnetic strip on each side so that I can attach it to the corner of a chalkboard. When a child needs to go to the restroom, he or she flips the correct sign to STOP. This lets the remaining boys or girls know that someone is out of the classroom and they must wait their turn. When that student returns to class, he flips the sign back to GO. If there are times during the day when I don't want anyone to leave the classroom (during a test or while I'm giving directions), I turn both signs to STOP.

Mary T. Spina—Gr. 4, Bee Meadow School, Whippany, NJ

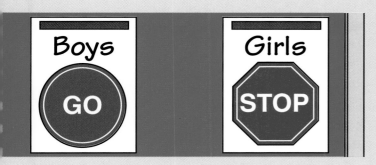

Student Job Board

Need a simple, easy-to-make display to help you keep track of classroom jobs? Divide a sheet of poster board into two columns; then divide the columns into sections equal to the number of classroom jobs. Write a job title and a brief description of it in each section. Laminate the poster board for durability. Next write each student's name on both sides of a pinch clothespin. Assign two or three students to each job by clipping their clothespins in the appropriate section. Each week move the clothespins in a clockwise rotation to give students new jobs. Students can readily see the jobs they are assigned to and what the jobs entail.

Virginia H. Kotok—Gr. 4
St. Margaret School
Pittsburgh, PA

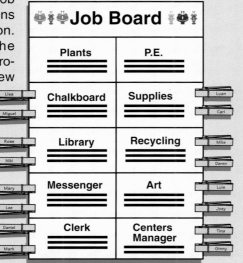

Wheel Of Fortune

Would you like your students to rush to their desks, get their materials ready, and listen attentively? Those are the positive results of my Wheel Of Fortune discipline plan. Each row of students has a baby-food jar. The goal is to fill your jar with marbles, which are awarded for positive behavior, staying on task, good study habits, etc. Once a jar is filled, everyone in that row gets to spin our class Wheel Of Fortune. Since my students determine the prizes featured on the wheel—lunch with me, candy, a homework pass, soda pop, etc.—they love every spin. Students catch on quickly and jars often fill up in a few days instead of weeks.

Debbie Cohn—Gr. 5, Desert Sage Elementary, Glendale, AZ

Substitute Plans

Each year I make a skeleton outline of my daily schedule. I keep a supply of copies both at school and at home. Whenever I need a substitute to take over my class, I simply fill out the form with my plans. This duplicated outline saves me from having to write out all of the details of my daily schedule every time I need a substitute.

Substitute Plans
Date:
Tues.: Lunchroom duty
Fri.: Morning & recess duty
8:05–8:10 Lockers
8:10–9:10 Period 1 (check roll, lunch count, supplies)

9:10–10:05 Math

Karen Womack—Gr. 4
Dardanelle Intermediate
Russellville, AR

File-Box Plans

Whenever my school system adopts a new textbook, I label a small index card with each chapter title. On each chapter card, I list the topics and page numbers that I plan to use. I also list workbook pages and other projects that I like to include in my units. On the back of the card, I add audiovisual materials and library books that I need for that chapter. I keep these cards filed in a small box on my desk. Each week when it's time to write lesson plans, I turn to my card file instead of dragging out those huge teacher manuals. Now I rarely forget projects, filmstrips, or books that I enjoy using!

Holly Bates—Gr. 4, Arlington Elementary, Anson, ME

The ABCs Of Positive Comments

Writing positive comments on a student's paper is important in building self-esteem. A problem I have, however, is using and reusing the same comments again and again. So I devised an alphabetical list of words and phrases to take the sameness out of grading. Use this list, or substitute words and phrases of your own.

A —	**A**wesome	N —	**N**eat
B —	**B**e Proud	O —	**O**utstanding
C —	**C**lever Writing	P —	**P**erfect or **P**ractically Perfect
D —	**D**ynamite Work	Q —	**Q**uite Good
E —	**E**xcellent Effort	R —	**R**ight On
F —	**F**antastic	S —	**S**uperior
G —	**G**ood Going	T —	**T**otally Great
H —	**H**ow Wonderful	U —	**U**nbelievable
I —	**I** Like This	V —	**V**ery Good
J —	**J**ust Super	W —	**W**ow
K —	**K**ing-Size Work	X —	**X**-cellent
L —	**L**ove It	Y —	**Y**ou've Got It
M —	**M**ighty Effort	Z —	**Z**ounds

Sandra Lowery—Gr. 4
Leavenworth, KS

Parent-Volunteer Notebook

I am always pleased to have parent volunteers help in the classroom. However, many times the helper comes while I am teaching a lesson, and I cannot stop to give her directions. I solved the problem by providing a special, looseleaf notebook for my volunteers (see the sample notebook page). As soon as my helper enters the room, she goes to this notebook and signs her name next to a job. With my explanations always available in the book, the volunteer can get right to work without interrupting me while I'm teaching. Not all volunteers feel comfortable doing certain tasks. Offering them choices encourages these helpers to return to my classroom again.

Sandra P. Neuhauser—Gr. 4
Halethorpe Elementary
Randallstown, MD

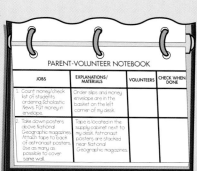

Beat The Teacher

To keep my students motivated to be on their best behavior all year long, I play a game with them called "Beat The Teacher." First I cut what looks like the top and bottom of a jar from construction paper. Then I connect the two cutouts with a five-foot piece of clear lamination and hang the resulting jar on one of our classroom walls. Each week I draw a gameboard in a small section of the chalkboard. One side is labeled "Miss Mertz" and the other side is labeled "4th Grade." As we proceed through our day, I award points to the class each time I see everyone following directions and working quietly. However, if I notice students who are off task or are being disruptive, I give myself a point. At the end of the day, if the students have "Beat The Teacher," I  place a cutout of a treat in the jar. (I use the same treat until the jar is full.) Some treat shapes that I have used include popcorn, chocolate chip cookies, doughnuts, Popsicles®, and ice-cream sundaes. When the jar is full, we celebrate our excellent behavior with a party featuring the treat in the jar.

Gwen Mertz—Gr. 4
Wyomissing Hills Elementary Center
Wyomissing Hills, PA

Test-Key Notebooks

If you have trouble keeping test keys at your fingertips, try this. Purchase a three-ring notebook for each subject. Use clear, plastic page protectors to fill each binder. Then place all original tests and their keys inside the page protectors. Problem solved!

Beverly Langland—Gr. 5
Trinity Christian Academy
Jacksonville, FL

SEASONAL IDEAS & REPRODUCIBLES

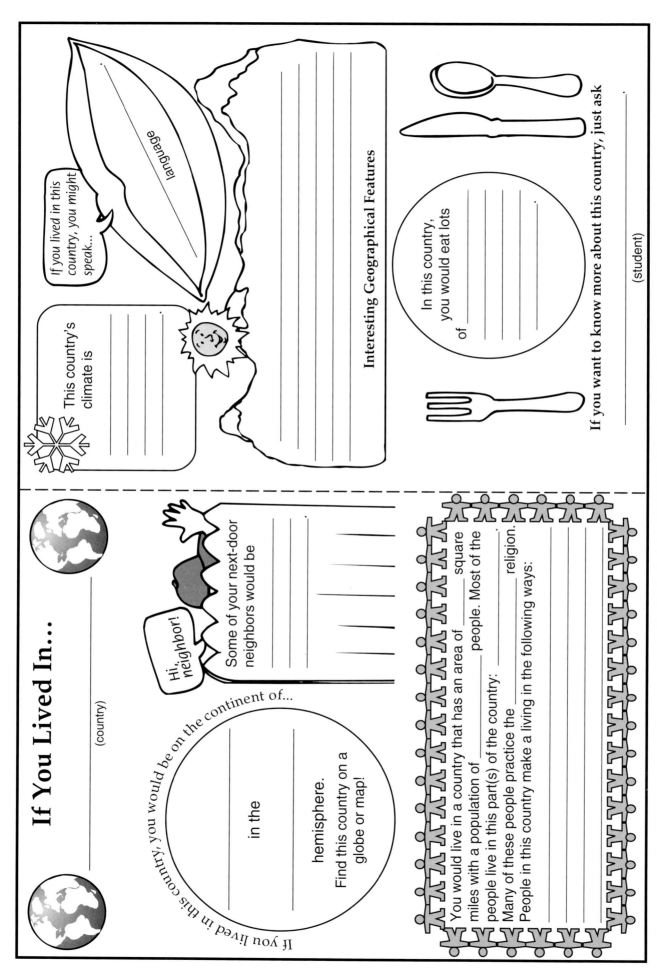

If You Lived In...

_____
(country)

If you lived in this country, you would be on the continent of...

Hi, neighbor!

Some of your next-door neighbors would be

_____
in the
_____
hemisphere.
Find this country on a globe or map!

You would live in a country that has an area of _____ square miles with a population of _____ people. Most of the people live in this part(s) of the country: _____
Many of these people practice the _____ religion.
People in this country make a living in the following ways:
_____
_____
_____

language

If you lived in this country, you might speak...

This country's climate is
_____
_____

Interesting Geographical Features
_____

In this country, you would eat lots of _____

If you want to know more about this country, just ask
_____
(student)

Note To The Teacher: United Nations Day is celebrated on October 24. Give each student a copy of this page and a United Nations member country to research. Pin completed forms to a bulletin board.

Halloween Headlines

The editor in chief of the *Hometown Gazette* is publishing a special Halloween edition. Several local authors have offered to write articles for this edition. For example, B. Lack Catt wants to write an article entitled "The History Of Superstitions." D. Ray Kullah has suggested a nature story called "The Life Cycle Of The Vampire Bat."

In the same vein, can you suggest articles that the following authors might write for this issue? Write each title in the blank beside the writer's name.

1. Jack O. Lantern: _____
_____

2. Candi Korn: _____
_____

3. Hal O. Weanmask: _____
_____

4. Bob Forapples: _____
_____

5. Frank N. Stein _____
_____

6. R. U. Skared: _____
_____

7. T. Rick Ortrete: _____
_____

8. Bea Safe: _____
_____

9. Esau A. Goste: _____
_____

10. Lotta Treetz: _____
_____

11. P. Art Teehost: _____
_____

12. Ima W. Erewolff: _____
_____

13. Madge Ickspell: _____
_____

Bonus Box: Now imagine that you are one of the authors listed above. On another sheet of paper, write an article suitable for the *Hometown Gazette,* using the title you suggested above. Write at least three paragraphs. Draw a picture to go with your article.

Turkey Tips

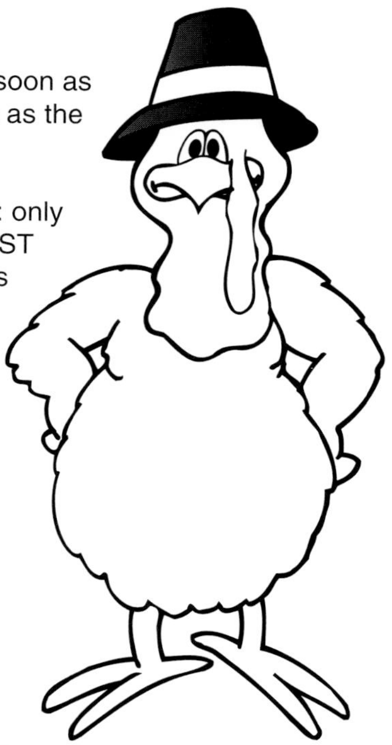

It's November, and Tucker Turkey has only one thing on his mind—SURVIVAL! As soon as he comes up with a tip on how to survive the Thanksgiving season (without winding up as the main course!), he writes it in secret code and sends it to his sister, Tallulah Turkey.

Tucker never uses the same code twice. All of his codes have one thing in common: only part of the letters in each word are used. For example, the message HANK EASES LAST PAIL could be translated "Help" by reading only the first letter of each word. Sometimes Tucker uses the second, third, last, or other letters in the words. And sometimes two letters from each word are used. Messages may also be read forwards or backwards.

Directions: Here are four messages that Tucker sent Tallulah. Each one uses a different code. Try to solve each one. Write your solution in the blank. In the second blank, describe how you broke the code.

1.
Break gravel with all this wet matter. Welcome Sheila's granddaughter. Don't waddle beside path. Stay boy. After echo, chill bananas.

Answer: _____
Code: _____

2.
Shopping List

nectarines
watermelon
onions
radishes
bread
ravioli
eggs
macaroni
rolls
asparagus
fig bars
doughnuts
ice cream
oranges
vitamins
apples

Answer: _____
Code: _____

3.
CHILD IDEALLY OBEYS. SHINE UNDER OTHERS. GET FRAME. ACT FORMALLY.

Answer: _____
Code: _____

4.
GET FREE CATCH DOC FRET ZEBRA PATH STYLE WATCH SWEET EARLY STEER GNU BLOB

Answer: _____
Code: _____

Note To The Teacher: See the bulletin board on page 51 for a way to use this reproducible.

'Tis The Season To Celebrate!

Celebrate the special days of December and January with the following creative activities.

Christmas

This December let students create a stunning wintry village that doubles as an Advent calendar. Have each child follow these steps:

1. On a piece of construction paper, draw and color a house from one of your favorite books.
2. Carefully slit the house's door so that it will open.
3. Place your house on another piece of same-sized white paper. Glue the two papers together, being careful not to glue the door shut.
4. Open the house's door and draw a holiday scene inside. Then trim around the outline of your house.

Arrange the houses on a bulletin board that has been covered with white paper (snow) and dark blue paper (the night sky). Add cotton snow, gold foil stars, and other student-made cutouts such as trees, sleighs, etc. Number the houses. Open one door each day until students leave for their holiday vacation.

Judith Brinckerhoff—Gr. 6, Hanaford School, East Greenwich, RI

Hanukkah

The Jewish holiday of Hanukkah will be celebrated this year on December 18–25. One important symbol of this eight-day festival is the menorah. Duplicate student copies of page 302 on white construction paper. Have each student complete the steps on the reproducible. Post the menorahs (with the center candles) on a bulletin board. Give each child an envelope in which to store his remaining candles. Each morning during Hanukkah (or the week before it begins), direct each student to remove one candle from her envelope, label it with something she is thankful for, and then staple that candle on her menorah. By the end of Hanukkah, you'll have a bevy of bright menorahs, burning brightly with thankfulness!

Beth Gress, Mt. Gilead, OH

Kwanzaa

Kwanzaa, a seven-day festival that begins on December 26, is a joyous celebration of African-American culture. Introduce students to the seven principles honored during Kwanzaa with *Celebrating Kwanzaa* by Diane Hoyt-Goldsmith (published by Holiday House). After sharing the book with students and listing the seven Kwanzaa principles on the board, divide the class into groups (one per principle). Direct each group to discuss its principle and design a poster illustrating it on a sheet of art paper. After groups have presented their posters, tape all seven posters together in order to make an instant Kwanzaa mural.

New Year's Day

Ring out the old and ring in the new! Have each student list negative habits he would like to stop on one paper bell, and positive habits he would like to begin on another. Have students attach their bells together with tape and ribbon as shown. Mount the bells and colorful streamers on a "Ringin' In The New Year!" bulletin board.

Julia Alarie—Gr. 6
Essex Middle School, Essex, VT

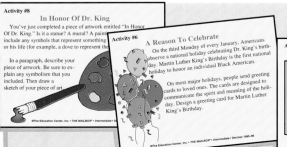

Martin Luther King's Birthday

To help your students celebrate Martin Luther King's Birthday on January 15, look no further than the ready-to-use activity cards on page 300 and 301.

Burning Brightly

Hanukkah is a Jewish holiday celebrated in December. During each evening of this eight-day celebration, a candle is lighted on a special candelabra called a *menorah*. A separate candle, called a *shammash*, is used to light each candle. Celebrate this holiday and all the things for which you are thankful by making your own menorah. Follow the steps below:

A Menorah Of Thankfulness

Name _____

Steps:

1. Color the menorah and the shammash candle in the middle.
2. Cut out the menorah (with the shammash candle) and staple it to a bulletin board.

3. Cut out the remaining candles and store them in an envelope.
4. Each morning of Hanukkah, label a candle with something for which you're thankful; then lightly color that candle and add it to your menorah.

Note To The Teacher: Use with the Hanukkah activity on page 301.

Name ______________________________ Christmas: magic square, using a calculator

Merry Moolah!

A distant relative of yours, Uncle Bigbucks, has offered you a one-of-a-kind Christmas present. On the gift box below, he's put a magic square comprised of 64 boxes containing the numbers 1–64. This square is "magical" because each column and row of numbers adds up to 260! But there are many more ways that Uncle Bigbucks's square is magical. In fact, Uncle Bigbucks will give you and your partner a $100 bill for each way that you can find. Just follow the directions:

Directions: On the back of this page, list as many ways as you can find that the square is magical. Use a calculator to help you. Each time you find a way that the square is magical, draw a $100 bill (100) on the tree. How much merry moolah can you earn?

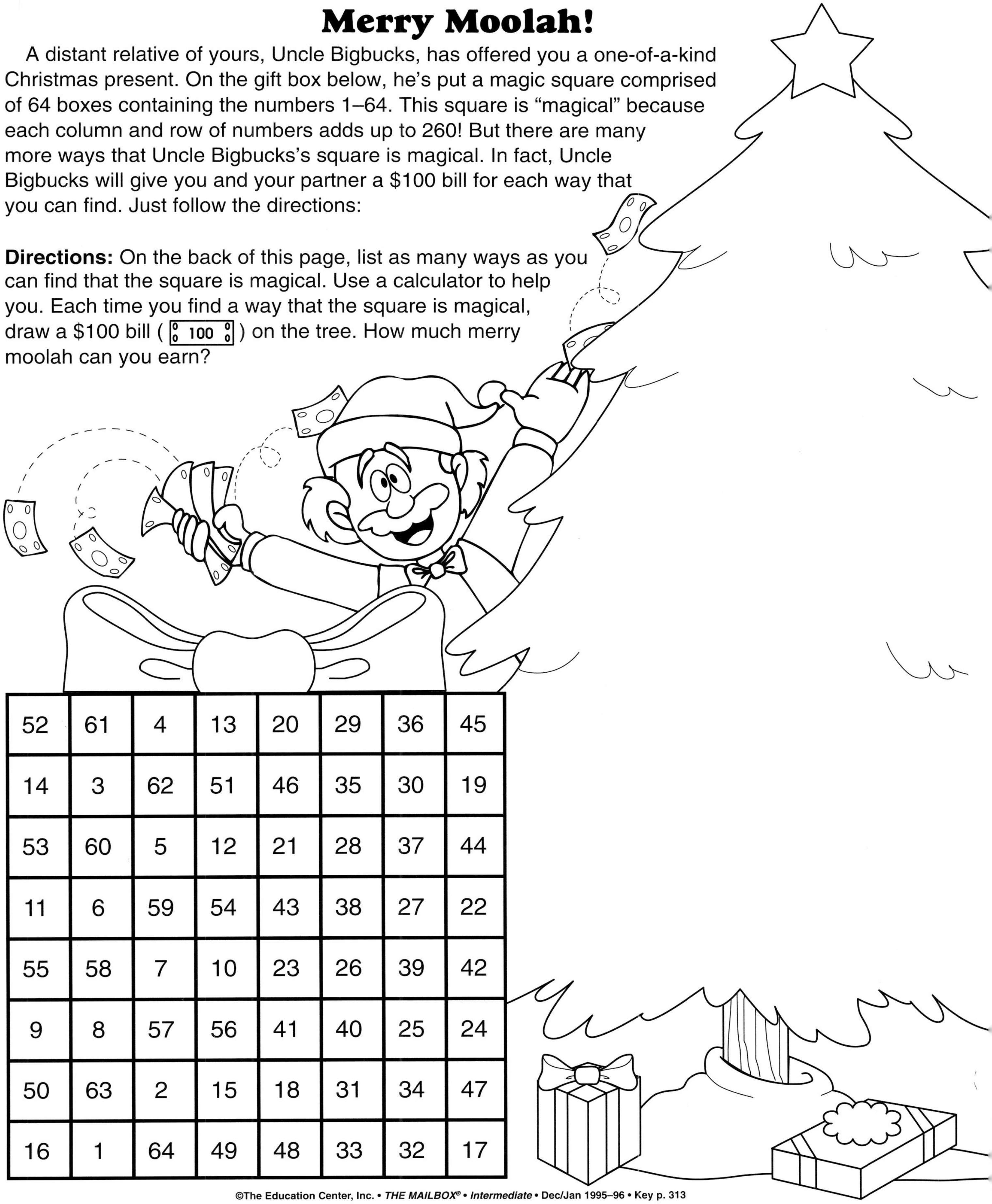

52	61	4	13	20	29	36	45
14	3	62	51	46	35	30	19
53	60	5	12	21	28	37	44
11	6	59	54	43	38	27	22
55	58	7	10	23	26	39	42
9	8	57	56	41	40	25	24
50	63	2	15	18	31	34	47
16	1	64	49	48	33	32	17

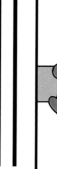

Here's what I think:

Activity #3
Speak Out!

Dr. King believed that he had a responsibility to speak out against violence wherever it occurred. And he did speak out against violence every chance he had.

What problem do you think you have a responsibility to speak out against? Design a poster that "speaks out" against this problem. Display it in your classroom.

Activity #7
More Work To Be Done

Dr. King would be happy about some of the positive changes that have taken place in America since his death in 1968. But what would he be sad about if he read today's newspaper or watched the television news?

The Nightly News

Pretend that you are Dr. King. You have just learned about life in America today. Write a speech in which you (as Dr. King) tell what you think are the most important problems for Americans to solve.

Activity #1
A Noble Example

The father of Martin Luther King, Jr., was a minister. After Martin graduated from college, he decided to become a minister too. He said that his father "set forth a noble example that I didn't mind following."

Because Martin admired his father so much, he was proud to follow in his footsteps. In whose footsteps would you like to follow as you grow older, get a job, etc.? Write a letter to this person explaining why you want to be like him/her.

Activity #5
A Committed Life

Dr. King was committed—or determined—to do everything he could to make sure all people were treated equally. He once said that when he died, he wanted "to leave a committed life behind."

What do you think Dr. King meant when he said he wanted "to leave a committed life behind"? What's one thing you are committed to doing before you die? Write your answer on your own paper.

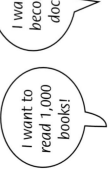

I want to read 1,000 books!

I want to become a doctor!

I want to help poor people!

I want to find a cure for AIDS!

Activity #2

What Are You Doing For Others?

Dr. King believed that it was important to help other people. He once said that the most important question anyone could ask himself was, "What am I doing for others?"

What are *you* doing for others? On a piece of paper, list ways you are helping other people at home, at school, or in your neighborhood or community. Then make another list of ideas that you want to try to do in the future. Meet with a friend to compare your lists, adding new ideas if you like. Post the list in your room at home to help you remember to follow Dr. King's example each day.

©The Education Center, Inc. • *THE MAILBOX® • Intermediate • Dec/Jan 1995–96*

Activity #6

A Reason To Celebrate

On the third Monday of every January, Americans observe a national holiday celebrating Dr. King's birthday. Martin Luther King's Birthday is the first national holiday to honor an individual Black American.

On most major holidays, people send greeting cards to loved ones. The cards are designed to communicate the spirit and meaning of the holiday. Design a greeting card for Martin Luther King's Birthday.

©The Education Center, Inc. • *THE MAILBOX® • Intermediate • Dec/Jan 1995-96*

Activity #4

Give Peace A Chance!

Dr. King encouraged blacks not to hate the whites who were mistreating them. He believed that there were peaceful ways to solve problems. Dr. King also believed that unfair laws could be changed if people peacefully protested them.

On a piece of paper, use colorful markers to write an acrostic poem about peace (see the example).

P eople committed
to love.
E veryone working
together.
A ll voices united.
C aring for all
people
E vermore.

©The Education Center, Inc. • *THE MAILBOX® • Intermediate • Dec/Jan 1995–96*

Activity #8

In Honor Of Dr. King

You've just completed a piece of artwork entitled "In Honor Of Dr. King." Is it a statue? A mural? A painting? Did you include any symbols that represent something about Dr. King or his life (for example, a dove to represent the idea of peace)?

In a paragraph, describe your piece of artwork. Be sure to explain any symbolism that you included. Then draw a sketch of your piece of art.

©The Education Center, Inc. • *THE MAILBOX® • Intermediate • Dec/Jan 1995-96*

Note To The Teacher: Use with the idea on page 297.

Heartthrobbin' Humdingers

Everybody likes to send (and receive!) Valentine's Day cards, right? Here's a chance for you to write some original valentine greetings that aren't of the ordinary romantic kind. Select one of the topics below. On another piece of paper, write a one-page letter or a rhyming poem of at least ten lines that could be sent for that situation.

1. a Valentine's Day greeting from one love-bug to another

2. a love letter from one Martian to another

3. a letter that could have been written from Juliet to Romeo

4. a valentine message to Wilma Flintstone from Fred

5. a greeting from one thorny rose to another

6. a message from a box of chocolates to its recipient

7. a Valentine's Day letter from a mother to a daughter who lives overseas

8. a memo from a florist to all his employees on Valentine's Day, the busiest day of the year

9. a love letter from one sneaker to the other sneaker in the pair

10. a Valentine's Day letter from an astronaut on the moon to his family back home on Earth

11. a message from a retiring cupid to the younger generation of cupids

12. a conversation between two diamond rings, each hoping to be purchased as a Valentine's Day gift

13. a note from an artist to his sweetheart, using only pictures and no words

14. a letter from a carpenter to a piece of wood he's crafting into a special Valentine's Day gift

15. a Valentine's Day message from the president of the United States to the entire nation

Bonus Heart: Valentine's Day once coincided with the day of an ancient Roman festival. What was that festival called?

"Phoney" Business

March 10 is the anniversary of the invention of the first successful telephone. In honor of this important date, here are some puzzles that even Alexander Graham Bell might find baffling!

Many businesses use phone numbers that, when replaced by the corresponding letters on the telephone, spell a word or phrase that describes the company's products or services. For example, a doctor's office might use the number 438-9355. Look at the matching letters on the telephone buttons:

The 4 matches G, H, and I.
Each 3 matches D, E, and F.
The 8 matches T, U, and V.
The 9 matches W, X, and Y.
Each 5 matches J, K, and L.

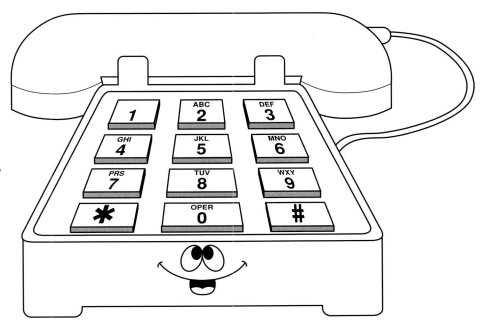

By selecting the right letter in each group of three, you could spell the words GET WELL!

Now try to spell a word or phrase that makes sense for each business below using the phone numbers given.

1. Sally's Styling Salon .... 288-4247 .... _____
2. Scott's Scuba School .... 938-7848 .... _____
3. Chuck's Chocolate-Chip Bakery .... 266-5437 .... _____
4. Frank's Fruit Tree Farm .... 672-4273 .... _____
5. Reta's Relaxing Recliners .... 748-3696 .... _____
6. Al's Automobile Cleaning Station .... 227-9274 .... _____
7. Phil's Photography .... 742-8873 .... _____
8. Sue's Service Station .... 427-7867 .... _____
9. Floyd's Flea Market .... 786-6243 .... _____
10. Buck's Butcher Shop .... 729-6328 .... _____
11. Sam's Supermarket .... 476-2379 .... _____
12. Hank's Hardware Supply .... 426-6377 .... _____

Bonus Box: Why can't Flora's Florist use a phone number that spells BOUQUET? Can you think of another word or phrase that *would* work?

Name____ Earth Day: addition, estimation

Earth Worth

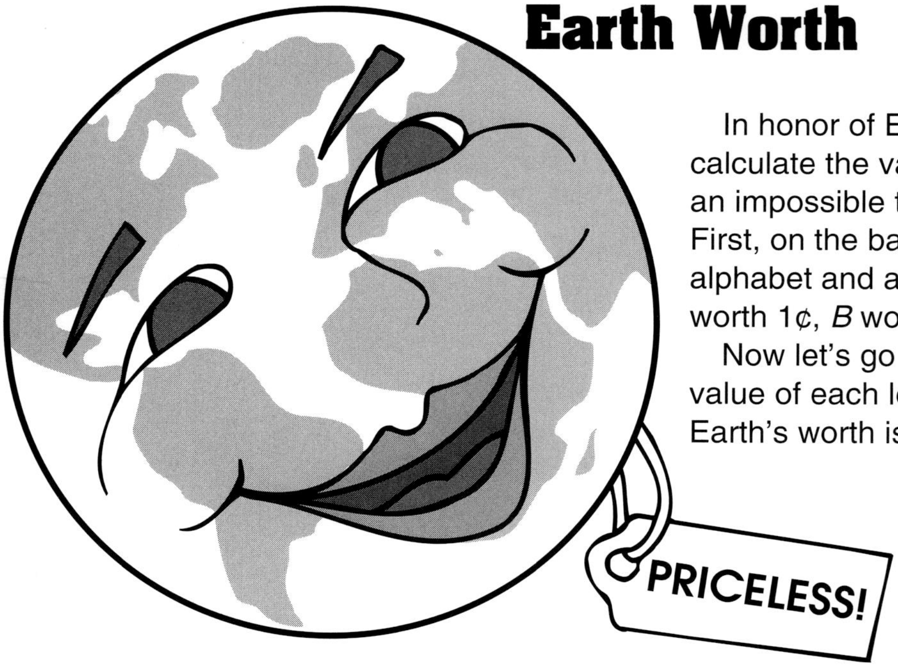

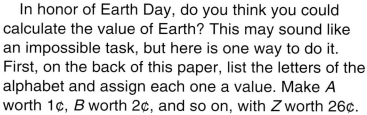

In honor of Earth Day, do you think you could calculate the value of Earth? This may sound like an impossible task, but here is one way to do it. First, on the back of this paper, list the letters of the alphabet and assign each one a value. Make *A* worth 1¢, *B* worth 2¢, and so on, with *Z* worth 26¢.

Now let's go back to the word *Earth.* Find the value of each letter. Add the five values together. Earth's worth is __________.

Look below at the different kinds of garbage you might collect or recycle on Earth Day. Using the method above, which one do you think will have the highest value? Circle it. Which one do you think will have the lowest value? Put an *X* by it. Now do the calculations and write your totals on the lines. Were your guesses correct?

1. eggshells = ____________________
2. apple peel = ____________________
3. meat bone = ____________________
4. milk jug = ____________________
5. scrap metal = ____________________
6. candy bar = ____________________
7. coffee filter = ____________________
8. bicycle tire = ____________________
9. tin can = ____________________
10. rusty kettle = ____________________
11. newspaper = ____________________
12. pop bottle = ____________________
13. plastic bag = ____________________
14. old shoe = ____________________
15. wood shavings = ____________________
16. pizza boxes = ____________________
17. broken toy = ____________________
18. empty carton = ____________________
19. soup label = ____________________
20. birdcage = ____________________

Bonus Box: List the other eight planets of our solar system. Which one do you think has the highest value? The lowest value? Do the addition and check your guesses.

"Eggz-acting" Problems

Easter eggs come in a variety of sizes and weights. Use the information in the chart to determine the weight (in ounces) of each hen's eggs. Show your work in each egg.

Jumbo	2.5 oz.
Extralarge	2.25 oz.
Large	2.0 oz.
Medium	1.75 oz.
Small	1.50 oz.

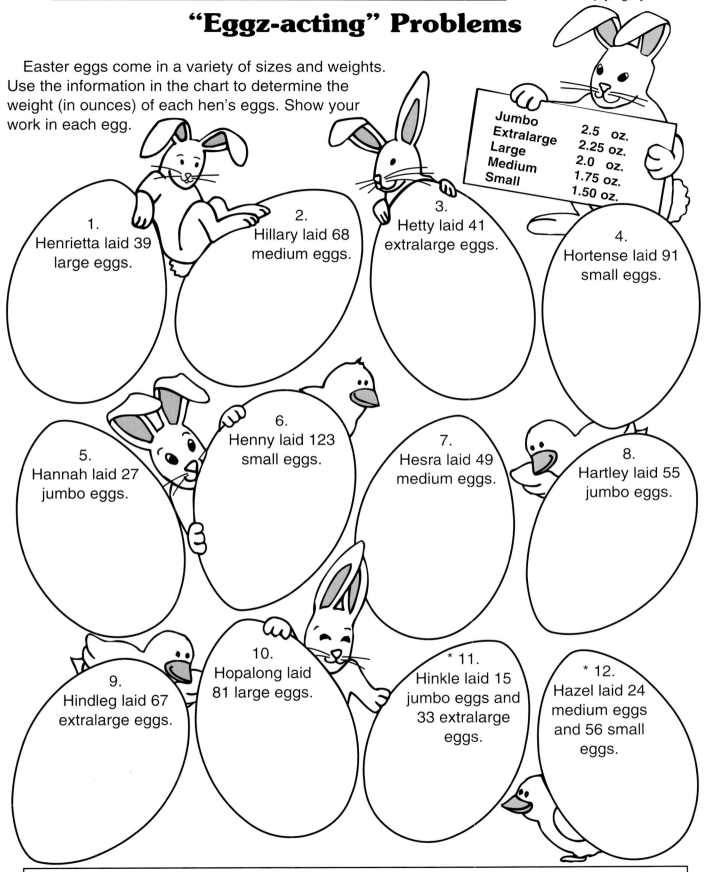

1. Henrietta laid 39 large eggs.

2. Hillary laid 68 medium eggs.

3. Hetty laid 41 extralarge eggs.

4. Hortense laid 91 small eggs.

5. Hannah laid 27 jumbo eggs.

6. Henny laid 123 small eggs.

7. Hesra laid 49 medium eggs.

8. Hartley laid 55 jumbo eggs.

9. Hindleg laid 67 extralarge eggs.

10. Hopalong laid 81 large eggs.

* 11. Hinkle laid 15 jumbo eggs and 33 extralarge eggs.

* 12. Hazel laid 24 medium eggs and 56 small eggs.

Bonus Box: Color the eggs according to this code: answers with two decimal places—pink; answers with one decimal place—green; and those with no decimal places—purple.

©The Education Center, Inc. • THE MAILBOX® • Intermediate • April/May 1996 • written by Laurie Vent • Key p. 313

Limerick Lines

May 12 is the birthdate of Edward Lear, an English poet famous for his nonsensical limericks. In honor of his birthday, let's take a closer look at this type of poetry. Here is an example of a silly limerick:

A starving lad from Timbuktu
Couldn't think of a thing he could do.
So he grabbed a fat 'gator
And he cooked and then ate her.
Now the young lad is no longer blue.

In limericks, the first, second, and fifth lines all end with words that rhyme with each other. These lines are each about eight or nine syllables long. The third and fourth lines are shorter and rhyme only with each other. They are each about six or seven syllables long.

To help you get started writing your own humorous limericks, here are some possible beginning lines. On another sheet of paper, develop as many as possible into complete limericks.

1. A dog who did nothing but dig
2. An old chef without any dough
3. A musician who lost all his notes
4. A chocolate milk cow named Daisy
5. A lazy and criminal crook
6. An author without any ink
7. The alien from outer space
8. There once was a young boy named Frank
9. A princess alone in a castle
10. A dragon who developed strep throat

11. One Martian with bright purple hair
12. A wee girl whose name was Samantha
13. A scientist going quite mad
14. A young pupil who knew all her math
15. The librarian we all called Sue
16. A robot with mixed-up new wires
17. An angry leopard who'd lost his spots
18. A teacher who loved to do knitting
19. There was an old cat in a tub
20. Someone living in Kalamazoo

Bonus Box: Pick one of your favorite original limericks. Rewrite it, add an illustration, and display it in the classroom.

Night Beat

To celebrate National Police Week (the week that includes May 15), each patrol officer in Maple City has been given a puzzling set of clues. The clues tell the officers which areas to patrol. The first officer of each shift who figures out the clues gets a special reward: a bonus vacation day!

Below is a map of the area Officer Gaines is to patrol, followed by the clues she has been given. How quickly can you help her schedule her night beat? Determine the time when Officer Gaines should check each site. Write the time on the sidewalk in front of each one.

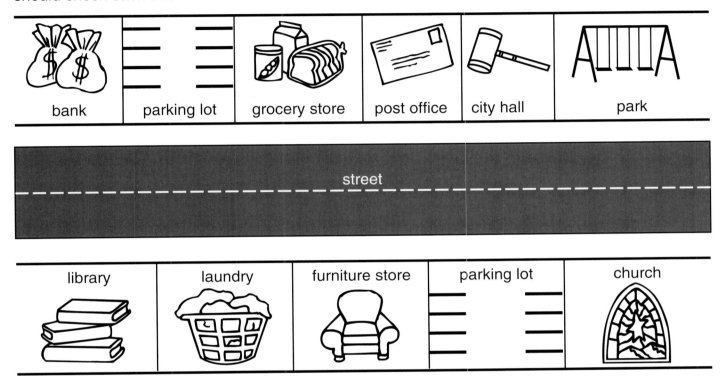

Clues:

1. Spend 15 minutes at each location.
2. Zigzag back and forth, up and down the street. Don't check more than *two* adjoining locations in a row.
3. Start patrolling the last location at 11:30 P.M.
4. Inspect the post office right after the furniture store.
5. Check the library an hour before patrolling the grocery store.
6. The laundry should be checked sometime after it closes at 10:30 P.M.
7. Inspect the church 30 minutes after starting at the library. Then go straight across the street to the park.
8. Check the grocery store at either 9:30 or 11:30 P.M.
9. Right after inspecting the bank, check the parking lot next to it.
10. Check the parking lot next to the church one hour after checking the other parking lot.
11. The bank should be checked promptly at 9:00 P.M. to be sure its security system is on.
12. The furniture store should be patrolled an hour earlier than the library.

Bonus Box: How many times in 24 hours does Officer Gaines's digital watch read the same backward and forward? (Examples: 7:07, 12:21, and 1:51) Write your answer on the back of this sheet.

ANSWER KEY

Page 55
Answers to bulletin-board questions:

1. a 3-leafed herb, a clover
2. three Hindu gods
3. California, Connecticut, Colorado
4. trivia, because it has nothing to do with the number 3
5. possible answers: arm, leg, toe, rib, etc.
6. Tripoli
7. 33
8. Examples of triangles:

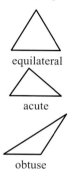 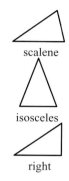

equilateral   scalene

acute   isosceles

obtuse   right

9. 12 toes
10. Answers will vary.
11. to recline on during meals (a couch extending around three sides of a table)
12. cares for and dresses hair (a hairdresser)

Page 90
Below are only a few of the possible answers. You may wish to make a composite classroom list to show students how many words they've found collectively. Be sure that students use dictionaries to verify unfamiliar words.

1. (forward): sort, tart, spin, trap, rasp, spot, roan
   (backward): tart, tort, part, taps, trot, tarp, tops
2. (forward): dead, deed, dean, Dane, nerd
   (backward): dare, darn, earn, dear, dean, deed
3. (forward): tact, data, fact, stat, dais
   (backward): cast, fits, said, cats, nota
4. (forward): rend, rear, pear, peel, peer
   (backward): rude, deep, line, raid, ripe, ride
5. (forward): spit, silt, rest, slit, soil, spot, pony, eons, pity
   (backward): tile, tine, lisp, line, lips, tips, nose, bier
6. (forward): star, daze, tied, sane, tare, size, died, dare
   (backward): rats, rant, dent, dean, dead, dirt

Bonus Box: Possible answers include:
1. apart (backward), ration (forward)
2. dared (backward)
3. disco (forward)
4. lucid (backward)
5. spoil, spilt (forward); loser (backward)
6. staid, sized, dazed (forward)

Page 91
Build-A-Word
Possible words include:

1. wreath
2. bread, beard
3. space
4. paddle
5. wheat
6. safety
7. rough
8. shawl
9. braid
10. jelly
11. break, brake
12. caller
13. lemon, melon
14. grand
15. roast
16. camper
17. apart
18. drink
19. flash
20. table
21. glue, luge
22. save, vase
23. went, newt
24. relax
25. party
26. prize

Bonus Box: Possible words include *endear* and *earned*.

Page 91
A Musical Journey
Possible solutions include:

1. piano
2. tuba
3. drum
4. fife
5. oboe
6. organ
7. lyre
8. flute
9. violin
10. cornet
11. gong
12. banjo

Page 94
Possible answers include:

1. quiet
2. fast
3. wet
4. proper
5. thorny
6. first
7. lumpy
8. big
9. single
10. miniature
11. funny
12. red
13. wooden
14. loud
15. gold
16. hot

Page 95
Possible answers include:

1. also
2. very
3. really
4. seldom
5. almost
6. never
7. indeed
8. slowly
9. farther
10. well
11. today
12. later or after

Page 107

Three's A Crowd!
Possible answers include:
1. c. only decimal with one-digit whole or d. only odd decimal
2. b. only two-digit whole, only even decimal; or c. only odd whole; or d. only decimal to tenths
3. c. only three-digit whole or d. digits not ascending
4. a. only decimal not equal to the other three
5. b. only one-digit whole or d. no zero in tenths place
6. b. only decimal to tenths or c. only decimal written in standard form
7. a. only decimal not equal to other three or d. only decimal written in standard form
8. d. only whole number

Pirate Patterns
1. 6.9, 7.0 (increase by 0.1)
2. 1.00, 1.01 (increase by 0.01)
3. 1.0, 1.2 (increase by 0.2)
4. 2.5, 3.0 (increase by 0.5)
5. 7.5, 7.8 (increase by 0.3)
6. 38.4, 76.8 (each number is doubled)
7. 10.5, 12.0 (increase by 1.5)
8. 24, 25.5 (increase by 1.5, then by 2.0)
9. 42.0, 47.5 (increase by 5.5)
10. 10.5, 14.0 (increase by 0.5, then 1.0, then 1.5, then 2.0, then 2.5, etc.)

Page 109

Black Moon	45.87 m
Eagle Talon	45.3 m
Caribbean Cruiser	42.9 m
Yo Ho Ho	41.35 m

Caribbean Cruiser	18.7 sec.
Yo Ho Ho	18.13 sec.
Black Moon	18.27 sec.
Eagle Talon	18.5 sec.

Black Moon came in second.

Eagle Talon	9.62
Black Moon	9.8
Yo Ho Ho	9.49
Caribbean Cruiser	9.73

Black Moon	5.34
Yo Ho Ho	5.43
Eagle Talon	4.9
Caribbean Cruiser	4.655
Total	20.325

Page 108

1. a. 6.8
   b. 60.08
   c. 16.008
   d. 60.8
   e. 0.008
   f. 0.08
2. 2—16.207
   4—6.9
   3—16.19
   1—16.26
3. 11.1, 11.069, 10.53, 10.507
4. 0.95, 60.05, 0.057
5. 9.7, rounded to the nearest whole, equals 10.0.
6. 17.76, rounded to the nearest tenth, equals 17.8.
7. 6.083, rounded to the nearest hundredth, equals 6.08.
8. 0.50
9. 60.9
10. 0.0076

They were both PIRATEs!

	Yo Ho Ho	Caribbean Cruiser	Eagle Talon	Black Moon	5,892.5 mi.	6,123.9 mi.	6,875.0 mi.	7,056.8 mi.
Kidd	✔	X	X	X	X	X	X	✔
Drake	X	✔	X	X	✔	X	X	X
Kirk	X	X	✔	X	X	✔	X	X
Morgan	X	X	X	✔	X	X	✔	X
5,892.5 mi.	X	✔	X	X				
6,123.9 mi.	X	X	✔	X				
6,875.0 mi.	X	X	X	✔				
7,056.8 mi.	✔	X	X	X				

Bonus Box: Captains Kidd, Drake, and Morgan were real pirates.

Try For 100%!

1.	a	11.	a
2.	b	12.	c
3.	c	13.	b
4.	d.	14.	a
5.	a	15.	c
6.	a	16.	a
7.	d	17.	a
8.	d	18.	a
9.	b	19.	a
10.	c	20.	b

a. 1/4

b. 3/4

c. 1/4

d. The idea of equally likely outcomes allows us to come up with a theoretical probability for an event. (Example: When tossing a coin, it is as likely to come down heads as tails.) Theoretical probability can only be determined when you know the number of equally likely outcomes.

Choices, Choices, Choices

1. 6 possible combinations using red-blue-green (3 x 2 x 1):

   rbg
   rgb
   brg
   bgr
   grb
   gbr

2. 24 possible combinations using red-blue-green-yellow (4 x 3 x 2 x 1):

rbgy	grby
rbyg	gryb
rgby	gbry
rgyb	gbyr
rybg	gyrb
rygb	gybr
brgy	ygrb
bryg	ygbr
bgry	yrgb
bgyr	yrbg
bygr	ybgr
byrg	ybrg

3. 120 different combinations (5 x 4 x 3 x 2 x 1)

4. 1 out of 24

1.	25%	9.	32 fluid ounces
2.	22 sixth graders	10.	$0.17
3.	$19.00	11.	24¢
4.	34 points	12.	27 inches
5.	20%	13.	23 girls
6.	33 years old	14.	28%
7.	26 weeks	15.	31 days each
8.	21	16.	18%

Bonus Box answer: The sum of each group of answers in a wedge is 100. The sum of answers that form each "circle" of the pentagon is also 100.

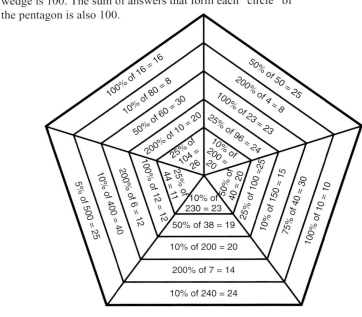

Page 128
Dandy Candies

	lollipops	mints	chocolate-covered pretzels	caramel apples	tins	plastic bags	plastic wrap	gift boxes
Matthew	✓	✗	✗	✗	✗	✗	✗	✓
Maggie	✗	✓	✗	✗	✓	✗	✗	✗
Mark	✗	✗	✗	✓	✗	✓	✗	✗
Megan	✗	✗	✓	✗	✗	✗	✓	✗

The Great Lollipop Lick-Off

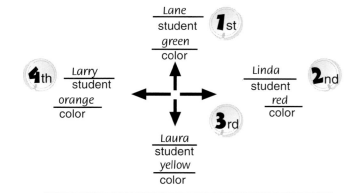

	1st	2nd	3rd	4th
student	Lane	Linda	Laura	Larry
color	green	red	yellow	orange

Page 143

1. Answers may vary.

   Aristotle agreed with Plato that the earth is a sphere, but based his decision on observable evidence. He noted that the shadow cast by the earth on the face of the moon was round. He also believed that temperatures close to the equator were hotter.

   Eratosthenes found a way to accurately measure the circumference of the earth by using a shadow cast into a dry well.

   Strabo was a genius at compiling information. He filled 17 volumes with the sum of the Mediterranean world's knowledge up to that time. He also divided the world into frigid, temperate, and tropic zones.

   Ptolemy set forth many of the cartographic principles still used by mapmakers today. In his attempt to represent a round world on a flat map, he came up with the concept of showing the earth on a globe.

   Pythagoras taught that the earth is a sphere and not in the shape of a disk. He also suggested that the earth, sun, moon, and planets revolved around a central fire. He put forth the idea that the world rotates.

2. Definitions are given below. Other answers may vary.

   cartography: the science or art of making maps

   climatology: the science that deals with climates and their phenomena

   ecology: a branch of science concerned with the interrelationship of organisms and their environments

   geology: a science that deals with the history of the earth and its life, especially as recorded in rocks

   oceanography: a science that deals with the oceans and includes the delimitation of their extent and depth, the physics and chemistry of their waters, marine biology, and the exploitation of their resources

3. Answers may vary. Below are some facts.

   Atlantis: based on an Egyptian legend passed down through the centuries and retold by Plato; a mythical island thought to exist west of the Strait of Gibraltar; occupied by people who descended from the sea god Poseidon; an earthly paradise where food was plentiful, the buildings were magnificent (coated with silver and gold), and the military was powerful; destroyed by an earthquake and a flood, swallowed up by the sea; as the legend grew over the centuries, myth insisted that the island miraculously continued to exist under the sea and would one day reemerge.

   El Dorado: the legendary name was applied first to a man, later to a city, and then to an entire country; the legend arose from an actual Indian custom of anointing each new chief with resinous gum, covering him with gold dust, plunging him into a sacred lake, and throwing gems in after him; Spanish explorers caught up in this myth named the chieftain *El Dorado* ("The Golden One"); later the name was applied to a fictitious kingdom of enormous wealth located on the Amazon River; explorers kept the myth alive to justify continued exploration and conquest.

4. **Sandwich Islands:** (now known as the Hawaiian Islands) named by Captain James Cook in honor of the Earl of Sandwich

   Greenland: named by the Viking explorer Eric the Red in hopes of attracting more settlers to the country

   Badlands: originally called *mako sica* ("bad land") by the Sioux; later called *mauvaises terres à traverser* ("bad lands to travel across") by French fur traders

   Red Sea: named for the masses of reddish seaweed found in its waters

   Yellow Sea: named for its characteristic color resulting from the rich yellow silt deposited there by the Yellow (Hwang Ho) and other rivers

5. United States—Mount McKinley
   Canada—Mount Logan
   Mexico—Citlaltépetl
   South America—Aconcagua
   Turkey—Mount Ararat

6. Possible answers include:
   Hudson—New York City
   Thames—London
   Seine—Paris
   Hooghly—Calcutta
   Parramatta—Sydney

7. Hoover—Colorado River
   Shasta—Sacramento River
   Pickwick—Tennessee River
   Fort Peck—Missouri River
   Grand Coulee—Columbia River

8. Strait of Hormuz—Iran and Oman
   Strait of Gibraltar—Spain and Morocco
   Strait of Dover—France and England
   Skagerrak—Denmark and Norway
   Windward Passage—Cuba and Haiti

9. Table Bay—South Africa
   Hudson Bay—Canada
   Guanabara Bay—Brazil
   Bo Hai—China
   Kiel Bay—Germany

10. Gibson Desert—Australia
    Kalahari Desert—Botswana
    Arabian Desert—Egypt
    Atacama Desert—Chile
    Mojave Desert—United States

Pages 152 and 153

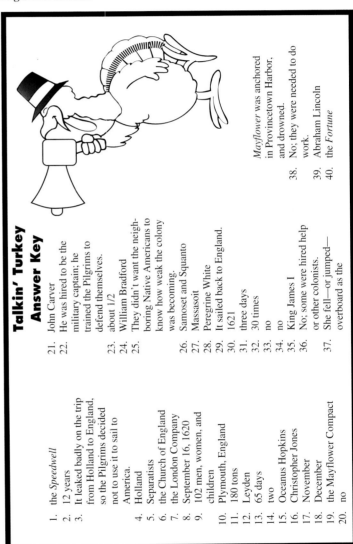

Talkin' Turkey Answer Key

1. the *Speedwell*
2. 12 years
3. It leaked badly on the trip from Holland to England, so the Pilgrims decided not to use it to sail to America.
4. Holland
5. Separatists
6. the Church of England
7. the London Company
8. September 16, 1620
9. 102 men, women, and children
10. Plymouth, England
11. 180 tons
12. Leyden
13. 65 days
14. two
15. Oceanus Hopkins
16. Christopher Jones
17. November
18. December
19. the Mayflower Compact
20. no
21. John Carver
22. He was hired to be the military captain; he trained the Pilgrims to defend themselves.
23. about 1/2
24. William Bradford
25. They didn't want the neighboring Native Americans to know how weak the colony was becoming.
26. Samoset and Squanto
27. Massasoit
28. Peregrine White
29. It sailed back to England.
30. 1621
31. three days
32. 30 times
33. no
34. no
35. King James I
36. No, some were hired help or other colonists.
37. She fell—or jumped—overboard as the
38. *Mayflower* was anchored in Provincetown Harbor, and drowned.
39. No; they were needed to do work.
40. Abraham Lincoln
41. the *Fortune*

311

Page 134

Answers will vary. Possible answers include:

1. Railroads were needed to transport supplies, soldiers, and weapons during the war. They were also needed to ship raw materials to factories.
2. Southern cotton growers needed the northern factories to process their cotton. During the war, the cotton could not be shipped to the North for processing.
3. Lack of adequate railroad track, wealth produced, farms, and bank deposits would all affect the South's ability to feed its soldiers and citizens.
4. Money was needed to finance all aspects of the war: salaries, uniforms, weapons, food, medical supplies, etc.
5. Because almost the entire war was fought in the South, the North was forced to invade the South. The Union army had to ship supplies across enemy lines and camp in unfamiliar and unfriendly territory.

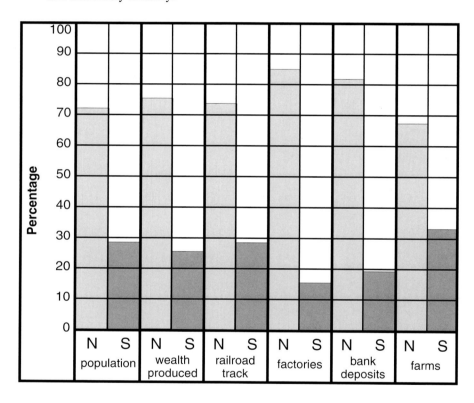

Page 296

1. Answer: EAT LITTLE AND STAY THIN.
   Code: Read the third letter of each word.
2. Answer: AVOID FARMER BROWN.
   Code: Read the first letter of each word in the list, starting at the bottom.
3. Answer: HIDE BEHIND THE TRACTOR.
   Code: Read the second and third letters of each word.
4. Answer: BURY THE HATCHET.
   Code: Read the last letter of each word, reading backwards from the end of the message.

Page 204
Bonus Box Answer:
Sarah Goode: folding cabinet bed
Sarah Boone: ironing board
Julia Hammond: device to hold yarn for knitting
Archia Ross: rack to keep trousers from wrinkling
Claytonia Dorticus: machine for embossing photos and a photographic print wash

Page 243
1. Turtle Wexler
2. Berthe Erica Crow
3. Judge J. J. Ford
4. Sydelle Pulaski
5. Otis Amber
6. Angela Wexler
7. Grace Wexler
8. Sandy McSouthers
Hidden message: He is not dead.

Page 160

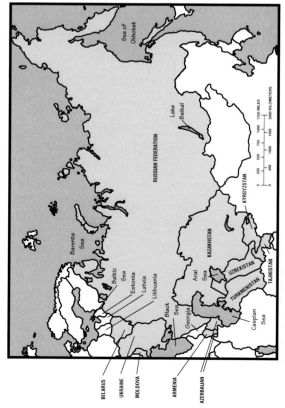

Page 299

There are hundreds of ways that Uncle Bigbucks's square is magical! Listed below are just a few examples:

- The four corner boxes plus the four middle boxes add up to 260.
- Any group of eight adjoining boxes (four boxes wide and two boxes high) adds up to 260. There are 35 such groups.
- Any group of eight adjoining boxes (two boxes wide and four boxes high) adds up to 260. There are 35 such groups.
- Any group of four adjoining boxes (two boxes x two boxes) adds up to 130. There are 49 such groups.
- Any group of eight boxes that form an octagon (for example: 14, 53, 6, 59, 12, 51, 4, and 61) adds up to 260. There are 25 such groups.
- In the first two columns of boxes, the sums of the side-by-side boxes are 113, 17, 113, 17, etc.
- In the second and third columns of boxes, the sums of the side-by-side boxes all equal 65.
- In the third and fourth columns of boxes, the sums of the side-by-side boxes are 17, 113, 17, 113, etc.
- In the fourth and fifth columns of boxes, the sums of the side-by-side boxes are 33, 97, 33, 97, etc.
- In the fifth and sixth columns of boxes, the sums of the side-by-side boxes are 49, 81, 49, 81, etc.
- In the sixth and seventh columns of boxes, the sums of the side-by-side boxes all equal 65.
- In the seventh and eighth columns of boxes, the sums of the side-by-side boxes are 81, 49, 81, 49, etc.

Page 302

Bonus Heart Answer: The festival was called *Lupercalia*.

Page 303

1. CUT HAIR
2. WET SUIT
3. COOKIES
4. ORCHARD
5. SIT DOWN
6. CAR WASH
7. PICTURE
8. GAS PUMP
9. RUMMAGE
10. RAW MEAT
11. GROCERY
12. HAMMERS

Bonus Box Answer: There is no *Q* on most telephones. The word *FLOWERS*, among others, could work.

Page 304

Earth = $0.52

1. $0.94
2. $0.88
3. $0.75
4. $0.83
5. $1.08
6. $0.68
7. $1.10
8. $1.11
9. $0.61
10. $1.76
11. $1.17
12. $1.21
13. $0.90
14. $0.78
15. $1.56
16. $1.43
17. $1.25
18. $1.50
19. $1.03
20. $0.49

Highest: rusty kettle ($1.76)
Lowest: birdcage ($0.49)

Bonus Box answer:

Mercury = $1.03 (highest)
Venus = $0.81
Mars = $0.51 (lowest)
Jupiter = $0.99
Saturn = $0.93
Neptune = $0.95
Uranus = $0.94
Pluto = $0.84

Page 305

1. 78.0 oz. (purple)
2. 119.0 oz. (purple)
3. 92.25 oz. (pink)
4. 136.5 oz. (green)
5. 67.5 oz. (green)
6. 184.5 oz. (green)
7. 85.75 oz. (pink)
8. 137.5 oz. (green)
9. 150.75 oz. (pink)
10. 162.0 oz. (purple)
11. 111.75 oz. (pink)
12. 126.0 oz. (purple)

Page 307

Hint: Suggest that students use clues 1 and 3 to list all of the possible time slots. Clue 3 says that the last location is checked at 11:30. Clue 1 says to spend 15 minutes at each location. Beginning at 11:30 P.M. and working backward to list 15-minute intervals results in the beginning time of 9:00 P.M.

9:00—bank
9:15—parking lot beside bank
9:30—furniture store
9:45—post office
10:00—city hall
10:15—parking lot beside church
10:30—library
10:45—laundry
11:00—church
11:15—park
11:30—grocery store

Bonus Box answer: There are 114 palindromic digital times during a 24-hour period.

Beginning at midnight: 12:21; then
1:01, 1:11, 1:21, 1:31, 1:41, and 1:51;
2:02, 2:12, 2:22, 2:32, 2:42, and 2:52.

Repeat this pattern with 3:00 through 9:00 (six times per hour for 1:00–9:00 equals 54 times); then 10:01 and 11:11 for a total of 57 times during a 12-hour period, and 114 times during a 24-hour period.

Index